THE CAP

THE CAP

How Larry Fleisher and David Stern Built the Modern NBA

JOSHUA MENDELSOHN

University of Nebraska Press

LINCOLN

Library of Congress Cataloging-in-Publication Data
Names: Mendelsohn, Joshua, author.
Title: The cap: how Larry Fleisher and David Stern built
the modern NBA / Joshua Mendelsohn.
Description: Lincoln: University of Nebraska Press, [2020] |
Includes bibliographical references and index.
Identifiers: LCCN 2020015427
ISBN 9781496218780 (hardback)
ISBN 9781496223845 (epub)
ISBN 9781496223852 (mobi)
ISBN 9781496223869 (pdf)
Subjects: LCSH: National Basketball Association—
Management. | National Basketball Association—History. |
Basketball—Economic aspects—United States.
Classification: LCC GV885.513 .M45 2020 |
DDC 796.323/6406—dc23
LC record available at https://lccn.loc.gov/2020015427

Set in Minion Pro by Mikala R. Kolander.

To Jen

Contents

Introduction . . ix

Persons of Note in the 1982–1983 NBA Collective
Bargaining Negotiations . . xiii

1. No Final Victories . . 1

2. Pleasantries and Unpleasantries, July 1982 . . 17

3. Survivors, August 1982 . . 35

4. That Brave Group of Guys Who Said "Fuck You," January 1964 . . 53

5. Larry . . 70

6. The Sport of the '70s . . 93

7. The Cap, 1979–1980 . . 108

8. The Right of First Refusal, Summer 1981 . . 127

9. David . . 157

10. The Moses Signing, September 1982 . . 180

11. The Big Item, October 1982 . . 195

12. Strike Date, January 1983 . . 221

13. War, February 1983 . . 241

14. Unbounded Pessimism and Cautious Optimism, March 1983 . . 257

15. Peace, April 1983 . . 273

Epilogue . . 285

Acknowledgments . . 303

Notes . . 305

Bibliography . . 343

Index . . 345

Introduction

In this business, only your work sustains you.

—LARRY FLEISHER

The first seed of this book was planted randomly. In the summer of 2012, Chicago Bulls Center Omer Asik, a free agent, signed a deal with the Houston Rockets. Under the collective bargaining agreement, Asik's old team, the Chicago Bulls, had a right to match the Rockets' offer. The Rockets, however, had structured the deal with Asik in such a way that made it nearly impossible for the Bulls to do so. Daryl Morey, the Rockets' brilliant general manager, was praised for being innovative in masterminding the deal to get his guy. I, as someone who followed these things, was deeply impressed with Morey's maneuvering. After the deal was announced, Bob Ryan, once described as the NBA's "ombudsman" was on ESPN talking about the Asik deal. Ryan said Morey's maneuver was neither new nor innovative. Ryan said center Moses Malone had poison pills in his free agent deal with the Philadelphia 76ers thirty years earlier that were more creative than Asik's. My ears perked up. I had absolutely no idea what Ryan was talking about. Despite being a die-hard NBA fan, armchair salary-cap nerd, labor lawyer, and NBA season ticket holder, I realized I knew almost nothing about the NBA's history.

I set out to find a book about it. I couldn't. Baseball history? Everywhere. You could read a straight line of history from 1890 to today from any angle. From Marvin Miller to Curt Flood to George Steinbrenner to collusion to the 1994 strike to *Moneyball* (in whichever form you enjoyed it) to Theo Epstein, the mining of the history

ix

of the sport was so directly entrenched with labor history and economics as to make it one story. The books and articles were endless and fantastic.

Basketball, however, was different. There was very little. There were the two phenomenal David Halberstam books—*The Breaks of the Game* and *Playing for Keeps*, which dealt with some of these issues. Harvey Araton, Bob Ryan, Bill Simmons, and, more recently, Jonathan Abrams had all written exceptional books about the history of the NBA. Of course, Terry Pluto's *Loose Balls* about the ABA is required reading. But, there was little else. There was a lot about games—there was less about the business. There was a lot about now. There was almost nothing about then. There was some about David Stern. There was much less about Larry Fleisher.

I did not know much about Fleisher when I started writing this book. My knowledge was limited to what was written in books about other sports. Much of it dismissed or limited Fleisher's import. I knew he was the head of the union *and* an agent at the same time, which felt sketchy. I knew his was the first union to agree to a salary cap. I had read the few lines in *Lords of the Realm*, the phenomenal history of the baseball business, which said that after agreeing to the cap, "[Major League Baseball Players Association chief] Marvin Miller was privately contemptuous of NBA Players Association chief Larry Fleisher." If the great Marvin Miller was contemptuous, who was I to think differently?

I was wrong. The more I read about Fleisher, the more I came to a clear conclusion: Larry Fleisher is one of the most influential people in sports history. He was brilliant, decent, creative, effective, and worthy of admiration. He was ahead of his time. He was Miller's equal—just different. Some of his perspective and approach—the creativity, the risk taking, the ingenuity—could help players in all sports today.

I obviously knew more about Stern than Fleisher entering into this project. I grew up watching David Stern. In writing this book, I found my research confirmed a lot of what I knew, liked, and admired about Stern, but looking at this time period allowed me to see a different side. In the time described in this book, Stern is not yet commissioner. He is putting the pieces together—building the business that would become the one we all love. He was smart, strategic, and visionary.

In many ways, the NBA in 2020 is the same business it was in the early 1980s. These men who built the sport in the early 1980s—Fleisher and Stern—had tremendous vision and foresight. They were both fantastic negotiators. The structure they built was also born of facts that are beyond Stern and Fleisher—court decisions, television deals, labor strife in other sports, and characters on both sides influencing decisions and actions. I tried to make what, to some, may feel like ancient history relevant to the modern game in very modern ways. Because, it very much is, and because this history has a tremendous amount to teach us. The league as it currently exists embodies the potential they both hoped for the NBA many years ago.

One final thing. This book is about the negotiation over the creation of the salary cap in 1983. It was written decades after that agreement was reached. We have the luxury of hindsight as to what would occur in sports, business, and labor relations. Now, in 2020, there is no need for a salary cap. There is value in forcing teams to spend, but there is no need for a limit. When you look at the modern game and what innovative GMs like Daryl Morey, Sam Presti, Sean Marks, and a dozen other equally brilliant front offices are able to accomplish in this complex, heavily regulated environment of professional basketball, wouldn't it simply be more fun to watch them use all of their creativity, smarts, and innovation in an open market?

In 1981 Los Angeles Lakers owner Dr. Jerry Buss said in response to complaints about how he ran the Lakers, "Sports should simply be part of the free-enterprise system instead of imposing all those useless restrictions." I agree with Dr. Buss—now more than ever.

To write this book was a pleasure, a privilege, and a challenge. It was also a tremendous amount of fun. I truly hope you enjoy it.

Persons of Note in the 1982–1983 NBA Collective Bargaining Negotiations

National Basketball Association (NBA)

Gary Bettman—NBA assistant general counsel

Russ Granik—NBA general counsel

Larry O'Brien—NBA commissioner

David Stern—NBA executive vice president, business and legal affairs, *chief negotiator*

NBA Outside Counsel

Joseph Barbash—Debevoise and Plimpton

L. Robert Batterman—Proskauer, Rose, Goetz, and Mendelsohn

Jeffrey Mishkin—Proskauer, Rose, Goetz, and Mendelsohn

NBA Labor Relations Committee

M. Douglas Adkins—vice president/counsel, Dallas Mavericks

Joe Axelson—general manager, Kansas City Kings

Alan Cohen—owner, New Jersey Nets

Angelo Drossos—owner, San Antonio Spurs

James Fitzgerald—owner, Milwaukee Bucks

J. Michael Gearon—president, Atlanta Hawks

Harry Glickman—general manager, Portland Trailblazers

Harold Katz—owner, Philadelphia 76ers

John "Jack" Krumpe—president, New York Knicks

Harry Mangurian—owner, Boston Celtics

Abe Pollin—chairman, owner, Washington Bullets

Larry Weinberg—owner, Portland Trailblazers

National Basketball Players Association (NBPA) Bargaining Committee

Junior Bridgeman—Milwaukee Bucks forward, NBPA treasurer

Fred Brown—Seattle Supersonics guard, NBPA vice president

Larry Fleisher—NBPA general counsel, *chief negotiator*

Charles Grantham—NBPA executive vice president

Bob Lanier—Milwaukee Bucks center, NBPA president

Maurice Lucas—Phoenix Suns forward, NBPA vice president

Steve Mix—Milwaukee Bucks/Los Angeles Lakers forward, NBPA secretary

NBPA Outside Counsel

James Quinn—Weil, Gotshal, and Manges

THE CAP

1

No Final Victories

The first day you started at the NBA, you had to read Larry O'Brien's autobiography: I think it was called *No Final Victories*. He believed you were never going to win everything, you were never going to win for all time, you negotiated the best you can and do the best you can and then try to win another time.

—RUSS GRANIK

In the first minutes of free agency, at 12:01 a.m. on July 1, 2016, Los Angeles Lakers General Manager Mitch Kupchak set out to rebuild his team. The Lakers were trying to vault back into NBA relevance. The retirement of Lakers legend Kobe Bryant and a string of down years had pushed the once-proud franchise to the periphery of the NBA. In those first moments, the first time teams could talk to players—well, talk to them legally—Kupchak decided to reach out to the agent for Timofey Mozgov, then a free-agent center who had just won a championship with the Cleveland Cavaliers.[1]

Mitch Kupchak was calling with what would become a very lucrative deal for Mozgov: a four-year contract worth $64 million dollars with an expectation that Mozgov would start for the rebuilding Lakers the following season. Mozgov quickly accepted. He would later claim that what appealed to him about the Lakers' offer was not the money—well, not entirely the money—but that he was excited about starting and playing for Luke Walton, the Lakers coach. After signing, Mozgov admitted he was not terribly familiar with his new teammates. "I'm not going to lie to you," he said. "I haven't seen them play a lot of games."[2]

Mozgov's contract was incredible: $16 million in the prior season would have placed the Russian center among the top twenty highest-paid players in the NBA, between Bulls All-Star Jimmy Butler and Wizards All-Star John Wall.[3] It would have him making $4 million more than the reigning MVP—Golden State Warriors guard Stephen Curry. Curry's wife, Ayesha, tweeted in response to the deal, "Mozgov making $4M more per year than Steph Curry has to be even more proof that the NBA is, in fact, rigged."[4]

He was an unlikely choice for such a massive deal. Mozgov was a dependable contributor for the Cavaliers in his season and a half in Cleveland. He had also been a solid rotation player in prior stops with the Denver Nuggets and the New York Knicks across the previous half dozen seasons. Mozgov's play in his season entering free agency was down a bit given his career, but not by much—he averaged seventeen minutes a game in 2015–16—using his time on the court to score a meager six points and grab just four rebounds.

Beyond his on-court performance, Mozgov's skills and player profile did not seem to fit in the modern NBA. The NBA was getting smaller, quicker, and more athletic with a focus on three-point shooting and "positionless" basketball. Mozgov's best attribute—being a massive, lumbering seven-foot-one, 275-pound center—was in heavy demand twenty years earlier but was out of place in the pace-and-space NBA. True, the Cavaliers with Mozgov had won a championship a month earlier—and make no mistake, the Lakers cared about championships—but Mozgov had played only a minor role in LeBron James's comeback against the Golden State Warriors, averaging under six minutes a game for the playoff run.

The most incredible part? Kupchak made his offer during the first minutes of free agency—presumably, before he feared the market for Mozgov, and everyone else, would go up. Mozgov was not the only player being courted with such offers, and the Lakers were not alone in offering them.

In October 2014 the NBA announced a new nine-year television agreement with its partners, Turner and ESPN, netting the league about $24 billion. The class of 2016 was the first free-agent class to benefit from that agreement, and during the summer of 2016, every team in the league had money to spend. Not only did they *have*

No Final Victories

money to spend, they *had* to spend the money—under the collective bargaining agreement between the NBA and its players, they were required to. Chandler Parsons, who averaged thirteen points and missed twenty games the previous season, went from the Dallas Mavericks to the Memphis Grizzlies for $98.5 million. Evan Turner went west—leaving the Boston Celtics for a four-year, $70 million dollar contract in Portland. Joakim Noah, who had only played in twenty-eight games the previous season, signed with the Knicks for $72 million. Mike Conley, the Memphis Grizzlies' point guard, signed a five-year, $153 million dollar deal—the most expensive deal in NBA history. In fact, six of the seven largest contracts in NBA history up to that point were signed in July 2016.

Decades earlier, the NBA, led by David Stern, and the National Basketball Players Association, led by Larry Fleisher, agreed to a deal. The more money the league made, the more the players made. The players agreed to a salary cap, a team limitation on salary, in exchange for a guaranteed percentage of revenue—most importantly, revenue earned from television, including cable. When the NBA's new cable agreement kicked in, 2016 was the first free agent class that benefitted, and the amount teams could spend on players spiked—leading to deals like Mozgov's.

When asked about it, Mozgov was up front: "I can't lie to you; I like it," he said, chuckling. "This is the way the NBA is doing business. Players are happy with the money going up. But it's not just about the players getting the money. The owners and the players association are getting money. Everybody's happy."[5]

• • •

On January 10, 1967, the bigger news of the day was that Red Auerbach had been ejected from the All-Star Game. Though he had retired the previous summer, what was meant to be a goodwill assignment, coaching the All-Stars, turned into a disaster.

Auerbach, the legendary Boston Celtics coach, had emerged from retirement only to try to lead the Eastern Conference All-Stars to a fifth-consecutive All-Star win. He couldn't. When the game started, Auerbach quickly picked up two technical fouls and got thrown out of the game in the third quarter for complaining to the referees. Auerbach, to this day, has the distinction of being the only individual in professional sports to ever be ejected from an All-Star Game.

Despite Auerbach's coarse language and jabs after the game—he said the referees would be best as "invisible non-entities"—the product on the court was spectacular.[6] The Western Conference scored a massive upset over the stars from the east, led by the hometown Warriors' All-Stars. Rick Barry—who would jump from the Warriors to the upstart American Basketball Association (ABA) a few months later and set off a firestorm that would engulf the NBA for the next decade—scored thirty-eight points. Warriors big-man Nate Thurmond pulled down eighteen rebounds for the Western Conference. This would be impressive against any team, but playing against Wilt Chamberlain, Bill Russell, and Willis Reed, the big-man talent from the Eastern Conference, made Thurmond's performance nothing short of incredible. For the Eastern Conference, Oscar Robertson led the way with twenty-six points, the only Eastern Conference player to score more than twenty.

Given the fireworks on the court and the sideline, the press would be forgiven for not focusing much attention on the pregame press conference held by the then fledgling National Basketball Players Association (NBPA). The NBPA, barely tolerated by the league, did not wield much influence. Its impact to that point had been minimal. There was no collective bargaining agreement, and the NBA and its owners had been dragging their feet for years on many of the proposals the NBPA had made. Even a few years earlier, when the NBPA seriously threatened to sit out the 1964 All-Star Game, demanding a pension from the owners, the effect was short term. The owners forgot or just ignored them. Now, in January 1967, three years after the threatened All-Star strike, the players were not much further along.

So, on January 10, 1967, led by their president, Cincinnati Royals guard Oscar Robertson, and general counsel, Larry Fleisher, the NBPA put forward a six-point plan for the future of the union and their sport. Emerging from a three-hour meeting with the players to discuss stalled pension-plan negotiations with the NBA—after having met with the owners that morning—Robertson expressed the will of the players that would serve as the roadmap for that union and every players' union for the next fifty years.

These were not requests by the players but demands. Both Robertson and Fleisher had been hardened by the experience of working in professional basketball. Years later in his autobiography, Robertson said of his relationship with Fleisher, "Larry and I shared one basic core understanding: when owners dealt with players, whatever they attempted was against our interest. That was our starting point. The league could prove that this was not the case, but we proceeded from that basic distrust."[7]

By January of 1967, Robertson had been president of the NBPA for all of eighteen months, but he had played in the NBA for several years. He was known for his combative relationship with the league and his team. He held out the previous season over a contract dispute after Royals chairman Ambrose Lindhorst told him that his contract was "not up for negotiation."[8] Robertson did not agree and refused to play. Fleisher had been working with the NBPA for about six years, all of it unpaid. Even without payment, Fleisher had doggedly fought the owners' disrespect in order to further the players' interests, all while holding down a full-time job. As recently as June 1965, the owners did not even allow Fleisher into meetings with ownership despite being an NBPA officer. J. Walter Kennedy, the league's commissioner, called Fleisher's presence at meetings "disturbing," and a sign of a "lack of mutual trust."[9] This was not a warm relationship and the NBA was not union-friendly. Neither Robertson nor Fleisher trusted ownership.

While the relationship with the players was turning adversarial, the circumstances for the NBA as a business looked promising. The league added a tenth franchise, the Chicago Bulls, and were looking at further expansion, planning to add two additional teams in 1968.[10] The league claimed that attendance was up 15 percent over the previous season, and Kennedy, who had recently inked a new five-year extension to be commissioner, believed that a twenty-team league in the not-too-distant future was likely.[11] "I don't think the owners will be satisfied with the 12-team league," Kennedy said the previous June.[12] They also had a stable television contract, and the Celtics franchise had recently sold for a record amount. "The NBA horizons are limitless," Kennedy said.[13] There was no reason not to improve the players' lot.

The substance of the plan Robertson put forward that day was nothing new—the league had heard such demands before, either from Robertson or Fleisher or Robertson's predecessor as president of the NBPA, Celtics star Tommy Heinsohn.[14] According to Heinsohn, much of what Robertson proposed in 1967 the league had already agreed to orally but simply had not followed through.[15] As the *Baltimore Sun* reported at the time, "There was nothing new or earth shattering in the demands. Almost all of them have been heard before, and in almost all cases, have fallen upon deaf ears." When outlining the plan to the press in January 1967, Fleisher said, "We have received only shabby treatment in our past dealings with the owners." Fleisher criticized the owners' prior conduct, saying, "They've continued their old-line policy of putting off to next week what they should settle today, like improved pension and health insurance plans."[16] Fleisher led the players' threatened strike at the All-Star Game three years earlier. He said that action made the owners aware that the players were serious, but there were still major issues unresolved.[17]

What made Robertson's demands different this time was that they were unambiguous, articulated together, and, most importantly, accompanied by a deadline. After laying out the proposed terms, Fleisher was stern and frustrated, "We are requesting a response from [Commissioner J. Walter] Kennedy and the owners by February 15."[18] There was no threat of a work stoppage involved if they did not receive a response—yet.

Robertson's plan had six points. First, Robertson called for a study of the present players' uniform contracts. Particularly, Robertson called for an investigation of the reserve clause—the clause in each players' contract that bound players to their teams, seemingly in perpetuity. "The reserve clause is stifling," he said, "there are cases where it has really hurt players." At the press conference before the All-Star Game, Robertson said the review of contracts would not revolve around dollars and cents. Instead, hoping that it would limit the threat, Robertson said they were calling for a study of options and players' rights to percentage of revenues.[19] Robertson's request seemed easy to accommodate. He was asking for a review—but in reality he was politely asking for free agency and an abolition of the reserve clause.

Robertson had publicly called for ending the reserve clause the previous summer—an unheard of position. In June 1966 Robertson

No Final Victories

said the NBPA called for "the elimination of the present contractual arrangement under which [players] are not able to negotiate with other teams in the league." Just wanting the ability to negotiate with other teams made Robertson a revolutionary. The headlines describing his statement blared, "Robertson leads revolt for negotiating freedom."[20] Celtics guard KC Jones said he believed the chances of NBA owners removing the reserve clause were nonexistent, lamenting that, "I don't see how the owners could consider throwing it out. If it means that a player would be free to negotiate the best deal for himself with any team in the league . . . I just can't see the owners eliminating that reserve clause."[21] Fleisher had loudly expressed his support for Robertson's ideas. In the mid-1960s, however, the reserve clause in all sports was alive and well, and the Supreme Court had upheld the practice in baseball going back decades. No matter what Robertson said, or how he said it, free agency was a pipe dream. The league had rejected Fleisher and Robertson's proposal, with Kennedy saying that the trend of the courts was to keep all professional sports free of antitrust legislation and that the reserve clause had been upheld as a "necessary evil."[22] So, in 1967, in the effort to move things forward, Robertson requested a review. To start.

Next, Robertson proposed that the league strengthen the players' pension plan by funding it with money the league earned from television, a new medium that appeared like it would be tremendously lucrative for the sport.[23] Once again, this was something that Robertson and Fleisher requested the previous year, when they asked for a share of television revenues for the players' pension. Everyone saw television as the future, and Fleisher and Robertson wanted a piece of it. The owners had simply tabled the discussion.

Third, the players wanted to create "National Basketball Players Properties Inc." This idea was similar to the group-licensing program created by professional baseball players months later. Fleisher compared the plan to a bottle-cap promotion that had run recently in pro football, saying that the players, not the owners, would reap the benefits.[24] This plan would have allowed the players to get money from their likenesses.

Next, the players wanted to establish a committee—comprised of Robertson and fellow players John Havlicek of the Celtics and Willis

Reed of the Knicks—to work with other players in other professional sports to strengthen players' rights.[25]

Finally, beyond the high-level policy desires, the players had practical concerns about their jobs. This was a union proposal after all and, no matter how special they were, the players were workers. They wanted to limit the NBA regular-season schedule to eighty-one games—they were concerned that the league's expansion would tempt owners to create eighty-eight games—eight against each opposing team in the league. On this issue Robertson was firm. "We won't play more than 81 games," he said. "I personally feel that 81 is too much, plus the exhibitions and playoffs, but we're committed to them now. But it shouldn't go any higher."[26]

Finally, Robertson called to limit the number of exhibitions and have players be paid for them. Specifically, the players requested that there be no more than ten exhibition games. According to Robertson, some clubs played as many as fifteen preseason games.

The six point plan outlined by Robertson was more than a significant milestone. It was groundbreaking. This was the first real declaration of rights and goals of professional players in modern sports history. Much of what he proposed seemed impossible at the time. Today players' rights to free agency, their likeness, television revenues, retirement safety, and a voice at work are not only reality but the foundation of NBA players' rights. Robertson also hit on issues and solutions that have remained at the forefront of labor relations in sports for the ensuing half century. Robertson made a statement of purpose as to what the NBPA could and should achieve. In retrospect, he had the force of will and vision needed to make it happen.

Robertson laid out the players' agenda—built around freedom, independence, and partnership. It was a visionary approach, well beyond what any other professional players' association had ever considered or articulated, much less accomplished. It was practical, but policy driven. It was reasonable. It was thoughtful. It met with a thud. In 1967 the owners still did not take the players seriously.

The date Fleisher demanded a response to the players' proposals from the NBA came and went. So, on March 1, 1967, the players announced that unless a deal was reached, the players would not play the playoffs. A strike date. It is forgotten now, but that was the first time any players' group had set a date for a league-wide walkout; it was set to coincide with the start of the 1967 playoffs, the most painful time for the owners to endure a strike. It spurred action—in the short and long term. Over the next half century, the players would achieve every goal Robertson laid out except one: the NBA season is eighty-two games, which is in direct opposition to Robertson's demand that players not play more than eighty-one.

At about the same time as the NBPA issued its six-point plan and Red Auerbach was thrown out of the All-Star Game in San Francisco, on the other side of California the launch of an upstart league, the American Basketball Association (ABA) was stirring. While the NBA was in San Francisco for the All-Star Game, executives for the ABA were having exploratory meetings in Los Angeles to talk about establishing the league the following season. The growth of the NBA and the viability of more teams caused entrepreneurs to consider competing with the league. Why shouldn't others get in on the limitless horizons Commissioner Kennedy thought possible for professional basketball?

About a week after the NBA All-Star Game and Robertson's announcement, rumors began to surface about the ABA in the press. The rumor was that Wilt Chamberlain had signed a contract for $150,000 to play and own the New York franchise of the ABA. Newspapers reported seeing a copy of his signed contract with the ABA. Mark Binstein, the acting chairman of the ABA, and then an assistant basketball coach at St. Peter's College in Jersey City, New Jersey, said that the league had gained momentum after a three-day meeting with Wilt Chamberlain, George Mikan, and other top executives in television and advertising who were interested in the venture. When reporters asked Chamberlain, then halfway through a three-year, $300,000 deal with the Philadelphia 76ers, about the ABA deal, he was noncommittal. Chamberlain said, "That's what they're saying, huh . . . Now wouldn't that be something?"[27] Chamberlain was the first, but not the last, player to use the threat of the ABA to try to improve his lot.

On February 2, 1967, the ABA introduced itself officially, led by Commissioner George Mikan who announced a ten-team league to begin in the fall. When asked if the ABA would attempt to poach NBA players, Mikan said, "We do not intend to raid the NBA for players. I have not read the present NBA contract. We would be stupid . . . not to ask players if they are not tied down. You have to respect contractual obligations, but if there is a player without a contract, we invite him to contact us."[28] Mikan also said he expected the two leagues to drive up salaries.

He also made several statements that were music to Fleisher and Robertson's ears. Mikan said, "When two people compete you show me a way it won't spiral cost. I'd like to be a 25-year-old kid now. The NBA isn't happy with our move. They try to give the impression there's no room for somebody else, but they're expanding."[29] Somewhere, Fleisher was nodding. Dennis Murphy, the owner of the Oakland franchise in the ABA was clear that they would get NBA players, saying about Wilt Chamberlain, "We know he'll be in our league and we are assured other superstars will be in also." Mikan, in referring to Chamberlain said, "We hope his position is such that he can join us. We would like to have Wilt, Oscar Robertson and any players like that who are available."[30]

"We simply believe there is room for two leagues operating independently," Mikan said.[31]

• • •

"I don't want you to read anything into this," Larry Fleisher said, smiling, as he lit up a cigar at the start of the press conference on February 3, 1976. "These aren't any of Red Auerbach's victory cigars."[32] In 1976 Fleisher was still the general counsel of the National Basketball Players Association, but his position in the basketball universe had changed. Dramatically. No longer denied entry into meetings with ownership, Fleisher had quietly become one of the most powerful people in professional basketball. As David Halberstam wrote of the late-1970s NBA, Fleisher was, "Perhaps, thought some observers, *the* most powerful man, excepting always whoever happened to run CBS sports at the moment."[33] Not only was he the head of the NBPA, he was one of the most powerful agents as well. For years, he took no money for his position as the head of the NBPA. The reason? It was not a noble gesture; it was a practical one—there was no money. He did not even work fulltime in basketball until 1971, ten years after he started with the NBPA.

Fleisher was important enough in 1976, however, to draw Auerbach's ire. Auerbach described Fleisher to legendary *Boston Globe* writer Bob Ryan as "some sort of Hitler reincarnate," after his Celtics lost Don Chaney, a Fleisher client, to the ABA. Regardless of his public image, Fleisher was certainly happy to appropriate the Celtics legend's postgame habit of lighting a victory cigar to commemorate NBA players gaining their freedom.[34] As one sports reporter for the *Baltimore Sun* wrote, "Auerbach never had one to match the victory Fleisher pulled off here at the expense of the NBA owners."[35] Fleisher called a press conference at the NBA All-Star Game in Philadelphia in February 1976 to announce a deal. This victory warranted a cigar.

The league and its players had reached a settlement to end the massive outstanding antitrust lawsuit the players had filed against the NBA six years earlier. In 1970 the NBPA, led by Fleisher and Robertson, had filed suit to block a proposed merger between the NBA and the ABA, which had spent the time, almost immediately from Red Auerbach's ejection, poaching NBA players, college players, and high school players and setting off a bidding war for professional basketball talent. Robertson and Fleisher's lawsuit was more than the polite request for review of the reserve clause that Robertson made at the All-Star Game in 1967. By 1970 Robertson and the NBPA were suing to have it thrown out entirely. They were tired of waiting. Player representatives for all of the NBA teams signed the lawsuit, along with the top stars in the league, with Oscar Robertson as the lead plaintiff. The *Robertson* case, as it was known, had been moving through the courts for six years.

The lawsuit claimed that certain key pieces of the NBA business were unlawful: the draft, the reserve clause, and the NBA's compensation rule, which allowed the commissioner to penalize teams who signed another team's players. All three were meant to artificially restrict the ability of players to switch teams, therefore restricting competition among business competitors. A clearly monopolistic practice likely to violate antitrust law. The true goal was to get an injunction to stop the ABA and NBA from merging—the inclusion of those three restrictions was a throw in. Fleisher's kitchen sink play. However, it was what stuck. The federal judge presiding over the litigation had given the players a favorable initial ruling, on February

14, 1975. A few months later, in a different case, a similar compensation rule in the NFL was struck down. The writing was on the wall that the NBA players were going to win. The owners were spending way beyond their budget for legal fees, and there was going to be a trial. By the start of 1976, under pressure, owners came to the table with the players. By February 1976 they made a deal to settle the case.

The settlement was a major milestone. Describing the scene to reporters at the February press conference, Ryan said, "We knew something big was up when Larry Fleisher, [Philadelphia 76ers guard] Fred Carter, [Boston Celtics forward] Paul Silas and [Detroit Pistons center] Bob Lanier were puffing victory cigars as they sat down to tell us about the *Robertson* case settlement."[36] It had taken so long to reach agreement—six years—that Oscar Robertson, the namesake and the head of the NBPA when the lawsuit was filed, had been out of the league for years by the time the deal was struck.

The NBA did more than agree to settle the case with Fleisher, it surrendered. The NBA had fought bitterly for six years, desperately trying to wait players out, hoping their resolve would break while running up costs they knew the players couldn't match. But in the end, it was they who caved. In truth, the NBA's aggressiveness was a tactical error—it bound the players together, gave them agency over the entire process. "The settlement appears to represent a near-total victory by the players," the *Los Angeles Times* reported.[37] Though Commissioner Larry O'Brien referred to the deal making as "give and take," a dissenting NBA owner described it as "us giving and the players taking."[38] Weeks later, news reports surfaced with headlines screaming "surrender" over O'Brien's face and the commissioner denying anonymous claims that he had capitulated to players.[39]

The settlement was massive and complicated—a staggered phase in of rights and rules over the coming decade that would mean the league's signings and transactions needed to be overseen by a federal court until 1987. That was the way Fleisher wanted it. He didn't trust the owners and wanted someone looking over their shoulder.

When he announced the deal, Fleisher, described as "owl-eyed" from days and nights of intense negotiation with the NBA, sat at a table flanked by several of his lieutenants prepared to divulge the settlement terms for the agreement that would bring freedom to the

NBA.[40] Fleisher, then forty-six, though universally described as understated, was clearly enjoying his moment of victory. It was the culmination of more than a decade of faith in players, work, growth, and building a sense of confidence in themselves. He tried to play down the deal as "something we can live with," but in reality it was a tremendous success.[41] There were other things he wanted for the players, namely, revenue from television. That would come. But on that day in 1976, Fleisher had to settle for free agency.

When the *Robertson* case was over, the future seemed bright. "This marks a new era in management-player relations," O'Brien said a few weeks later when the NBA and its players finalized the agreement. "The primary interest is that of the fan and . . . this will keep the emphasis on the court instead of in it." Paul Silas, president of the NBPA, said, "This will make for happier times for all of us."[42]

• • •

Silas was wrong. The chaos that began in the '60s, continued through the '70s and into the early '80s. The *Robertson* settlement fixed one set of problems and created another. There were no final victories—certainly not in the NBA.

The NBA had spent decades in a precarious position financially and legally. The NBPA, like every other sports labor union at the time, wanted player freedom and ever-higher salaries. Comically poor ownership for many franchises, weak television revenue, and a set of rules that limited the NBA's oversight of owner incompetence further exacerbated the situation. As a result, in 1983 the NBA and its players made a novel settlement—a salary cap. The agreement was a compromise intended to end the chaos that had gripped the sport since the 1960s. The salary cap, then and now, is a partnership—a profit sharing agreement—the more money the NBA makes, the more money the players get. The deal that was made in 1983 is not simply a lid on salaries that owners had attempted, unsuccessfully, to push on the players in 1980, and again in 1982. The deal in 1983 focused on redistributing income from the sport among players and owners, while distributing accountability among owners to avoid incompetence. It provided everyone with a stake in the business. In settling in 1983, the players gave up the possibility of infinite salaries—a tremendous concession given the salary inflation in previous years and the rosy projections for the NBA business moving forward. What they gained, however, was a guaranteed piece of the greater revenue pie and free agency to play where they wished; a combination that did not exist before in professional sports but became the framework for the NBA, NFL, and NHL. The players got a seat at the table. There is a belief now that this agreement, this economic structure that now governs the NBA, was an inevitability, the outcome of destiny for professional sports. It, most certainly, was not.

On several occasions over the difficult, complex ten-month negotiations, both sides attempted to walk away. The owners attempted to implement draconian proposals. The players threatened a strike. Both Fleisher and Stern proposed abandoning the proposed salary cap entirely. Both had constituencies to keep together—this was more of an issue for Stern, who had owners attempt to derail his agreement at the last moment. A salary cap built on revenue was complex and uncharted, and neither side was certain of what would occur. Both sides made proposals that they believed would help them at the time—but in hindsight would never have entertained.

Fleisher would take heat for the agreement—to agree to a cap on salaries is antithetical to what a union was supposed to do. Though he believed the cap to be temporary when agreed to—to help the league get back on its feet—Fleisher would vehemently defend the agreement, saying that to become partners in the business was a tremendous accomplishment. Before that, and without it, the players were chattel. When the agreement was reached, NBPA treasurer and Milwaukee Buck Steve Mix turned to David Stern, then the executive vice president for legal and business affairs for the NBA, and summarized the nature of the agreement. "Hi partner," Mix said to the soon to be commissioner.[43] For ownership, the Bulls' Jonathan Kovler said, "I hope the players get a lot in TV revenue because that means the league will be healthy."[44]

Kovler got what he wanted. The NBA now earns a lot in TV revenue. In 2016 revenues soared because of the new television deal, and the salary cap increased, meaning there was a massive influx of money teams could—nay, *had*—to spend on players. The league attempted to convince the new head of the NBPA, Michele Roberts, to agree to "cap smoothing," which would gradually increase the cap to avoid such inflation in salaries and avoid situations like Mozgov's. The union, seeing no reason to add yet another artificial restriction on player salaries, declined. Roberts would say later: "It would be quite counterintuitive for the union to ever agree to artificially lower, as opposed to raise, the salary cap. If we ever were to do so, there would have to be a damn good reason, inarguable and uncontroverted. There was no such assurance in place at that time."[45]

So, when 2016 hit, the increase was massive—not 5 percent or 8 percent, but about 30 percent. Free agency in 2016, the first year the spike impacted players, was pandemonium. The vision Robertson described in 1967 and that Fleisher had moved toward in 1976 and the goals of the deal he made for television revenue in 1983 were realized. Free agency in 2016 was how both sides—the NBPA and the NBA—envisioned the best-case scenario of the salary cap and partnership they agreed to in 1983. As a result, nearly thirty-five years after the cap was instituted, more than twenty-five years after Fleisher died, and about fifty years after Fleisher began to covet television money for players, Fleisher's vision of player mobility and faith in the NBA on television came to life. Though Fleisher had been dead for years and all but forgotten from the public consciousness, the goals of the deal he made in 1983 and the roadmap that Robertson laid out fifty years earlier were realized.

• • •

When Kupchak signed Mozgov in those first moments of free agency in 2016, he had been a part of the Los Angeles Lakers franchise, in some form or another, for thirty-five years. He had joined the team as a player in the fateful summer of 1981, when free agency first came to the NBA in earnest, thanks to Fleisher's *Robertson* settlement. As part of that first wave of free agents, Kupchak signed with the Lakers, having completed his contract with the Washington Bullets amid a league-wide spending spree, not that much different from 2016. When he signed with the Lakers, Kupchak had been with the Bullets his entire career, not exactly a star, but like Mozgov, he had helped his team win a championship. He signed a seven-year, $5.6 million dollar contract, less than one tenth of the value of Mozgov's, but massive at the time. His agent in that deal was Larry Fleisher.

Kupchak's deal with the Lakers was panned by many throughout the NBA, with league executives like Jerry Colangelo of the Suns and Carl Scheer of the Nuggets going on the record to deride the deal, and Kupchak, as being a poor value. The owner of the Bullets, Abe Pollin, had been close with Kupchak, and saw his deal as a sign that the league had passed him by, and rumors were growing that he would sell the team. As the *Los Angeles Times* reported at the time, "Is free agent Mitch Kupchak worth $5.6 million over seven years? . . . some NBA general managers, fearful of the large salaries free agents are commanding, called the figure absurd." Kupchak himself derided the deal, just as Mozgov did thirty-five years later, saying in response to whether he was worth the money, "No. I don't think any athlete is worth that much money. But I was in the right place at the right time in the right system."[46]

2

Pleasantries and Unpleasantries, July 1982

We met for 1 hour and 20 minutes and only 15 minutes were
related to collective bargaining. The rest of the time was spent on
pleasantries and unpleasantries.

—LARRY FLEISHER, July 29, 1982

I disagree. We spent 20 minutes on collective bargaining issues, and
the rest on pleasantries and unpleasantries.

—DAVID STERN, July 29, 1982

On June 1, 1982, the collective bargaining agreement between the
NBA and its players expired with little fanfare. The players did not
strike. The owners did not lock them out. Despite the claims of run-
away salaries and teams bleeding money over the life of the previous agreement, both sides let the CBA expire quietly and without
urgency for a new one. In fact, at the time the contract expired, the
NBA and the NBPA had not even met yet to discuss their next agreement. The NBA had not even finalized its proposals. For the most
part, on June 1, 1982, the people relevant to the upcoming collective
bargaining negotiation—Commissioner Larry O'Brien, NBA Executive Vice President David Stern, and NBPA General Counsel Larry
Fleisher—were distracted by the end of the NBA season. The day the
CBA ended was also the third game of the NBA Finals between the
Los Angeles Lakers and the Philadelphia 76ers, taking place in Los
Angeles, after the teams had split the first two games at the Spectrum
in Philadelphia. No matter what the circumstances, the action on the
court took precedence.

The Lakers, led by their young star Earvin "Magic" Johnson and their old star Kareem Abdul-Jabbar, were trying to win their second championship in three years. After a tumultuous season in 1980–81—a humiliating first round playoff upset for the defending champs coupled with massive public dissension among the players aimed primarily at Johnson—the Lakers entered 1981–82 embroiled in drama, even as they remained overwhelming favorites to win the Western Conference. If the end of the 1981 season was about the Lakers' players feuding among themselves, then the start of the 1981–82 season was about the team revolting against its coach, Paul Westhead.

Westhead was entering his third full season as head coach of the Lakers in 1981. His tenure as head coach coincided directly with that of the team's owner, Dr. Jerry Buss, and Johnson, who had been drafted weeks after Buss took over in 1979. Westhead had been hired as an assistant to Jack McKinney, who had grown up under Dr. Jack Ramsay and the Portland Trailblazers before being hired by Buss to be the Lakers head coach. Before the start of his first season, McKinney had been injured in a bike accident and was unable to coach. Westhead took over the job of a lifetime.

After a championship as a rookie coach in 1980 and a disappointing second season, Westhead had a new idea for the 1981–82 season: he wanted to implement a new offense. This was the era of offensive and defensive "systems" in the NBA—Hubie Brown had built one in Atlanta to much success and fanfare, and the NBA being a copycat league, Westhead was looking to copycat. The benefit of a system was that it removed responsibility from the play on the floor. Success? The system worked. Failure? The players couldn't adapt to the system. Doug Moe, the coach of the Nuggets, said of Brown's system: when his team lost "early in the year, he said it was because they had lousy players; when they started to win it was good coaching."[1] For a coach, and perhaps a coach on the hot seat who had overseen a failure the previous season, it seemed like a no-lose situation. The system Westhead devised for the Lakers was complicated; it required more play calling from Westhead from the bench and less of the freewheeling style that Magic, and the Lakers, were known for.[2] As Magic said later, Westhead "violated one of the fundamental rules of sports, politics, business, and just about everything else: if it ain't broke, don't fix it."

Westhead's system was an immediate and unqualified disaster, both on the court and with the players. The Lakers started the 1981–82 season with a 2-4 record, and Johnson and other players said they were unable to get into the flow of their new offense. After a twenty-six-point drubbing in San Antonio, Johnson was aloof with reporters, sitting alone at the airport with his headphones on, saying, "Sometimes I just have to sit in the sunshine and think." Westhead was upset with the players' reluctance to accept his offense and preached patience, saying cryptically, in defense of his system, "The almond tree bears its fruit in silence."[3]

While the Lakers won the next five games after the San Antonio blowout, all of the wins were close and the team teetered. After a win in Utah, the tension boiled over. As the Lakers went to the dressing room, Westhead pulled Johnson aside for a private conversation. It did not go well. When Johnson emerged and spoke to the media, he demanded a trade.

"I can't play here anymore," Johnson said. "I want to leave. I want to be traded. I can't deal with it no more." The media and his teammates were stunned. Johnson was asked if he was serious—he had just signed a twenty-five-year contract the previous summer that was set to start in two years and run through 2009. Johnson replied, "Definitely. I haven't been happy all season. I've got to go." Regarding Westhead specifically, Johnson was asked if he wanted him to leave Los Angeles, to which Johnson said, "Yeah. We don't see eye to eye on a lot of things. It's time for me to go."[4]

Lakers owner Jerry Buss was shocked by Johnson's trade demand when the news got back to him. Buss, who orchestrated the twenty-five-year, $25 million contract for Johnson, was tremendously close to his young superstar. He was told of Johnson's demand while at the Forum watching the Los Angeles Kings, the NHL team he also owned. Buss responded by preaching calm. Described as someone who did "everything he [could] to project a swinger's image," according to the *Los Angeles Times*, Buss said, "The main thing you learn the longer you're in sports is don't overreact, don't panic, sit back and talk to everybody, then make the moves that are necessary based on what you've discovered."[5] Despite Buss's Zen response, Westhead never coached another game for the Lakers. He was dismissed within twenty-four hours of Magic's demand. Buss replaced him with two coaches: Jerry West, running the offense, and Pat Riley, running the defense. After some confusion—West had not exactly agreed to that—West stepped aside and Riley took over.

The rest is history. From the minute Riley was installed as coach the Lakers went on a tear, winning sixteen of their first eighteen games. As Magic proclaimed in December, just a month after Westhead's firing, "It's show time again."[6] The name stuck. There was no more discussion of trading Magic. Under Riley's coaching, the Lakers won fifty of seventy-one regular season games and finished with the best record in the Western Conference, despite Westhead's system failure in their first eleven games. In the playoffs, the Lakers remained dominant, sweeping its two playoff series entering the Finals with the Philadelphia 76ers.

By the time they got to June 1, the third game of the Finals, the day the CBA expired, the series with the Philadelphia 76ers had just gotten interesting. After winning Game One, the Lakers were coming off their first loss in forty-six days, a 110–94 loss to the Sixers in Game Two. The Sixers had been the first team to beat them in six weeks. Before the loss, the Lakers were loudly stating their goal of being the best team in the history of basketball, by winning all twelve playoff games and sweeping all three series. Riley saw the record as a motivating factor, something to keep his unbeatable team engaged. As *Sports Illustrated* recounted in response to the loss, "The Los Angeles Lakers hadn't been playing other basketball teams so much as they had been playing history, and history didn't seem to know how to stop a fast break." After the Game Two loss Magic, seemingly disappointed to be playing only for a championship, said, "We had a chance to do something no one else had done. Now we have the chance to be the champs. I guess we have to focus on that."[7]

Unlike the Lakers playoff dominance, the Sixers had to scratch and claw their way into the Finals. The Sixers had been one of the dominant teams of the NBA in the late 1970s and early 1980s, but they had very little to show for it. The Sixers were the greatest beneficiaries of the merger between the ABA and the NBA in 1976 because they were able to acquire the ABA's best player, Dr. J. (Julius Erving), from the New York Nets. Though the Sixers had the best overall record over

Pleasantries and Unpleasantries

the previous six seasons, neither they nor Erving had won a championship.[8] There were fears the team was on the downswing.

Running into the Lakers in the Finals in 1982 was like running into a buzz saw. The Sixers were a tick older and slower than the Lakers, and it showed. The Sixers and the Lakers played a similar style, but the Lakers were simply better at it. The Sixers had been a strong transition team all season, but the Lakers made them look slow. As Sixers guard, and NBPA player representative Clint Richardson said, "We were trying so hard to get our baskets and it seemed as if they were getting theirs so easy. Sometimes it makes you wonder why you even bother to go down to the other end to play defense."[9]

The Lakers would go on to win the 1982 NBA championship in six games, giving Magic Johnson his second title in his first three seasons in the NBA, and frustrating the Sixers, their fans, and their owner, diet magnate Harold Katz, when they came up short yet again. When asked during the Finals about their championship futility, Katz flatly denied reports that he had planned to break up the Sixers if they were unable to win a championship. "All I ever said was we might need to make some changes. I never talked about totally breaking up the team. I'm not the kind of guy that goes and does rash things. Everything I do is based on a business decision that might better the team," Katz said.[10] After another season and another disappointing result, the Sixers were entering a crucial offseason.

So, despite the CBA expiration in early June, it was not until the end of July that the NBA and the NBPA got together for their first bargaining session. Regardless of the difficulties the NBA faced coming out of the *Robertson* settlement, by 1982 things were looking a little bit better for the NBA. Not great, but better. The NBA under O'Brien had been committed to improving its position in the sports landscape. In 1979 the league hired an outside PR firm, and the NBA began to look at syndication of games and taking a larger role in the league's broadcast marketing. Leading all of those initiatives, which had shown early positive result, was David Stern. At the gate, despite years of decreasing attendance, attendance league wide was up almost 10 percent in 1981–82, with nine teams reporting increases of 1,100 fans per game.[11]

Most importantly, that winter the NBA, led in negotiations by Stern, had signed a new four-year broadcast television deal with CBS, USA, and ESPN worth $88 million—a minimal increase in the fees for the rights.[12] This was in a period in which the value of other sports' broadcast rights was exploding. The NFL, Major League Baseball, and even college basketball were all seeing massive exponential increases in broadcast revenue—each new broadcast deal basically doubled the league's payout. Not so much for the NBA. Though the value of the deal had increased, the league's imprint on broadcast television, which was crucial in 1982, would be much smaller in the next agreement. The deal called for as few as four games on CBS, and a maximum of twenty-eight games, compared to forty in the previous season. Additionally, CBS agreed to televise the All-Star Game and up to twenty-three playoff games. The big move for the NBA was to shift some of its games to cable, with both USA and ESPN networks televising forty NBA games.[13] In truth, the value of the contract was in those CBS games—they paid exponentially more than the cable networks.

The Finals ended on June 8, later than any finals in the history of the NBA. The late end to the season was not accidental—it was to save the NBA embarrassment. The NBA, tired of starting its season in mid-October as the World Series was dominating the headlines, began the 1981–82 season in late October to have the sports landscape to itself once the World Series ended. In addition, starting the season in late October and having its Finals in June had the benefit of timing the Finals so they were outside of the crucial sweeps network ratings periods in May. As a result, the NBA Finals, which were not strong enough for CBS to run during sweeps, were aired live on the network, which paid them for the first time in years.[14] So things in the NBA were better. They were certainly not good.

• • •

David Stern, executive vice president for Business and Legal Affairs and nominally the second most powerful person in the National Basketball Association (though by all accounts even then he was the most powerful), walked into the Berkshire Hotel in midtown Manhattan on July 29, 1982 intending to remake the business of basketball. Stern was at the hotel for the first day of negotiations for a new collective bargaining agreement between the NBA and its Players Association. The agreement would be the second after the *Robert-*

Pleasantries and Unpleasantries

son settlement in 1976 and the first with Stern as the chief negotiator. The stakes for these negotiations, and for Stern, were high—in some corners, there was concern that the future of the NBA itself was at stake. The league claimed it was hemorrhaging money, and several teams, mostly the old ABA franchises, were in danger of folding. Six years after the *Robertson* settlement, the NBA was a mess. Well, a mess from the owner's perspective.

Publicly, the owners placed the blame for the NBA's economic troubles on rising player costs; the loosening of player movement and the increase in economic competition for players' services achieved through Fleisher's machinations, the *Robertson* settlement, and the ABA/NBA war had led to a dramatic increase in salaries and benefits. The problem was, the owners claimed, the sports' profits couldn't keep up with the escalating salaries. The league's accountants said the NBA had lost $13 million for the season ending in 1980, up from $8 million the year before, and that day Stern would tell Fleisher and the NBPA that the losses had reached $20 million league wide in the 1981–82 season. Some believed those numbers, which were staggering to begin with, were too conservative because they failed to take into account the high interest rates that less stable teams were paying on the massive debt they had racked up.[15]

There was a deeper concern that professional basketball was rotten from the inside. Television ratings were weak compared to other major sports, and attendance was spotty, even in big markets like New York and Chicago, where the game should have been thriving. As the *Chicago Tribune* said, "When formidable teams in New York and Chicago fail to draw capacity crowds regularly, something dramatic is wrong."[16] In smaller markets, like Indiana, San Diego, Cleveland, and Utah, the circumstances were even more bleak. The perception of drug use among players, especially cocaine, was everywhere. An article in the *Los Angeles Times*—which the NBA later vehemently denied—entitled "NBA and Cocaine: Nothing to Snort At," placed the number of NBA players who used cocaine at 40 to 75 percent of the entire league. Frank Layden, then general manager of the Utah Jazz, was quoted as saying, "There is not a team in the league you can confidently say does not have a drug problem."[17]

There was also concern about the racial makeup of the NBA. As

Stern said, years later, "There was a fair amount of discussion of the fact that the NBA was predominantly black on the playing court. It became fashionable to discuss whether a black league could ever succeed in a predominantly white country." Stern hated that argument. "We never had a doubt that that was a non-issue but that's something that was widely dealt with in the press."[18]

The NBA was unsure how to improve the game. They looked at every possibility—whether the changes were to come from within the game itself, the stands, or the television set. In 1981 the NBA league office asked every team to assess the fundamental nature of the game and make recommendations through a questionnaire.[19] They sent the questionnaire to a broad spectrum of basketball luminaries to gain insight, including Fleisher.[20] Some people thought the league should implement a zone defense. Others thought they should extend the shot clock to thirty-four seconds. Some thought the league needed more white players. Wayne Embry, the former player and front office executive, who the *Chicago Tribune* believed could admit the race problem *because* he was black, said, "If the argument that we don't have enough white players is legitimate—and it might be—then the zone might be the answer. The 24-second clock has developed basketball into a game of speed and quickness. And the consensus is that black kids are quicker, have more speed, and jump better. There are a lot of good white players, kids who might be a step slow defensively, but who can shoot and pass, who you could hide in a zone defense."[21]

There was hope for the future—if the league could hold on—in television. Cable television. As Sonny Werblin, president of Madison Square Garden, put it, "a lot of teams are looking for the revenue from cable and pay TV as the savior, but that help is three or four years away, and by that time a lot of these clubs and owners will be long gone."[22] The MSG network, which had started a few years earlier, was a massive, unexpected success, and the Seattle Supersonics, among a number of NBA franchises, were planning to have their own channels to broadcast the games—and keep the advertising revenues—themselves. The NBA was closely monitoring the growth of this avenue, especially Stern, who had been leading the initiative since the mid-1970s. They had reached deals with USA and ESPN in their most recent agreement and had explored league-wide deals with

Pleasantries and Unpleasantries

HBO as far back as 1976. There was an expectation that every team would have their own channel within a few years.

While owners wanted to blame the players for the rising cost, in their hearts (and in private and even, sometimes, with newspaper reporters) owners agreed that they themselves were also a major problem in creating the economic issues the NBA faced, for a number of reasons. As a basic matter, there was too much turnover among owners. The NBA had twenty-two different sales between 1972 and 1982, nearly four times as many as the NFL. From 1971 to 1981 the NBA had forty-five different ownership groups, and several teams, including the famed Boston Celtics and Houston Rockets, had cycled through five different ownership groups in the previous ten years.[23]

The turnstile ownership cycle resulted in serious instability and short-term thinking. As Fleisher described it, these owners "buy in and take a very active role for two years or so, until the novelty wears off. Then they begin to disappear and are gone completely after four years, maximum five."[24] Also, with that much turnover, the NBA had more than its fair share of bad owners who were focused on the fame of owning a team and the short term of the franchise. The union called this group of owners the "used car salesmen." Not just a pejorative term: at one point in 1983, three of the NBA's twenty-three teams were owned by salesmen from the same car dealership. Bad owners exacerbated the existing problems through short-term thinking, deferred payments, fiscal irresponsibility, and always expecting some sucker to be ready to buy their franchise.

The problem was that it was not altogether clear that there were many eager buyers ready to purchase NBA franchises by 1982, and that perceived lack of prospective owners would impact collective bargaining. Celtics owner Harry Mangurian said, "Over the years, the owners would meet with Fleisher to make a collective bargaining deal, and they would cry to him about how much money they were losing. He would tell that it wasn't his fault, and that if they didn't like it, sell. There would be another fool waiting to buy it. Fleisher always counted on that next fool to keep things going for him," he said. Now, it was different. "I am currently the chairman of the committee in the league that deals with ownership and expansion and there are no more fools out there. There are no more buyers."[25] As the merry-go-round slowed down, the NBA got stuck with several really bad franchises with very bad ownership groups. Monumentally bad. Egregiously stupid. For example, Ted Stepien of the Cleveland Cavaliers. Stepien, who was described by a fellow owner as someone who "thinks with his mouth open," traded every future draft choice for the better part of the next decade and responded by overpaying bench players. There was also Donald Sterling, an egomaniac who had submarined his own franchise, made public statements that it was his intent to lose, and failed to make basic payments. (Joe Axelson, the vice president of operations for the NBA, said in a confidential memo to O'Brien of Sterling that he "apparently thinks the fans pay to see him and not the team.")[26]

On the other hand, shrewd owners in big markets, like Dr. Jerry Buss of the glitzy Los Angeles Lakers, used the strength of their markets to keep their stars, sign better players, and write off the failures. Buss used his business acumen to make more money than before, increasing the Lakers' advantage over smaller markets. Buss scared the hell out of owners in smaller markets because of the possibility of dominance by coastal teams—if Buss could afford to pay Mitch Kupchak almost a million dollars a year for seven years and have him sit the first three quarters of the season in the first year of the contract and *not play at all in the second year,* how on earth could the Indiana Pacers, who could not afford to pay Kupchak to *start,* compete?

In addition to the sheer volume of owners coming in and out the door, there was also the issue of how the owners in the NBA were and should be economically accountable to one another. In short, they weren't. Unlike other sports, NBA teams, though partners as franchises, were not really bound to one another financially. At that time NBA teams did not share gate receipts as they did in Major League Baseball, and though they did share television revenue, it was not nearly as large a portion of team income as the national TV deals were for the NFL.[27] Efforts to make teams more accountable to one another had died in the NBA's Board of Governors meetings. As a result, there was little that bound them together, or, more importantly, that made them accountable to one another. Teams were little fiefdoms run as separate businesses. In the early '80s, teams were not even required to make financial statements or budgets available to one another, which

Pleasantries and Unpleasantries

made their relationships more opaque.[28] As a result, the interests of various teams were not aligned, and since owners were coming in and out of the league so quickly, they were not incentivized to make longer-term decisions. Teams were deferring costs well into the future. During the early '80s nearly half of the players in the league had some amount of deferred compensation.[29] Bob Ryan of the *Boston Globe* was more succinct: "What the NBA has . . . is a generally excellent product that is hampered by mismanagement."[30]

Under the current framework there was actually very little the owners could do about the dominance of Buss or the incompetence of Stepien and Sterling. Since the demand to buy teams was not as high as it was in baseball or football, and the risks of ownership seemed so much greater, the NBA generally had to accept people with the money to pay, regardless of their character. Additionally, those teams that were making money were not terribly interested in sharing revenues and saving owners from themselves for a number of reasons.

First, there were the old NBA and ABA franchises. The NBA/ABA settlement that had merged the leagues in 1976 had been an angry peace. The NBA owners exacted hefty financial concessions from and put limitations on the old ABA franchises, putting them in considerable debt, and the legacy NBA owners simply had no appetite for helping them. Then, there were expansion teams. Donald Carter, owner of the Mavericks, resented his cost of expansion (he had joined the NBA in 1980) and had no plan to share revenues with other owners. "They made us dance naked, dance naked and dance naked," he said, using naked dancing as a stand-in for expansion fees. "They won't get any sympathy from me to bail them out."[31] In preparations for collective bargaining negotiations in 1982, the NBA league office raised the possibility of establishing a line of credit in case of a player strike. During one meeting, several owners said that they would "be unwilling to place their credit on the line to assist weaker clubs in borrowing necessary funding."[32] This was not a cohesive group.

That was the landscape Stern was working in as he hoped to achieve what felt impossible in professional sports in the early 1980s—he wanted to limit player salaries. Not only that, he wanted to get the players to agree to the rollback through collective bargaining. Stern and the NBA could not act unilaterally; they needed Larry Fleisher, who had made his life's work improving the rights and earning power of NBA players, to agree with their vision of the NBA's future. Stern may have had his own goals, but they did not seem likely to be achieved.

Unlike Stern, Fleisher's constituency was cohesive. Their position was clear. The players' view was that the economic circumstances in the NBA were the owners' problem. For the players, the *Robertson* settlement achieved much of what they wanted. A ten-year phase in of rights escalating in the players' favor, until—it was expected— total unbridled free agency would enter when the settlement ended, after the 1986–87 season. It was a compromise—as any settlement was—but there was a plan to institute free agency for players as well as limitations on the onerous player draft. To top it off (and of crucial interest to Fleisher), all activities relating to player restraints, movements, and freedoms were to be overseen by a federal court for the decade the settlement was in place.[33] That way, no matter what games the owners played—and they would and did play games—there would be someone looking over their shoulders who had the power to make the owners heel. Fleisher's view of the importance of this issue is embodied in an op-ed he penned in the *Washington Post* in 1979 entitled "Courts Provide Player Clout to Challenge NBA," which included a cartoon with a suited owner leaning over a table scowling at a jerseyed player sitting across from him. Over his shoulder and clearly on his side—?—a stern-looking judge with a gavel staring back at the owner. In 1982, from the player's perspective, the system the settlement created, though imperfect, seemed to be working the way it was intended.

As a result, while Stern was trying to remake the business of the sport, the status quo was just fine for Fleisher and the players. There was very little interest on the player's side to provide givebacks at all. Fleisher knew whose fault the issues—if they existed at all—were. In fact, early on in the negotiations when Stern was unable to get the players to agree to the cap, he asked Fleisher if the players had any proposals to save the league money. Fleisher's response? "Get better owners, with more money, who market better."[34] He wasn't wrong.

Certainly, there were things the union wanted to achieve in these negotiations—Fleisher arrived at the Berkshire Hotel with five pages worth of proposals—things like increasing minimum salaries and benefits. But in reality, if he had to make any changes to the status quo he really wanted just one thing—a piece of television revenues. Buried on page three was a proposal, simply written among improvements to medical care and increases to per diem, requiring "payment to the players for the right to use, distribute or license any performance by the players on network and local broadcast TV, pay TV, cable TV, cassette or other means of distribution known or unknown." He had been going after a piece of television revenues for a decade, back to the early 1970s. If there was hope in TV, Fleisher wanted a piece.

• • •

By the time negotiations between the NBA and its players kicked off in July 1982, they were expected to be slow, drawn out, and tense. The terrain was fraught, and the likelihood of a work stoppage was significant. Historically the NBA and its players, generally, and Stern and Fleisher, specifically, had a strong, constructive relationship. Despite a few close calls, the NBA and its players had never had a strike or a lockout in decades of bargaining. In prior negotiations strike dates had been called, lockouts had been threatened, sabers had been rattled, but last-second negotiations occurred, and each time, no games were lost. As the *New York Times* described the relationship between Fleisher and Stern, "Since the 1960's, David Stern and Larry Fleisher have stared at each other across the bargaining table, sometimes screaming, sometimes laughing, but always able to work out a solution."[35] In 1982, however, no matter how jovial the relationship, the NBA was not immune from the trends in the broader sports landscape. Attempts by management in other sports to limit free agency, less draconian than what Stern was proposing, had led to turbulent times in the early 1980s. The players in each of the three major sports had been on similar trajectories: their unions were established and ignored in the 1960s, they made gains and eventually achieved free agency in the mid-1970s, and by the early 1980s they were defending their achievements amid bitter owners who saw their costs grow profoundly with increased players' rights. By 1982 these battles were reaching a crescendo. The Major League Baseball players had gone on strike the year before over free agency issues, costing the league a considerable amount and ending in a victory for the MLBPA, and its Executive Director Marvin Miller, which amounted to protecting what they had achieved. The National Football League, who had an especially tense relationship with its Players Association, and specifically the NFLPA's Executive Director Ed Garvey, were deep in very adversarial negotiations for a new agreement in the summer of 1982. The NFLPA had agreed to very limited free agency in the last round of negotiations, and players felt duped. When that agreement ended, the players wanted a greater percentage of league revenues and were preparing to strike over it, which they did in the fall of 1982. As a result, at the start of negotiations Stern did not know exactly what to expect or what response his proposals might provoke. The NBA had always had the most positive labor relationship in professional sports, but they had never had negotiations like these before.

That first session, in late July, was well attended. Stern was flanked in the conference room by NBA General Counsel Russ Granik; outside attorneys Joseph Barbash of the law firm of Debevoise and Plimpton; and Jeff Mishkin of Stern's old law firm, Proskauer, Rose, Goetz, and Mendelsohn. As for the players, they were represented by Fleisher and Charles Grantham, Fleisher's top aide. In addition, the players were represented by Jim Quinn, the NBPA's outside counsel from Weil, Gotshal, and Manges, who had litigated the *Robertson* case, as well as two players, Milwaukee Bucks center and NBPA president, Bob Lanier and Steve Mix, a forward who had just completed his contract with the Philadelphia 76ers and who was also the union's treasurer.

Stern began the negotiations. After an agreement to keep things out of the press, Stern made an opening statement. Though this was a negotiation, and not a trial, Stern wanted to make clear the overarching concern for these negotiations and to frame the deliberations on his terms. Stern said he wanted to begin by discussing "broad concepts."[36]

Stern, then thirty-nine, was the executive vice president of the National Basketball Association, having previously served as general counsel and outside counsel to the NBA. At five feet nine inches tall, the players he negotiated with towered over him. Stern, with a bushy moustache, was known for his penchant for three piece suits, thin rimmed glasses, and being effective while staying out of the public eye. As the *Boston Globe* described him, "He looks like a lawyer and sounds like one."[37] Stern had been involved in pro basketball since the mid-1960s and had served as one of the NBA's main lawyers in the *Robertson* case. (In fact, it was his name on the intrusive, harassing subpoenas to players during the course of the *Robertson* litigation, which were intended to threaten and cajole them into dropping their ultimately successful antitrust action.) He had negotiated the NBA's television deals and was intimately familiar with the economic issues the NBA faced. In fact, it was Stern who had laid out for Commissioner O'Brien the economic concerns each of the ABA teams faced, including the liens on the owners' property when they entered the league in the 1970s. Stern had been involved in previous rounds of collective bargaining negotiations and other transactions with the NBPA and with Fleisher—those that led to the *Robertson* settlement, and the collective bargaining agreements in 1977 and 1980. This time, however, was different.

Stern described the current circumstances in professional basketball. He said that "the NBA grossed approximately $116 million in the 1981–82 regular season; that the average player salary for that season was about $218,000; that total player salaries were approximately $64 million which, together with approximately $6 million in costs for player benefits accounted for approximately 60% of regular season revenues; and that total league operating expenses were approximately $135 million . . . and therefore the league suffered an operating loss of $20 million."[38] Stern continued, "In light of these figures as a business matter, the NBA owners would be wiser to use their equity in their teams for other investments rather continuing to engage in basketball operations at a loss." Stern said, "However, the NBA is committed to continuing its operations in the hope of achieving financial benefits both for the owners and the players. To do so, however, the NBA and the players must reach agreement on a means of stabilizing or moderating players' salaries."[39]

Fleisher was cool to Stern's position immediately—it would be hard not to be, given that Stern was saying the NBA continued to exist in spite of itself. Fleisher said he was "surprised and pleased" to learn that player salaries accounted for 60 percent of revenues—he had always believed they were higher. He rejected Stern's argument about the return on investment and that it had never been a criterion for ownership. Fleisher said "there were a number of ways that the owners could ease the financial difficulties of some of the weaker teams, such as by sharing gate receipts or local broadcast TV and cable revenues."[40] Fleisher put the burden on Stern to put his house in order.

If Stern's NBA bona fides were strong, the person sitting across the table was an NBA blue blood. By 1982, Larry Fleisher was an institution in professional basketball, with over twenty years in these fights. Stern would be involved in NBA labor negotiations for the next two decades, but this was the only time in Stern's tenure where the chief negotiator on the other side—Fleisher—had more experience in professional basketball than he did. Fleisher accepted the unpaid position of general counsel to the fledgling Players Association in 1961 as a thirty-year-old tax lawyer with little labor experience. He was recruited to help establish a pension plan for the players. Going far beyond that initial request, Fleisher quietly racked up stunning victories over NBA owners for decades. Fleisher led the 1964 threatened strike to derail the All Star Game, the 1967 threatened strike that almost cancelled the playoffs, the *Robertson* antitrust lawsuit that created free agency in basketball, and the fight to stop the merger of the ABA and NBA both in Congress and in the courts. He also negotiated the first collective bargaining agreement in basketball history, in 1967, and every one thereafter. In addition to his union work, Fleisher was one of the most powerful agents in the sport, acting as representative for many of the league's top players. He was well respected throughout the league and known for his understated but effective style. The market that Stern wanted curtailed—the benefits the players enjoyed—amounted to Fleisher's life's work. He and the players were not about to give them back.

In addition, in 1982 when these negotiations began, Fleisher's position was as strong as it had ever been—both legally and politically. Legally, the *Robertson* settlement provided comfort—there was a federal judge overlooking anything the owners tried to do for the next five years. Politically, with his members, Fleisher had tremendous credibility. After twenty years of running the NBPA and achieving unimaginable success, Fleisher was firmly in control, respected, and successful. As negotiations dawned, a source told the *New York Times*, "Fleisher doesn't have to worry about going back to his players and explain all his actions. . . . Fleisher's been doing this since

1963. He knows all the answers. He doesn't need his players' permission to do anything."[41] He was no pushover, and Stern would not be able to get what he wanted easily.

Fleisher was curt. At fifty-one, Fleisher was stocky but still had a full head of mostly brown, close cropped hair, he wore glasses and spoke with a detectable, but not overwhelming, New York accent. He said that "under no circumstances" would the players ever give up what they had achieved in the *Robertson* settlement. He quoted from the settlement agreement, which required the players to "negotiate the best available terms without limitations or restrictions of any kind."[42] Fleisher said that the *Robertson* agreement prevented the players from agreeing to any salary moderation plan, and the players would never agree to discuss it. Quinn said that negotiating over such a provision would amount to the union breaching its fiduciary duty to the plaintiffs of the *Robertson* case. Fleisher said that teams can limit their desire to pay players, but that the Players Association "will not consider any collective agreement that limits the amount players can earn."[43] For good measure, Fleisher said that the NBPA was prepared to "do what the players did in baseball."[44]

Stern asked if Fleisher, despite his position, was willing to listen to the details of the NBA's proposal on what they called "salary moderation." They did not have a written version of their proposal yet—Stern advised that it would be delivered the next week—but the NBA wanted to make an oral presentation. Fleisher said that "while there was no point discussing it," he would listen to their proposal. This was often Fleisher's technique in bargaining. To always let the other side speak more, to listen, to let them lay out their position.

Barbash, who had been hired by the NBA because of his experience negotiating union contracts in the airline industry, laid out the NBA's salary moderation proposal, which was simple and crude. It took the total salary paid to players from the previous season, divided it by the number of teams, and made that the limit. The total salary for players in the previous year, 1981–82, amounted to $64 million. Split among the twenty-three teams, that would be a team salary limit of $2.8 million dollars.[45] Under the proposal, that would be the amount teams could spend moving forward. No teams would go above that amount, but there was no obligation to spend anything at all. Deferred salary would be discounted, and guarantees would remain on the books even if the players were no longer playing. Teams that were already above the limit would have their current contracts "grandfathered" and could continue to sign new players at the minimum salary.[46] It was not well received by Fleisher. He had rebuffed this proposal three years earlier.

In addition to the salary moderation proposal, the league also proposed the end of guaranteed contracts and an expansion of the league's program for confidential treatment and rehabilitation for players with personal problems and drug and alcohol abuse.[47] Stern said that there was a "strong feeling" in the NBA that guaranteed contracts had a negative impact and should be phased out, and that the elimination of those proposals was a "bedrock" of further negotiations.[48]

Stern agreed that the NBA would deliver to Fleisher a written proposal later in the week. Fleisher said they would immediately file with the special master overseeing the *Robertson* settlement to determine the legality of the NBA's salary moderation proposal. Believing it eroded the benefits of the *Robertson* settlement and was patently illegal, Fleisher's position was that even offering it was illegal.

After bargaining, Fleisher and Stern were asked by the press about what had happened in the session. "We met for 1 hour and 20 minutes," said Fleisher, "and only 15 minutes were related to collective bargaining. The rest of the time was spent on pleasantries and unpleasantries."

"I disagree," said David Stern. "We spent 20 minutes on collective bargaining issues, and the rest on pleasantries and unpleasantries."[49]

3

Survivors, August 1982

*While I would have expected some of the more Neanderthal owners
to have sent us these demands, your past record vis-à-vis labor
would have led me to believe that you would not have participated
in such a clear anti-union set of proposals.*

—BOB LANIER

Bob Lanier was not one to suffer fools, especially not from NBA ownership. Lanier, starting center for the Milwaukee Bucks, had been president of the NBPA since 1980, when Paul Silas had stepped aside. Lanier was imposing, a force at the bargaining table, but not in a pound the table way; at six feet eleven inches tall and 250 pounds, he was a force by virtue of his presence.[1] As David Stern said, "Bob taught me not to be afraid of size. Having him glower at me from across the table was intimidating for a bit, but I got over it."[2] Lanier was tremendously respected by both sides and had a long post-playing career working for the NBA—even acting as a go between for the league and the union during some of the labor bouts of the 1990s. When Stern went into the Basketball Hall of Fame in 2014 he invited just five men on stage that he felt embodied the NBA's best—Russ Granik, Bill Russell, Magic Johnson, Larry Bird, and . . . Bob Lanier.

In 1982 Lanier was one of the oldest players in the league. Lanier's career, though Hall of Fame caliber, had not been smooth. A heralded college player and top pick, Lanier always dealt with serious obstacles—his knees, losing, personal tragedy. Though he had played in the NBA for twelve years, he had never even sniffed the NBA Finals, much less a championship. His teams had never gotten past the second round of the playoffs. He bore no illusions about the glory of being a pro basketball player. "Basketball is a game because it's fun and it's a job because I get paid," Lanier said.[3]

The CBA negotiations that began in the summer of 1982 between the NBA and the NBPA occurred at a very specific point both in Lanier's career and life. "Lanier is a survivor," the *Washington Post* would write in May 1983, as part of a feature on him as his Bucks made a playoff push. The article was one of several written about Lanier during the early 1980s' period that shared a theme. Lanier as survivor, as the warrior in winter. The *Washington Post* article was entitled "Lanier: Winding Down in Pain and in Growth."[4] In 1981 the *New York Times* ran a piece about Lanier entitled "For Bob Lanier, a Tough Season."[5]

As a player he was still effective in the early 1980s, but no doubt slowed by injuries and time. "There are certain things I can't do anymore," he said at the time. "The adjustment is more in your mind, because when you can't do what you want to do and have to be satisfied with inconsistent performances, you start to question your self-worth and you start asking yourself if it's all worth it—the pain, the mental anguish. If the realization is that you can't be a productive part of your own dream, then it's time to wake up. My time is close."[6] So, if after fourteen years in the NBA Lanier was not yet a champion, he was certainly a survivor.

Born in 1948 in Buffalo, New York, Lanier grew up very poor and very big. By the time he was a sophomore in high school, Lanier was six foot six and 240 pounds, a fifteen-year-old boy in a grown man's body. Despite his tremendous physical gifts, Lanier's high school coach cut him from the basketball team, wanting him to play with kids his own age and size before playing seriously, to still have some fun before basketball got serious, which for a player of Lanier's caliber it certainly would. Lanier's coach, Nick Mogavero, saw that Lanier was tremendously talented beyond his physical stature but also that his coordination was slow and he tended to tire out quickly. Mogavero was concerned that if he put Lanier up against bigger, older, tougher kids, it could result in injury and derail his progress. Mogavero consulted with local physiologists at the University of Buffalo about Lanier—an incredible level of enlightenment displayed for a high school coach in 1963. The experts concurred and agreed that an injury was likely for Lanier and that more time would benefit Lanier long term. So, even though he could help the team, Lanier was cut.[7]

Lanier, still a kid, was devastated and furious. He wanted to prove the coach wrong. He worked out intensely, focusing on agility and skills all year long. "It probably was one of the best things that could have happened to me," Lanier said years later of the cut. "I feel that it was a turning point in my life. It made me really focus on what I needed to do to get where I wanted to go." Lanier made the team as a junior, but Mogavero was gone to another job. He never told Lanier why he had cut him—Lanier believed it was his playing ability. When he learned nearly three decades later why Mogavero had cut him—to protect him—Lanier said, "If he cut me for those reasons, then he was a very perceptive and compassionate coach, and a hell of a human being. And I appreciate it."[8]

After a star high school career, "Buffalo Bob" wanted to go to Canisius College but was rejected because of his grades. Instead, he went to St. Bonaventure, near Buffalo. He was an All-American in his senior season and the Bonnies seemed poised to win an NCAA championship, or at least seriously compete for one. They won their first twelve games of the 1969–70 season, then, after a loss to Villanova, the Bonnies won their next thirteen, finishing the regular season ranked in the top five in the nation. They cruised through the first two rounds of the 1970 NCAA tournament with double-digit wins. To get to the Final Four, they would have to beat Villanova, the only team they had lost to all year. The Bonnies were up sixteen at the half, and a victory and Final Four appearance for Lanier and the Bonnies seemed all but assured. But there was always a catch for Lanier. In the second half, leading by eighteen, Lanier was guarding the lane when Villanova guard Chris Ford, who would later be Lanier's teammate in the pros in Milwaukee, lost his balance and bumped into Lanier's knee. Lanier crumpled to the ground, the collision tearing the medial collateral ligament in his knee. After being treated on the court, Lanier refused to be taken out of the game and continued playing on the injured knee until he simply couldn't anymore. As the *Washington Post* reported at the time, "After an agonizing trip down the court, he had no choice and walked off the court to a standing ovation."[9] When Lanier got hurt, the Bonnies were up eighteen. They would increase that lead and win the game. It was a Final Four berth for a team, and a school, that did not reach the Final Four. This was St. Bonaventure—not Kentucky. But the celebration after the game was muted.

"That's that," Lanier's teammate Greg Gary said after the game after hearing that Lanier would undergo surgery to repair the ligament. They had no shot without Lanier. "Oh we'll show up," Gary said about the Final Four date, "but we'll be playing with an empty feeling."[10] The Bonnies would lose to Artis Gilmore and Jacksonville, and Lanier's college career would end in a hospital bed.

Within days of his injury and surgery, Lanier's focus moved to the pros. In truth, the professional leagues' focus on *him* had existed for months, even years, before he was ready to leave St. Bonaventure. Lanier's college career, and specifically its end, coincided with the greatest war for talent in professional basketball history. As *Sports Illustrated* reported, "Within the larger drama of St. Bonaventure's quest for a perfect season and an NCAA tournament bid is a smaller drama between Lanier and the warring pro leagues."[11] In 1970 there were loud rumors of a merger between the upstart ABA and the NBA, but the ABA was fighting aggressively to sign players at the same time it was negotiating for a merger with the NBA. In its third year, the ABA changed strategy from signing established players, like Wilt Chamberlain, Rick Barry, and Oscar Robertson, to signing college, and even high school, talent. It was easier. They had struck out the previous year with UCLA star Lew Alcindor, who signed with the Milwaukee Bucks after a dramatic circumstance in which both leagues were told to make a single offer—their best. The ABA had not taken Alcindor at his word—and tried to bluff, lowballing him in its first offer to sign him up for the league. He ended up in the NBA. The next year, in 1970, with a strong class led by Lanier and LSU guard Pete Maravich, the ABA was ready to pounce. The ABA held their draft in secret in January, well before the college season ended, to get out in front of the NBA. Then, the ABA got busy signing players. Throughout the winter, the ABA announced signing after signing of top college players like Rick Mount of Purdue, Mike Maloy of Davidson, and Dan Issel of Kentucky (signed to the nascent Kentucky Colonels for $1.4 million—more than Alcindor).[12] No matter the status of the

Survivors

merger, the ABA continued to sign players, infuriating the NBA and frustrating merger efforts. On March 12, a few weeks before the end of the college season (when the NBA would begin to sign players), ABA commissioner Jack Dolph was asked about progress toward a merger between the leagues. He said he had not attended the meetings with the NBA. The reason? "I was too busy signing basketball players," he said.[13]

Where Lanier would go professionally was a major concern. Even with the injury, Lanier was expected to be a top pick, and by mid-March, one of the last few without a clear professional option. The New York Nets of the ABA had tried to sign Lanier as a junior the previous season, but his father, Bob Lanier Sr., nixed it. He told Lanier to stay in school. "I know you're going to be a superstar, but I don't want you to be a *dumb* superstar," his father said. So, Lanier stayed in college, but the intensity on him grew. He received so many calls from scouts, agents, and reporters his senior year that he asked the school not to give out his phone number.[14] The Nets drafted him again in 1970. Two days before the game against Villanova, the *Washington Post* reported that the ABA had the inside edge on him and four of the other top ten college seniors.[15]

The NBA felt like it was stuck in place. By the end of the NCAA tournament, the NBA had not signed anyone or even held its draft. The salary scale for rookies was exploding. The ABA recognized it had to pay a premium for talent to play in a less established league. Desperate to survive, they paid. If the NBA was going to sign any of the top players, they would have to pay too. Fleisher, who had spent nearly a decade unable to make headway with the league, loved seeing the salaries rise, but he was concerned. If the reports were true that ABA/NBA merger was imminent, that would kill the market. That's what teams were telling players, and players were frightened. In football, the merger between the National Football League and its rival, the American Football League, deflated player salaries, and it had not recovered. This type of salary explosion had never happened before, and it may never happen again. On March 19, the NBA took the unusual step of moving up its draft from March 30 to March 23, the day after the season ended, to allow teams to sign players or at least compete with the ABA.

Pistons GM Ed Coil told the *Detroit Free Press* that the Pistons, who had the top pick, would draft and sign Lanier. Lanier still had an offer from the Nets.[16] According to Roy Boe, owner of the Nets, their offer to Lanier topped $2 million, between salary and fringe benefits, and included a ten-year loan for Lanier to invest in businesses.[17] As Bob Ryan put it in the *Boston Globe*, "The New York Nets have reportedly offered all of Long Island and half of Connecticut."[18]

On March 23, Lanier became the first overall pick in the 1970 NBA draft. After which Lanier remained non-committal but seemed to be leaning toward the NBA. "I don't know yet who I'll sign with," he said. "It's real good to be drafted first by the Pistons, but it didn't surprise me. There's more prestige and competition in the NBA."[19]

The bidding war for Lanier was over quickly—the NBA was desperate. He was drafted on March 23, and by the morning of March 25, the Pistons scheduled a press conference. The NBA had lost most of the other top prospects, but not Lanier. Lanier took less to sign with the Pistons over the New York Nets. Why? Lanier insisted on being paid in cash as opposed to the more complex ABA style of deferred compensation, which would later be found to be much less than what was reported. Norman Blass, Lanier's lawyer who negotiated the contract, said the offer to Lanier by the Nets was a "funded contract, which would have included payment over an extended period. It was a very very good and substantial offer but we feel the Detroit offer is better overall."[20] Fleisher agreed with Lanier's approach, saying of the ABA deals, "There is no real way to determine the true value of these contracts" due to the complex web of insurance payments, annuities, deferred compensation, real estate, and stock options. "Personally, when I'm negotiating contracts I get cash for my clients and let them do the investing themselves," Fleisher said.[21]

The press conference announcing Lanier's signing was held at Buffalo General Hospital, since Lanier was only a few days removed from the injury he received playing against Villanova.[22] The news conference was in the hospital's cafeteria, where Lanier addressed the media from a wheelchair with, as the *Washington Post* reported, "his leg in a bulky, plaster cast."[23] The NBA was so desperate to sign a player that they wanted to make sure the news got out that they could sign players, too—even if their athletic superstar was stuck in massive cast.

Blass said that the deal Lanier signed with the Pistons was "the largest contract ever signed by a professional athlete." Lanier was anxious to start playing. "I'm just waiting to go" he said from the hospital.[24] He said he chose the NBA because of "prestige, better competition and security."[25] Apparently his friend Willis Reed of the Knicks had lobbied Lanier to join the NBA. Lanier's father, Bob Sr., was over the moon. Quoted in an article entitled "Lanier's Father Likes Rich Pact," the elder Lanier said, "It's nice to have a million dollar baby."[26]

The war between the leagues was not over, but Lanier was certainly a winner. "Those were no voluntary payments the NBA made to Lanier and Maravich," one ABA owner told the *Washington Post* after Lanier went to the Pistons and Maravich to the Atlanta Hawks for $1.5 million. "The money was paid as a result of the war." The ABA, undeterred and unmerged, said they were moving on to veteran players as well. "Every ball player in the NBA is a sitting duck," an anonymous ABA owner said soon after Lanier's signing.[27] It didn't even matter if the players were worth it. As the ABA's own spokesman said, "The NBA and the ABA spent a lot of money signing players and let's face it, some of these people aren't worth that much money."[28] There was hope the leagues would merge soon. They would not. Fleisher, surrounded by Lanier's friend Reed and others, announced the filing of the *Robertson* lawsuit the following month. The war between the ABA and NBA would go for another six years.

Once he got to the pros, it was not easy for Lanier on the court. The knee injury he suffered in the regional final had not fully healed. "I wasn't healthy when I got into the league," Lanier said later. "I shouldn't have played my first year. But there was so much pressure from them to play, I would have been much better off . . . if I had just sat out that year and worked on my knee."[29] As a child, Lanier was protected—his coach had done all he could to protect Lanier's massive body from injury, even if it meant losing on the court. As an adult, there was nothing Lanier could do. He struggled with knee injuries his entire career, having eight knee surgeries. He was never without pain.[30]

Lanier was a leader on the court, in the community, and in the union. He was not afraid to buck the league. In 1972, while playing in an unsanctioned All-Star Game between NBA and ABA All-Stars, promoted by Fleisher, NBA owners told players they would be fined for cooperating. Lanier spoke publicly, saying that if anyone was fined for cooperating all of the players would "quit."[31] Fleisher walked back Lanier's comments, but he had an ally. Lanier continued to be involved in the union, serving as secretary treasurer since 1975, before the *Robertson* settlement.[32] Lanier smoked a victory cigar next to Fleisher in 1976 and became president of the NBPA in 1980. Lanier, along with former NBPA President Paul Silas, had been a part of a lawsuit against the NBA in 1979, claiming that players should be entitled to their image and that money spent on cable should go to the players. The lawsuit had been dropped as part of the 1980 settlement, but, as Silas said, "That's something that will be an important part of the negotiation three years from now."[33]

On the court Lanier's teams struggled. Even if he played well, his team didn't. His Pistons teams in the 1970s were bad, cycling through coaches and players and never getting past the second round of the playoffs. He suffered tremendous criticism in Detroit. Lanier was the All-Star, the best player, and yet the team continued to lose year in and year out. He struggled with his knees; he kept playing when he was injured from that fall against Villanova, even years later. "You look at Bob Lanier's knees and the pain almost shouts at you," George Shirk of the *Philadelphia Inquirer* wrote. "They are crisscrossed with scars, and they look unsturdy for those of a man his size."[34] Bucks team doctor, Dr. David Haskell, said that Lanier has "some of the same trouble that a 70-year-old man might have."[35] "I don't know how he plays," one of his trainers said later in his career, "The X-rays look like he has a bunch of sand in his knees."[36]

After over nine years in Detroit, Lanier finally asked for a trade early in the 1979–80 season. He was traded to the Milwaukee Bucks in February of 1980. The Bucks, with Quinn Buckner, Marques Johnson, and Junior Bridgman, could actually compete for a title. The Bucks were strong when they acquired Lanier midseason, but once he arrived, they went on a run. In the first game he played for the Bucks, they won on a last-second shot. Lanier thought the winning shot had missed. As *Sports Illustrated* said, "[Lanier] was so conditioned to losing he had forgotten all about game winning shots." The Bucks finished the season 20-6, with the second-best record in the league in that time period. Free from the baggage of his time with the Pistons, his play reached its highest level. Lanier said, "I don't have the emotional burden. Here I help on defense, set picks and pass the ball, things I do well anyway. It makes life easier. My playing time has gone down but the Ws are up." Though the Bucks lost in the second round of the playoffs, the future looked bright. Asked if they could win the title, Lanier said, "Yep, yep and yep. It might be destiny."[37] With a young core, Lanier was finally close to his first elusive NBA title.

However, there was always a catch for Lanier. In October of 1980, at the start of his first full year with the Bucks, with expectations high, Lanier's father was killed in a hit and run car accident. Bob learned of his father's death after landing at the airport. He had difficulty coping with it. While the Bucks succeeded in starting the season, Lanier struggled. "I just was not zeroing in on my game. Especially early in the season," Lanier said. "I'd come down the court and I'd see the image of my father. It was hard to shake." Don Nelson, the Bucks' coach, said, "You'd see Bob lose concentration out there, but only briefly. I know he's tried not to bring his personal problems onto the court. But in spite of everything that has happened to him, he has played really well."[38] Lanier was a survivor.

In reality though, Lanier was not holding together well. In February 1981, a few months after Bob Lanier Sr.'s death, his wife of eleven years, Shirley, called him and told him she was leaving him and taking their children. Though she had supported him after his father died, she was leaving. "Things with Shirley and me had been building over the years," Lanier said. "She claimed I was isolating myself from the family, Maybe she was right, and I hadn't realized." Lanier looked at his conduct rationally. "I've been moody. I've thought too much about myself, and I've taken my frustrations at work—like not winning championships—home with me."[39]

"It's a funny thing," Lanier said in 1981, "your whole life you strive for the American dream. And it seemed like I had it. Then, suddenly everything comes apart. I felt like I was in quicksand. Something like that makes you put the championship in perspective. I want to win it—I want it very much, to be a winner, to vindicate all those years in Detroit. But if we lose, well I know it's not the end of the world. I mean in relation to the rest of your life, to your family, your home—what is it? I don't think I ever really questioned it before."[40]

• • •

After the NBA and the NBPA's first bargaining session on July 29, both sides moved the venue of negotiations from the bargaining table to the legal arena. Stern and Fleisher were both maneuvering in the summer of 1982, and it was those machinations that would yield the power in negotiations. Regardless of what they said publicly, the NBA was trying to set the union up to agree, or be forced to agree, to its "salary moderation" proposal. For years they had investigated the ability of the NBA to implement the proposals they wished, and the mechanisms by which they could do so. The day after their first negotiation—when Stern and Fleisher had spoken of unpleasantries—the NBA filed a charge with the National Labor Relations Board, the federal agency that regulates union-employer negotiations. The NBA's charge alleged that Fleisher and the NBPA were violating federal labor law by refusing to bargain over the salary moderation proposal they had made verbally in the previous negotiation.[41]

The owners were tired of losing before the special master overseeing the *Robertson* settlement. (It should be noted that the special master for the first few years of the *Robertson* settlement, Telford Taylor, was a squash partner and friend of Fleisher—the NBPA had done quite well before him.) As a result, the owners were hoping to move this circumstance from the special master's jurisdiction to the NLRB. There, to refuse to bargain over a mandatory subject is a clear violation of the National Labor Relations Act.

The NBA's theory was simple and reasonable. Under the NLRA, both parties in a labor negotiation, the union and the employer, have topics they are required to bargain over called "mandatory subjects," and issues they can choose not to bargain over, or, "permissive subjects." There was no doubt that Fleisher was refusing to bargain over the salary moderation proposal—he freely admitted it. The issue was whether it was a mandatory subject. Issues like wages and health benefits, which impact the day-to-day lives of the employees the union represents, are mandatory subjects of bargaining. More opaque issues, like indemnities or the scope of the group the union represents, which do not impact the terms and conditions of employees' day-to-day lives, are permissive, and the law allows either party not to get their deal derailed by the other party insisting on discussing permissive subjects. Clearly, the NBA argued that the nature of player salaries, or a salary cap, related to the wages of the employees and therefore was a mandatory subject, and the union could not duck it. Fleisher would have a hard time arguing otherwise and thus would not be able to simply ignore the league's proposal. The NBA's legal theory took a benefit normally reserved for employees and used it against them, something that would inform its approach in later CBA negotiations. Throughout the following decades, the NBA would utilize the NLRB regularly in its negotiations in order to gain leverage.

Calling the salary cap proposal a mandatory subject had an added benefit for the NBA; it would raise the pressure on Fleisher to bargain on the league's terms. Parties to a labor negotiation are not obligated to reach an agreement on issues; they are only obligated to bargain in good faith. If at the end of the negotiations the parties have gone as far as they can go and do not see eye to eye on a mandatory subject, an employer can argue that they have reached an "impasse." In those circumstances, employers are allowed to implement their last proposal regarding mandatory subjects. Consequently, if the NBA could establish the cap as being a mandatory subject, they were beginning the process of backing Fleisher into a situation where such a policy, in some form, could be implemented, and the players would either have to strike or negotiate to avoid it. It was forcing Fleisher, who was ever able to find a new tactic, to look down the road at a situation he did not want to be in. This issue, the idea of a salary cap as a mandatory subject to assert a negotiation impasse, was the strategy that Major League Baseball would try ten years later in its epic strike of 1994–95.

While the league went to the NLRB to determine whether the salary cap plan was a mandatory subject of bargaining, the players went to Judge Carter, who oversaw the *Robertson* settlement. The day after the first bargaining session, the NBPA filed an ex parte temporary restraining order, which directed the NBA "not to enter into, adhere to, or take any steps to implement or effect, any formal or informal agreement or limitation upon the individual or total player salaries by any NBA team or all NBA teams."[42] Simultaneously, the players commenced an action with the special master asking that the league be stopped from making a salary moderation proposal because it undermined the intent of the *Robertson* deal. Fleisher's demand for an injunction was denied, but the special master would hear the case in August.[43] Stern and Granik were clear that the salary moderation remained a proposal, and they did not agree that making the *proposal* violated the *Robertson* settlement. In a memo to owners outlining the negotiations they said, "We wish to emphasize, and have so represented to Judge Carter, that the salary moderation plan, like all other demands, is still only a proposal subject to negotiation with the Players and has not been implemented by the NBA. It remains, however, a fundamental element of our negotiating goals."[44]

The legal maneuvering on the nature of the salary moderation proposal slowed negotiations down as both sides pursued legal avenues— the NBA with the NLRB, and the NBPA with the special master. Though the NBA had a strong legal position at the board, the union was not concerned about it; they believed that the special master had the trump card over the labor agency. Bob Ryan, always with his finger on the pulse of the issues in the NBA, recognized the nature of the problem stating, "The owners and players are on a severe collision course, because the former party, whose accustomed role in the scenario is to listen to union demands, is instead coming to the table as an aggressor. The owners, in effect, want something back this time, and unions don't like to give anything back."[45]

• • •

The document began: "The NBA proposes a plan for moderating wages and enabling teams to compete for players on a more equal footing while still permitting individual negotiations between players and teams. This 'salary moderation plan' would prescribe the total amount of compensation teams could pay out annually to players' salaries."[46]

As promised, on August 5, 1982, just a week after the first bargaining session, with both sides pursuing their respective legal avenues, the NBA sent over its initial proposals to the Players Association for a new collective bargaining agreement. The six-page document included twenty-two numbered proposals on a myriad of issues. However, nearly all of the six pages proposed considerable givebacks by the players.

The NBA's proposals were aggressive, beginning with proposal #1: their salary moderation proposal. What was laid out should not have shocked Fleisher and Lanier; it was the same program Barbash had explained the week before, and a similar proposal to the one Fleisher had rejected in 1980.

Though that was their most important proposal, there were many others, each more draconian than the last. If agreed to, any or all of the NBA proposals would greatly limit players' rights and earning power. The NBA proposed to outlaw guaranteed contracts, no-trade clauses, renegotiation of existing agreements, and even incentive and performance bonuses.[47] They wanted players earning over $100,000 to fund their own benefits and were even proposing a requirement for coach travel for players—quite the request when dealing with bodies that were over seven feet tall.[48]

The proposals were accompanied by a cover letter by Commissioner O'Brien (who had not attended the first negotiation session) addressed to Lanier. Lanier had been an officer in the union since before O'Brien was commissioner, and the two had worked as principals (though not direct negotiators) on the *Robertson* settlement and the collective bargaining agreement in 1980. O'Brien's letter to Lanier was sanguine about the state of the league, hoping it would soften the blow of the proposals, which he must have known would not be well received.

Lanier and O'Brien had more in common than just basketball or labor relations. They were both survivors. As Lanier had overcome disappointment and tragedy, so had O'Brien, on a scale few others could understand. The period from 1960–75 was almost certainly one of the most tumultuous in American history. Very few people felt it—lived it—as much as Larry O'Brien did. There was almost nothing in the American political theater that touched Americans lives that had not touched O'Brien's life personally. The idealism, the violence, the disappointment, all of it. He had been assistant to two presidents and the chairman of the Democratic National Committee during Watergate admist a lifetime of high-level political work. As a close aide to President John F. Kennedy, it was O'Brien who had swept into office with tremendous hope in 1961, and it was he who sat in the back of Air Force One in November 1963 with the casket, next to Jackie Kennedy, who was still covered in the president's blood. Five years later, it was O'Brien who was campaign manager for President Kennedy's kid brother Bobby, in his quest for the presidency in 1968. After a victory in the California primary, Bobby Kennedy, too, was murdered. O'Brien, who had retired to his nearby room to get room service, found out about Kennedy being shot when he was unable to get anyone on the phone to order. "That's it," O'Brien said, without even seeing what happened. In retelling the scene, O'Brien said, "In Dallas, I had not been able to believe that Jack had been shot, in Los Angeles I never doubted that Bob had been. I sat frozen, watching the reports on television. I couldn't move." O'Brien went back to Washington. After Bobby Kennedy's death, he wrote, "I went home and remained there for several days. It was a mood I had never known before. Following President Kennedy's assassination I had been swept along by Lyndon Johnson and the legislative program, but now I had nothing to do and nothing I wanted to do."[49]

O'Brien believed that in politics, and in sports, things moved slowly and change could not be expected overnight. He believed there were no final victories—he wrote a book by that title. He took particular pride in retelling a story from the West Virginia 1960 primary when he was working for then senator John Kennedy. O'Brien had been asked by Kennedy to go see what the landscape was for him in far flung states—Indiana, California, West Virginia. The Kennedys had unlimited resources, but in West Virginia in 1960, unlimited resources didn't matter. When O'Brien attempted to barrel into the state to convince West Virginians to support Kennedy, with promises of the White House and favors, money had not been persuasive, but showing respect was. O'Brien spent long hours in the lobbies of county clerks waiting for meetings. It was the waiting that opened doors, not the brashness. Things moved slowly.

Historically, in professional sports there are really only two types of people who are hired as commissioners of sports leagues: career insiders, or people who serve a very particular purpose to the league. Have a gambling problem? Major League Baseball hired Judge Kenesaw Mountain Landis to be commissioner and to establish law and order. Want to get a television deal? The NBA hired J. Walter Kennedy, a publicity man who the owners thought would give them their best shot. Want to get a salary cap? In the 1990s, the NHL went to one of the lawyers who negotiated the first salary cap in the NBA and hired Gary Bettman away from the NBA. If you don't have an immediate need, leagues tend to hire insiders who know the industries—Pete Rozelle in the NFL, Rob Manfred in Major League Baseball, Adam Silver, Bowie Kuhn, and, yes, David Stern, who was regaled as the "insiders choice" when he became commissioner in 1984.

O'Brien was hired to serve a specific purpose: to make deals. He was named commissioner of the NBA in 1975 to settle the NBA's issues— whether the antitrust issues, the merger with the ABA, or the *Robertson* lawsuit with the players. If he could reach a new television agreement with CBS (one of his clients during his brief spell as a consultant in the early 1970s) then all the better, but O'Brien was hired to make a deal. With everyone. So he did.

After the *Robertson* case, O'Brien said, "When I first took this job everyone told me that there were two truths: The 18 owners could never agree on the time of day and the players association would be totally intransigent against everything. I found this to be totally inaccurate on both counts." O'Brien said he saw opportunity. "It was hard for me to conceive that there wasn't an avenue of agreement to be explored. I had dealt with an arena where there was a lot of give and take and where we were able to make two branches of government happy. So, I couldn't believe that there was no common ground between owners and players."[50] Though some saw the agreement he reached to settle *Robertson* as caving into the players, the truth was that the owners had very little recourse. They were going to lose at trial, they were spending more money than they had, and as O'Brien said, "Why not get the best you can instead of nothing."[51]

In his first year as commissioner, O'Brien was hailed as a hero: he settled *Robertson*, merged the two leagues, and negotiated what seemed to be a rich new broadcast deal with CBS. After the flurry of agreements in 1976, O'Brien had, in some ways, served his purpose to the NBA. By 1982, for the most part, people saw O'Brien as a figurehead. Certainly the union did. "Larry O'Brien was a politician, much more so than a sports business guy," Grantham said.[52]

As described by David Halberstam, "Larry O'Brien seemed surprisingly passive about his job (other than being present from televised ceremonies on the occasion of title games)." Halberstam described him as "an oddly disengaged commissioner, a man more than a little disappointed in the way his life had turned out, as if somehow the bright promise all those young men had sensed in early 1961 had never quite been fulfilled. He generally did what his staff pushed him to do during the late seventies and early eighties, but he did it without passion or real interest."[53]

Perhaps it was that disengagement that made it easier for O'Brien to reach deals with the Players Association. He did not have the same resentment of the union or childlike wonder for the sport that Commissioner Bowie Kuhn had in baseball. His deals with Fleisher and the Players Association over the years were simply that, deals—not life or death. If you don't like this one, you'll get 'em next time. There were no final victories.

However, the negotiations set to begin in 1982 were expected to be difficult. O'Brien, always a dealmaker, had prepared his owners for difficult and tense negotiations—something he had not done in the 1980 negotiations. At the start of preparations for bargaining, O'Brien wrote to the owners: "I predict that our negotiations for a new agreement will be extremely difficult, perhaps the most difficult the league has ever faced."[54] At the end of the Board of Governors meeting in June 1982, O'Brien pushed the owners to support the proposals, including the salary moderation proposal. In approving the proposals, the meeting minutes reflect: "Commissioner O'Brien reiterated to the board the need for unity and strength as the League embarks upon the difficult task of readjusting the inequities of the current financial position of the Players and the NBA."[55]

In his letter in August to Lanier, probably drafted in some measure by Stern, O'Brien maintained a similar somber tone. He wrote: "As you know, although fan interest in our sport is at an all-time high, the NBA teams are collectively suffering very severe financial losses. The enclosed proposals represent our collective views after considerable study and thought as to the best method for addressing the League's financial problems while attempting to preserve 276 jobs for professional basketball players whose average salary now exceeds $218,000 per year. You and your colleagues may have your own views as to how we can best achieve these goals, and the NBA's negotiating committee will be prepared to consider your ideas." O'Brien was seemingly attempting to come off as conciliatory—having spent decades in high-level national politics, he was no stranger to negotiation or compromise—but in the end he came off as patronizing. O'Brien attempted to end his note on a high point saying, "The NBA has been a pioneer among sports leagues in its relationship with the Players Association, and we have worked together over the years, in a constructive way, on such difficult problems as free agency, violence and drug abuse. I am hopeful that this spirit of cooperation will continue as we jointly begin to address as the bargaining table the future of professional basketball."[56]

O'Brien's proposals were dead on arrival. Bob Lanier may have been a survivor, he may have endured personal and professional adversity, but he was not a fool. He had earned the highest contract in history days after having serious knee surgery; he saw the importance of the market and represented his members well as president of the union. The next day, Bob Lanier issued his response on NBPA letterhead—drafted by Fleisher and Quinn. After complaining that the *New York Times* seemed to have a version of O'Brien's letter before Lanier had even had a chance to review it, which was a breach of their understanding to keep negotiations out of the press, Lanier turned to the proposals. Lanier (and Fleisher and Quinn) did not mince words. "I am somewhat shocked to find your signature on the letter attached to the proposals," he wrote to O'Brien. "While I would have expected some of the more Neanderthal owners to have sent us these demands, your past record vis-à-vis labor would have led me to believe that you would not have participated in such a clear anti-union set of proposals."[57] Lanier was not holding back. "It is inconceivable that any management group, even in the worst of times, would have proposed something as barbaric as the six pages sent to us by your office. You have proposed to eliminate every single advancement made by players since 1967. Larry, I assure you this is not going to occur."[58]

Lanier was unmoved by the NBA's claims of loss and gave him a history lesson. "The plaintive cries of poverty presented in your letter are nothing new. Up to 1967, before the clubs agreed to negotiate with us, we were told that the league was skirting bankruptcy. In 1970, when they attempted to merge, we were told that disaster loomed. In 1971 and 1972, in the hearings before Senator Ervin, we were told that financial ruin was around the corner. In 1975 and 1976 during the antitrust case and during the period of settlement, we were told that the league could not survive. And here we are once again hearing the same old song."[59]

Lanier said, "I too share your concern about professional basketball," and tried to finish his letter on a positive note by saying, "Clearly we are not even going to talk about those things that are illegal, both from an antitrust and Robertson Settlement Agreement point of view. However, we are willing and desirous to talk about everything else. I sincerely hope we can now move ahead in a constructive manner."[60]

The NBA and the NBPA had their second bargaining session about a month after the first, on August 25, 1982. With the litigation pending before the special master and the NLRB, the parties did not get much further than their first session. As O'Brien summed it up in a memo to league personnel after the meeting: "Although the session lasted more than four hours, it was wholly unproductive with respect to any significant financial issues."[61] O'Brien stated that "the players have been informed that, perhaps in contrast to prior negotiations, the economic state of the League, as a whole, has caused the NBA teams to become united in their position; the players claim to be equally united and have expressed concern that perhaps the NBA owners are not aware of the players' resolve." As was reported in the *New York Times* after that session, "The groups are apparently in no rush to agree on a contract."[62] That appeared to be an understatement.

4

That Brave Group of Guys Who Said "Fuck You," January 1964

What can be said is that these players, who talk so often of the
importance of "the right mental attitude toward a game," spent the
day negotiating instead of resting, thinking of retirement pay instead
of basketball.

—LEONARD KOPPET, *New York Times*, January 15, 1964

Go tell Bob Short to go fuck himself.

—ELGIN BAYLOR, January 14, 1964

The 1964 NBA All Star Game was supposed to be a crowning achievement for the NBA and was expected to showcase the best of the NBA,
its players, and its past. Most importantly, the 1964 NBA All-Star
Game would mark the first time the All-Star Game had been broadcast live on television. Professional basketball had always been a minor league on the professional sports landscape and was hoping to
take a more meaningful place in the sports landscape alongside Major League Baseball, the national pastime, and the National Football
League, the sport that was built for television. The hope was that the
professional game could become more popular than the college game,
or at least as popular.

No owner had more skin in the game than Walter Brown of the
host and perennial champion Boston Celtics, a team he also founded.
Brown loved the All-Star Game, believed in it, and had the vision and
persistence to allow the other owners to let him promote and host
the first NBA All-Star Game back in 1951.[1]

By 1964 the NBA All-Star Game had grown considerably but still lagged far behind Major League Baseball's All-Star Game in import and in dollars. Brown's plan for the 1964 game was ambitious. Instead of just the one game, he planned for a triple-header of basketball: first, a game with the original Celtics players from the 1920s; then an old-timers game including Bob Cousy; and finally a main event, the top-twenty All-Stars in the NBA.[2] Most importantly, the league sold the rights to broadcast this event to ABC Sports. The hope was that broadcasting the game on the new medium would raise the profile of the fledgling league. It was a tryout.

However, the players, and, more specifically, their union president, Celtics forward Tommy Heinsohn and the union's general counsel, Larry Fleisher, also saw the 1964 game as their opportunity to fight for their pension. The All-Star festivities often served as a de facto league convention and operated as one of the few times a year when players, owners, and league personnel were all in the same place at the same time. For the NBPA, the All-Star Game was often the only time they could get an audience with the owners for "union" issues—the opportunity to raise concerns like fines and limits on exhibitions and travel. It was also often the best opportunity to discuss, or at least attempt to discuss, their nascent pension, which was their most important issue.

The players believed a pension was crucial, and they were all aware of the possibility of being destitute after they retired without it. They also knew that the baseball players had gotten their pension from the proceeds of the All-Star Game and hoped they would be able to do the same, as it seemed only fair.[3]

The National Basketball Players Association was founded in 1954 by Celtics guard Bob Cousy. In 1954 the NBA was only eight years old and was not a clear shot to succeed as the dominant pro basketball league in the United States—there were several professional basketball leagues at the time.

When Cousy founded the NBPA, he had never been in a union and did not have strong labor connections. Cousy sent a letter to one player from each of the eight teams in the league about unionizing. He identified players who were veterans, respected, and not likely to be retaliated against. He asked what their issues were and what the

That Brave Group of Guys

interest was from their teammates. Within three weeks he had heard back from every team except one—the Fort Wayne Pistons. Their owner, Fred Zollner, was publicly against the union and threatened to cut any player who was involved with the NBPA.[4]

In conceiving of the NBPA Cousy did not make the determination that there was some labor need for a union, but rather a practical one. According to his biographer, Cousy founded the union "not because he had some ideological belief in the rights of labor, but from the pragmatic view that in a league as fragile as the NBA the players needed to have a strong voice, that they had almost as much of a stake in the league as the owners did. It was Cousy's belief, one shared by many players, that for the league to be assured of survival it had to become more big league, less bush league." Cousy, when asked whether it was his job to run the union said, "It's everybody's job. We can't go around apologizing because we're professional basketball players. We've got to have pride—pride in ourselves and in our teams and in our league. What's good for the NBA is good for us all—and what's bad is bad for us all. We need a players association, so we can fight for these things."[5]

Cousy also felt, probably rightly, that he was one of the few players who would not be retaliated against for such a stand.[6] This was important; the strength of the union in the NBA, especially in the early years, was that the stars took a large role. First was Cousy, but later Tommy Heinsohn and Oscar Robertson, not to mention John Havlicek, Bill Bradley, Lenny Wilkens, Bill Russell, and Bob Petit all took leadership roles and put themselves on the line to forward the lot of players. Had it not been for the stars who were well respected by ownership and crucial to the league at the gate, the players would probably not have been able to wrangle the concern or interest of management. Even with them, they struggled.

Through the 1950s Cousy had very limited goals for the nascent Players Association. First, the NBPA wanted to limit the number of exhibition games—teams played as many as twenty for which the players were not paid. However, once Cousy started to establish the union, as is regularly the case in unionization, he became the sounding board for players—they would complain that some players got preferential treatment; they would complain about referees.

In the late 1950s there was some progress. At the 1957 All-Star Game there were rumors that the NBPA would affiliate with the AFL-CIO or a national union. Seeking to cut off the problem, NBA commissioner Maurice Podoloff scheduled a competing meeting with the players, in which he proposed a "family plan," because the NBA was a family. Podoloff suggested that the players have a vote by each team for representatives and that they have those individuals attend the league's Board of Governors meetings. "There is an element of soundness to everything proposed by you men," Podoloff said at the time. Podoloff told the players that he was in the process of negotiating a lucrative television contract with the National Broadcasting Corporation, and that "an outside organization might have a bad effect on this type of deal." Podoloff also proposed making player issues the first topic at the upcoming owners meetings. Cousy and the players accepted Podoloff's offer. Cousy said afterward that "the subject of affiliation with a national union will receive continued consideration of the players association. We are relying on Mr. Podoloff's promise that the board of governors of the National Basketball Association will bargain in good faith on April 15, 1957."[7] At the owners meeting on April 15, the NBA agreed to recognize the NBPA and to meet annually with player representatives. However, despite some minor changes in fine procedures, contract procedures, and meal money, that was as far as they had gotten.

It was not benign neglect—Podoloff was not a friend of the union—he had been explicitly told to stall and not to agree to anything. As he was described in 1957 by the *Boston Globe*, "The best defensive man in the NBA is a guy who stands only five feet two inches. Name: Maurice Podoloff. Club: the owners. Position: President of the League."[8] Further, Podoloff and former union president Bob Cousy did not get along, to say the least.[9] Podoloff was often dismissive and insulting to the union when it was run by Cousy, and later to Fleisher, letting the players sit in the lobby of owners meetings and refusing to meet them.[10]

Making matters worse, Podoloff was joined in leading NBA labor relations by Fred Zollner, owner of the Detroit Pistons. Between Podoloff and Zollner there was simply no hope of real progress. Zollner was as anti-union as could be. Despite owning the world's biggest manufacturer of pistons, Podoloff, through whatever fashion, had no unions in any of his business interests.[11] This was an outlier in an industry—automobile manufacturing—that tended to have a strong and powerful union presence, especially in the 1940s and 1950s. Needless to say, with Podoloff and Zollner in charge, the NBA was not friendly to the nascent NBPA.

In 1960, Celtics star Tommy Heinsohn, who had taken over as head of the union from Cousy, Dolph Schayes of the Syracuse Nationals, and Richie Guerin of the Knicks went to the owners meeting in Philadelphia to discuss a pension plan with the owners and flesh out what was agreed to between Cousy and the owners.[12] Despite the meeting, nothing happened. For the next few years this became the pattern. In January 1961, in attempting to reach an agreement with the owners over a pension at the owners meeting, the owners agreed to begin paying $500 a year for their retirement, and the owners pledged to match those contributions.[13] Despite their promises, the owners did not actually match the contributions.

Fleisher became involved in 1961, when a classmate from law school who did tax work for some of the Celtics, got him in touch with Heinsohn. Fleisher, who did not take a salary, mostly "represented the players as a hobby in those years."[14]

In 1963, after years of delay and frustration in accomplishing a workable pension plan, Heinsohn asked the owners to include Fleisher in their yearly meeting. The owners refused, stating that Fleisher was not a player and they did not want outside individuals at their negotiation. Another year, another brush off by the NBA.

• • •

By 1964 Heinsohn and Fleisher were deeply frustrated at the lack of progress. The players had reason to hope that things were changing, in the form of new NBA commissioner J. Walter Kennedy. In September 1963 NBA commissioner Maurice Podoloff stepped down and was replaced by Kennedy, a former public relations director for both the Harlem Globetrotters and the Basketball Association of America. Kennedy had been hired because of his relationship with television—and the possibility that he could get the NBA on it.

When Kennedy took over for Podoloff, Heinsohn and Fleisher saw an opportunity to move things forward.[15] In the fall of 1963, Fleisher and Heinsohn told Kennedy that they wanted to meet about the pension plan at the All-Star Game in 1964.[16] In November 1963 Kennedy relayed Heinsohn's request to the owners, who turned it down. Kennedy sent a letter to Heinsohn stating that in 1962 Heinsohn had been forwarded a specific pension plan and that the league had not received a response in the ensuing two years. As a result, Kennedy said that ownership was not going to meet with the players until they received a response. This response did not sit well with the players.

It was an inflection point. The players had tried to be patient. They had tried to give the owners the benefit of the doubt. However, they also knew they had leverage at the All-Star Game in 1964 and were tired of being ignored by the owners. In anticipation of the high profile game and the broadcast rights, the player representatives agreed that they would hold a meeting the day before the All-Star Game in Boston and devise, as Heinsohn called it, "forceful action."[17]

Heinsohn, both the president of the Players Association and a Celtic, attempted to prepare Walter Brown, the owner of his team, for problems at his All-Star Game. Heinsohn and Brown had a close relationship. Brown was not Zollner. Brown was known by Celtics players as being fair and generous, and he was often a more sympathetic ear for contract negotiations than the difficult and stingy Red Auerbach.[18] In fact, during a time of limited salary growth and negotiating rights for players, Brown was well known for fairness. Players would simply leave their contracts on Brown's desk, knowing they would receive a fair deal.

Brown was more than a fair negotiator—he was a man of principle and courage, best known for breaking the color barrier in the NBA, drafting the first African American, Charles Cooper, in 1950. When Brown picked Cooper at the draft, the owners meeting in Chicago went silent. "Walter," said another owner, "don't you know he's a colored boy?" Brown simply responded, "I don't care if he's striped, plaid or polka dot, so long as he can play."[19] Cooper immediately telegrammed Brown to thank him, saying, "Thank you for having the courage to offer me a chance in pro basketball. I hope I'll never give you cause to regret it." Years later, Cooper, who had a solid NBA career, said, "I am convinced that no team would have made the move

That Brave Group of Guys

on blacks then if the Celtics had not drafted me early." As Red Auerbach would say of Brown, "There were a lot of things I learned from Walter but I think the biggest thing he taught me—and this was by example—is that a man is a man is a man, the old Gertrude Stein crap. He told me, 'Take a man for what he is and what he does, and forget everything else you've heard about him.' Walter really believed that. He never gave a damn about a person's color, religion, nationality or anything else. He simply cared about the man."[20]

For Tommy Heinsohn, Walter Brown was more than just a fair-minded owner. They had a closer relationship than that. Heinsohn, in addition to his role as a player for the Celtics, also held a job as an insurance salesman in the offseason and actually handled Brown's personal estate.

Heinsohn, prior to the game, told Brown about the planned meeting of players, about their pension, and about the frustration the players had felt over ownership's conduct to that point. Heinsohn approached Brown and said, "I anticipate a problem at your All-Star game." Heinsohn said, "If you are going to run a banquet, the players are planning to run one of their own because they want to use it as a meeting in regard to the pension."[21]

Brown did not respond well to the proposed banquet. "I don't have a pension," he told Heinsohn. "Why should you guys have one?" Heinsohn reminded him that the players had attempted to settle the matter for years but had been unable to.

Heinsohn was disappointed by Brown's response but was undeterred. It cannot be underestimated what a difficult thing Heinsohn did by putting his personal situation, his good relationship with the owner, and his premier event in jeopardy in the interest of serving all players. Brown was no villain; Heinsohn was taking a massive risk alienating him.

The players moved forward. The All-Star Game was scheduled for January 14, 1964, and the players set a meeting the night before, the thirteenth, in Boston, to plan strategy. That meeting didn't happen. A massive blizzard hit large parts of the country and many of the players had difficulty getting into town in time for the All-Star Game, much less the night before. Heinsohn met them as they came into town.

There were twenty All-Stars from all over the league, many of whom would become the first generation of true NBA legends. For the Eastern Conference the All-Stars were: Oscar Robertson, Wayne Embry, and Jerry Lucas from Cincinnati; Bill Russell, Sam Jones, and Tom Heinsohn from the Celtics; Hal Greer and Chet Walker from the Philadelphia 76ers; and Len Chappell and Tom Gola from the New York Knicks. From the Western Conference: Jerry West and Elgin Baylor from the Lakers; Wilt Chamberlain and Guy Rodgers from the San Francisco Warriors; Walt Bellamy and Terry Dischinger of the Baltimore Bullets; Lenny Wilkens and Bob Petit from the St. Louis Hawks; and Don Ohl and Bailey Howell from the Detroit Pistons.

The morning of the game Heinsohn met with Kennedy and Zollner, who was still the owner's point person on labor issues.[22] While no lawyers were there, Heinsohn was flanked by the union's pension committee, comprised of players. Fleisher, as was the practice at the time, was not allowed in the meeting. The meeting was tense. According to accounts from players and the union, it was the same lip service they had been dealing with for years. Kennedy agreed to put the matter before the owners at the next Board of Governors meeting. Zollner would not even concede that, which made the meeting more tense.[23]

Eventually, Zollner left the meeting, leaving Kennedy alone with the players. The players implored him to behave differently than Podoloff had, and said that they had heard promises before. Kennedy, hearing the players concerns, claimed to put in writing the commitment to raise the pension issue at the next NBA Board of Governors meeting.[24] Whether this meeting yielded an agreement depends on who you ask. According to some accounts, mostly those coming from management at the meeting, an agreement was reached for a pension plan. Management agreed that if the players accepted the plan proposed by the owners the previous year, the implementation would be taken up at the next owners meeting in February.[25]

The players, however, did not think they had a deal. According to Heinsohn, there was no agreement, and the players left "humiliated, angry and determined to establish [their] dignity, at the least." The players unanimously agreed that there would be no All-Star Game unless and until there was a written commitment to a pension plan.[26]

After the meeting, Fleisher caught up with the players and asked

That Brave Group of Guys

to see the agreement they made, the document. He was told by the players that nothing had been signed. Fleisher was furious. He called Kennedy three times during the day and asked to meet to discuss it. Kennedy failed to return the calls, further infuriating the players.[27]

As the players trickled in from out-of-town flight delays, Heinsohn updated them on the frustrating situation. Heinsohn believed that the players were wary of oral consent from the owners that was not supplemented by action. The fact that they had no written document and Fleisher was unable to get Kennedy on the phone only made it worse. As the afternoon continued, the level of anger rose. As Heinsohn said, "Too often, both under Bob Cousy and myself we were given promises of action and nothing happened."[28]

As more and more players got past the storm and into town, the idea of a pension to be considered by the league in the future did not sit well with them.[29] When the Cincinnati contingent, led by future NBPA president Oscar Robertson and Wayne Embry met Heinsohn in the lobby of the hotel, Heinsohn told them the players were meeting in the Celtics locker room to discuss whether they would play. "The agenda is very short," Heinsohn told them. "Some of us have been negotiating with the owners for a players pension plan and we're going to take a vote on whether we should play tonight if the owners won't commit to address our demands."[30] As Fleisher said later, "The players . . . met with all the other players available. It was agreed that nothing had been gained, and all they had was a promise from Mr. Kennedy that the pension would be discussed in the future."[31]

At six o'clock, just before game time, Heinsohn, Petit, and Petit's young teammate Lenny Wilkens went to Kennedy's hotel room to tell him they would not play without a guaranteed pension.[32] Once again, the meeting was tense. Heinsohn told Kennedy they wanted a meeting with the owners before the game or else they would not play. Kennedy refused, stating that the Board of Governors would not meet with the players before the game.[33] Kennedy then turned, not to Heinsohn or Petit, but to Wilkens—playing in his first All-Star Game, just twenty-six years old, and younger than both Petit and Heinsohn. According to Wilkens, "Kennedy looks right at me, the youngest guy in the room and the one who he sensed was the most likely to buckle under pressure. 'Lenny' he said. 'You mean to tell me that you're really going to strike this game?'" Wilkens gave a nod and whispered that he would. Kennedy shook his head and said he would go back to the owners.[34]

Heinsohn said later that the decision to even threaten to strike the game came as a result of the owners conduct over the years, and that the players were forced to extreme action because the owners were not taking them seriously. Heinsohn said, "We were not militant people by nature or background but were forced to challenge the owners one-way attitude in some way."[35] This would be the story of nearly every conflict between the NBA and its players, both in 1964 and in later situations—years of delay turned players who simply wanted to make a deal into combatants.

Kennedy then went back to his owners. They were not about to give in to the players, and they were not going to be forced to a meeting by a threat. As Kennedy said, "I contacted each of the club owners over a two hour span, at which time each indicated his refusal to attend such a proposed meeting."[36] Both sides were at an impasse.

The players, fully dressed in uniform for the game, along with Fleisher, met in the dressing room at the Boston Garden to plan next steps. Heinsohn stood to speak: "We have not made any progress with the owners, what do you want to do?" They all recognized the precarious nature of the league's finances and the importance of television to growing the game.[37] They knew a potential strike could damage the league. They also recognized how important the pension was for their future.

Heinsohn, always one to know the value of insurance given his non-basketball career, had taken the wise step of having all of the player sign a written document that they would not play absent an agreement.[38] "If it got a little sticky, I wanted everyone to know he was on record with his signature," he said. Heinsohn was aware he was sticking out his neck; it was his hometown and he was pushing the owner of his team in the middle of the event that ownership valued the most. He also knew that some players would waffle if things got tougher.

Kennedy then came down to the locker room and explained that he simply could not get all the owners together in time. The nature of how this discussion went is different based on the player describing it. Some describe Kennedy as being reasonable and attempting to make a deal, apologetic that he could not assemble the owners in time on short notice. Others saw Kennedy as nasty, aggressive, and resentful. According to Embry, Kennedy entered the room angry. "You sons of bitches. You had better play this game or else," Embry remembers Kennedy yelling, sweating profusely and beet red. Embry also recalled that Kennedy refused to speak with Fleisher in the room, despite the players' demand that he be included. Kennedy said Fleisher was simply a representative, and that this was a legal meeting. The players stood firm, saying that they would not play under those conditions and that the game would not go on national television as scheduled. Kennedy told the players they would ruin the league by delaying or cancelling the game. Kennedy was told that they had attempted to deal with this issue for years.[39] Kennedy left once again to see if he could get the eight owners together before the game to finalize an agreement.

While Kennedy was gone, Larry Fleisher officially became the first employee in the history of the National Basketball Players Association when Heinsohn and the other players elected him an officer of the association and gave him official status.[40]

Meanwhile, on the court, the various legends' games that Brown had called were happening despite the turmoil in the players' locker room. The old-timers game, starring Bob Cousy and Bill Sharman in the East and George Mikan from the West excited the crowd while the drama for the current All-Stars unfolded.

For the players in the locker room it was a tense waiting game as Kennedy attempted to go back to his owners to develop consensus. Fleisher and Heinsohn would give periodic updates, but no one was clear as to what was going on. At seven thirty the players took an actual strike vote. It was 18–2, with the only dissenters being Wilt Chamberlain (who thought the league would fold) and Len Chappell (who feared he would be cut).[41] The player most willing to play was Wilt Chamberlain.[42]

On Kennedy's side, the owners were irate. Some of them tried to force their way into the locker room. Heinsohn, who had planned for this possibility, assigned a cop he knew from Boston, who was sympathetic to the players, to the door to protect them from angry owners. Heinsohn told him not to let anyone in unless Heinsohn gave the okay.[43]

First came Bob Short, owner of the Los Angeles Lakers. Short fought to get into the locker room but was unsuccessful. He sent word to his players: Elgin Baylor, then the team's best player, and Jerry West. Short told them to "get their fannies on the court if they knew what was good for them."[44] Short said later, "I ordered Baylor and West onto the floor, but I did not say they would be fired. I just wanted to talk to them. They were being talked into doing wrong things by Heinsohn. If I had been allowed in the meeting, I would have shown them where they were wrong."[45]

Baylor and West held firm, which Heinsohn believed was key. Heinsohn said, about Baylor, "If he, or anyone backed down it would have been all over." Baylor's answer was short and sweet, "Go tell Bob Short to fuck himself."[46]

At 8:25, with a tip off at 9:00 p.m., the owners caved. Kennedy entered the dressing room. "We have a problem," he said.[47] He could not get the owners together in time for a meeting, but he would personally commit to convincing the owners to provide the pension plan if the players played the game that night. In truth, it was not that far from his prior position, or even his initial one. He agreed to introduce the disputed pension plan at a Board of Governor's meeting either in February or May, depending on how many of the owners would be present at the meetings.[48] According to Embry, Kennedy said, "The owners have agreed to a pension for you guys. Now get your asses out there and play ball."[49] Heinsohn asked him if he would step outside for the players to discuss the proposal.[50]

When Kennedy left, the players debated how to proceed. They went around the room discussing what to do.[51] Some wanted to wait for a written agreement or until the owners made some deal to guarantee the plan, unwilling to rely on Kennedy's oral representations, the same such promises they had been given for years. Others were willing to play, believing they had proven their point. Heinsohn spoke last.

Heinsohn said he believed the game should be played—he believed that with Kennedy as the new commissioner there was a new opportunity to set a new course, but that the players should have a plan if

That Brave Group of Guys

the owners once again broke their word. Heinsohn said, "I thought we had made our point with Commissioner Kennedy and we should trust him until we found out otherwise, then we would take stronger action next time. I sincerely believed we had spotlighted the issue and there was no practical sense in antagonizing the owners, the fans and everyone unnecessarily."[52]

As Heinsohn said after the game, "It was the consensus that we'd play and await further action from Mr. Kennedy. He assured us he will recommend a course of action to the league on the pension plan."[53] Fleisher said the players "didn't like the way the agreement had to come about, but they feel that in the end it will all turn out all right."[54] After the game, an anonymous player said he only played because of television commitments. "We were ready to refuse to play because we feel the owners have been putting off a pension plan and have not been fair about it."[55] At 8:55 Bob Petit came out of the dressing room meeting and notified Kennedy that the All-Stars would play.[56]

As the players were introduced to the crowd, Kennedy held a hastily assembled press conference where he immediately blasted them. So much for Heinsohn's hope. Kennedy blamed the players, stating that the pension plan had been under consideration when he took office in September, and that it was Heinsohn's job to either accept or reject the proposal.[57] Kennedy told the press he had reached agreement with the players that morning, and that they had reneged on their agreement.[58] Responding later, Heinsohn said, "the players definitely wanted to play the game. Some had battled the storm and disrupted transportation to get here . . . We wanted to play the game but we wanted to meet with the Board of Governors first." Heinsohn also said, "I am not at liberty to divulge what our action would have been if Mr. Kennedy hadn't met with us."[59]

The players had five minutes to shoot around before the game, which started about fifteen minutes late. The Eastern Conference defeated the West 111–107, delighting the over thirteen thousand fans in the stands and many more watching on television on ABC.[60]

The quality of the game itself was different depending on who was asked—Embry said it was "one of the greatest games ever."[61] The *Hartford Courant* called it "marvelously balanced." The *New York Times*, however, called it "lackluster," and stated that no one could say "whether fatigue from travel difficulties or absorption with pension problems was the cause."[62] Robertson won the MVP and, as described by Leonard Koppet in the *New York Times*, "[was] a star among stars no matter what else [was] happening."

Though he would later be praised in the press as a statesman for agreeing to the salary cap twenty years later, the proposed strike of the All-Star Game did not endear Fleisher, or the players, especially Heinsohn, to the press. In fact, it was Kennedy, and not Fleisher or Heinsohn, who was credited with making the deal. Several newspapers referred to Kennedy's successful appeal to the players in getting it done and lambasted the players' efforts.[63] The *Los Angeles Times* headline the next day screamed that the request to have a pension in writing was a "Player Revolt."[64] The *Boston Globe* printed a parody column, with a large picture of Alfred E. Newman from *Mad* magazine, mocking the player's relationship to union activity. "If an athlete's gonna get ahead," the article said, "he's gotta get with the labor movement, and know about strikes, pension plans and collective bargaining." As the column continued, "The fans don't generally realize the bondage we're in but our situation isn't too different from what the coal miners used to be. Did you ever see the dressing rooms at Boston Garden? They're like a mine."[65]

After the game the *New York Times* had two stories about the NBA All-Star Game the previous day, one an analysis, the other a thinly veiled game recap that spent a significant amount of time criticizing the players. As Leonard Koppett wrote, "The National Basketball Association's lifelong knack of finding some way to tarnish its best moments manifested itself again tonight as the East defeated the West 111–107 . . . This time it was the players, not the owners, who spoiled the chance to have the NBA, still struggling after 18 years for a true major league image, put its best foot forward. By bringing to a head an old grievance about not having a pension plan, they came within minutes of a public relations disaster."[66]

• • •

Beyond the press and public comments, after the game, tensions remained high between players and owners. As legendary *Boston Globe* columnist Will McDonough reported, "a serious rift between man-

That Brave Group of Guys

agement and players has been created over the threatened strike Tuesday night." Oscar Robertson said he would not sign his contract if the league did not follow through on its promises. He was not alone; several unnamed players made similar threats.[67]

Additionally, it was not altogether clear that Kennedy's word was gold, or even reliable—these were the early days of the league and commissioners. It was not clear what Kennedy could actually do. As McDonough pointed out in the *Boston Globe*, "The danger point is this. Kennedy is not an owner, and the owners are the ones who pay the salaries. They are bound to be miffed at the sequence of unsavory events when they meet, and the player pension plan might not come that easily."[68]

And the owners were definitely miffed at what the players did. First, was Bob Short of the Lakers. Short, who said, "I have always given my players whatever they ask. If they want a pension, I'll give them one but it was a foolish thing the players did in Boston." Short blamed Heinsohn, saying the players "must realize that we don't get any half a million dollars from television like football and baseball. There's only so much to cut up and the players get their share."[69] Red Auerbach, the great Celtics coach, shared Short's comments, saying the players "are rushing things. Their timing was all wrong. They didn't go about it the right way."[70] There were players who were told they wouldn't play another game in the NBA after the threatened strike.[71]

Just as no one had more skin in the game than Walter Brown, in light of the threatened strike no one was angrier than Brown either. "That incident at the Garden the other night was brutal. I'll tell you one thing: it destroyed my thinking about these men," he said.[72] "If I had known [about the strike] they'd never have gone into that dressing room."[73] Brown vowed, "I'll never walk into a Celtic's room again after that exhibition the other night."[74]

Beyond just the business, Brown was hurt personally. "Of all nights, to get tough, just before an All-Star game. I'm sick about it. I have the highest payroll in basketball . . . and there were three of my men in that room. Tommy Heinsohn, Bill Russell and Sam Jones, all well taken care of by me. What were they saying?" Brown continued, "I've tried to bring that basketball game of the week here, for nothing, and can't get it on TV . . . so can't we do this thing the right way—by sitting down and straightening things out without calling a strike vote?"[75]

Heinsohn bore the brunt of Brown's ire. Brown called Heinsohn the "No. 1 heel in sports."[76] Though Brown did not intend to trade Heinsohn, he said, "If I had a team in Honolulu, I would ship him there."[77]

When Heinsohn responded he did so diplomatically. He did not attack Brown, but he did not back down either. "This fight for a pension has gone on for a long time," he said.[78] Heinsohn was clear that he was not going after Brown, saying, "Mr. Brown, I'll always admire as a great man," and the most unfortunate part of the dispute was that "it happened in Boston and happened to one of the owners who is behind the Players Association 100%."[79] Heinsohn said "These men have been asking me, 'what's cooking on our pensions, Tommy?' and I've been stymied . . . I have a duty for these men too, and it's been sidetracked. So we ran into trouble. I'm very sorry. So are the players."[80]

Within days of the game, Heinsohn tried to settle his issues with Brown personally. They had a twenty-five-minute meeting—Heinsohn wanted to emphasize that there was no attempt to insult Brown personally.[81] Brown was still furious. As described by *Boston Globe* columnist Bud Collins, Brown, at that meeting, "sat there while Heinsohn talked, his chins sagging deeper into his hand."[82] The image was printed in the *Globe* with Heinsohn and Brown showing significant frustration. Brown refused to comment, other than to say, "I have nothing to say. Nothing has changed. Heinsohn didn't tell me anything I didn't already know. I'm burned up and I'm sore about it. It was a fine way for any of my players to treat me. My first obligation is to those people on the seats."[83] Heinsohn said, "I'm sorry Walter feels this way, nothing personal was intended. This was an unfortunate affair that got all misunderstood."[84] Heinsohn, who was "looking frustrated and puffing on a cigarette," went further, stating, "The big tragedy is that we haven't been able to have a meeting of minds with the owners . . . if we had had the Monday night meeting with the owners, all this would not have happened."[85]

Heinsohn said, "If we were unreasonable, okay. But I don't think we are unreasonable, particularly since we were promised this thing two years ago.[86] I've done nothing to be ashamed of. I've tried to head the organization to do what the players wanted."[87]

That Brave Group of Guys

In the end, even though it created ill will in the moment, the players' gambit worked. In February, the Board of Governors confirmed the pension plan.[88] In May, the Board of Governors gave final approval. The plan, which had been proposed by Pistons owner Fred Zollner two years earlier, was less generous than those in the NFL or MLB, but the players had achieved what they wanted.[89]

Despite their protestations and complaints about what happened in Boston, the owners and Kennedy also got what they wanted—a television deal. At the same meeting that they announced final approval of the pension deal, in May 1964, the owners announced a national television contract with ABC. ABC would show sixteen Sunday afternoon games, including playoffs.[90]

Finally, all of the principals were rewarded. Kennedy received a new four-year contract.[91] Heinsohn was reelected president of the union.[92] Despite the discomfort, everyone got the result they wanted. The players had a union and a pension. The owners had a lucrative television contract. And the commissioner had a new four-year deal. It was the first threatened strike in sports history, Marvin Miller had not even taken over the MLBPA, but the NBA players, led by the selfless and courageous conduct of their stars and Fleisher, got a foot in the door. It would not be their last.

Fleisher later told his friend and colleague Jim Quinn that he never felt more alive than during that fight for their pension at the All-Star Game in 1964 and said, "As long as the guys stick together, the owners can't win."[93] It was his first great victory. A half century later, while looking back on the history of the league, David Stern, who was in law school at the time of the 1964 All Star strike, discussed the trajectory of the league. He said, "The credit really goes to those guys, led by Larry in '64, who weren't going to play that All-Star game. That brave group of guys who said 'fuck you.'"[94]

5

Larry

There should still be a sufficient number of players left in the league
who appreciate the unpayable debt to Larry Fleisher. In case no one
has informed the younger ones: It wasn't always this good, and each
time you look at that paycheck, you should offer a prayer on behalf
of your greatest benefactor.

—BOB RYAN on Larry Fleisher's death in 1989, *Boston Globe*

Larry Fleisher passed away suddenly in May 1989. Very suddenly. He
had been playing squash, a favorite pastime, at the New York Athletic
Club on Central Park South in New York City, when he collapsed in
the shower room. He was pronounced dead several hours later, presumably of a heart attack. He was only fifty-eight years old. "It's a horrible shock to us," said Charles Grantham, Fleisher's longtime aide
and his successor as executive director at the NBPA. "Every player
who has ever played in the NBA knows that Larry did more for professional basketball players and, indeed for all professional athletes,
than any other person associated with the game."[1]

Fleisher had left the NBPA the previous fall, but he had not retired from the business of basketball. He was going to be an agent full
time—to take a vice presidency at the powerful International Management Group (IMG), the massive agency conglomerate started by
Mark McCormack to lead their nascent basketball practice.[2] He had
big plans—IMG, which had a long history of successful representation in golf and tennis was new to team sports and wanted to invest
in basketball with Fleisher at the helm.

Fleisher had left the NBPA in triumph. The 1988 collective bargaining agreement, the first after the salary cap in 1983, was the most player-friendly agreement he had ever achieved, and the gains they made were accomplished through the most daring and radical maneuver in a career full of them. Sure, in the new agreement Fleisher agreed to maintain the salary cap (which he firmly believed to be a temporary measure to protect the league in 1983), but he cut the draft to two rounds, got players to free agency faster, and secured a more "free" free agency system, better even than in baseball.

That last agreement in 1988 had not come easily, and it should already be apparent that none of them did. Each agreement Fleisher reached with the NBA required its own creativity and toughness. With every new negotiation, Fleisher reinvented his positions and changed his tactics. With the *Robertson* settlement and the collective bargaining agreement ending in 1987, at the bargaining table the players proposed to undo the salary cap, the draft, and the other anticompetitive aspects of the NBA business as part of their proposals. Fleisher saw the NBA doing well and no longer believed that the players should be parties to artificial economic restraints. In a memo to players at the start of negotiations he said, "The players believe that it is no longer in their self-interest to accept any of the existing restrictions on their economic freedom." Fleisher told his members that they had agreed to such a plan as a "stop-gap measure only and with absolutely no intention that it be continued beyond a fixed period in order to allow certain of the NBA clubs to 'get back on their feet.'"[3]

Fleisher did not get far with his proposals at the bargaining table with Stern (now commissioner), Granik, Bettman, or the owners. They liked the cap and wanted to keep it even though the NBA was in better times. So, with both the *Robertson* settlement and the CBA set to expire, Fleisher and Quinn went back to court in 1987—filing an antitrust lawsuit against the NBA that said the salary cap, the NBA draft, and free agency restrictions were antitrust violations. They were—and frankly, still are. Precedent said, however, that such anticompetitive systems were lawful if they were a part of a collective bargaining agreement or as part of the *Robertson* settlement. This doctrine was called the Non-Statutory Labor Exemption to the antitrust law—which was originally established to protect unions from lawsuits that labeled them anticompetitive institutions (it was somehow anticompetitive for a group of employees to fight together for better terms of employment) but became what professional sports leagues used to hide their anticompetitive conduct. But, the settlement was ending and the CBA was expiring, so Fleisher and Quinn argued that that should remove the NBA from that exception and that it should be subject to damages under antitrust law. Slam dunk for the players, right? Wrong. The players lost in district court, with the judge finding that the labor exemption continued in the NBA even if the agreement and the settlement expired because there was a labor *relationship* between the league and the NBPA.

Once again, Fleisher (with Quinn's help) found a new path. The judge had held that the existence of the union and the ongoing relationship between the parties—with or without an agreement—insulated the NBA from antitrust violations. So, Quinn had an idea: if the agreement wasn't the catalyst and the relationship between the union and the league was, what if there was no union at all? What if the NBPA ceased to represent the players? Then, certainly the NBA's unlawful conduct could not be shielded. As Quinn would say later, "I don't see how any court, certainly any appellate court, would find a labor exemption without a labor union. There can't be a labor exemption when there is no collective bargaining agent acting for the union."[4]

It was shockingly simple. They called the plan "decertification" and Fleisher began making noise about it—when else?—at the 1988 NBA All-Star Game. Just as he had done in 1964, 1967, 1976, 1980, 1982, 1983 and scores of times in between—the All-Star Game was Fleisher's time to stir trouble. He also announced in the players-only meeting, at the 1988 All-Star Game where they decided to act on the plan, that he would step down from the NBPA when they reached a new collective bargaining agreement.[5] The player representatives voted unanimously to decertify the union but not to strike the playoffs or the All-Star Game. "We think it's necessary," Fleisher said of the maneuver to decertify. "We get what we want without striking. The benefits of that are more than the benefits of having per diem and pension benefits in the collective bargaining agreement."[6] Fleisher's since retired counterpart in baseball, Marvin Miller of the MLBPA, thought Fleisher's strategy was absurd, saying, "For a union to decertify itself to the National Labor Relations Board is equivalent to suicide. Members of a union may want to decertify the union when the union leadership has failed to assert itself or when there is corruption. I've never heard of a union advising its members to vote the union out of power."[7]

"What we have done," Fleisher said at the time, "is innovative, unique, radical and painful. But maybe it would finally jolt the team owners out of their little cocoons and bring them to their senses and realize that they have been violating the players' rights for a long time."[8] It was a risk only Fleisher could take—nearly thirty years in the job, deeply experienced, and trusted by the players. Only someone with his clout could kill the organization he created.

So, the players, led by Fleisher, started the process of getting rid of the union. "They felt the union couldn't help its members," Fleisher said of the players at the All-Star break. "[The NBPA] was being turned on their heads and was hurting the players. The owners need the union more than the players do. They need to have somebody to deal with. Now they have to do it individually. That means a lot of individual negotiations and a lot of grief."[9]

It was a radical move—beyond radical. Such a thing had never even been considered. What would happen? What about all of the other benefits the players enjoyed? "There's some danger of chaos. We are going into uncharted waters," Fleisher said. There was risk for the players, but the real danger was for the owners. With nothing to protect them, every player could become a free agent. There would be no salary cap. Fleisher envisioned a world in which "every college player could write every team and say the draft is illegal and I want to negotiate with you."[10]

Stern talked tough, saying he would not accept an "invitation to chaos," but the NBA was stuck—they had been caught flat footed by a strategy that was tremendously innovative. Within two months, Stern and Fleisher made a deal—their last deal. Fleisher's gambit worked. It worked so well, in fact, that Players' Associations in other sports would spend the next thirty years trying to recreate its success—and often hired Quinn to do it.

When the deal was reached, Fleisher was proud and contemplative, like a player retiring in the immediate afterglow of a championship. Fleisher said, "There are times when the lawyer in me and the association head come into conflict. The lawyer still thinks he could have beaten them in court. But the association head wants an agreement. Sometimes what you think is 'right' isn't pragmatic. What do I care if there's a salary cap if the average salary will become $900,000 or a million? I still think the draft should go, but we can live with this. And the free agency is a real breakthrough. I'd still like to get it down to nothing, but effectively, every player who is any good has a chance either to be a free agent or to have leverage."[11] Fleisher still believed the cap was temporary, and it was his intention to get rid of it.[12] But that would be someone else's problem.

With the deal done, Fleisher left the NBPA in the fall of 1988. After twenty-seven years at the helm of the NBPA, he was moving on. He was the longest tenured union head in sports history. He claimed he wanted to leave after twenty-five years but joked that he stayed on because "it took two years longer to complete the new agreement."[13] There was a belief that part of his reasoning for leaving was that he was tired of complaints about his conflict of interest in being an agent and the head of the union.[14] The complaints over the conflict between being an agent and the union head were getting louder. The issue of who would take over when he left was complex and frustrating for Fleisher—there had been fierce and vicious battles over his successor. He felt that he would get the last deal done, and move on to something else.[15]

Fleisher was excited about working at IMG. His plan was to look at foreign players as a source for the NBA—a relatively untapped market. As in everything he did, Fleisher saw trends before others did. In his years running the union, Fleisher had made it one of his traditions to organize international trips for players in the off-season. They would go all over the world—Mexico, China, Yugoslavia, Brazil, Africa.[16] After a few years, Fleisher realized that if the players played a few games, the money from those games would fund the entire trip. So, he began organizing basketball games against local talent in the countries they visited. The players saw it as a vacation and a chance to see the world—the local players saw it as an opportunity. These trips showed Fleisher how good basketball was in other places. The players they played against in these games were good! They could play! He wanted to bring these players to the NBA. Part of why Fleisher went to IMG was that they had such an international presence; IMG's footprint had been in golf and tennis, and Fleisher could use their international reach. He was also pleased to be working with his sons. Once he was set up at IMG, he was interviewed about what he liked about his new position. "Now I do a lot of thinking and have time to work on other things with my sons," he said.

Just as he left the union, Fleisher reached a deal with the USSR to negotiate on their behalf for players to reach the United States—including future NBA players Sarunas Marcilonus and Arvydas Sabonis. The NBA was claiming territorial rights to the Russian players based on their draft. Fleisher didn't buy it. "It's our position that no team has legal rights . . . and we'll go to court to prove it."[17] Classic Fleisher. When he died he was prepping young Yugoslavian center Vlade Divac for the NBA draft—Divac was expected to go in the first round. The future was bright. Fleisher was a young man. Before he could even really start, he was gone.

Fleisher's funeral was incredible; it showed the diversity of love and respect that Fleisher had engendered. The speakers list only proved his importance—former client, now senator, Bill Bradley; Oscar Robertson; Paul Silas; John Havlicek; David Stern; Howard Cosell; Quinn; and MLBPA executive director Don Fehr.[18] Even Fleisher's former nemesis Red Auerbach was there. They had buried the hatchet a few years earlier.

Bradley eulogized his former agent and friend. "If the task of a labor leader is to improve the financial position of his members then Larry Fleisher is the most successful labor leader of the twentieth century," he said. [19] "He conceived a strategy and held the players together in collective bargaining. He built a monument to honesty, common sense, persistence and the power of solidarity."[20]

Oscar Robertson said Fleisher "was honest. He was a genuinely honest guy."[21] At the end of his eulogy, Robertson broke down crying and said, "I'll always cherish his memory."[22] David Stern, who wept openly at the funeral of his longtime adversary, said Fleisher was "a remarkable man and a personal friend, an effective union leader who always worked for the good of the sport of basketball."[23]

• • •

Fleisher was born to Claire and Morris Fleisher on September 26, 1930.[24] Claire, who had five other children pass away, doted on Larry, her only child.[25] Though he was raised in the Bronx and became a labor lawyer, Fleisher's father was an employer. Morris Fleisher, a Russian immigrant with left-leaning politics (he was a member of the Communist Party) owned a small printing shop in Manhattan but required that his employees be union members. Fleisher said that his father "believed there was no employer in the world as good as a union," and that "no matter how reasonable or fair an employer is, if he gives his employees something, it is coming out of their pockets."[26]

From a young age, Fleisher was bright and a whiz with numbers. He finished high school at sixteen. He went to college at NYU and then Harvard Law School. After law school Fleisher earned a masters from NYU in business, specializing in taxes.[27] Fleisher briefly went into the army after graduating from NYU. As part of that process, the army had an intelligence exam. To no one's surprise, Fleisher scored very high. Fleisher was put in charge of identifying inefficiencies in the army's operations, and he wrote a paper that was widely used, on how to run things in the most efficient manner.

When he got out of the army he began putting his considerable education to work. Fleisher began by working at an accounting firm, which led to a small law firm with a few friends from law school. That led Fleisher to Martin Brody, who at the time was the chairman of the board of Restaurant Associates, a restaurant and hotel company with over two hundred restaurants, including a number of the top restaurants in New York.[28] Fleisher rose to become chief operating officer of the organization—combining his knowledge of efficiency, economics, and law.

Then, out of the blue, one of Fleisher's law school buddies contacted him and asked if he would help a group of Boston Celtics with an "organization." The players knew they wanted benefits—their careers were short and uncertain—but didn't know how to do it. Fleisher loved basketball and he couldn't say no. They couldn't pay him, so they didn't. Frankly, they never did. While he was still at Restaurant Associates, Fleisher started working with Tommy Heinsohn and the NBA players, and he often hosted their meetings and press conferences at restaurants he ran in his day-job. Fleisher didn't see what was going to happen in basketball; he didn't know how things would grow and change. He just liked basketball, liked the players, and respected them and wanted to help them.[29] He thought they were being treated unfairly by the owners, and he wanted to fix it. So, he did.

At the bargaining table, Quinn described Fleisher as being "intentionally enigmatic" to the other side. Though collective bargaining negotiations were always theatrical—Stern was known as a yeller—Fleisher was not particularly fiery and preferred not to give his cards away early. "His negotiating style really was very low key," Quinn said.[30]

"They never really knew what he really wanted," Quinn said. "That was a benefit because often times what would happen is we would be in negotiations and Larry would be relatively quiet and be listening back and forth and we would make them make the proposals and then reject them, and they would have to come back and come out with something else and that was a pattern over a long period of time but he was very good at getting what he wanted to get ultimately." Quinn said of Fleisher that "his great strength was he knew what the key issues were that were going to matter the most to the players."

In addition to posture and temperament, Fleisher was terribly creative and willing to gamble—a characteristic that was crucial to someone who was attempting to build an economic structure that no one had conceived of. Being an accountant allowed him to see the economic impact of what was proposed, and being a tax lawyer allowed him to think in terms of exceptions and loopholes. "He was a whiz with numbers," Quinn said. "He could see a bigger picture of how it would all fit together."[31] Fleisher's creativity was mixed with aggression and courage that led to him taking the lead. Fleisher had a lot of firsts in sports labor—most of them. He threatened the first strikes in sports, led the first lawsuit against the basic tenants of a league, and was the first to decertify the organization he ran. When he ran into a roadblock with players or owners and something seemed insurmountable, he would simply come up with something else.

Fleisher didn't have to be certain he would win when he started something or even know how it would go. When the players filed the *Robertson* lawsuit, the aspects that became the most crucial pieces of the case—the attacks on the draft and fights for free agency—were throw-ins. As Oscar Robertson himself said of filing the *Robertson* case, "You have to expect to lose when you get involved with some of these situations." They knew they were right but they didn't expect to win. It didn't matter. The risk forced change. In the late 1970s, when the players filed a lawsuit claiming that they were entitled to the value of their likeness on television in sports, Quinn, who filed the suit, said they believed it was probably "bullshit." It was—Quinn would lose that argument in a court decision in baseball in 1986. However, it was that lawsuit that gave players leverage in negotiations in 1980 and allowed them to fight off the first iteration of the salary cap. Fleisher believed that just because you could lose, just because you thought your argument was bullshit, that didn't mean you didn't try.

Fleisher tried to educate the public, but he had no illusions of his ability to sway public opinion toward players in labor disputes. As Cosell said, "More than any other sports union leader, Fleisher comprehended the suspicion and hostility of the fans toward unionization and he never counted on public support for his cause. Knowing that anti-union attitude so well, Fleisher moved carefully all along, standing up for his players, but in a manner designed to alienate the public as little as possible. He never fooled himself for a minute that he was living in a climate that was favorable toward labor."[32] Regardless, Fleisher tried. As Bob Ryan wrote in his eulogy of Fleisher: "From a media standpoint, Fleisher was a great pro. Recognizing the inherent difficulties most members of the press have in grasping legal minutiae, he invariably synthesized important matters in an entertaining (he had a wicked sense of humor) and illuminating manner."[33]

Philosophically, Fleisher preached that the stars were crucial to the success of the union, or as his son Marc described it: Fleisher believed the NBPA derived success from the "top down." Not only did stars need to be involved in the organization, but they needed to be at the top, in leadership positions. They had the power: the owners were afraid of them and their fellow players respected them. Fleisher believed that each team's top player needed to be the player representative. And when the NBPA filed a lawsuit, which they did routinely under his leadership, every player representative would sign their name. It was a union, after all. Whether it was Fleisher or circumstance, the caliber of the men who were leaders in the union in this period was astonishing. The presidents of the NBPA were men of tremendous character—Heinsohn, Robertson, Paul Silas, Bob Lanier, Junior Bridgeman. He also had strong involvement at other levels from Hall-of-Fame-caliber players—Bill Bradley, John Havlicek, Lenny Wilkens, and many others.

In addition to his work at the NBPA, Fleisher maintained a private practice as an agent and lawyer for players. Fleisher's first client was Bill Bradley, and his first negotiation was when Bradley, a Rhodes Scholar, was returning from Oxford to the New York Knicks. While studying in England, Bradley was unsure he even wanted to play professional ball. The Knicks were desperate to sign him, thinking of Bradley as a great white hope who could sell out Madison Square Garden. What was an existential crisis for Bradley was a negotiation opportunity for Fleisher—who Bradley eventually hired to represent him in negotiations with the Knicks. Negotiations with the Knicks were difficult. Bradley, through Fleisher, was seeking the largest salary in the history of the NBA. After tough negotiations, the Knicks were willing to meet Bradley's salary demands on one condition: he had to be willing to give 25 percent of his "ancillary" income to the Knicks. Bradley asked Fleisher what ancillary rights were; Fleisher said they were from commercials. Bradley had told Fleisher and the Knicks he did not intend to do any commercials. "Looks like they don't believe you," Fleisher said. "Looks like I got what I wanted; 25 percent of nothing is nothing," Bradley said.[34] Fleisher's role as an agent was born.

Through the '70s and '80s Fleisher represented many of the top players. In addition to Bradley he represented John Havlicek, Earl Monroe, Paul Silas, Lenny Wilkens, Mike Dunleavy, Geoff Petrie, and Maurice Lucas, among many others. He had deep relationships with the Knicks—he often represented half the team. Fleisher was proud of having bright clients. In addition to representing them, he would go into business with them as well. He and Havlicek owned a number of Wendy's franchises because Havlicek had a relationship with Dave Thomas, the founder of Wendy's. Fleisher brought Junior Bridgeman of the Bucks in—he would become the second-largest owner of Wendy's franchises.

Being an agent informed his approach for collective bargaining. Fleisher was skilled at stretching the limits of the CBA and the rules he helped negotiate—he knew how the document actually worked. Unlike Marvin Miller, who only dealt with owners and general managers when it came to collective bargaining negotiations or grievance and arbitrations, Fleisher was a regular collaborator with them. As union head he would negotiate better terms in the collective bargaining agreement, then, as an agent, he would spend the next three years stretching its limits. As one assistant GM told the *Boston Globe*, "Fleisher knows the collective bargaining agreement better than anyone alive. He should. He's written it. He's lived it."[35]

His dual role did not come without controversy. There were always questions about whether being an agent and running the union was a conflict of interest for Fleisher. Though he was cleared by the New York State Bar Association, a fact that Fleisher was always quick to point out, like it or not there was an appearance of impropriety. Some believed Fleisher's conflict would result in routing player appearances and endorsements that came into the Players Associations to his clients. It drove the league, and many owners, crazy. The media was critical of this dual role, and some, including the *Wall Street Journal*, opined that Fleisher's circumstance contributed to the bush league image of the NBA. As the *Journal* wrote in 1982, "The NBA puts up with the sort of intramural dealings that other big-time sports leagues have long since cast off . . . Larry Fleisher, who heads the NBA Players union, doubles as the personal agent for several of the league's top stars."[36]

Fleisher believed there was no conflict between his union work and his agent work for two reasons. One, he had been doing it for years and never tried to hide it. As he said, "The whole world knows about my situation, and I only represent players . . . I know more than other agents know, which helps me do a better job."[37] When Steve Johnson, one of his clients, was asked about Fleisher's roles, he said, "When he's representing the players, he's trying to get what the player association wants. When he's representing me, he's negotiating in my interest."[38] The second reason Fleisher used to defend his positions was that the players benefitted—they never paid him a salary for running the NBPA. He was not pocketing money on both ends. Fleisher ran the union on a shoestring. He didn't take a salary at any point in his leadership. He was paid for expenses. He never had more than two people working full time for the union—his longtime aide Curtis Parker and, later, Charlie Grantham.[39] He had hired Grantham, at first, part time. Grantham was the head of admissions at the Wharton School at the University of Pennsylvania and would have to be on the road for the college. That meant he could go and visit locker rooms while working for Penn and only be a part-time employee of the NBPA. That suited Fleisher's needs perfectly.

Teams and owners across the league would try to use Fleisher's dual role to cleave players away from him and the union. It didn't work. One example came from Fleisher's representation of Celtics guard Don Chaney and his helping Chaney play out his option and leave the Celtics for the ABA. Chaney had been a favorite of Red Auerbach and was negotiating with the Celtics in the summer of 1974. Auerbach, who had a long history of tough negotiating with players, did nothing different with Chaney. "Red gave us a figure and he wouldn't go above it. And he wouldn't," Chaney said.[40] Auerbach ignored Fleisher, Chaney's agent, and spent months having the calls he placed directly to Chaney ignored. "If Red could get [Chaney] on the phone for five minutes, he'd have him signed. Which is precisely why Chaney was smart enough to hire Fleisher in the first place," said an anonymous Celtic player.[41]

Chaney held out. Auerbach suspended him. Then, Fleisher got Chaney a deal in the ABA. Auerbach went nuclear. He blamed one man, Larry Fleisher. "I think Chaney got a snow job from Fleisher," Auerbach said after Chaney signed a deal to play in the ABA. "I'm very surprised that such a player as Don Chaney . . . would listen to a man who speaks for the NBA Players Association and who also represents athletes in negotiations with teams."[42] Auerbach's comments were echoed in the hometown *Boston Globe*. "Who the hell is Larry Fleisher?" Bob Ryan wrote in his column on Chaney's decision. "Like Auerbach, I don't understand why Chaney elected to place his future entirely in the hands of Mr. Fleisher, whose credibility is suspect, since he is the director of the NBA Players Association as well as an agent for players in both leagues."[43] Even Heinsohn, by then the coach for the Celtics, turned on Fleisher. "Fleisher's a brilliant man. It's not what Fleisher told Chaney but what he didn't tell him. Errors of omission . . . Do you think Fleisher told Don 'hey listen to what

Larry

the Celtics have to offer'? Did he talk about the stability of the NBA against the ABA? Of course not. He's got a vested interest in keeping the ABA alive. This guy gets the players down to Acapulco after the season and gets them all steamed up. He's a regular Jimmy Hoffa."[44] It didn't work. Chaney would finish his career with the Celtics, returning in 1977. Red and Fleisher would bury the hatchet a few years later, when Fleisher asked Auerbach to coach a team on one of his NBPA trips to the Soviet Union.[45]

No matter what ownership tried, Fleisher was trusted by the players—he had been their greatest champion. "He [has] the unquestioned support of the players," the Boston Globe would say, in the spring of 1983.[46] Quinn said there was tremendous faith in Fleisher—rooted in the Robertson case. "There was huge trust among the players. Number one because of the Robertson fight, the fight itself. The NBA made a tactical error because they insisted on taking so many depositions, almost a hundred As a result, all of these players felt invested in the whole process. They were part of the fight. That had a huge impact over the years."[47]

Though Fleisher threatened work stoppages and strikes over and over again—in '64, '67, '73, '80, '83—he was always worried about a strike for basketball players. He believed basketball players were different from their counterparts in baseball or football. Fleisher had deep concerns that the players may not have enough history behind them to successfully strike the way baseball players did—they didn't go through the minor leagues. He also had concerns that basketball players didn't have the discipline to save and to not collapse during a strike. He was concerned that a strike would never work, and that unlike baseball, which had a lot of success with industrial warfare, it could be devastating for the NBA.[48] Because of Fleisher's deep concerns about a strike, he believed that the best way—arguably the only way—the players could make real accomplishments economically was through other mechanisms: competition or litigation. He found, early on, that to combine both was his springboard.

• • •

On April 16, 1970, Larry Fleisher announced that the biggest stars in the NBA were *suing* the NBA. Well, *all* of the players (except one) were suing the NBA—he just happened to make the announcement surrounded by some of the NBA's biggest stars—Oscar Robertson, Bill Bradley, Willis Reed, and Kevin Loughery of the Baltimore Bullets.[49] The suit was filed to stop the merger between the ABA and the NBA and to question the league's practices on antitrust grounds.

In April 1970, a month after Bob Lanier signed his deal with the Pistons from a hospital bed, the NBA and ABA were set to merge, creating one league. Fleisher feared this consolidation would end the bidding war for players' services—and hamper salaries. Fleisher and the NBPA quickly brought a lawsuit to stop the merger. Fleisher said that, "consummation of an ABA/NBA merger would irreparably impair the rights of all the players by depriving them of the opportunity to negotiate."[50] If NBA players could only negotiate with one league, salaries would certainly collapse. "The appearance of the ABA provided an escape route for the players—providing at least one other group to bid for their services," Fleisher said when he announced the suit. He brought the lawsuit on behalf of all current and future NBA players against the NBA, its (then) fourteen teams, and the American Basketball Association, in what would become known as the *Robertson* case, named for the NBPA president, and lead plaintiff, Oscar Robertson.

When Tommy Heinsohn retired after the 1965 season, the NBPA was facing an uncertain future. The organization's stature was in no way secure and the selection of his successor was critical. Kennedy's All-Star Game promises had not manifested the way anyone had hoped, and there were likely big fights on the horizon. There certainly was no collective bargaining agreement, and Fleisher was still persona non grata in meetings.

One player laid out the circumstances facing the union at that time perfectly, stating, "Playing conditions were still dismal. . . . Whoever was going to take over the union would have to be intelligent, dedicated to the players' interest, and willing to spend an enormous time for the cause. It needed to be a star . . . a premier player, someone who played so well that the league couldn't punish him. Someone who would also impart courage to other players who were somewhat timid and insecure about their futures. Since there were more and more black players coming into the NBA, it also followed that the new head of the union should be black."[51] Luckily those were the words of Oscar Robertson, Fleisher's pick.

Robertson was a perfect choice and a huge get for the NBPA. Robertson's election moved leadership of the union outside of the mighty Boston Celtics for the first time. It had been crucial that the best team was involved in the establishment of the union, but the next phase would require engagement throughout the league. More importantly, Robertson was a star and he was black. The players in the NBA by 1965 were largely black, and Fleisher and Heinsohn wanted to make sure that the organization was representative of the players. Fleisher also wanted to make sure that he had firepower at the top of the union. Robertson said that the quality of his play insulated him from retaliation: "The caliber of player I was—they could not do things to Oscar Robertson. That's why they asked me to be a part of it."[52]

Robertson was anxious to take over the union. Almost immediately the posture was more combative than under Heinsohn. Robertson saw the players as workers, and the union as being no different from any other industry's union. When asked if basketball players were special in the world of labor relations he said, "They are special. Special workers . . . No matter what you do, it's a form of work."[53] Robertson's viewpoint was informed by experience. Heinsohn had respect and admiration for Celtics' ownership and maintained a close relationship with Walter Brown. Robertson's feelings were harder. Robertson was angry that the players did not have health insurance, they stayed in second-class hotels, team trainers did not go to road games, players did not get paid for preseason, and there was no All-Star break. He had almost no respect for the management of his team, the Cincinnati Royals.

Robertson's approach to labor relations was built on two tenants. First, was communication—with his fellow players and with Fleisher. Robertson trusted the judgment of NBA players. He believed that if he communicated properly, advised them, they would make the right decisions. He believed that was the reason for their success under his leadership, saying, "Communication was the biggest strength that we had."[54] Robertson's other tenant was mistrusting ownership. Robertson said, "Larry [Fleisher] used to say that I had the one great talent necessary for an effective labor negotiator: always distrust the other side."

It was no surprise then, by 1970, that Oscar Robertson was the lead plaintiff in a lawsuit against the NBA. The sides had moved far past Podoloff's "family plan" from the '50s, the trust of Kennedy in the '60s, and Robertson's proposed review of the reserve clause a few years earlier. Now, the NBPA was going to court with *Robertson* as the lead plaintiff.

The *Robertson* complaint made two basic allegations. First, that the NBA/ABA merger should be stopped because it would create a monopoly in professional basketball and harm competition for players' services. Second, that basic aspects of the NBA business—the draft, reserve clause, and, later, the compensation system were in and of themselves anticompetitive and unlawful.[55] Fleisher said at the time of the filing that the lawsuit was not a direct attack on the reserve clause—that position would change later—but rather the suit was intended to maintain the competition of the two leagues.

The lawsuit was an audacious act and a tremendous risk. As Fleisher's attorneys put it when the case settled, the lawsuit was "the first challenge in any professional sport to the entire system of player allocation inherent in the practice of professional sports leagues and was the first class ever filed seeking to eliminate restrictions upon competition for players movement."[56] Outside of older cases that held that Major League Baseball was not subject to antitrust law, there was no precedent here—either about sports in general, or basketball in particular. The NBA players simply felt that the NBA was an unlawful monopoly, and the time had come to change it. As Robertson said later, "We felt it was improper and wrong legally, morally and otherwise for me to tell you hey I don't like you, I'm going to give you 50,0000 dollars that's all I'm going to give you . . . if you don't like it you'll never play a game of basketball."[57] Fleisher prided himself on being reasonable but the *Robertson* case was about doing what was right. As Fleisher's wife Vicky said of Fleisher's talent, "It's not stubbornness exactly. It's more like integrity and perseverance and doing what he believes is right."[58]

Three days after the lawsuit was filed, the players received a temporary restraining order blocking the merger between the leagues. On May 4, about two weeks after the suit was filed, the judge in the case issued a preliminary injunction forbidding "any merger and non-competition agreement between the competing leagues."[59] If the NBA and ABA wanted to merge, they would need either agreement from the players or specific Congressional approval. The players won the first battle. Fleisher was not convinced the parties would reach a deal—either through bargaining or through Congress. "I don't believe you're going to change the reserve rules meaningfully though bargaining. It's been tried. The owners just don't want the players to move."[60] Not everyone shared Fleisher's pessimism. Red Smith would write in the *Washington Post*, "We are coming to the end of the feudal age in sports. Ownership of people is on its way out."[61]

After the judge's initial ruling, the forum for resolution moved to Congress. Given the ease with which the NFL and AFL had merged in 1966, the NBA and ABA hoped they would have a similarly smooth process. Fleisher and the basketball players were doing everything they could to stop it. They didn't strike—they testified. In 1972, Fleisher, Robertson, Bradley, and others testified as to the impact of the merger on players and how allowing the NBA and ABA to merge would be devastating.

In his impassioned opening statement, Fleisher said, "We will introduce evidence which will show the one-sided nature of the employer-employee relationship in professional basketball, unique in the sense that except for other team sports no similar relationship exists in the United States. We believe there is no reason for a system to exist which deprives the player of his right to negotiate freely for his salary. We will show that to grant a merger for the owners' economic necessity will be absurd . . . We will have witnesses indicate the various side benefits that exist, namely, interest in the construction and ownership of stadiums, concession rights, ownership of cable TV companies, et cetera. In addition, we will show where individual owners have used public funds, through the use of municipal stadiums, for their own advantage. . . . We will show what appears to be a paper loss on the operation of a franchise is, in most instances, a substantial gain."[62] Robertson was more succinct in his testimony, saying that players needed the competition between the two leagues: because "If my NBA team were to fire me, I could get a job in the other league. With a merger, there would be no place for me to go."[63]

Fleisher's testimony focused on the race aspect in basketball. As he said, "We will have testimony before this committee indicating the adverse effects that the passage of the proposed legislation would have on the black minority in the United States. We will show that pro basketball, a sport in which over 65 percent of the players are black, has a unique place in the lives of hundreds of thousands of black children. How Congress treats the economic rights of black basketball players who have escaped the ghetto by hard work will be noted by all black Americans."

The play by Fleisher, Bradley, and Robertson worked. The merger stopped. The Senate subcommittee unanimously refused to allow a merger as it was, leaving the NBA and ABA with little to do but continue to compete for players while the lawsuit worked its way through the courts. The Senate did provide a framework for the leagues to merge, but it required protections for players in order for any such bill to be made. Specifically, the reserve clause would have to go. "They put things into the merger bill that I don't think owners in either league can live with," Commissioner Kennedy said after the Senate issued its position.[64] The parties were at an impasse.

After the congressional failure the focus returned to the lawsuit and what the impact would be. Ed Silver, the owners' negotiator, and future commissioner Adam Silver's father, said that to change the economic system of the NBA would lead to chaos. As he said in 1973, "The owners say they can't believe the sport will survive if the kind of open arrangement the players want comes into being. There's a tremendous investment in players. They're paid tremendous salaries. If they're going to be free to make deals with anyone, the owners fear all the better players will be playing for the wealthier clubs. And, without competition the sport will suffer and ultimately die."[65]

Fleisher bought neither argument. He argued that the teams were talking about losing balance they never had. "They say all the best players would go to the rich teams," Fleisher said. "Well, the Celtics won all those years under the owners' system, with the draft and reserve rules." Fleisher did not believe that free agency would cause chaos, saying, "you won't find most of the stars flocking to a few teams. They want to play. They'd rather be playing one place than sitting another. Sure, there are some prostitutes. But most players are not interested in money alone. My true belief is that a free enterprise system, where players are able to go where they feel they're needed, will produce more balance than we have now." Fundamentally, Fleisher's theory of the NBA's resistance was simple: "All change is objected to on the theory that it will destroy."[66]

In 1973 Fleisher began working with Jim Quinn, a young attorney at Weil, Gotshal, and Manges, the outside firm handling the case for Fleisher and the players. They met when Quinn was called into a room with the senior partners from Weil, Robertson, and Fleisher, who was smoking a cigar. What a room for a young lawyer to walk into. Quinn found Fleisher to be easygoing and likeable, and they hit it off quickly. "What endeared me to Fleisher early on was he treated young lawyers as well as the senior partners. Everybody was the same to Larry," Quinn said.[67] Fleisher and Quinn would become close friends and build a friendship and partnership that would extend for the rest of Fleisher's life. Lucky for Fleisher, Quinn became one of the country's best trial lawyers right at a time when he needed one.

After losing in Congress, the NBA's plan in the *Robertson* case was to spread the players thin—taking hundreds of player depositions doing everything they could to force the Players Association into dropping the case. "The Players Association didn't have any money," Quinn said. "Litigation is expensive and they were barely just paying our firm's expenses. Basically, the firm was underwriting the case; the players couldn't afford it and the league knew it. So they started to do every conceivable thing to make us spend money, endless motions, moving for summary judgment." The NBA demanded depositions—not only from the plaintiffs but from dozens of players. There was no reason for it. The NBA would subpoena extensive documents from players—information players would never have. It was harassment intended to run up the bill. Many of the subpoenas were signed by a young lawyer—David J. Stern—at the NBA's outside law firm, Proskauer, Rose, Goetz, and Mendelsohn.

"My job was to delay," Stern said, years later, "and Bill Bradley is perfect [for a deposition] because he doesn't know how to be dishonest. So I'm asking him, 'What were you doing when you were at Oxford shooting around? And he says, 'I would bounce the ball . . .' and this goes on for about five days. Remember, lawyers are like soldiers.

Larry

You have empathy for the soldiers on the other side. The parliaments make the wars. The lawyers go in and fight it out."[68]

•••

As year after year of the *Robertson* case continued, the NBA's prospects for actually winning the case dimmed. "I must confess," Judge Carter wrote in February 1975 when he issued the crucial decision that denied many of the NBA's motions and made clear that a trial would happen, "that it is difficult for me to conceive of any theory or set of circumstance pursuant to which the college draft, blacklisting, boycotts and refusals to deal could be saved from Sherman Act condemnation, even if defendants were able to prove at trial their highly dubious contention that these restraints were adopted at the behest of the Players Association."[69] Judge Carter advised that "the life of these restrictions, therefore, appears to be all but over, although their formal internment must await further developments in this case." Judge Carter's decision held that a merger between the leagues was unlawful and that "Any merger or non-competition agreement between the NBA and the ABA without Congressional approval . . . would be unlawful and defendants are presently under injunctive restrictions in that regard."[70] After five years of litigation, the owners had achieved almost nothing.

"These cases have now achieved dimensions which make this letter, without question, the most serious and important letter I have ever written to you," George Gallantz, Stern's mentor and the NBA's lawyer wrote to Commissioner Walter Kennedy in 1975 after Judge Carter's decision. Gallantz conceded that "unless some decision favorable to professional sports comes down in time to influence [Judge Carter], we have no reason for optimism at the trial court level. The amount of damages that could be awarded is almost too astronomical to contemplate. The award by a jury would have to be trebled . . . and attorneys fees added." Gallantz said that "although the legality of the present methods of operating professional athletic leagues will ultimately be passed upon by appellate courts—and quite possibly the United States Supreme Court—it is no exaggeration to say that an adverse result in the case, if not ultimately reversed, threatens the very existence of the NBA." Gallantz advised Kennedy to consider settlement.[71] Within a few months of Carter's decision, Kennedy stepped down as commissioner, and O'Brien was installed.

Fleisher also sent a memo to the players after Judge Carter's decision, but it struck a much more positive tone. Fleisher wrote: "Judge Carter last week issued a momentous ruling on our antitrust case against the NBA. His opinion, which ran close to a hundred pages, is in my opinion sensational, brilliant and devastating to the NBA." Fleisher continued, "While the case is not over and still requires a trial, and while the NBA will probably continue to fight us, it is a major victory that can only strengthen our position enormously."[72] The trial was set for May 3, 1976.

On December 30, 1975, another gift happened. A judge ruled that the compensation system in the NFL was unlawful. Almost immediately the NBA owners sought to settle the *Robertson* case. Fleisher was not optimistic. Regardless of movement, Fleisher did not yet see a deal. "They don't ever want anybody to be free and they want to own a player. That's the primary hangup. They refuse to give up. Without settling that, it's inconceivable or worthwhile to try and go forward."[73] The big issue was compensation. Fleisher was also clear that this practice had already been found to be unlawful. "That's exactly what a judge found to be illegal in pro football."[74]

Over the next month, after some fits and starts between Fleisher and the NBA to settle *Robertson*, at the All-Star Game in Philadelphia, Fleisher finally lit his victory cigar. After six years, the *Robertson* case was over. To complete the deal, they negotiated all night—working in O'Brien's hotel suite with owners, players, Fleisher, and retired players (represented by Oscar Robertson) working toward a deal.[75] Twenty minutes before the NBA's Board of Governors meeting O'Brien made the deal he was hired to make. Fleisher, emerging from the negotiating session, said, "There is no single major unresolved issue left. There is enough of an agreement for me to go to the players tomorrow and tell them we have arrived at an understanding. I'd say the percentage is more than 50 that the Robertson case will never go to trial." O'Brien echoed Fleisher's optimism, stating, "I am a pessimist by nature, and I'm optimistic about this."[76] Owners, too, were optimistic. "If O'Brien makes an agreement with Larry Fleisher, he has the prestige to deliver the owners," Buffalo Braves owner Paul Snyder said.[77]

Fleisher described the reasoning for making a deal, and, as always, he was pragmatic. "We are delighted. We came to terms for two reasons. Anyone would have to be totally foolish not to read the handwriting on the wall in recent court decisions. And secondly, the players have spent an enormous amount of money fighting this thing. It was clear to us the owners would have continued this fight for three to five more years."[78] However, he believed the players were resolute, saying, "The players were determined to see it through after all the time and effort we've expended, even if we had to camp on the courthouse steps."[79]

O'Brien was simply happy to have a solution. "We have taken a giant step eliminating horrendous litigation," he said.[80] "I have been in a lot of things over my lifetime, and I have to be impressed with what has happened."[81] "It was a business judgment we had to make and I think it was a sound one," O'Brien said after the deal was made. "The only other answer was pursuing the case to its ultimate and I'm certain that would have been disastrous."[82] Forty years later, Stern said that the most significant day in NBA history was when the league settled *Robertson*.

With the litigation in the rearview, the future was bright for the NBA. "It was a remarkable job," the *Chicago Tribune* said about the deal. "The decade of renewed interest, growth and prosperity for pro basketball that lies ahead didn't seem possible before O'Brien cut the Gordian knot." In an article in the *Chicago Tribune* entitled "NBA's O'Brien a Miracle Worker," O'Brien was praised: "Even those who don't like basketball will reap the benefits of the backbreaking effort by this cool, competent old pro to find an acceptable solution, heal the scars, and reverse the depressing trend of lawsuits, court fights and escalating bitterness. All this, mind you, in eight months on the job as NBA commissioner." "Getting this settled is like an anvil dropping off my back. Now we can move ahead in a lot of areas," O'Brien said. "The future of the NBA is limitless," he said, sounding like his predecessor J. Walter Kennedy ten years earlier.[83]

When the case settled, the impact was astounding. The injunction the players achieved in 1970—which kept the rival leagues competing—increased the median salary of players from $35,000 in 1970 to over $100,000 in 1976.[84] When the case was settled, and the NBPA's lawyers advised the court how long they had spent, it ended up being 13,546 hours, the equivalent of nearly eighteen months of nonstop work.[85]

"What we have accomplished here is a structure for NBA growth and progress in the next decade," O'Brien said, defending his deal. Almost immediately, O'Brien was fighting off angry owners, who believed that the great dealmaker had, in fact, simply surrendered to Fleisher and the players. O'Brien, however, was moving on to his next obligation. "Our television committee is meeting now with CBS on a new long-term contract and those negotiations look promising."[86]

6

The Sport of the '70s

The NBA as a television attraction has been almost a model of
consistency in recent years—downward.

—Jack Craig, *Boston Globe*, 1978

The NBA's relationship with CBS felt like a mistake almost from the
minute the partnership started. By the early 1980s it felt like a bad
marriage. Though they had extended their agreement on several occasions, each time the negotiations were unpleasant. In 1976 and 1978
CBS expressed tepid interest in retaining the right to broadcast NBA
games and little appetite in paying more for the privilege of doing so.

In the 1960s the NBA's future on television was bright. After the
threatened strike at the 1964 All-Star Game, Walter Kennedy—who
was hired as commissioner, in part because of his ability to get the
NBA onto TV—was able to sell a package of NBA games to ABC. The
NBA's initial agreement with ABC was modest—a two-year commitment to show Sunday afternoon games and a few playoff games. The
payout to each team was $100,000 per season—peanuts compared to
broadcast deals for the big time leagues like the NFL (who made over
$1 million per team per season) or Major League Baseball (varied by
team but significantly more). The money was secondary—it was the
first real agreement that the NBA had to regularly broadcast its games.

There was no better place for the NBA to be than on ABC in the
mid-1960s. ABC sports was led by the great Roone Arledge, who was
as close to a philosopher-king as could exist in televising sporting
events. (David Halberstam described him less favorably as a "huckster-
dramatist.")[1] Arledge singularly believed in the importance of tele-

vision to sports but also in the reciprocal importance of sports to television. As he wrote in 1966, "Having exclusive rights to the NFL or the World Series or the Army-Navy game is damned near like owning a space shot or the Pope's visit. It has transcended the normal concept of a sports event and become nearly a national institution."[2]

In terms of presentation, Arledge was ahead of his time. He dismissed the old approach to televising sports: a camera mounted around the playing field, and an announcer trying to describe the play on the field or court. His goal was, as he said, to "get the audience involved emotionally. If they didn't give a damn about the game they might still enjoy the program." Arledge focused on atmospherics: cranes and blimps to get pictures overhead, shots of the crowd and environment, a microphone meant to get the thud of the ball on a football punt. "We asked ourselves," he said of his viewpoint to broadcasting, "if you were sitting in the stadium, what would you be looking at? The coach on the sidelines, the substitute quarterback warming up, the pretty girl in the next section. So, our cameras wandered as your eyes would."[3]

In addition to simply presenting sports better than anyone else, Arledge actually *believed* in professional basketball, specifically, in the NBA. He saw the NBA of the 1960s as a franchise that was about to take off—Wilt Chamberlain and Bill Russell were a rivalry that was made for television. Even though, as he said, he "couldn't tell the difference between a screen and a pick and roll," when he bought the rights he intended to make it a hit with the American public.[4] "Physically, professional basketball is an excellent sport for television," he said around that time. "It's played in a confined area and the cameras can be placed to show the agility, finesse and contact."[5] Arledge gave the NBA the full ABC Sports treatment. He placed cameras around the arenas, attempted to humanize players, and tried to give them miniclips to provide the viewer with an understanding of who they were.[6]

Arledge's investment paid immediate dividends for the NBA and for ABC—albeit modest ones. The NBA's ratings improved each year it was on ABC—from a 7.4 share in 1966, to 7.6 in 1967, 8.3 in 1968, and 8.6 in 1969.[7] The original two-year commitment ABC made to the NBA in 1964 was successful, and it begot more agreements between the league and the network, keeping them there through the early

1970s.[8] ABC was so pleased with the steady growth of the NBA that after creating Monday Night Football in 1970, Arledge considered creating "Monday Night Basketball" when the NFL season ended.[9] The NBA was not rating nearly as high as the NFL or even Major League Baseball, but that would come in time. The steady increase in ratings and viewership led Kenyon and Eckhardt, one of the country's largest ad agencies, to issue a detailed report that called the NBA "the sport of the '70s." The report said, "The 1970s are a time of protest, revolution and emotionalism . . . America, in many ways, has become a ghetto society and basketball in many ways is a ghetto game . . . almost all levels of society can identify with basketball's simplicity and relative democracy."[10]

In 1970 the partnership between the NBA and ABC reached the big time—Kennedy and Arledge signed a three-year agreement that nearly quadrupled the value for NBA broadcasting rights—$17 million over three years.[11] When the agreement was reached, ABC was promoting the NBA, expanding its footprint onto weekends and in primetime. Why wouldn't they? For ABC, NBA ratings were up 12 percent over the prior year.

With the NBA's broadcast rights up after the 1973 season, ABC and the NBA renewed negotiations in November 1972. There were rumors that the negotiation between the league and its longtime broadcast partner were simply a formality.[12] Arledge offered a four-year deal worth $35 million. ABC's offer was strong but certainly not astronomical—over $3 million a year above what the NBA had received under the old agreement, nearly doubling the value of the rights and continuing the slow and steady growth of the league. They were still well behind the NFL or MLB. According to Arledge, in January, 1973 he was advised by Kennedy that the agreement was approved by the NBA's Board of Governors 13–4, and that the only issue was whether the NBA wanted a three-year deal or four-year deal to remain with ABC.[13] From Arledge's perspective, they had a done deal. Then, the NBA went quiet.

Arledge may have thought he could rely on Kennedy, but Kennedy did not have control over his owners. The Board of Governors, according to Kennedy in later testimony, was the scene of "much dissatisfaction with those terms," and the owners were deeply unhappy with what Arledge was offering. Halberstam described the dynamic at this time as Kennedy being a "nice man fighting hard to hold on to a job, wary of stepping on the toes of his owners who more and more treated him with open contempt."[14] One particular owner, Jack Kent Cooke of the Lakers, was furious that so many of his games were on national television, limiting the amount he could make on pay TV. ABC had been successful, but they had focused on the superstars, Chamberlain and Russell, and the big markets, Boston, Los Angeles, and New York. As a result, ABC was cannibalizing the local broadcast rights for owners, costing Kent Cooke, and the other owners in big markets, a lot of money. Cooke and Arledge had clashed over the presentation of NBA games before—the Lakers had refused to move seats from in front of the television cameras, resulting in people's heads popping onto the screen at crucial moments in the ABC broadcast. Kent Cooke had been working on other owners in big markets—Ned Irish of New York and Franklin Mieuli of San Francisco—roiling them against the ABC deal for the same reason, to convince them that there was more money to be made in another deal and in ridding the NBA of ABC, and Arledge.

While Arledge thought the deal was done, Kent Cooke and his representatives set out to find a new broadcast partner. That wouldn't be easy. Under its contract with the NBA, ABC had a right to match any outside offer the NBA received for broadcast rights. *Even if* the NBA was able to find a partner that would pay more, ABC could simply match it and keep the Lakers on TV every week. Arledge likely would. More money from another network wouldn't fix Kent Cooke's problem.

Barry Frank, Arledge's former assistant and now Kent Cooke's representative at IMG, met with the Lakers' owner at the New York Plaza hotel. The goal of this meeting was to strategize how to get around ABC's right of first refusal, or to find, as Alan Rothenberg, Kent Cooke's lawyer, was alleged to have said, "as many ways as we can . . . [to] fuck ABC."[15] The NBA would only have one shot to dislodge its games from ABC. So, Frank came up with a plan. ABC showed college football games on Saturday afternoons. It was a cash cow for the network and certainly worth much more than the NBA. What if they were able to get another network to agree, as a term of their contract, that they would show NBA games on Saturday afternoons

The Sport of the '70s

during those weeks? ABC would never match that deal and imperil college football, and Jack Kent Cooke would be free to make money on the Lakers.

Luckily there was a network looking to add sports at the time—CBS. CBS was desperate; having recently lost the NHL to NBC and having lost the Olympics entirely, CBS was in trouble. The NBA presented an exciting opportunity to improve their sports offerings. CBS outbid ABC—barely. The NBA agreed to a three-year deal worth $27.3 million, an increase in $3.5 million per year, but only about $300,000 per year above ABC's offer—divided among the seventeen teams at the time, the increase was minimal. More importantly, as part of the deal, CBS was required to show games on Saturday afternoons the first seven weeks after the World Series to get around ABC's right of first refusal. Neither the NBA nor CBS would be desperate to have early season games on; players played their way into shape in those days, and the outcome of a game in November was not terribly important. Both sides inserted that clause to push out ABC.[16]

As a result, on the evening of February 28, 1973, Rothenberg, representing the NBA, presented Arledge with the NBA's final proposal based on their deal with CBS. ABC was happy to match the economic terms of the deal but ABC would not—could not—forego the revenue from college football. Arledge tried to salvage the deal; he had worked with the NBA for nine years, built a successful relationship there, and saw one of his investments disappearing. Immediately after receiving Rothenberg's proposal, Arledge sent a telegram to Kennedy seeking a meeting be arranged. He wanted to improve ABC's offer and sought to change the schedule to make it work, even including a prime-time NBA game. Kennedy declined, saying, "I have no present intention of calling a meeting of the team owners on the short notice you have suggested." In a last ditch effort to save the partnership, Arledge proposed extending the deadline for negotiating a new agreement between ABC and the NBA. Kennedy declined this offer as well.[17] Arledge was livid. "Walter Kennedy is acting in a very dishonest manner," Arledge said. "He's a very weak man."[18] And with that—a fruitful nine-year partnership was undone.

With no other option, Arledge went to court. Arledge's lawsuit alleged that the NBA and CBS "undertook a campaign of studied, calculated and deliberate action to improperly, unjustly and illegally interfere with the business and contractual relations between ABC and NBA."[19] CBS' defense was that they had done exactly what ABC alleged, and it didn't matter. Bill MacPhail, head of CBS Sports, filed an affidavit saying as much. ABC moved for a restraining order and a preliminary injunction to keep the NBA on ABC to stop the move to CBS. Both motions were denied.

In the end, ABC and Arledge lost in court and CBS got the contract to broadcast the NBA. Their initial victory began what would become a deeply unhappy relationship for both parties for much of the next two decades. CBS had paid for the league, but it was not clear that they believed in it. The ratings were low to start. CBS did away with a lot of Arledge's showmanship. They abandoned the Saturday games—the flashpoint to get ABC out of the deal—within a year.[20]

One piece of CBS' new in-game presentation stirred Fleisher's ire. When Arledge broadcast the games, ABC ran an in-game segment in which NBA stars would play one-on-one, with the champion winning $15,000. The piece had been a success with ABC. Not only that, the players and the Players Association got a payoff for the use of their likenesses. When CBS took over NBA broadcasting rights in 1973, they dropped the feature—choosing instead to do filmed segments, some of which included player likenesses, others didn't. This infuriated the players, who individually (the champion) and collectively (the union) lost a substantial amount of money when the network changed. Fleisher called foul on the change in practice. CBS did nothing. Fleisher decided to pull players out of on-camera interviews until they got paid.[21]

The NBA was furious—Kennedy filed a grievance that the Uniform Player Contract required the players to make reasonable promotional appearances. Kennedy was right. Fleisher admitted it but said the halftime interviews were commercial, not promotional. Fleisher said "any filming of players without their okay is a violation of privacy, and a violation under their Uniform Player Contract."[22] This was more a power issue than a legal one. CBS had paid dearly for the NBA—they wanted the players.

For five weeks in the fall of 1973, the players refused to appear on CBS interviews, frustrating the network and forcing it to the table.

With a weak legal hand, Fleisher still won. Fleisher, the NBA and CBS met late into the night, reaching an innovative deal. Fleisher got the players paid every time they did an interview before, during, or after a game. More importantly, Fleisher got the players a cut of the highlight revenue for NBA films. "Nobody else in professional sports has that kind of deal," he said afterward. "It's a landmark. For the first time, it's recognized that the players have a right to their own privacy—and if they're to be used by anybody for commercial purposes, they have to be compensated."[23] Fleisher learned a few things from this fight: TV was important, the players had power, and they should be paid for appearing on television.

With or without the players at halftime, on CBS, NBA ratings declined over the years. Precipitously. After peaking in 1973, with 10.0 rating, the NBA went down to 9.3 in 1974, 8.9 in 1975, and 7.2 in 1976. After the ABA/NBA merger, ratings improved slightly then declined again. As one reporter put it in 1978, "The NBA as a television attraction has been almost a model of consistency in recent years—downward." There were myriad reasons people proposed for the decline: the players didn't care; the game was boring; there were too many black players, which alienated white audiences; free agency made teams inconsistent; guaranteed contracts; violence on the court was alienating fans. The race issue was pushed aggressively in the media—77 percent of NBA starters were black and there was concern that white audiences simply couldn't relate. As the *Boston Globe* wrote on this issue, "There are no ratings or surveys to support this premise but there are also none to refute it. In such a dilemma, myths reported often enough become accepted as truths."[24]

There was, however, one additional reason for the NBA's cratering ratings. The NBA's move to CBS had garnered the NBA a powerful and vengeful enemy with the ability to impact their ratings directly—Arledge. When the CBS deal was done, Red Auerbach fought the move, saying that the NBA had been well served by Arledge and ABC, and the decision to move was shortsighted. At the end, when the deal was done, Auerbach said to his NBA colleagues, "You don't really think a man like Roone Arledge is going to take this lying down, do you?"

He did not. Almost immediately after the NBA moved to CBS, press reports referred to Arledge's "crusade against the NBA," and that he was "looking for sheer revenge" and to "bury the NBA in the ratings in order to avenge the league's jump to a rival network."[25] Within a year, his retaliation against the NBA had a name worthy of Arledge—it was simply called "Roone's revenge."

Arledge created a block on ABC on Sunday afternoons that eviscerated the NBA on CBS. He made a Sunday afternoon version of the *Wide World of Sports*, and a show called *Superstars*, where athletes and celebrities would compete in events other than their specialties. The block was a massive hit.[26] *Superstars*, described by the *Boston Globe* as "blessed by Arledge's production and promotion finesse . . . was an immediate ratings smash."[27] The NBA's ratings cratered in the face of Arledge's juggernaut.

Regardless of the difficulties with CBS, O'Brien, the newly crowned commissioner, negotiated a new agreement with the network in 1976, increasing the worth of the NBA's rights from $12 to $18.5 million dollars a year.[28] The agreement came at an important time—after the *Robertson* settlement but before the merger with the ABA, when O'Brien's shine was brightest. CBS signed the deal despite decreasing ratings for the product. "We had some difficulties with our ratings," Robert Wussler, head of CBS Sports, said when the deal was reached. "Basketball has been slightly off but we are confident over the long haul in the inherent strength of basketball. We at CBS are delighted to be continuing our relationship with the NBA." CBS hoped that with *Robertson* settled, the NBA and ABA would merge. Their agreement contained economic sweeteners if new teams were added to the league. O'Brien, hoping to maintain his leverage with the ABA, claimed that the new deal and its high rates had nothing to do with a potential merger. Wussler came clean, "I understand Larry's position but we're optimistic that something with the ABA . . . merger or amalgamation . . . will happen."[29]

CBS may have publicly said they were delighted, but privately it was less of a partnership. Poor ratings have that impact. The NBA had attempted to negotiate with NBC and ABC, but CBS was the only "legitimate" offer the NBA had received.[30] When the details were negotiated, outside counsel David Stern and NBA attorney Russ Granik met with Alan Levin of CBS. The two had gone to counter some of CBS' proposals in the broadcast agreement. With the NBA ratings poor, and the NBA's leverage weak, CBS was not interested in making further concessions to the NBA in any area. In a memo to O'Brien, Granik said that despite the negotiation skills of Stern and Granik, "all of Mr. Levin's responses carried some statement to the effect that if we did not accept this position we had no deal. If we did not like it, we could talk to Bob Wussler," then the head of CBS sports.[31] CBS was deeply concerned about the future of the NBA. One of the hold ups to a deal was CBS trying to terminate the contract if there was an "unacceptable game," namely if there was a players' strike, or if the expansion caused a "severe dilution of NBA talent."[32] The NBA did negotiate one term of utmost importance in that 1976 agreement: the ability to negotiate an independent agreement with cable companies.[33]

The NBA on CBS did not improve in the new agreement. CBS simply did not know what to do with the NBA. Ratings were declining. They tried to change the teams that they broadcast. At one point, they tried focusing on regional games rather than national. That didn't work. Then they went back to concentrating on the bigger markets—Knicks, Lakers, Celtics, Sixers. That didn't work either. As Bullets coach Dick Motta put it, "How many times do you want to see Dr. J?"[34] There were issues with the broadcasters themselves—CBS changed them every year. Former players as broadcasters struggled: Elgin Baylor was described as "incompetent," Oscar Robertson "lacked warmth," and Rick Barry was "boorish."[35] Nothing was working.

The 1976 agreement provided an option to CBS after two years; so just two years later CBS and the NBA were negotiating again, this time after the merger with the ABA. The NBA remained in a very weak position, arguably weaker than before the merger. In the fall of 1977 CBS made three proposals for four-year deals for NBA rights: first for around $59 million, then for $62 million, and then a four-year $67 million for the four years beginning in 1978, all less than what the NBA had previously gotten.[36] O'Brien rejected them all. Eventually, despite poor ratings, Wussler proposed a four-year, $74 million agreement to keep the NBA on CBS. While other sports' rights values were exploding—CBS proposed to keep the rights values basically flat with the last year of the 1976 agreement. O'Brien countered with a four-year offer worth $88 million. According to O'Brien, after he made the offer, he and Wussler agreed to "have further discussions shortly." Within a few days, however, it was announced that Wussler would be leaving cbs—plunging the nba negotiations into jeopardy.[37] Wussler was in trouble with congressional probes investigating whether or not cbs had cheated on a tennis tournament and had to abruptly resign.[38]

When Wussler left, the nba scrambled. O'Brien arranged a meeting with Gene Jankowski, head of cbs, who said "negotiations would be halted" until a replacement for Wussler was named. When Frank Smith eventually took over at cbs Sports in March 1978, he had a very different view of the nba than Wussler did.

In a humiliating meeting with O'Brien and Celtics owner Irv Levin, Smith told O'Brien and Levin that not only was the nba's $88 million offer rejected, but the $74 million offer that Wussler had made was off the table. From Smith's perspective, there should be no further discussion of extending the nba on cbs, and he could not understand why they were negotiating two years before their deal was up.[39] Smith told O'Brien that he would never have made the $74 million dollar offer and that Wussler had not been authorized to make it. According to internal nba documents, at the time Smith "[took] the position that if he had been involved in these negotiations from the outset, he would not be discussing a figure of anything like $74,000,000 for a four-year nba contract. In fact, he is in favor of dropping all negotiations at this point, simply picking up the two-year option, concentrating on improving the product and hopefully the audience acceptability and looking at the entire matter anew at some undetermined later date."[40]

O'Brien tried to backtrack. He asked Smith to maintain the $74 million offer. Smith declined; his view was that the nba's counter of $88 million amounted to a rejection of cbs' proposal, negating the $74 million proposal Wussler had made. O'Brien said that the nba had never had a full opportunity to act on the $74 million, and that to take the deal off the table would create "a credibility problem for cbs."[41] O'Brien, ever the dealmaker, was desperate for a deal.

Smith then asked if O'Brien would accept the $74 million if it were offered. O'Brien said in that moment, that he could not accept on behalf of the league. Then, according to O'Brien, "Smith then said that, although the offer was no longer outstanding, if we would accept $74,000,0000, he would recommend acceptance by his management since the offer had been made by a CBS representative, even though without authority."[42]

O'Brien went back to the NBA owners with his tail between his legs. Could they simply reject the non-offer from CBS? Probably not. The NBA's broadcasting chief, George Faust, wrote the commissioner a dark memo about the NBA's marketability. First of all, CBS had a right of first refusal, deeply limiting the NBA's value to other networks. (It should be noted that after its tussle with ABC years earlier, CBS would not allow the maneuver again. They were only obligated to match economic terms to retain the NBA, no other.)[43] In addition, and more importantly, there was simply nothing to match. Faust told O'Brien, with the non-offer pending, that "there appears to be no viable network currently available, with which to negotiate a contract for the NBA. I do not believe that ABC-TV would even consider such a negotiation, for many reasons and in view of NBC-TV's currently successful agreement with the NCAA it does not seem feasible that they would be a possibility."[44]

Faust believed that to reject the offer from CBS would be passing on money that the league desperately needed. They were in trouble. Rejecting the CBS offer would forego $5 million in revenue over the next two seasons, and having just negotiated the merger, "this would seem to be a particular hardship on the four financially struggling ABA clubs." In addition, Faust said that to reject CBS would be "gambling on reopening the negotiation at some future date for a new agreement starting in 1980–81 and beyond with no assurance that we will be in any better position to negotiate at that time."[45]

The NBA had little option. There was one additional benefit to the CBS deal. As Faust told O'Brien, "There is also the public relations value of a new television contract at substantially increased rates, despite a somewhat retrogressive rating picture, that connotes a sense of 'coming of age' or increased 'respectability' for the NBA."[46] O'Brien had a frank phone conversation with the owners, outlining their limited hand. Part of the documentation given to owners was a chart with the rights values going up as the ratings went down. O'Brien had been able to confirm with Smith that CBS would honor the deal. The NBA took the deal and spun it as a victory. The NBA would remain on CBS until at least 1982. In an act of profound humiliation, the NBA was forced to accept an offer that wasn't there at all.

While relations with CBS were at their nadir, the NBA had hope that cable television would limit the ability of CBS to humiliate them going forward. In 1979 the *Los Angeles Times* made a prediction about future of television. It was shockingly accurate. "Twenty years from now," they wrote, "when television channels may be as plentiful as radio stations are today, they'll talk about the old days of television when three networks dictated what Americans could see—the days before the cable explosion."[47] How the NBA would handle that explosion was of keen interest—to Stern and to Fleisher.

• • •

Cable, which had existed since the 1940s, was created to help individuals who lived in mountainous regions, who were unable to get television signals from out of the air. By the 1970s, cable providers were looking to expand; the focus was no longer on the inability to get signals but on the ability to get more channels into American homes. No longer was there a scarcity of networks; there was now a glut, and sports was an obvious filler.

In the 1970s, cable led to giant, profitable businesses seemingly out of nowhere. In 1970 Ted Turner bought WJRJ-TV—a local television station in Atlanta, Georgia. He renamed it WTCG, which stood for "We're Turner Communications Group." Then he bought the rights to three thousand movies and began to pump the channel across the country. He then tried to figure out how to have sports programming as well. So, he bought teams—surely the rights came with them. First, Turner bought the Atlanta Braves in 1976 and later the NBA's Atlanta Hawks and the Soccer Chiefs. In 1976 Turner began to supply the stations over satellites that broadcast the local channel across the country, the first "superstation."[48] As Stern would say later, Turner "was cable when cable wasn't cool."[49] By 1979 Turner's business model was unassailable. His Southern Satellite company began providing WTCG to cable companies for ten cents a subscriber. By the late 1970s Turner was earning $300,000 a month in profit.[50]

Turner was not the only one cashing in on the cable boom. In 1978 there was a network in New York, a joint venture of Madison Square

Garden and the "UA-Columbia cablevision corporation" that began showing Knicks and Rangers games. It was tremendously profitable—immediately. The *New York Times* reported in 1978: "The Madison Square Garden network, as it is temporarily called . . . made almost $500,000 in revenues." Robert Rosencrans, president of UA-Columbia, was mystified by the instant success. "We got into this last April because we were looking for additional ways to make cable relevant, but things started coming together rapidly and all of a sudden we had ourselves a new business," Rosencrans said.[51]

"I don't know where we're going with this," Rosencrans said. "We have no master plan, and are doing it piece by piece." Within a year they were reaching 1.3 million households and were carried on one hundred cable networks. The network made money two ways: through cable subscriptions and advertising. It was tremendously lucrative. "Our basic business in cable television is subscription, not advertising," Rosencrans said. "Every time we fill a gap left by commercial television, we satisfy a segment of our audience. Ratings are of no consequence to us if there is customer satisfaction. That's a fundamental difference between cable and broadcast television."[52]

There started to be more competitors in cable. Getty oil invested in a small cable network called the Entertainment and Sports Programming Network, or ESPN. In 1979 ESPN's president, Bill Rasmussen, predicted they would have 4 million subscribers in a year. "I know it's a bold, kooky, wild approach but it's a logical vehicle. There's a stock market channel. So why not all sports?" Rasmussen asked. By 1979 revenue from cable was $1.5 billion dollars, when only 14 million of 73 million U.S. households were connected. Plans were, that number of families would close to double by 1981.[53]

The NBA saw an opportunity in cable and they tried to capitalize. In 1976 Stern negotiated with CBS to allow the NBA to achieve its own cable deal independent of their network agreement. Almost immediately, the NBA attempted to find a cable partner. The NBA tried unsuccessfully in 1976 and 1977 to reach a league-wide deal with a new operator, Home Box Office (HBO). In 1977 the NBA attempted to identify—if only for itself—what role it would play in cable and who owned what. Who owned which games? Could away teams broadcast their own games? What if a team had national reach? Russ Granik sent a memo to the Board of Governors outlining what the territorial rights would or should be.[54] There were more questions than answers.

There was a concern—long an issue in sports—that cable would cannibalize interest and the more lucrative broadcast deal with CBS. They were having difficulty stopping cable providers from broadcasting games against their wishes. At one point Granik enlisted Red Auerbach to stop rogue cable providers from broadcasting NBA games without their permission. Larry O'Brien specifically believed that cable could hurt the game of the week on CBS. "We've got to protect our property rights as far as the rip-off of distant signals is concerned," O'Brien said. "Our product is going to the viewers without any remunerations to us."[55]

However, the NBA continued to push for a cable deal. By 1979 Stern was negotiating, on behalf of the owners' television committee, in earnest with two companies. First, Rasmussen's all sports startup based in Connecticut—ESPN (which in his memos to the NBA Television Committee, Stern simply described as "ESP," ignoring the N) and UA-Columbia Cablevision, who had successfully, the year before, begun the MSG network.

Stern wasn't interested in simply selling rights fees. He wanted a partnership approach—this world was growing and the NBA should be a part of it.[56] In the end, Stern picked UA-Columbia Cablevision over ESPN because they offered more money as well as a partnership.[57] He was not going to take a shortsighted approach.

The three-year agreement with UA-Columbia Cablevision was to have them broadcast a doubleheader on Thursday nights on cable. Set to coincide with the end of the CBS deal in 1981, the NBA would sell them forty regular-season games and ten playoff games that would not be on CBS. The money was peanuts—Stern had wrangled $7,500 per regular season and $10,000 for each playoff game with a guarantee of $400,000 per year. Split between twenty teams, that wouldn't pay a player's minimum salary, but it was a start. There were clear incentives in case of growth of the league and for ratings (which Stern expected), and the NBA would be given advertising spots to use or trade.[58]

Though they didn't reach a deal on broadcasting games, Stern still found a way to work with ESPN. In 1980 Stern negotiated a deal with

The Sport of the '70s

ESPN to allow them to show a highlights package. The NBA would send ESPN tapes of every game played every week. ESPN would create a weekly highlights package of twenty-four minutes in duration for the NBA. The highlights would be owned by the NBA, but ESPN would have an exclusive license to show it for the first forty-eight hours. There was no money changing hands, but Stern was broadening the reach of the NBA (and getting free highlight reels).[59] He also consolidated power by getting the Board of Governors to agree that NBA Properties, run by the league office, should have the "exclusive right to market all tapes, films, video-cassettes and videodiscs involving NBA teams or any footage of games between NBA teams."[60] Even if relations with CBS were hard, the future on cable seemed promising. Stern was creating a beachhead on cable for the NBA that would run out of the league office—his league office.

7

The Cap, 1979–1980

The difference between a good negotiator and a bad
negotiator is that the good one knows when someone
has him by the proverbial balls.

—ANGELO DROSSOS

In the late 1970s there was considerable resentment among NBA owners over the *Robertson* settlement. Despite the end of the war with
the players and the ABA, player salaries were not going down, but
up. The system they created—compensation—that was intended to
depress salaries was not working, and Fleisher won every case before the special master. Salaries rose. As Cavaliers GM Bill Fitch said
in 1977, "We ended the war to keep from going broke, but if you go
broke in peacetime as well, what is the use of continuing business?"[1]

Though the *Robertson* settlement would run through 1987, the
collective bargaining agreement signed at the time of the *Robertson*
settlement expired in the spring of 1979. Several owners saw the negotiations for a new deal as an opportunity to strike back. Jim Fitzgerald, owner of the Milwaukee Bucks and a member of the NBA
Labor Committee, said of upcoming negotiations, "I promise you
there will be fireworks." "No longer is it a matter of what the players
want," he continued. "Instead, it is what we want. We've got a lot of
ground to make up."[2]

Part of the reason for the owners' urgency with the 1979 negotiation was that they were worried the negotiation could be their last
chance before the market changed again. In 1981 the next phase of
the *Robertson* settlement would begin. The fear was, once free agency

got freer, that the big markets would dominate. As one anonymous owner told the *Chicago Tribune*, the right of first refusal system, the next phase set to begin in 1981, "will enable the two richest NBA franchises, New York and Los Angeles to sign anybody they want and buy championships the way the Yankees did. Unless the NBA can reach the kind of parity the NFL has between big and small franchises, the owners believe some teams will go bankrupt and fold."[3]

For the players, the 1979 negotiations would be led by Fleisher. That much was clear. The NBA's side of negotiations was much murkier. There were factions and groups—the owners were divided. As one anonymous source told the *Chicago Tribune*, "In every showdown, Fleisher wins because he speaks for all players. The owners can't agree on anything."[4]

For the NBA, Alan Rothenberg, the chairman of the NBA Labor Committee, was the chief negotiator. Rothenberg was not an owner but an outside attorney best known for representing Jack Kent Cooke, who owned the Lakers, and for his starring role in taking the NBA away from ABC and over to CBS in 1973. He was joined in leading the negotiations by Howard Ganz, a partner at the law firm of Proskauer, Rose, Mendelsohn, and Goetz in New York, the law firm of David Stern and the NBA's outside labor counsel for decades. Ganz acted as the eyes and ears of Larry O'Brien, who did not attend negotiations, but who, along with Stern and then NBA deputy commissioner Simon Gourdine, was kept abreast by private memo correspondence from Ganz. In addition to the lawyers, the NBA had a labor committee made up of owners who had a divergent array of views about how to fix the league's economic problems. Some were moderate like Alan Cohen of the Nets. Cohen was known as "Bottom Line Cohen" for his willingness to reach deals.[5] On the other side were Jim Fitzgerald of the Bucks and Angelo Drossos of the San Antonio Spurs—both fierce labor hawks in smaller markets, who were looking to extract a pound of flesh from the players and from Fleisher. Fitzgerald wanted an end to guaranteed contracts. Drossos wanted a salary cap—a mechanism he created and introduced in these negotiations.

The NBA's proposals were intended to provoke the union. As Ganz put it in a memo to O'Brien at the outset of negotiations, "In addition to requests for changes believed to have a reasonable chance of success, the NBA proposals as delivered . . . contained a 'roll-back' or elimination of certain benefits and a revision of various terms enjoyed by the Players Association." This was Ganz's kind way of telling the commissioner that the NBA was making proposals meant to pick a fight—in addition to the ones with a reasonable chance of success.

The league's strategy was to overwhelm Fleisher with proposals and isolate him from his membership. Fitzgerald said, "We will be on offense this time, and Fleisher will be hit with so many plans he won't know where we are coming from." An anonymous owner said on the eve of negotiations, "We will present the players with as many as 20 different plans, and many of them will be designed to put Fleisher in an uncomfortable position that exposes his conflict of interest. One of them will be to cut player salaries across the board. The money that is taken away from the players will be placed in a pot for distribution among the players as they see fit. Then Fleisher will have fighting within his organization. At the same time, Fleisher, wearing his other hat of player agent, will suffer loss of revenue due to the lower player salaries."[6]

All of that was the prelude to negotiations that began later in the summer of 1979. After telegraphing their intention to dump a myriad of plans on Fleisher, the NBA did exactly that. Rothenberg's first proposal was a wage scale for players where compensation was keyed to factors like the players' positions in the draft, length of service, and performance.[7] The proposed collective wage structure would end individual negotiation for players. Under the NBA's proposal, player salaries would be reviewed by an eleven-person review board—three players, three coaches, three general managers, the chairman of the NBA's Competition Committee, and a League Office representative. At the end of each season, that group would rank players at each position. The top five would receive $30,000–$50,000 increases; the next five $15,000–$30,000 increases; and the third five would get $5,000–$15,000. Players would get increases based on team success, minutes played, and any honors the player achieved in the previous season.[8] When players became free agents, they could go to the maximum in their range.

The players made proposals that were "intentionally modest," as Ganz wrote to O'Brien during negotiations.[9] Given the *Robertson* settlement, the players were fine with the status quo through 1987. The players' main issue outside of *Robertson* was cable revenues—getting a piece of what looked to be a booming business moving forward. Since 1970 the collective bargaining agreement between the NBA and the Players Association contained language that said that the parties would agree to disagree as to whether the players were entitled to any piece of cable revenue, or "pay TV, Cable TV, or any form of cassette or cartridge system or other means of distribution as yet unknown."[10] Both sides reserved their rights. In 1976 both sides agreed not to engage in work stoppage over this issue.

By 1979 Fleisher saw an opportunity. However, Fleisher did not make a proposal about cable revenue. Thinking he would be unlikely to achieve these gains in negotiations, Fleisher, as he was wont to do, had gone to court to get players a piece of the upcoming cable bonanza. In 1979 NBPA officers Paul Silas, Bob Lanier, and Butch Lee commenced a lawsuit in New York that claimed that the use by cable companies of players' names, pictures, and performances violated New York State's right to privacy laws. The suit was aimed at the nascent MSG network and the Knicks.[11] It was, as were all of the legal approaches made by Fleisher, tremendously creative, and the ramifications were tremendous. Quinn, who filed the lawsuit, was unsure about its likely outcome. In describing the suit in 2018, Quinn said, "We had come up with this notion, which was probably bullshit, but because cable television had just come in and was just starting, each team was going to have its own cable contract and that was significantly increasing or would significantly increase over time that we filed a lawsuit saying we should have a separate share of the cable money because we never waived our rights with regard to that. It was based on the right of publicity."[12] Publicly, O'Brien was defiant. "Naturally, the league says players have no more right to cable TV money than they have to commercial TV money," O'Brien said.[13]

In bargaining, the NBA proposed that the players simply waive their rights to cable revenue. That was a non-starter. There was no reason for the union to agree to a complete waiver of rights they could win in court. During those early negotiations in the summer of 1979, Fleisher expressed a willingness to gamble on the outstanding *Silas* lawsuit. As Rothenberg wrote to O'Brien in September, the

"PA's position is that if they lose, while they intend to pursue their claims in collective bargaining, they realize they would have a lesser negotiating position. If they win, however, their negotiating position will be enormous because, among other things, they may very well have the right to an accounting and, therefore, a very significant money damage claim."[14] There was little incentive for Fleisher to agree to what the owners had proposed—especially if they continued to propose gutting the economic benefits for players. A source told the *Chicago Tribune*, "Larry keeps telling us he can't talk about cable TV money because the players filed a lawsuit to force the NBA to share it with them. He's confident of winning the case, and with the enormous potential of cable revenue not far down the road that decision could affect all sports."[15]

Privately the NBA was concerned about Fleisher's cable lawsuit—deeply concerned. The potential liability was massive, and given Fleisher and Quinn's track record of beating them in the court, the NBA had reason to worry. In the late 1970s Stern and Granik had spent a considerable amount of time investigating and identifying how cable could benefit the NBA. Though the cable agreements Stern negotiated with ESPN and UA were small in the late 1970s, everyone expected they could grow astronomically. As Ganz wrote to the NBA's negotiators, "while the amount of potential liability has not been estimated, it should be noted that the damages claimed by plaintiffs may not necessarily be limited to the license fees received from the cable companies by the NBA and/or NBA clubs. Plaintiffs will probably claim the right to an accounting and a share of the profits made by cable companies."[16] With the lawsuit pending during negotiations, it was not clear what would happen, but it did give the players leverage.

Between the collective wage proposal and the cable proposal, Fleisher said that the NBA's proposals were the most regressive he had ever seen and would undo all of the benefits the players had negotiated to that point.[17] Both were rejected.

The NBA was not surprised. When they made the collective wage proposal, they knew Fleisher would never go for it. The owners quickly abandoned it in service of their real proposal, a salary cap created by Angelo Drossos, owner of the Spurs. As Ganz wrote to O'Brien after

Fleisher's rejection, "When, as expected, this was rejected, a plan for limiting total team payroll was put forward."[18]

The proposed system looks somewhat like the modern NBA—a soft salary cap with a tax on those teams who go over it. Drossos's proposal called to limit each team's payroll at the average salary for the prior season divided by the number of teams in the league. Those above the average were frozen, and those below could continue to spend. Teams could exceed the cap, but 50 percent of its excess payroll would be distributed to the rest of the teams in the league—what amounted to a luxury tax.[19] The cap was in no way tied to revenue. Each year, the cap would increase by 5 percent. Drossos's proposal even had a "stretch" provision, providing that players who were released would only be counted for half of their actual payroll obligations for cap purposes. Though proposed by the NBA in 1979, such a provision would not appear in the NBA until after the 2011 collective bargaining agreement.[20] Needless to say, Drossos's plan was well thought out.

Fleisher rejected this proposal too. So much for the owners' plan to overwhelm him into making a bad decision. At the table, Fleisher asserted that the Players Association would never agree to any "direct or indirect limitation on a player's right to seek and negotiate for whatever salary he wishes."[21] He disagreed with the proposal for the same reason he rejected Stern's similar proposal three years later—it violated the *Robertson* settlement, limited player movement, and constituted a giveback he had no interest in providing. As a compromise, at one point in negotiations Fleisher joked that the NBPA would agree to a salary cap. He proposed a cap of $10 million dollars per team, which at that time was about five times the highest payroll in the league. As Deputy Commissioner Simon Gourdine said in a memo to O'Brien, "The Players Association has said it would agree on a team payroll ceiling which is so high as to be meaningless."[22]

Though Drossos was committed to the cap, many on the owners' side, including Ganz, Rothenberg, and Cohen believed that Drossos's system was not realistic. They believed that the NBA could not achieve it without taking a players strike, and with the league struggling, a strike was simply not a fight worth picking. Drossos, a former boxer, was spoiling for one.

‧ ‧ ‧

Today, for all of the Harvard lawyers and MIT MBAs poring over the language of the NBA collective bargaining agreement, looking for exceptions and interpretations, there may not have been a salary cap if not for a staged arm-wrestling hustle by Angelo Drossos in a bar in San Antonio in 1958. Red McCombs, then just a young car salesman, walked into the Dragon Lady bar on main street in San Antonio looking for trouble. McCombs, who admitted he had been "drinking pretty good" before he walked in, saw Drossos and another man, just patrons in the bar, arm wrestling. McCombs thought he could take the winner. "Well, Angelo set me up by letting me win two or three times," McCombs said of their ensuing arm wrestling matches. "So I put some money down and he beat me really bad. I knew I had been set up, but instead of getting mad, I just laughed it off . . . We formed a great relationship that night."[23] They became quick friends. Drossos went to work for McCombs at his Ford dealership. Fifteen years later, when professional basketball called McCombs, he called Drossos.

In 1973 the Dallas Chaparrals, a nonentity in the ABA for five seasons, were on the brink of bankruptcy. The Chaparrals had horrible attendance even by ABA standards. In the hopes of filling their seats, the team began making moves, trading a number of its players. The remaining ones protested—they were concerned that the Chaparrals were trading black players for white players to boost attendance. The players threatened not to play. With the team expected to fold, the ABA decided to reach out to McCombs, who had been involved in minor league football to potentially take over—and save—the franchise.[24] McCombs brought Drossos along. Drossos convinced the owners of the Chaparrals to let them lease the team for two years with an option to buy at the end. They leased the team for $200,000.[25] Drossos took over ownership of the Dallas Chaparrals of the ABA in 1973, moved them to San Antonio, and renamed them the Spurs.[26]

Angelo Drossos was an unlikely NBA owner. He became an NBA owner by virtue of being an ABA owner. And he was only able to be an ABA owner because of the unending dysfunction of that league, its horrible management and racism. Drossos was a hustler. He spent fifteen years promoting and managing boxers, running bars, even instructing dance. Drossos ran a Coney Island hot dog stand in San Antonio, was a car dealer, and a stockbroker. However, for Drossos, running a basketball team was a perfect fit.

From the minute he took over the Spurs, Drossos found his calling. Terry Stembridge, Drossos's first hire with the team, said, "Angelo Drossos fell in love with running a basketball team. I mean head over heels in love. He truly did. He learned a lot very fast, he was tough and he was gutsy." Drossos saw himself as a different type of owner. As he said, "There are two kinds of owners of pro sports teams. The first is the guy who sits in the backseat and lets the GM run the franchise. The second is the guy who is a 'hands on' owner."[27] Implied in the statement was that Drossos saw himself as the latter. The Spurs were an immediate success—by ABA standards. San Antonio was happy to have a major league franchise, and Drossos ran it as best he could. They had better attendance than their cross-state rivals the NBA's Houston Rockets, despite Houston being both a larger city and the Rockets playing in the more established NBA.

Drossos's skills were well known—he was described as both "unconventional" and a "ruthless negotiator."[28] As Drossos said, "The difference between a good negotiator and a bad negotiator is that the good one knows when someone has him by the proverbial balls."[29] While certainly effective, Drossos was a difficult personality. Former Spurs broadcaster Terry Stembridge described him as "unique." George Karl, the first player Drossos signed when he bought the Spurs, said, "Personally, he was kind of a bulldog, in-your-face kind of guy, but he had a lot of love for people involved with him."[30] Those were statements from the folks who *liked* him. As the *San-Antonio News Express* said *in his eulogy*, "Diplomacy was not among Drossos' finer qualities."[31] He was quick to anger and, having been a boxer, was known to threaten physical retribution to those who disagreed with him. During one Spurs game in the ABA days, Drossos came out of the crowd to pick a fight with the opposing team's coach, Larry Brown. "Hey, you wanna have it out with me?" Drossos asked. Brown ignored him, saying, "What's with that guy?"[32]

Drossos had an uncanny ability to turn nothing into something, and the Spurs afforded him unique opportunities to do so. Soon after he took over the team, he convinced the city of San Antonio to help him get the concession rights at the HemisFair Arena—where the Spurs played. Drossos ran the concessions not only for basketball but for everything. Drossos then went to the cola companies. As they are today, in the early 1970s Coke and Pepsi were in the midst of a vicious unrelenting war. The arenas were the frontline—both companies wanted any arena they sold at to be exclusive. Complicating manners was that Coke was the radio sponsor for the Spurs and, therefore, should have had an advantage in negotiating for exclusivity. Not with Drossos. Somehow he convinced both Coke *and* Pepsi to become cosponsors for the Spurs. They both advertised on the radio, they were both available at the arena, and the Spurs made a lot more money than if either had been exclusive.

Having successfully hammered out the concessions to his advantage, Drossos then moved to consolidate his ownership of the Spurs. Drossos had only agreed to a lease with an option to buy after two years. Almost immediately, the Spurs in San Antonio were clearly a success—certainly compared to the Chaparrals. Halfway through the first year of the lease, Drossos made a very aggressive bluff. He went back to the Chaparrals' owners in Dallas and said he was giving them back the team. After their failures in Dallas, they didn't want the Chaparrals back even though the Spurs were successful. Drossos convinced them to sell him the team for half of what they had agreed as the option to buy two years later.[33] Something from nothing.

Drossos's Spurs were one of the success stories of the ABA. That put Drossos in a strong position when the merger talks with the NBA got serious. Drossos was one of a small cadre of ABA representatives at the NBA Board of Governors meeting in Hyannis Port in June 1976 when the leagues tried to merge. After years of war, the ABA was running out of steam. Several ABA teams had petitioned to join the NBA the previous season, which was believed to be an act of desperation. Several teams had already folded or were about to. Though O'Brien wanted a deal, Drossos knew that the NBA, in his words, "had him by the balls." After several days of intense negotiations, it looked like a deal would not happen. Drossos told O'Brien he was out.

"I'm not making any deal," Drossos told O'Brien during an impasse in negotiations. "It's like building a house. You start out thinking you'll spend $30,000. Then you decide to add a bedroom, then there are cost overruns and the next thing you know it's $60,000. It cost you double what you expected. That's what has happened here. The NBA should just go on doing what it does and the ABA will do whatever it will do next." O'Brien called Drossos back in to try again. Drossos made the ABA's final offer—O'Brien declined. Drossos went back to his room, despondent, to pack his things and return to San Antonio. The future was uncertain for the Spurs and the ABA. He got a knock on the door asking him to come a conference room. When he walked in, Mike Burke owner of the Knicks gave him a hug. "Welcome to the NBA," he said.[34] The NBA had decided to accept Drossos's last offer.

The NBA agreed to absorb the four strongest teams from the ABA— Drossos's Spurs, the New York Nets, the Indiana Pacers, and the Denver Nuggets. Each ABA team would pay $3.2 million to the NBA and were not allowed to share in television revenues for four years.[35] The ABA teams would be described as "expansion" teams. (Stern and Granik would adhere to this absurd nomenclature for the ABA teams for years, even in internal NBA documents.) The ABA teams would not be involved in the upcoming draft, and the Nets would have to pay the Knicks $4.8 million for playing in their territory.[36] Though it was a peace, the NBA wanted to punish the ABA teams.

After the deal was reached, Drossos returned home to San Antonio. A raucous crowd met him at the airport. The people were excited about the city's entrance into the big leagues. Drossos was not nearly as happy. "This is no time to break out the champagne," Drossos said. "This isn't a good deal. We paid dearly to get in." Between the fees to the NBA and to the ABA teams who folded, Drossos needed to take out a massive loan. The bank had not wanted to make such a payment—but they wanted the Spurs to exist.[37] The financial limitations would directly impact Drossos's view of many NBA initiatives, especially collective bargaining.

However, regardless of economics, just as he had thrust himself into ownership when he bought the Chaparrals, Drossos became a hub of NBA owner politics. "I always felt like one of those church workers," he said of his work on intra-league matters, "you know, you kind of laugh at those guys but the church doesn't work without them." "He threw himself into it emotionally," Jerry Colangelo of the Suns said.

"I think he always represented the city and the franchise in the way any fan would want them represented."[38]

For an owner who was a tough negotiator, short on money, and popular with his fellow owners, Drossos was a natural fit to have an explosive relationship in collective bargaining with Fleisher and the NBPA. During negotiations, both in 1979 and after, Drossos would pace in the room trying to raise the tension. The union was unsure if the pacing was intended to intimidate them, but for the most part the players simply laughed. Though Fleisher was known to be low-key, he had a number of blowups with Drossos over the years, more so than with other owners. Fleisher was not alone. "He didn't like me," Grantham says now of Drossos, "he said one time he was going to kick my ass."[39]

• • •

During the 1979 CBA negotiations when Fleisher rejected Drossos's cap proposal, Drossos was not one to simply give up and accept Fleisher's rejection. He got Coke and Pepsi to agree to sponsor the Spurs together—surely he could make Fleisher heel. As Ganz wrote to O'Brien in September 1979, "The Committee's focus on a salary limitation plan and the Players Association's steadfast refusal to entertain any such arrangement have provoked a considerable amount of heated discussions—especially with Drossos." According to Ganz, Fleisher never used the words strike, but he "made clear that the players will not agree to any salary limitation plan and will do 'whatever is necessary' to resist such arrangement."[40]

By September, after a number of sessions, the parties were at an impasse—mostly due to deep divides on the owners' side about how to proceed. Ganz sent a memo to O'Brien, who had not been at negotiations, with the intention of explaining the divisions among ownership, or as he put it, "to give you some feel for the divergence of views within the Labor Relations Committee."

Drossos and Fitzgerald wanted the salary cap, or more explicitly, they wanted a fight with the players. Drossos said he was a "hawk" and that "he was ready to take a strike and lose $1,000,000 and that he would attempt to persuade the Board of Governors to support his position."[41] Given his standing with the other owners, it was possible he could convince them.

Fundamentally, Drossos believed, according to Ganz, that "unless the Players Association agrees to some sort of payroll limitation arrangement, the NBA should not compromise on any of the traditional issues that thus provoke a strike." Drossos objected to anything that could push the parties to a deal. As Ganz wrote, "Drossos has objected to Rothenberg's discussing possible areas of compromise on these other issues with Fleisher."[42]

On the other side of the table were the moderates—Ganz, Rothenberg, and Cohen—who believed what was on the table with Fleisher was an excellent deal and that the likelihood of getting Fleisher to agree to any salary limitation was nonexistent.[43] Rothenberg had attempted to work around Drossos, negotiating with Fleisher on all of the issues other than the salary cap plan. By September 6, Rothenberg and Fleisher had come close on everything other than the cap and cable revenues—the two big-ticket items.[44] The moderates believed they had wrangled strong concessions from the union in the proposed agreement—a limitation on deferred money was likely to limit salaries moving forward. Rothenberg's belief, according to Ganz, was that "the deal is attractive enough, and the owners disinclination to force or take a strike strong enough, so that the Board will not support the Drossos position."[45]

Regarding cable, for some reason, the owners themselves were not terribly concerned. Ganz expressed frustration at this disinterest in the cable television issue in his memo to O'Brien on September 20. "I stressed the importance to the NBA of its resolution during these negotiations . . . however, there was little discussion of the matter, and my sense was that it was not regarded as terribly important (except perhaps for reasons of strategy) by those in attendance yesterday."[46]

Staff was different. Simon Gourdine, deputy commissioner, argued that the NBA should not take the potential for cable lightly. As he wrote in a memo to O'Brien in October 1979: "with the relaxation by the FCC of cable restrictions, many believe that cable is on the threshold of enormous commercial success. Therefore, the suit by the Players Association challenging the cable companies' (and by implication the NBA and its teams) right to use players' likenesses, could have a serious adverse effect on a revenue source of the NBA. I think that assuming the Players Association retains its posture of 'rolling the dice' on the outcome of the litigation, the NBA should be prepared to unilaterally implement a proposal (in the event of impasse) which confers all future rights to the players' likenesses to the NBA and its teams." What Gourdine was advocating for was to create an impasse so the NBA could enforce its terms to require players to grant their likeness to the league. Though he recognized there were legal concerns: "If such a plan is possible, it seems that the Players Association is least likely to strike over what may be 'windfall income' somewhere in the future."[47] While Gourdine may have been right, there does not seem to have been any interest from the owners in pursuing that.

After a meeting of the NBA Labor Committee on September 19, 1979, Ganz again wrote to O'Brien, as well as Stern and Gourdine. This time, he said, though there was some dissent on issues, there was a desire to accept the package outlined by the moderate wing of the negotiating committee, but Drossos and Fitzgerald remained holdouts. Ganz advised O'Brien that "Drossos and Fitzgerald are of the view that the NBA should not make an agreement with the Players Association along the lines tentatively proposed, unless the Players Association agrees to some form of team payroll limitation (Drossos) or the elimination of guaranteed contracts (Fitzgerald). Both acknowledge that the Players Association will not voluntarily agree on such matters and they propose a return to the bargaining table and an insistence by the NBA upon the present level of benefits and/ or cut-backs in certain areas . . . as a method of forcing such an arrangement. If an impasse is reached, they believe that the NBA should make a final offer to the Players Association which, assuming its rejection, would then be implemented unilaterally. Drossos and Fitzgerald are prepared to take a strike and intend to ask the Board of Governors to support their position."[48]

The owners' insistence on the cap triggered threats on both sides in anticipation of the Board of Governors meeting in late September 1979, after the Labor Committee meeting. There were rumors of a work stoppage if a deal wasn't reached. "The owners are in a fighting mood," a source told the *Chicago Tribune* before the Board of Governors meeting. "They believe Fleisher is refusing to negotiate the key issues, confident he can wear them down. Word is going around that the players will walk out before the playoffs, but I wouldn't be surprised if the owners beat them to it with a lockout when they're convinced a strike is inevitable."[49] Fleisher said on the eve of the Board of Governors meeting, "There is no chance of approval for any agreement restricting our right to bargain individually. If it comes to a strike, it comes to a strike."[50]

Beyond Drossos, however, the stomach for a strike was limited on the owners' side. At the Board of Governors meeting, Rothenberg went, according to the minutes of the meeting, "line by line" through his memorandum, attempting to implore the owners to the agreement he thought was reasonable.[51]

There was still no deal—so negotiations continued. In November 1979 Fleisher began to move on cable. Though he said he could not force the individual players to drop their lawsuit or waive their rights, and that while he would not agree to having the lawsuit dropped, Ganz wrote that Fleisher said "he might agree to take no action (whatever the outcome of the lawsuit) during the anticipated three-year term of a new collective bargaining agreement."[52]

In mid-January 1980, Howard Ganz and Ed Silver wrote a memo to the NBA Labor Relations Committee. The memo was drafted to push the Board of Governors generally, and Drossos and Fitzgerald specifically, to an agreement. Ganz and Silver said there were three options: "1. Continued negotiations 2. Unilateral implementation or 3. Lockout." The memo emphasized that the players, with the agreement expired, could strike at any time. Continued negotiation, the lawyers said, "would be of significant advantage to the NBA. It would insure 'labor peace' for the duration of the season, and deprive the Players Association . . . of its most potent weapon."[53] Though they discussed the possibility of unilateral implementation, Ganz and Silver seemed hesitant and thought the process to be risky, particularly as it related to the cable television issue. Their view was that since the NBA was currently being sued by Silas and the players, *and* was subject to the *Robertson* settlement agreement, *and* because they had taken the position that they were not obligated to share cable revenues, any unilateral implementation of any policy could hamper their position in the future. The memo seemed drafted to push the owners to a deal.

By early February 1980 the players were threatening to walk out over the cap issue. "There's no way we'll start another season without a contract," NBPA president Paul Silas said. In terms of attempting to force the cap, Silas said, "We believe that's against the law. Right now, negotiations have broken off and we're not even talking with them." On the eve of the All-Star Game, O'Brien preached calm. "There have been no threats or rancor on either side. A player walkout would be difficult for the league, but I don't believe it will happen." Silas said to expect a "dramatic announcement" after the players' meeting at the All-Star Game.[54]

At the All-Star Game the sides reached a deal. The NBA dropped their cap proposal. Fleisher said he was surprised by the NBA's movement. "We came to the All-Star meeting on Friday still far apart from the owners. I was surprised when they made an acceptable contract offer, because a group of owners wanted to test the union by pushing us into a strike," he said.[55] It was obvious who Fleisher was referring to.

When Rothenberg made a presentation at the Board of Governors meeting on February 3, 1980, on the day of the All-Star Game in Washington, he was pushing for a deal, as he had been for months. He said that they had reached an agreement with Fleisher based on the terms Ganz and Silver had sent around in January. They had achieved one additional concession—though they were unable to get Fleisher to dismiss the suit entirely, he would agree to have "the action discontinued without prejudice and not to reinstitute it or a similar proceeding for a period of 7 years." Rothenberg further told the Board of Governors that "all members of the Labor Relations Committee except Mr. Drossos recommended that a new collective agreement be entered into." Drossos responded saying he believed "the proposed agreement with the Players Association was not a favorable one for the NBA," and that he opposed the agreement. His former ally, Jim Fitzgerald of Milwaukee, moved to have the agreement approved by the Board of Governors, and the agreement passed 16–6.[56] Drossos was defeated.

The Players Association agreed (for itself and its members) that they would not sue over cable or pay TV until the conclusion of the

1987 playoffs. Nothing stopped Fleisher from bargaining over it in the next round of negotiations, which would be after the 1982 season.[57] "The important thing is that the Players Association gave up its right to sue over cable revenue," Simon Gourdine said after the agreement was announced. "They can go on strike later if we don't cut them in on it, but we got as much out of the agreement as they did."[58] It was obvious to everyone that cable television would be a big part of the next negotiations. Gourdine said that cable TV "will come up in 1982, I'm sure."[59] As the *Chicago Tribune* reported, "In the next contract, the [NBPA] will try to negotiate for some of the cable TV pie, expected to be worth millions by then."[60]

O'Brien said, "I am proud there was never any rancor expressed by either side," and that this was the product of good faith bargaining. Fleisher said, "I will certainly recommend acceptance. This proposal is the product of hard negotiations, and we think it's a major step forward."[61]

The issues loomed large and the framework became clear. What the NBA and its players negotiated in 1980 was a ceasefire: The players and the owners stuck with the system they had—the players would put off their fight for cable revenues, and the owners would withdraw their proposal for a cap. They kicked the can down the road. Grantham calls this "a boxing period," a time when, due to low ratings and economic hardship, neither side had the stomach for a war.[62]

• • •

After the agreement with the players, the NBA's business continued. When the NBA's Board of Governors met in June of 1980, there was a motion to approve the sale of the Cleveland Cavaliers to a new owner, Ted Stepien. The Cavaliers had been in chaos, cycling through four owners in just two months. Though Stepien had purchased the team on the public market—it was sold on the stock exchange then—he still had to be approved by the NBA's Board of Governors prior to taking control.

Stepien was a local Cleveland businessman and had made his money founding the Nationwide Advertising Agency out of Cleveland, Ohio. Nationwide was known for "recruitment advertising," which is a fancy way of saying he was the king of the "help wanted" section of local newspapers—all of them, in every city across the country. Nationwide was known for doing everything related to hiring—they would write, design, lay out, and place the hiring advertisements. They could also find interviewing facilities, schedule with candidates, and even handle the interview itself. Stepien started the business in 1947 with five hundred dollars he had borrowed from his father. The growth of Nationwide, as described in a fawning piece in a business trade journal, "is not so much a testimony to one man's creative genius," referring to Stepien, "but rather an example of capitalizing on an advertising vacuum."[63] In almost every assessment, analysis, or description of Stepien there are two themes: first, that he was not a business genius or a genius of any kind; second, that although he was tremendously successful, his success was in spite of himself.

Stepien's interview with the Board of Governors was different from those with many of the other owners who purchased NBA franchises. Stepien had made a series of racially insensitive statements about African Americans and Jews in his various attempts to purchase local Cleveland professional sports teams. In a prior effort to purchase the Cleveland Indians, Stepien had referred to their ownership as a "Jewish clique." In 1979 Stepien said about the Cavaliers, "This is not to sound prejudiced but [if I owned the team] half the squad would be white. I think people are afraid to speak out on the subject. White people have to have white heroes. I, myself, can't equate to black heroes. I'll be truthful, I respect them but I need white people. It's in me. And I think the Cavs have too many blacks. 10 of 11. You need a blend of white and black."[64] These were not his only insensitive statements prior to entering the NBA.

The NBA was concerned about Stepien's comments. As the *New York Times'* columnist George Vecsey put it, "The owner of sports franchises rarely scrutinize new applicants on moral grounds, but are usually satisfied if a new boy's check doesn't bounce higher than the top of the stadium. However, Stepien made the faux pas of talking out loud about racial quotas in a sport where 70 percent of the players are black."[65]

Rather than apologize, Stepien defended himself. Stepien told the *New York Times* before his meeting with the Board of Governors that those statements were "in a context of marketing," and that "they do not mean I'm prejudiced."[66] He told *Sport* magazine, "I happen to be a street guy. When I grew up you were a Dago, you were a Polack, you were a Jew, you were a black. And those were forms of endearment. Now I think people are more sensitive to them."[67] Even on the eve of his meeting with the Board of Governors, Stepien doubled down on his positions on race. "I'm from Pittsburgh originally," he said, "and I know the Pirates suffer a lot due to too many black faces. People are afraid to say it, but it's true. The Pirates won a pennant one year and drew fewer than a million fans."[68] Stepien's numbers were, both emotionally and factually, wrong.

The NBA was concerned about legal liability from Stepien's comments and issues that could come from players. Several of the black players on the Cavaliers said they would not play for Stepien if he were approved by the NBA. Campy Russell, who had played the previous six seasons in Cleveland and had been an All-Star said of Stepien, "If he can find four or five white guys who can help us win, I'd like to see it."[69]

At the Board of Governors meeting Stepien was questioned extensively about his racist and anti-Semitic comments by his fellow owners, almost to the exclusion of his finances. Stepien was asked whether he would choose a team that was half white. Stepien said he would play the best players regardless of race. Stepien was asked about the "Jewish clique" comment. He denied saying it "in an anti-Semitic way"—whatever that meant.[70]

After the meeting, Stepien said, "They heard that I was anti-Jewish and anti-black and I had to explain my position. Then I asked how many of them told Polish jokes or listened to Polish jokes. And I think they got taken aback by that. If I said that in Cleveland there was a Jewish clique, I meant that as a form of endearment. They were sensitive to that if they were Jewish. We ethnic people also feel that we're discriminated against, in business and in other areas. I grew up with the same feeling of insecurity and minority feeling as everybody else. I still feel it in business. I'm excluded, not openly, from certain financial circles. I know that."[71] After the meeting, Larry Weinberg of the Portland Trailblazers said, "Stepien told us he has a Jewish lawyer and Jewish friends, and told us 'you can call me other things, but I am not a bigot.' He was very emotional. I think people were impressed."[72]

In the end the Board of Governors saw Stepien as a necessary evil. The NBA was desperate. The Cavs were in trouble; Stepien had money and was prepared to take over. No matter his views, he was approved by the Board of Governors unanimously. After the vote, Weinberg said, "I had some serious questions, and I raised them. I also called friends in Cleveland, who said Stepien tends to spout off on occasion and that they may not like him personally, but that bigotry was a mislabel."[73] Irv Levin of the Clippers said, "He is enthusiastic about rebuilding the Cleveland team and financially able to do it. I don't have to be buddy-buddy with him."[74] Not the most ringing endorsement from the members of his new fraternity.

Stepien left the meeting wounded. "I feel a little resentful at having to defend myself," he said. "They took things out of context. I'm not a racist. I don't know if I want to join people if they don't want me."[75] Stepien was surprised by the substance of the meeting, saying, "They heard about my so-called views but I thought they were going to interrogate me on my finances." They probably should have.

After the meeting Stepien was the proud owner of his hometown Cleveland Cavaliers. Stepien was described by Bob Ryan in the *Boston Globe* as "yet another semi-eccentric" NBA owner who spent his first time in front of the national sports media describing the physical specifications of his nineteen-year-old daughter, a finalist in the Ohio Miss America pageant. Stepien described her as "stacked and very good looking." He also added, "I'm her coach."[76]

On the basketball side, Stepien was positive. "I like all the ingredients," he said of the team he was assuming control over. He said that fans should expect "no wholesale changes" from his ownership.[77]

Stepien was also clear, however, that he intended to run the basketball operations. Stepien would have purchased the team months earlier, but he insisted that Cavaliers president Nick Mileti resign as team president so that he could run the team's basketball operations unobstructed. "I certainly don't want to buy an organization I can't run," he said.[78] Mileti stepped aside as part of the transaction when Stepien assumed ownership. "For that kind of money, I'd better be involved . . . It's the type of involvement that gives you national exposure," Stepien said.[79] As Bob Ryan described him, "He appears to be a forceful man who can't wait to start running the team on a day-to-day basis."[80]

8

The Right of First Refusal, Summer 1981

Angelo Drossos had the idea of a salary cap. Ed Garvey from the
NFL[PA], his idea was to say to the owners, "I want to share the
revenues," and they said, "Absolutely never, we'll shut down before
we do," and they did. What we did is say to the players: "How about
if we share revenues? If we share revenues, you give us a salary
cap." . . . That's where we came up with it, by borrowing ideas that
had been forwarded and rejected in an earlier negotiation.

—DAVID STERN, 2004

Before the 1960s there were no real unions in sports.[1] There was a
nominal one in baseball, one in football, and another in basketball.
Overall the unions in these sports were, at best, weak trade associations, sometimes funded by the leagues themselves. There certainly
were not work stoppages or regular collective bargaining negotiations
that could upend the status quo. Players unions were disorganized
and weak and the people who ran them thought they could accomplish very little. So, they accomplished very little.

Beginning in the 1960s, things started to change. Partly because
they began to hire professionals to run the organizations. Fleisher
was first, brought into the NBPA by Tommy Heinsohn in 1961 after
seven years of minimal progress. Then Marvin Miller came to the
MLBPA in 1966, recruited by Robin Roberts and Jim Bunning, after
about twenty years of futility. Then Ed Garvey came to the NFLPA
in 1971, brought over from the law firm handling a promising antitrust litigation on behalf of NFL players. Throughout the 1960s and
'70s, these Players Associations not only started to gain traction but

they also made significant economic improvements for players. They reached collective bargaining agreements, achieved independent arbitration, minimum salaries, and pensions, among other benefits. Due to their growing clout, they were formally recognized by the leagues they bargained with as representing the players. These gains empowered players to take bolder action in support of further gains—work stoppages, lawsuits, public statements. Sportswriters lamented that the sports page began to look like the business page, but the impact the MLBPA, NBPA, and NFLPA were making was clear.

This progress certainly did not come easily. Owners aggressively fought every change, especially at the beginning. They began by ignoring the unions —and the men who ran them. Improvements only occurred either as a result of force, by courts or arbitrators, or as a result of the threat or actualization of work stoppages. Fleisher and the NBPA had used such threats to great success in 1964 and 1967, and Marvin Miller would undertake the first strike in sports in the early 1970s.

By the 1970s all major sports unions were going after the same main goal, free agency: The simple ability of players to change teams and play in a circumstance they wished to play in. First the MLBPA achieved it through an arbitration award in 1975 (after failing in the famous Curt Flood case), then the NBPA through the *Robertson* settlement in February 1976. Finally, the NFLPA, after a 1975 court decision, negotiated limited free agency in 1977. In some ways, that achievement of free agency was a high-water mark. Almost immediately the owners attempted to put the genie back in the bottle to return to the times of perpetual ownership of players. Since 1975, in one way or another, the major players associations have been playing defense, with those early victories the touchstones of union success.

Nineteen eighty-one was a crucial year in the evolution of the various organizations, their sports, and their leaders, especially Garvey at the NFLPA. The three players unions, who in most instances had been pursuing the same goal in the 1970s—free agency—were dealing with the aftermath of their success differently. The MLBPA and its leader, Miller, were under assault as the owners attempted to implement a compensation plan for free agents who left their former teams—a similar circumstance to the unmitigated disaster that had befallen the NBA from 1976–81. In basketball the concern was less about free-agent compensation—which had been a giant failure—and more about an overall effort by the league to rein in salaries. Fleisher, like Miller, was simply attempting to protect the free market as much as possible in light of the assault from ownership. In the NFL in 1981, however, Garvey was doing something different; he was moving away from free agency and seeking a percentage of the NFL's gross revenues. It was a significant turn; in an era of evolution and change, there were many unorthodox ideas considered and implemented in sports, but it was not clear that this move away from free agency made much sense. But it did make sense for Ed Garvey.

There is a desire now, in light of how the industries have moved, to believe that these changes and economic structures in sports were inevitable and preordained. They, most certainly, were not. The MLBPA had no inherent power. The NBA was not predisposed to a salary cap. The NFL was not—by virtue of its sport—required to have weak free agency. The individuals at the top of these unions and leagues shaped the policies, perspectives, and outcomes of their sports. Decisions they made impacted the trajectory of their sports—in good ways, and bad. They had different philosophies and approaches. For the unions, these were new organizations. There was no roadmap.

Leading the MLBPA you had Marvin Miller, the now deified (and properly so) executive director. He had taken over the ballplayers union at the age of forty-eight—with a long career in labor relations as chief economist to the powerful steelworkers union before working in baseball. He was a trade unionist first, last, and always, and that was how he viewed the MLBPA. In baseball he built a trade union, the strongest he could find. He educated, empowered, and listened to his members—bringing along in baseball players a group of people who were deeply skeptical of unions. They became the most powerful union on the planet. He tried to meet every player in his bargaining unit. He encouraged them to come to meetings, board meetings, team meetings. He wanted them to come to the union office when they were in New York. "This is *your* office; this is *your* union," Miller implored them to take ownership.[2] He was patient. He explained the bargaining process. Miller was building something. There would be no shortcuts. Tim McCarver, one of the early leaders, said, "The most remarkable thing to me, looking back, is what a patient man Marvin Miller was. He realized how disparate his knowledge of negotiating and contracts was from ours. So he educated the player reps and they educated the rest. It was a very slow, methodical process. He never let the cart get before the horse. Everything was building from a base."[3] Miller, like Fleisher, believed that a rising tide lifted all boats. He also cultivated stars among his leadership—Tim McCarver, Joe Torre, Reggie Jackson, Robin Roberts, Steve Rogers.

He let the players guide the MLBPA's approach and build its power. In 1972 Miller oversaw the first strike in professional sports when his membership struck over a pension issue. The strike did not occur because of Miller's recommendation but over his objections: he did not believe his members were ready for it. In the end, it was their union, and it was their decision. He respected his membership. In terms of staffing, Miller surrounded himself with strong union professionals—Dick Moss, with a history at the steelworkers, was his general counsel, and later, Don Fehr, hired from a union-side law firm in Kansas City. When he retired from the MLBPA in the early 1980s he had only one rule for the players in finding his replacement: hire someone with experience in labor relations. He was not trying to reinvent the wheel but rather to put a lifetime of experience into it. Their approach was to be the most powerful union they could in the ways that the most powerful unions had been. Solidarity, organization, and communication were the ways to build power. It was tremendously successful.

Who was on the other side mattered, too. In baseball you had the famous "Lords of the Realm"—the owners in baseball—who resisted any question of their power over the game. They were not going to be told what to do by Miller. Miller was not only a trade unionist but a Jewish trade unionist. Owners referred to Miller as "that gimpy-armed Jew bastard," mocking both his religion and an injury from birth that limited his use of his arm.[4] For much of Miller's tenure, Bowie Kuhn was commissioner of Major League Baseball and maintained an almost childlike view of the sport he oversaw. Kuhn did not come from the world of labor relations; he was a white shoe corporate lawyer. He could not understand Miller as professional trade unionist and negotiator or the organization he was dealing with. He couldn't understand why Miller put the needs of his members above those of fans. As he wrote in his autobiography: "There was about Miller the wariness one would find in an abused animal," but Kuhn felt he had a better relationship with Moss, in his view, because "in the first place, he was a real baseball fan and liked to talk about the game."[5] This was an economic relationship, not two friends talking about last night's game.

Major League Baseball was simply unprepared for professional labor relations when Miller arrived. When Miller and Moss were unleashed on baseball, they were shocked at the incompetence they saw on the other side. "It was incredible," Moss said of his impression of Major League Baseball when he began at the MLBPA. "This was a labor-relations scene from the thirties in the mid-sixties."[6]

Bruce Johnston, who was a negotiator for US Steel and knew Miller and Moss from their steelworker days, said that it was the lack of maturity of baseball as an industry that made Miller and Moss so successful, not necessarily the men themselves. He said Moss was a "secondary player on a topflight legal team," and Miller was "certainly competent but you could have found two thousand guys like him." Johnston said that their success came from the fact that Miller and Moss were experienced and then "turned loose on an industry that was, in terms of labor relations, naïve and illiterate. The owners were a loose amalgam of highly individualistic entrepreneurs who are the worst people in the world to deal with labor. They're impatient, egocentric and exasperating to represent."[7] Most importantly, these distinctions had an impact on outcomes. In 1981, when the right of first refusal was beginning in the NBA, Miller was asked about its potential application to Major League Baseball. Miller, who by that time had raised issues with it, told the *Los Angeles Times* that the concept had come up once during negotiations in 1976 but that "the owners rejected it out of hand."[8] He was no longer interested—he had a better deal. By resisting the union, the owners in baseball often ended up with worse deals.

In basketball, Fleisher was at the top of the NBPA—pragmatic, economical, but principled. Though he had less traditional labor experience than Miller when he took over the NBPA, he understood and cultivated solidarity, especially after the All-Star strike of 1964. As his friend Howard Cosell said, "Fleisher was the ultimate pragmatist in a field where few pragmatists are found."[9] Fleisher ran his organization differently than Miller. In his mind the NBPA was more of a trade association on behalf of NBA players—operating with a lean staff and utilizing the courts to gain leverage. Fleisher, like Miller, believed strongly in the importance of member leadership and communication. He was tactical, willing to gamble but fiendishly creative and innovative. While Miller used the tools of trade unionism like a master, Fleisher invented new ones not considered. Miller could not comprehend decertification, it offended him so. Fleisher used it to reach a deal. This was an era of experimentation. Miller saw his foray into baseball as a laboratory for new ideas. So did Fleisher. There was uncertainty as to the terrain, what would work, what wouldn't. Neither was right or wrong, just different. In 1972 Miller achieved salary arbitration for his players to great acclaim, as salaries skyrocketed. In 1975 Fleisher rejected it as part of the *Robertson* settlement. In 1976 the owners in baseball rejected the right of first refusal (restricted free agency) out of hand. That same year the NBA accepted it.

In the NBA, management was O'Brien, Stern, and Granik and, even further back, Ed Silver. The relationship was cleaner, easier. More businesslike—even a partnership. In the early 1970s, even with the *Robertson* case burning, there was not tremendous animosity between the sides. There were strong positions, but the relationship was more productive. In 1973, at the height of the *Robertson* litigation, the *Los Angeles Times* ran a long story on the labor relationship in the NBA entitled "NBA Players Militant . . . Still Get along with Owners," with a subtitle that read, "Personalities May Be Key in Harmonious Relationship," putting the focus on the trust between Fleisher and Ed Silver. "Our relationship has been fairly good . . . and we don't have anybody in ownership trying to destroy the association," Fleisher said.[10] Even after *Robertson*, the relationship was stronger. O'Brien believed that there were no final victories. Fleisher wanted to push the NBA, but it was not personal. As Granik said about that time, "[Fleisher] was the guy you had to deal with, and he had a very professional view of things. His job was to make the best deal he could for his players without hurting the league. He understood if you pushed too far, it wasn't good for anybody."[11] Fleisher once told an NBA owner, "My job is to take you right up to the brink of bankruptcy, but no more."[12]

Then, at the NFLPA, you had Ed Garvey. The *Los Angeles Times* said that Garvey "speaks with more animation, and perhaps less diplomacy, than Marvin Miller and Larry Fleisher, his counterparts in baseball and basketball."[13] In comparing Garvey and Fleisher at the time of the *Robertson* settlement, Alan Goldstein of the *Baltimore Sun* noted, "Unlike his football counterpart, Ed Garvey, who has an uncanny knack for creating headlines and unrest, Fleisher has consistently maintained a low profile. And while the football union has been ripped by dissension amid cries for Garvey's head, the basketball players have remained firmly united behind Fleisher for over a decade."[14] Ray Grebey, Major League Baseball's chief negotiator through some of the most bitter labor wars with Miller, once sat next to Garvey at a law school symposium and felt compelled to remark, "I've never sat next to someone as self-righteous as you, Ed." What was left unsaid was that he spent much of his time sitting with Miller, whom he detested, under much higher stakes.[15] For his part, in the 1970s Miller once excoriated Garvey for attacking the MLBPA's achievements and exaggerating the NFLPA's. After a three-page letter, in which Miller carbon copied Garvey's entire member leadership, Miller ended the letter by saying, "I agonized along with the football players during their struggle. I hope they eventually will achieve terms and conditions which they want. But it serves no useful purpose to falsify the record by citing losing efforts as exemplary and by falsely depicting another organization's successful efforts."[16]

Garvey was polarizing and brash but no one denied he was brilliant. "People either love him or loathe him," *Sports Illustrated* wrote of Garvey in February 1982.[17] "You bet he's abrasive," Bill Curry, Garvey's champion and president of the NFLPA said in 1974.[18] As the *Boston Globe* put it, "Garvey, you must understand, can offend just about anyone. He is quick to stick a needle into anyone other than himself, defensive to the point of being defenseless and can personalize virtually every management labor issue."[19]

Garvey had a very combative relationship with the NFL, agents, and even some of his players. Garvey ran the NFLPA in an unorthodox manner. He was not like the true believer Miller, who practiced what he preached. Nor was Garvey a business-focused labor leader like Larry Fleisher who ran the union on a shoestring, never taking a salary. Garvey was politically active and saw the NFLPA as part of the broader labor movement. He believed it was important for the NFLPA to join the AFL-CIO. He envisioned and attempted to create a broad sports-labor coalition and used NFL player's dues to fund the founding of other sports unions, including soccer, drag racing, and rodeo. He became the executive director of some of these organizations at the same time he was in charge of the NFLPA.

By 1981 NFL players were well behind their cohorts in other sports in terms of salary.[20] The free agency he had negotiated for in 1977 was an instant disaster. Rather than try to improve the free agency he negotiated, in 1981, Garvey had a new idea. He began spinning free agency as a negative, something that would never work in the NFL. He argued that the NFL was socialistic, and that the only fair thing would be for NFL players to get a "percentage-of-gross," meaning that players would get a percentage of the gross revenue the NFL earned—from television, from ticket sales, from everything. Garvey's plan proposed that the NFL would convey the gross earnings to the union who would then distribute the revenues to players on a uniform basis. Garvey's proposal in 1981, which was tremendously complicated, would eliminate the ability of players to negotiate for their own contracts. There would be a union scale, similar to the initial collective wage proposal the NBA had made to Fleisher during the 1980 negotiations.

Garvey had not always been against free agency. In 1974 Garvey unsuccessfully attempted to achieve free agency through a training camp strike, which lasted about six weeks. The issues were unclear; Garvey said the players were focused on "freedom demands." The strike was rocky from the start. When he took the players out on July 1, the owners who were especially combative in the NFL did everything they could to cut Garvey from the players and to make the strike about him rather than the issues. George Halas, the legendary owner of the Chicago Bears, attacked Garvey directly. "The position of Ed Garvey with his huge no cut contract is the sweetest of all because he stands to lose nothing but an argument," Halas said.[21] Garvey was a clear figure on the picket lines, reveling in the theater.

His counterpart for the owners, John Thompson, said that based on Garvey's conduct on the picket line, "it does not appear he's ready to resume bargaining any time soon."[22]

Negotiations went nowhere. After about a month of striking with no progress, players began to return to training camp and cross the NFLPA's picket line. Garvey had not built an organization like Miller; he dealt with considerable dissent. When Bob Parsons, punter and tight end of the Chicago Bears, was the first Bear to cross the picket line on July 30, he said, "I admit I don't know what's going on with this strike. Garvey's screwing things up."[23]

Garvey was unable to avoid problems of his own making. On August 4, five weeks into the strike, Roger Staubach, quarterback of the Dallas Cowboys, crossed the picket line and walked into Cowboys training camp. In response, Garvey said, "I'm glad I wasn't at Pearl Harbor with him." The only problem was that Staubach had gone to the Naval Academy and served years in the navy. For Garvey to make a Pearl Harbor joke was in very poor taste. In addition, Staubach was quite popular and respected. After hearing Garvey's statements, the soft-spoken Staubach was angry. "Normally, I wouldn't say anything about it," he said. "But talking to a Navy man about Pearl Harbor . . . I just thought that was uncalled for. Garvey has been that way. He's made some strong statements about people who don't listen to his party line. If he hadn't said Pearl Harbor, if he'd just said, 'Staubach's a scab' I wouldn't have said anything." Garvey immediately apologized. He sent a telegram to Staubach saying, "I did not mean to criticize you. I respect your individual decision."[24] Unlike Fleisher and Miller, Garvey was sniping at his stars, not working with them.

Condemnation of Garvey for the Staubach stunt was somewhat universal even in the midst of a strike. Tom Mack, an offensive lineman for the Rams who would later go into the Hall of Fame, released a statement the next day saying, "I would like to make clear that there are few men who command more of my respect for integrity both on and off the field than Staubach. I hope further comment about individual personalities will cease as they can only be confusing and inflammatory." He still defended the strike, saying, "I continue to believe the issues are genuine."[25]

Rams owner Carrol Rosenbloom used the opportunity to take a

swing at Garvey too, saying, "My business experience, and that of other owners in the league, is that strong labor organizations traditionally negotiate responsibly, intelligently and ethically—unlike the current association leadership." Rosenbloom later clarified that he only meant Garvey, not players.[26] The owners were successfully making the walkout Garvey's strike, not the players'.

By mid-August Garvey was out of options—players were returning to camp with or without his say-so. He called for a two-week "cooling off period," and though he did not end the strike, he sent players into camp. He claimed he could pull them back out, but no one believed him. As Robert Markus wrote in the *Chicago Tribune*, "Anyone who has ever seen a 30-year-old defensive tackle sweat through two-a-day drills in the dog days of summer must realize the futility of asking him to leave camp after two weeks of agony and face the prospect of getting into shape all over again."[27] The strike was over, without much of anything having been accomplished.

After the strike, Garvey took responsibility for its failure, saying, "The strike collapsed and we lost." Garvey, who cavalierly said he thought a strike would be fun before they went out in 1974, seemed to intimate a desire not to strike again, saying, "It's clear, by the attitude here and elsewhere that we will try and avoid another strike . . . Very few of the players I have talked to told me they wouldn't pay their dues." The NFLPA was deeply weakened. At the Bengals' team meeting, they attempted to select a new player rep, but as Pat Matson said, "There wasn't enough dues paying members of the association to make the vote stand up."[28]

Money was an issue for the union and Garvey was struggling. This was not a problem in baseball because Marvin Miller created a group-licensing program, which funded the union independent of management or dues. This was not an issue in the NBA because Fleisher took no salary and ran the union on a shoestring.

For Garvey, however, dues were crucial. In 1975, on the eve of training camp, Garvey admitted that the NFLPA was $200,000 in debt. "We've had to borrow money just to keep the doors open," Garvey said. "We can't go through another year without a contract and survive as a union."[29] Not exactly the pillar of strength, especially in dealing with the NFL who had power, resources, and intent to limit

The Right of First Refusal

the union's impact. In admitting that membership had shrunk to 750 dues paying members, Garvey said the decrease was "primarily because the owners [had] taken away the checkoff in their continued effort to break the union," referring to the ability of employees to have union dues removed directly from their paychecks.[30]

Garvey said that because of the change "the player reps [had] to go around and collect checks from each member . . . and you know how that goes."[31] Garvey also admitted that the decrease was also because his 1974 strike had failed. "We didn't think the owners would play exhibition games with rookies and free agents, but they did. We thought the rookies would honor the picket lines, and that was probably unrealistic of us."[32] There was no real way to fix NFLPA's problems without raising more money. In 1976 Garvey was asked whether the NFLPA was in debt. His response: "Yes it's true. But I'm not particularly concerned about it. We are paying it off as we can. I suspect we'll have to raise our dues."[33]

They had no agreement after the strike ended in 1974. As they negotiated a new agreement with the owners, the debt followed them. In 1977 the NFLPA finally reached a collective bargaining agreement with the NFL for the first time in seven years. Finally, Garvey was able to achieve pension benefits and severance pay. Garvey also got a union shop, which would help Garvey's economic problems. When the agreement was reached, Garvey was asked where the power for the union would come from in the next negotiation. His first answer was the union shop provision; he said it would give him the money for communication, litigation, and, yes, a strike fund.[34]

A union shop is a crucial benefit for any union to prioritize, and the ability to raise funds through member dues allows a union to grow and develop, but Garvey was forced to make a very deep concession to achieve a union shop—he gave away real free agency. Almost immediately after the collective bargaining agreement, the NFL announced a massive new television deal. Garvey had made a gigantic miscalculation.[35] The free agency deal that they made was terribly unfavorable. In fact, in the three years after the agreement, only one player had actually moved in free agency.[36]

The dues issue remained a noose around the NFLPA, even in the late 1970s. In 1979 Garvey accused the NFL of racism, in failing to hire minorities for administrative positions. Rozelle suggested Garvey was making the claim to take the heat off himself, and Rozelle said he "had heard 'rumblings' from some players that Garvey had taken $200,000 from the players' union to form a similar union in the North American Soccer League."[37]

Though he certainly had his supporters, he was disliked by many of the players he represented, in addition to player agents. Howard Slusher, who was one of the top NFL agents of his time, was critical of Garvey. He said, "While Marvin Miller thrives on his players being enriched, Ed Garvey sees that as a threat. He thinks if they're real wealthy, they won't need the union. Football has no exemption from antitrust and has had great success in the courts, and he threw it all back. He had the NFL on the ropes and he chucked it all back. Ed Garvey simply cares about Ed Garvey."[38]

So, beginning in January of 1981, about a year before the NFL collective bargaining agreement expired, Garvey began making noise about what the NFLPA intended to achieve in their next deal. He said he believed that free agency was "dead" and the players would "seek a percentage of owners gross revenue instead."[39] Garvey began to float the idea that players should get 55 percent of revenues, the amount they had gotten before the AFL-NFL merger. "The last contract has become a cruel hoax that we created in an attempt to make individual negotiations work," he said. "The league outsmarted us, and in the meantime, agents have become an impossibility for the most part. By sharing in the gross revenues, the players can become partners with the owners as the league grows and you won't need individual bargaining. It will eliminate holdouts and bad agents."[40] He said, "If the league gets a larger television contract, a bigger part of cable television and raises ticket prices, we'll grow with them."[41]

Eventually, however, 55 percent of revenues was not enough for Garvey. "The general feeling was that 55 per cent was too low," Garvey said in July. "We want to research the entertainment industry to see what labor industries receive before we settle on an exact figure we'll ask for."[42] By November of 1981 he was proposing 65 percent of revenues. Garvey quoted one player as saying, "Who thought of 55 percent? We should get 85 percent."[43]

Garvey was also clear, not only that his percent of gross idea was crucial, but that any other idea—say free agency—was bad, and that the union should not pursue it. "Free agency will not work in professional football," he said.[44] "Individual negotiations cannot work in a monopoly like the National Football League," he said. Garvey also claimed that players were not even interested in free agency in the next contract. In identifying potential proposals though, he said "there had been some discussions about seeking a clause in the 1982 contract that would free a player to negotiate with other teams after three years of service." "But that's not a big thing at this point," Garvey said.[45]

He even tried to argue that NFL players had not wanted free agency in the first place. "When we talked about free agency in 1974—and we took surveys afterward—a lot of our people thought that free agency wouldn't help them," he said. "This time they can see a percentage of the gross will help virtually every player."[46]

Garvey had considerable support for his idea, but he also had skeptics. Garvey agreed, "Some quarterbacks like it, some don't, but generally speaking, most quarterbacks will be doing better than they're doing now."[47] Many players were critical of both the percentage of gross idea and the move away from free agency. Jack Lambert of the Steelers said, "I will not strike and I will cross the picket lines if a strike is called by the NFLPA on those issues. I am much more concerned with our freedom, the opportunity to move from one team to another." When asked about Garvey's demand for 55 percent of gross, Lambert said, "Ed Garvey is in the wrong country."[48]

The NFL rejected Garvey's proposal out of hand, stating that they did not intend to be partners with the players union. Though they said the rejection was firm, Garvey's rhetoric was heated. "They also said in 1970 they'd never discuss the powers of the commissioner. In '74 they said they would never agree to impartial arbitration or altering the Rozelle rule. They did. And they will negotiate over part of the gross. It's only a matter of time," Garvey said.[49]

"His gross revenue idea is preposterous," one league executive told the *Washington Post*. "There is no way anyone is going to agree to it and he knows it. A strike seems inevitable."[50]

• • •

While Ed Garvey was moving away from free agency, the summer of 1981 was also when the NBA came closer to it. It was the beginning of the next phase of the *Robertson* settlement—the part that made Fleisher light his victory cigar at the All-Star game in 1976. It was the first year of the "right of first refusal," or what is now called restricted free agency. Under the *Robertson* settlement, the right of first refusal system was to run for five years. Then, in 1987, it was expected that players would achieve free agency.

The system was simple: free agents could negotiate beginning on May 15, the day after the NBA finals had ended. When they came to terms with a team they would sign an "offer sheet," which listed the terms of their agreements, and forward a copy to their old team. The old team would have fifteen days to match it on its terms.[51] Not yet unrestricted free agency, but it was hoped this would be a much more free market than the compensation system.

This was new territory for professional sports, and it was not clear what the impact would be. Many expected a freer market would lead to higher salaries. Fleisher believed the system would benefit the lower level players saying that they "will have greater movement, and they'll benefit the most." There was optimism that this system would be good for management as well. Carl Scheer, general manager of the Denver Nuggets, said, "I think the new system will increase salaries but I think that it will allow teams to hold onto their best players. It could work in management's favor."[52] There was also considerable concern that the system would allow the big markets, New York and Los Angeles, to have an outsized impact because of their financial advantages, similar to what the New York Yankees had done in baseball in the late 1970s after free agency was implemented there.[53]

Within a few weeks of the new system, the impact was clear: salaries had exploded. As *Sports Illustrated* put it, "there's evidence that Right of First Refusal will bring about an escalation in pro basketball salaries that will recall the increases resulting from the battle waged for players by the NBA and ABA from 1967."[54] Other teams made moves, but the escalation came mostly from the action of two owners: Dr. Jerry Buss of the Los Angeles Lakers and Ted Stepien of the Cleveland Cavaliers. Both spent a lot of money in the offseason of 1981—Buss had it, Stepien didn't. What Buss did was expected; what Stepien did wasn't.

• • •

Jerry Buss was known to like "fast cars, fast women, and fast scores in business." In a piece in the *Los Angeles Times*, after his purchase of the Lakers in 1979, it was said that "by day, [Buss] is a calculating tycoon whose every mood in his multi-million dollar business is carefully thought out . . . But by night, there is very little he won't chance." Though Buss had a PhD in physical chemistry—he was described as someone who "does everything he can to project a swinger's image."[55]

Buss had never been shy about spending money since taking over the Lakers, in fact he was more aggressive than anyone else in the league. He often increased his players' salaries mid-contract—when he didn't have to. By 1981 Buss had increased nearly every Laker's salary in the time since buying the team. He gave Kareem Abdul Jabbar a raise from $650,000 to over $1 million; Jamal Wilkes from $350,000 to $600,000; Norm Nixon from $65,000 to $400,000; Michael Cooper from $35,000 to $250,000;and Jim Chones from $250,000 to $350,000.[56]

Buss's largesse had incurred the wrath of his fellow owners. They feared his cavalier increases were pushing the league salary scale beyond what other markets could sustain. Buss simply didn't care; he believed that the higher salaries were part of running a sound business, *his* sound business. "I have a certain income from the Lakers," he said. "Also expenses and profit. Truthfully, whatever I pay players is no one's business, except for the joy everyone gets gossiping about the numbers." Buss made his team building decisions a reflection of his business acumen, saying, "If any owner can show me that he, too, has income expenses and profit, and operates within those parameters, then fine, I have no quarrel with paying trillions."[57]

In the summer of 1981 the Lakers were at a crossroads, the first such bump in the magical ride of Jerry Buss's Lakers ownership. In his first month in charge, Buss's Lakers drafted Magic Johnson, and at the end of his first year, the Lakers won the NBA championship. His second year, however, was different. As the *Los Angeles Times* reported after the season, which ended with a first round playoff loss to the Houston Rockets, "Buss' money brought happiness, but not another championship."[58]

Magic missed forty-five games in the 1980–81 season with torn cartilage in his knee, sitting out from Thanksgiving until the end of February. While the Lakers struggled without Magic, they didn't collapse. Magic's injury allowed Norm Nixon, the Lakers' first-round pick just two years before Magic was drafted, to resume his role as the Lakers' lead ballhandler.[59] When Magic returned toward the end of the season, Magic assumed his prior role. Nixon stewed.

On March 30, 1981, two days before the Lakers' first-round playoff series with the Rockets was set to begin, a story appeared in the *Los Angeles Times* detailing Nixon's conflict with Magic and his impact on the team. "I thought Magic would come in and have to adjust to our game but we had to adjust to him," Nixon said. "The first thing they said in training camp that year was that Kareem and I had been handling the ball too much." Nixon reconciled his frustration with a prediction, "Anyway, 15 years from now, everyone will have forgotten Magic," Nixon said.[60]

Two days later, the Lakers lost the first game of their series to the Houston Rockets at the Forum. The Lakers had entered the playoffs in third place in the Western Conference, won fifty-four games in the regular season, and had home-court advantage in the series.[61] It was clear, however, even before that first game, that something was awry, the players were not interacting as they had all season. As the *Los Angeles Times* reported, "One clue came before Wednesday's upset: the recent lack of handslapping among the Lakers. That's a Magic Johnson trademark that is as much a sign of affection as anything else."[62]

After the second game against the Rockets, which the Lakers won, Johnson spoke about the issues surrounding the team. "Things are different," Johnson said, stating the feeling in the locker room relative to the prior season. "I can't say it's jealousy because I might be wrong. I feel kind of upset, kind of let down. This is the first time I've been involved with something like this."[63]

Johnson had heard Nixon's statements and some rumblings that he had received too many endorsements. "They think I hog the endorsements," he said. "I turn half of them down. I don't go out looking for publicity. I don't tell writers to write about me. . . . When you win, everyone knows you . . . I don't know if it's jealous [sic]," he said. Johnson was clearly hurt by his teammates' feelings, especially Nixon's. "If [Nixon] wants the ball more he can have it. I don't need the ball." Johnson seemed resigned, "I try to involve my teammates in the game before I get myself involved. And now, to have them focusing on me, like I did something wrong. I don't know." He was disappointed in their play: "I figured we were just waiting for the playoffs before we started really playing. But the playoffs are here."[64]

Two days later, the Rockets and the Lakers played the rubber match. With the Lakers on the brink of elimination, Johnson had a terrible game. He made only 2 of 14 shots, missing 6 of 11 free throws, and missing two crucial free throws in the final minute. In the end, the Rockets beat the Lakers, again, at the Forum, 89–86, sending the Lakers home early—the game ending with an air ball from Magic.[65]

After the game, Kareem left without speaking to the media. Magic, upset about the loss, said, "The way I look at it, we won the championship last year and everybody came at us this year. There's a lot to be thankful for, but right now I'm down." Jamal Wilkes said Johnson's statements "definitely did not help and might have been a distraction."[66]

Buss was described in the aftermath of the Lakers' loss as "outwardly calm but his Coors can seemed to be shaking just a little." He was furious over the Nixon story and blamed the local papers for both the dissension on the Lakers and their early loss. "I thought it was a cheap blow when they publish stories like that just before the series," he said of the Los Angeles Times reports leading up to the series. "I think most people feel they would like to see the papers more supportive of a team entering the playoffs. I didn't see any articles on the fantastic love and camaraderie shared by the Lakers."[67] Several days later, the Los Angeles Times ran an editorial defending its conduct, stating: "Apparently, [Buss] would have preferred that Times readers believe nothing was amiss, that the players stopped their handslapping merely because they decided it was gauche."[68]

Needless to say, the defending champions were staring down the barrel of a crucial off-season. Buss stated that changes would be made. Days after the season, Buss spent six hours picnicking with Johnson in Palm Springs. Buss described the meeting as a "philosophical discussion—on how to accept losing. Magic's not very used to losing, and neither am I." After Johnson, Buss planned to meet with Wilkes and Abdul-Jabbar. After meeting with the players, Buss planned to meet with his coach, Paul Westhead, and finally his general manager, Bill Sharman. "Over the next 10 days," Buss said. "We'll decide which direction we'll take."[69]

There was certainly the possibility that Buss would wade into the right of first refusal, though Buss said he intended to spend money only as a "medium roller."[70] In terms of free agents, Buss was non-committal about going after any of the top ones—Kings guard Otis Birdsong, Nuggets guard Alex English, or Bullets forward Mitch Kupchak. "We'll see what needs to be done and then we'll do it," Buss said.[71] Buss was certain of one thing, he wanted Rockets' center Moses Malone, who was set to be a free agent the following season. "He's the player I want and I'm going to get him. He becomes a free agent after next season. Believe me, he'll become a Laker."[72]

. . .

Ted Stepien of the Cleveland Cavaliers was not Dr. Jerry Buss. He was not the shrewd businessman or the suave ladies man. As one NBA owner said, "He thinks with his mouth open."[73]

Almost immediately from his assumption of ownership, the Cavs were plunged into chaos. A few days after he took control, Stepien announced a new personnel director, Bill Musselman. Musselman had been out of professional basketball for four years. Musselman had been dabbling in real estate and the stock market when he got the Cavs job. "I bet I went to more Padre home games last year than anybody," he said when announced.[74]

How then did Musselman get into Stepien's orbit? Flattery. When Stepien bought the team, Musselman engaged in a "high pressure salesmanship of such people as Billy Martin . . . and Ballard Smith, president of the Padres. They lobbied on Musselman's behalf with letters and phone calls, and by all accounts, Stepien was star struck. Just talking to Billy Martin sent chills through his body."[75] Stepien's hiring practices did not improve.

A week after Stepien took over, his coach, Stan Albeck, decamped to San Antonio. Albeck got out after one meeting with Stepien. Well, part of one meeting. In the middle of his first meeting with Stepien,

The Right of First Refusal

Albeck walked out, left town, and next emerged as coach of the Spurs.[76] Stepien demanded compensation from the Spurs—Albeck was in the midst of a three-year contract.[77] He received none. Two days later, Stepien announced that Musselman was now his coach instead of general manager. As general manager, Stepien tabbed Don Delaney, who had previously served as the coach of Stepien's professional softball team.[78] He had no prior NBA experience.

Once management was in place, Stepien began dismantling the team. Stepien inherited a promising, if middling, team—the Cavaliers had gone 37–45 the previous season and just missed the playoffs. First, the Cavs traded Campy Russell, their best player, who had questioned Stepien's racist statements. Then they traded Foots Walker to the New Jersey Nets. Stepien began trading draft picks—that's where he did his real damage. First, Stepien traded a 1984 first rounder to Dallas for Mike Bratz. Then in late October, around the start of the season, the Cavaliers made a few trades that, according to the New York Times, caused "consternation to mount around the league," trading two more first-round draft choices to Dallas (1983 and 1986) and then making another move for Kim Hughes, who was immediately placed on the injured list. One general manager told the New York Times that Stepien's series of transactions was "exceptionally poor." Stepien defended the moves, saying, "Although we don't have a first round draft choice until 1985 or 1986, we are well stocked with youth for the present."[79] When the dust cleared, the Cavaliers had only four players left from the previous year's squad and one first round pick until 1987 (which Stepien would trade away in February 1981).[80] "How can they build?" one rival executive said, "They have no draft picks and only one player."[81]

Eventually, the NBA stepped in. After an early season loss against the Lakers, which left the Cavs 4-8, Stepien was summoned to New York for a meeting with O'Brien, Gourdine, and NBA director of operations Joe Axelson.[82] O'Brien told Stepien that there were complaints from owners and general managers about his reckless trading. There was concern that the team, which had already been twenty-first out of twenty-two teams in attendance, would go under. Stepien was incensed. "What did they expect?" he said. "I didn't inherit the

Los Angeles Lakers or Philadelphia 76ers. I bought a team whose financial plight was so bad the banks refused to lend them money."[83]

After the meeting, the NBA released a statement that Stepien had agreed to "a brief moratorium on trades, during which the league's director of operations, Joe Axelson, and other members of the league's office staff [would] confer with Cleveland management on a number of operational matters. Following this, for a period to be determined, but not beyond this season, the Cavaliers [would] consult with Mr. Axelson and obtain prior approval from the league office prior to any future trades." Axelson said kindly, "The Commissioner feels that the Cavs need a breathing spell, as far as trades are concerned."[84]

Stepien was furious at the NBA for letting the information of his reprimand get out. "It was supposed to be a secret meeting," he said. "And then [O'Brien] leaks it to the world by sending Telexes to the entire world notifying them of his actions. That was uncalled for. Aren't we a league? Do they want to embarrass one of their franchises? I want to know what's behind all this. I'm putting $2 million into the team this year. It's my money, not their money." Axelson said O'Brien never made any promise of secrecy. He said that absent going public, "How else were we going to notify the other teams that there was a trading ban with Cleveland?"[85] Though O'Brien lifted the trade embargo on November 26, Stepien's Cavs were an abject disaster.[86]

Stepien also made changes to the in-game presentation at Richfield Coliseum. While every new owner tries to make their mark, Stepien's in-game presentation changes were . . . not traditional. Stepien created and oversaw the casting of the "Teddi-bears," a thirty-three-member dance troupe that would do a polka if the Cavaliers won.[87] In a shock to no one other than Stepien, the Cavs struggled on the court and there were not very many polkas.

With the losses came criticism. Intense criticism. Pete Franklin, a popular Cleveland radio host, was relentless. Franklin hosted a five-hour call-in show five nights a week on WWWE, the Cavaliers broadcast partner, and Stepien was a regular topic. "This guy," Franklin said of Stepien early in that first year, "is a megalomaniac who's dumb. The worst thing about him is that he is dumb. I don't mind you quoting me because he's a schmuck, a dodo head. This team is on support machines."[88]

The Right of First Refusal

Stepien did not react well to criticism. He believed that given his level of investment he should be beloved in Cleveland. At one game against the Clippers early in the season, Stepien accosted Doug Clarke, a writer for the *Cleveland Press*. Stepien sat down next to him at half-time, and, according to Clarke, "Started talking in a loud aggressive tone, jabbing me in the chest with a forefinger." After finishing his rant, Stepien walked away and called Clarke a garbage writer. Clarke responded, "You're a garbage owner with a garbage coach."[89] Then a man approached Clarke and said, "Just write about the Cavs . . . leave the owner alone." When Clarke asked who the man was, thinking he may be an usher, the man said "I'm gonna break your face. Then you'll know who I am."[90]

As Stepien's first season as an owner wore on, somehow, it got worse. By December he was threatening to move the team to Pittsburgh.[91] By February Stepien had sued wwwe, the radio station that broadcast Cavs games, and Franklin for $10 million dollars, for presenting "unfair reports on the team" and for "malicious, reckless, willful and wanton" conduct by the station.[92] It was an absurd lawsuit. Franklin was unconcerned about the pending litigation, saying, "The suit is like everything else associated with Ted Stepien—a joke."[93] By late February 1981, Stepien was threatening to move the Cavaliers somewhere—anywhere. "I can only give Cleveland next year to support us or I'm moving the team to Pittsburgh, Minneapolis, Louisville or Cincinnati," he said to upi.[94] By the spring of 1981, the Cavs' future was bleak. Stepien had traded every Cavaliers draft choices through 1987, and as the joke went, the Cavs next first-round pick was in seventh grade.

On March 29, 1981, the Cavaliers finished their first season under Ted Stepien, getting blown out by the Washington Bullets 138–103, finishing the season a very poor 28-54. They lost sixteen of their final nineteen games and finished the season on a seven-game losing streak. Musselman's flattery had not gotten him a long leash with Stepien. He was fired in early March. He was replaced as coach by softball impresario Don Delaney. When Musselman was fired the headline screamed, "Musselman out, novice in as Cavaliers coach," which, somehow, was generous to both men. Attendance was dreadful. Stepien lost a staggering amount of money—$3 million in his first year.

As the 1981 offseason dawned, Stepien was a year into being an owner, with little to show for it. He wanted to make his Cavaliers competitive. He had burned every bridge—with the fans, his city, the players, and the league. He did, however, have an option to improve his team. The right of first refusal was where Stepien saw an opportunity to remake his team—quick! He could actually sign players, pay them more than other teams, and build a winner in Cleveland. He was the first to jump into it.

Immediately after the end of the Finals, free agency started. Otis Birdsong, the top free agent, found himself negotiating between six teams. If Stepien was going to get him, he had to blow away the competition. He did. Ted Stepien offered Birdsong's agent, Bob Woolf, a deal worth over $1 million a year. Stepien also agreed to have a bonus of fifty cents for every seat sold over five thousand to each of the forty-one home games. Such an offer was astronomical. To understand: the million-dollar yearly contract placed Birdsong at the top of the NBA's salary pyramid next to Moses Malone and Kareem Abdul-Jabbar as the only million-dollar players in the NBA.[95] "Otis' offer is crazy," Kansas City general manager Jeff Cohen said when he heard of it. "He's a good guard, but not a game breaker. Now he's on the same level financially as Kareem Abdul-Jabbar and Moses Malone. If that amount is acceptable for a good guard, then Larry Bird will have to get two million a year and Kareem five."[96]

Stepien, Woolf, and Birdsong celebrated the offer sheet, the first signed under the new system. "It will be difficult for anyone to match this offer," Woolf said. "This is a landmark situation, the first of its kind. This proves Ted Stepien is working hard to make Cleveland a winner." Birdsong was equally positive. "I feel really good about everything," he said. "Cleveland has a good nucleus. They are talking about getting another new player, and, along with me, we can make the Cavaliers a big winner."[97] Stepien was surprised he was the first to jump into the fray. "I'm surprised we were the first ones to come out of the blocks on free agent bidding," he said. "The day Boston beat Houston, I thought a half dozen teams might be in there bidding. I was concerned that I might be a Johnny come lately, to tell you the truth."[98]

Even though Cohen believed "one million dollars for a guard [was] the most insane thing [he'd] ever heard of," Kansas City quickly matched the offer on Birdsong and traded him to the New Jersey Nets.[99] Stepien was surprised to lose his free agent signing. "I wasn't totally familiar with the third-party aspect of the system. Losing Birdsong was a little bit of a surprise to us," he said.[100]

Three days later, Stepien struck again, signing the second player under the right of first refusal. Stepien signed center James Edwards, formerly of the Pacers, to a four-year, $3 million offer sheet. Once again, Edwards was a solid contributor, but the offer was considerably more than what he expected in the market. "This is a good place to play," Edwards said. "Cleveland is definitely a team on the move. It just needed a couple of players."[101] Before he was done, Stepien would sign several more players under the system. Scott Wedman, of Kansas City, signed a five-year, $4 million offer. Bobby Wilkerson of the Bulls signed an offer sheet worth twice what the Bulls, his former team, had offered. "We weren't really shopping around for an offer after we negotiated with the Bulls but Cleveland made the offer and it's tough to refuse," Wilkerson's agent, Steve Ferguson, said. "Bobby's certainly happy. It's sure a lot more money than we'll ever make."[102]

Between Birdsong, Edwards, Wedman, and Wilkerson, Stepien drew the ire of his fellow owners. "He set the early free-agent pattern by offering crazy salaries and we're going to have to live with it," one anonymous owner told the *New York Times*. "It seems the average going price of a free agent is $750,000; some of them had been getting less than $200,000."[103]

There were concerns that the bar Stepien set would force other teams to sign massive deals. The Edwards deal would force the market for centers higher. The Sixers would have to pay Daryl Dawkins, a much more promising center, significantly more money. And, of course, Moses Malone was going to be a free agent the following season and the price for him would be out of this world.

Other owners were getting involved in the free agent market as well: Sam Schulman of the Supersonics signed Alex English of Denver—who had rejected a two-year offer from Stepien—and Steve Hawes of Atlanta to offer sheets. The Nuggets spent the fifteen days after receiving the English offer sheet trying to trade him. They couldn't, and so they kept him at the higher rate. "We couldn't afford to give him up without compensation," Scheer said. "We had too much invested."[104]

And, of course, Buss was lurking. He signed Mitch Kupchak to a massive offer sheet that the Bullets could not match. "Kupchak may not be worth $900,000 a year to the Bullets or any other team in the NBA, but he would be worth that to us," Buss said.[105]

"So far it has been some kind of disaster," Bob Ferry, GM of the Washington Bullets, said of the new system, "The market value of the players has not been proportional to their abilities. I think the team that set this all off was Cleveland."[106] Jerry Colangelo of the Suns said, "It's not in the best interest of the league to get involved in such ridiculous negotiations."[107]

At the Board of Governors meetings in June, his fellow owners questioned Stepien about whether he actually had the money to pay the contracts he signed. Afterward, Stern said, "The owners asked Stepien certain questions about his finances. The answers he gave regarding his ability to pay appeared to satisfy them. Nationwide Advertising Company, a very successful advertising agency, of which he is the sole owner, has lent the Cavaliers more than $4 million. Each team is responsible for its own obligations."[108]

Stepien defended himself. "It's all right when a Red Auerbach or a Jerry Buss spends money for a free agent, but when Ted Stepien does it, from a nonplayoff team, then it's not all right."[109] Stepien continued, "I had to induce them to come to an unglamarous market," he said. "I bought into a bad situation and have backed it with $4.5 million of my own money. I didn't create free agency but as long as it's there, I want to take advantage of it."[110]

Stepien said, "This year, in my first season, we won 28 games and had no draft choices. My only avenue of escaping last place was the one I took. Since somebody else set up the rules we went after it. I criticize the other owners for not doing their homework. We signed our players. Kansas City and Indiana should have signed theirs . . . If I had three first-round draft choices like New Jersey, I wouldn't have had to do this."[111] In truth, Stepien was not wrong.

Fleisher was dubious of the drama: "We cannot understand the apparent fear that exists over last week's free agent activity. The right of first refusal was negotiated in 1976, specifically to give the NBA owners a chance to get ready for it. Now that it is here they are expressing shock. What did they think would happen?"[112]

The Right of First Refusal

Within a few weeks of Stepien's free agent splashes, the NBA economy was rocked again. On June 26, three weeks after Stepien's follies, Jerry Buss announced that the Lakers had signed its star, Magic Johnson, to a twenty-five-year, $25 million contract. The contract, which was not set to begin until 1984 was set to run through 2009.[113] It quickly became the richest, longest contract in all of sports.

After the Lakers were eliminated from the playoffs, the problems in Lakerland simmered. In early May, weeks after the Lakers' season had ended, Buss met with Magic and Nixon in Las Vegas and all sides discussed how to work through it next season.[114] While the hope was that the summit had fixed the issue with the Laker guards, Magic went on television and admitted there was tension on the team and that the Nixon article had a lot to do with it. When asked if it led to the poor showing in the playoffs, Johnson said "it would have to because there was tension there and nobody was easy. Everybody was thinking about why this happened at this time or is there any truth to the article." When asked if he could play with Nixon, Johnson said, "I can play with him, but there's going to have to be a trade in there somewhere."[115]

Buss tried to neutralize the issue with cash. In signing Magic, Buss said that any problems within the Lakers that may have existed were resolved. "How much would he get right now? A million and a half?" Buss said. "How much next year? Two million? Somewhere in there, I'm sure. So paying $1 million a year covers all his basketball playing." Buss continued, "I know that $1 million a year past basketball sounds exorbitant. But consider this: 14 years from now, the average secretary—not good ones, mind you, but average—will be making $60,000 a year. So Magic's services, as coach or GM or whichever direction we mutually choose to take, are worth $1 million a year to me."[116]

According to Dr. Buss, Magic had approached him about a deal. "He came to me and said, 'is there some way we can work it out so I don't have to go on the open market someday and be bid on like a piece of property? I like you, the team, the city and I want to stay here permanently.' I told him, 'Magic, it will be difficult because we'll have to figure in inflation.' But we worked it out."[117] Magic, who would speak a few days later, said that Buss "did this out of the goodness of his heart. He made me an offer and I couldn't turn it down. He didn't have anything more to offer."[118]

Buss was not concerned about the impact of the Magic signing on the broader league, repeating again his belief that the current restrictions were worthless. Buss said, "I want to stress this: If everybody decides the object is to make money, what's the difference what we pay players? It becomes a nonsensical question. There should be entirely open markets in sports, total free agentry, players selling themselves to the highest bidder. True, most of the good players would gravitate to the big cities, but isn't that the case in most walks of life? Sports should simply be part of the free-enterprise system instead of imposing all those useless restrictions."

Just as they had with Stepien's moves, other teams reacted to the Magic signing with consternation. But unlike Stepien's moves, they were also fearful. Stepien was a fool, but Buss was not. Jerry Colangelo of the Phoenix Suns said, "I'm worried about the rippling effect to other franchises. Many of us have financial limitations. It's tough to retain competitive balance when things like this take place. At least in concept, Jerry Buss should be more attuned to how moves like this affect everyone else. One franchise may prosper, but any franchise is only as good as the rest of the League."[119]

Some others, like Frank Layden of the Utah Jazz, were more sanguine. "Jerry Buss is free to do as he pleases. A lot of people may be outraged, but not me. I don't care what other teams do with contracts. We decide what's fair, what's right, for our players. Besides, I believe in the free enterprise system. And if no one breaks the rules, who's to say who should get what?"[120] Eddie Donovan of the Knicks was also not as alarmed. "In basketball, you can't buy a championship. If you bought the whole East or West all-star team, you still might not win. You need players to complement each other, and usually you can't buy that."[121]

While Buss may not have cared about the rest the league, he did care about the impact on *his* team. After the Magic signing, Buss was asked whether it would cause the same drama it had the previous year. "I don't see why," he said.[122] Almost immediately Buss had issues with Kareem. As the *New York Times* reported, "Abdul-Jabbar's initial dissatisfaction, according to sources, began with published reports that Buss would try to sign Moses Malone of the Houston Rockets. The relationship further widened when Johnson's $1 million a year contract for 25 years was announced recently."[123] Additionally, Jabbar was upset because, according to a source, "Buss went and singled out someone else to teach the business to."[124]

Buss, who had been so vocal in his love of Magic, had some work to do. He called in each of the Lakers' players for private meetings in an effort to smooth over the problems about the Magic contract. He met with Abdul-Jabbar last. In late July, Kareem advised the Lakers that he would like to be traded—either to the Knicks or the Nets, returning him to his home in New York. Buss offered what he could—more money. Abdul-Jabbar quickly relented, saying, "Any rumors that you might finally get rid of me were a bit premature."[125]

Though Abdul-Jabbar was happy about his new deal, he was also frank. "In ways, a basketball team is like a family. If you pick one person out and put him in front of everyone else and say 'this is my favorite child' other people in the family are definitely going to be affected by it." Jabbar also said, "Some members of the team wondered if their value lay in competing for the affection of the owner, rather than in what they do on the court."[126] Magic, from his basketball camp in Michigan, was pleased. "I can tear up my contract now if it causes problems on the team. I just want to win. I don't wanna do anything to keep us from winning. We had enough little problems last year. We definitely don't want any problems with the big fella."[127]

Buss's money had brought problems and solutions. The question entering 1982–83 was whether it would bring another championship.

The one person Buss did not want to be compared to was Stepien. "The difference between the Lakers and Cleveland is that we can afford the salaries we're paying. If you have to go to your other businesses to get funds, that's cheating. You pay what you can afford." Stepien said, "I don't argue with Jerry Buss paying Magic Johnson whatever he wants. It's ok for him to pay big money or for Red Auerbach, but when I do it I'm a Midwest jerk."[128]

• • •

On June 12, 1981, the Major League Baseball Players Association went on strike, over exactly the system that was leaving the NBA—compensation for free agents. The relationship between Major League Baseball, its players, and its union were different from the NBA. The owners were intentionally hostile. Ray Grebey, the owners' hired negotiator, reveled in provoking Marvin Miller and the players. The strike had its seeds a year earlier, when Grebey issued a press release misrepresenting their agreement. Miller had not forgiven Grebey. Grebey enjoyed calling Miller "Marv" at the table, knowing he hated it.[129]

"Are you really going to strike?" Grebey asked Miller, hours before the players walked out.[130] The owners in baseball, as they seemed to do every time they negotiated a new agreement, had totally misread the players. They were going to strike, and it became the first midseason strike in professional sports history. Both sides dug in. As Calvin Griffith, owner of the Minnesota Twins said, "It's like two soldiers in foxholes facing each other. Both are absolutely convinced that he has God on his side."[131]

While out on strike the baseball players were considering suing the owners and the television networks, claiming that they had a right to a share of the revenues, similar to the claim Fleisher had filed prior to negotiations in 1979. When asked about it, Fleisher said that the MLBPA "have a very good chance of winning. It's a unique question. It has not come up before. Based on the memos we did at the time, I'd say they have a better than even chance of winning."[132]

The baseball strike was something the other sports were following closely with both the NFL and the NBA collective bargaining agreements coming up the following year. Garvey was aggressive, looking at the NFL through the lens of a strike. "They've given us confidence that it can be done and done effectively. All we have to do is stand together like the baseball players have."[133]

Fleisher applauded the baseball players, stating, "This will have a dramatic impact. This shows that athletes are not going to sell out their fellow workers. The owners said they were too greedy to give up their salaries. They've shown that they're willing to stand together if they're properly organized and understand the issues." While Fleisher applauded the baseball players, he did not believe it made basketball players more likely to strike. "If this proved to be a failure by the players early on our owners would have put us to the wall on everything. But if the baseball players prove they can stay together, it may have a moderating effect in basketball."[134]

When MLB and the Players Association finally reached an agreement on July 31, there was no fondness between the parties—only deep bitterness. At the press conference announcing the deal, Miller and Grebey would not shake hands. Miller would not be in a photograph with him. In the meeting Grebey approached Mets outfielder Rusty Staub, thinking him to be a friendly face. "You're a liar. You're always going to be a liar and you're not going to be my friend," Staub said.[135]

• • •

After the off-season of 1981, NBA owners began looking to the expiration of the collective bargaining agreement the following year. They were not the only ones. That summer Larry Fleisher testified in Congress in favor of legislation to make baseball subject to antitrust law and overturn an outdated precedent from 1922 that identified baseball as a game, not a business, and thus not subject to antitrust legislation because it did not constitute interstate commerce.

During his testimony, Fleisher was asked about Garvey's percent-of-gross idea. Fleisher did not think it fit in basketball. He said that the percent-of-gross concept was "the position that the football players association has taken, saying that one of the great difficulties they have had in negotiating contracts with their players is that there is no need for any of the teams to compete since they start off the season ahead of time fully subscribed to. That has not been the case in professional basketball, where there has been an equalization of the CBS and ABC national television funds. They have been competing and have been going out so I do not see why that would change."[136]

As part of that testimony, Fleisher was also asked about the NBA, specifically the economic health of the game and the impact of cable television. Fleisher said bluntly, "I believe that the revenues that are going to be generated to professional basketball through cable and pay TV are going to greatly outweigh the revenues that have been generated up until today in radio or television." In a nod to upcoming negotiations, he continued, "Therefore, from the players' point of view and assuming I do my job and other people do their jobs in negotiating properly for the players, they are going to share in that growth revenue."[137]

Tom Railsback, a member of the committee and a Republican from Illinois, asked Fleisher about the likelihood of a battle at the bargaining table. Fleisher responded, "I started getting gray hairs talking about these wars in the next couple of years . . . I do not perceive in basketball that we are going to have wars. I could be wrong but I do not perceive that at this time. However, I think that . . . may well end up being very true in some of the other sports."

Railsback responded, "You are not as gloomy as far as basketball is concerned."

Fleisher replied, "I try to be optimistic all the time."[138]

9

David

I grew up in Stern's Delicatessen. He has his meat wrong.

—DAVID STERN, 2010

The Deli. Stern's Delicatessen. Nearly every description of the man who would become the most important commissioner in the history of the NBA, and possibly in all of sports, will take you to the Chelsea section on the West Side of Manhattan in those years following the Second World War. Stern's Deli was located on Eighth Avenue between Twenty-Second and Twenty-Third Streets—just ten blocks from Madison Square Garden, where the New York Knicks, David Stern's favorite childhood team, played.

David Stern was born on September 22, 1942, twelve years after Fleisher. Both were children of Russian immigrants and both had fathers who shaped their approach to work.[1] Though he was not necessarily poor, Stern's upbringing was simple and surrounded by deli meat. "It was comfortable. At least, I always thought of it as comfortable," Stern said.[2] Later in life, when he, as commissioner of the NBA, had a private car taking him from the wealthy suburb of Scarsdale to New York City every morning, Stern said that his life was still simple, but that his view of simplicity had changed.

The deli was a crucial part of both the David Stern myth and the actual David Stern. "I was an expert at using a mop, as well as doing the counter service and cooking," Stern once said of the work he did there.[3] The man who would become a master marketer of basketball heroes was loathe to give interviews about himself, but he still had a hand in crafting the narrative around *him*. That narrative prominently displayed Stern's Deli and the lessons he learned from a working-class childhood that he took to the top of corporate America. "There was no better way to prepare yourself for a job that demanded a good deal of skill with the public, David Stern thought, than working behind the counter in a deli,"[4] David Halberstam wrote of the commissioner in 1999. "From Corned Beef to Caviar," was the headline of an in-depth feature in *Sports Illustrated* praising Stern's rise and reign in 1991. Hard work, respect, customer satisfaction: those were the things Stern learned at the deli and transferred to the NBA.

He also used Stern's Deli and his working-class childhood as a cudgel. In 2010, in the midst of his last round of collective bargaining negotiations as commissioner, Stern and then NBPA executive director Billy Hunter were engaged in a contentious battle that would lead to a lockout. The parties were far apart and Stern was claiming teams were losing money. Hunter called those representations "baloney." Stern's response? "I grew up in Stern's delicatessen," Stern said. "He has his meat wrong."[5]

As a child, Stern loved sports—not just basketball. Later in life, when Stern wanted to explain the economic issues in basketball, one of his favorite rhetorical devices was to compare baseball to basketball. He would also compare basketball favorably to baseball—use his love and knowledge of the game he didn't work in to make his point about the sport he did.

Stern also grew up a basketball fan, and in New York that made him a Knicks fan. Being a Knicks fan has always been a frustration, and the 1950s were no exception. Stern would go to see Harry Gallatin and the Knicks. Often he would see them lose. Sometimes he would go alone, able to use a school card to get a cheap ticket. Often he would go with his father, William Stern. Stern learned from and admired his father. On the day he was named commissioner, Stern said, "I used to go to the games with my father. There were doubleheaders then, and even though the Knicks weren't very good, they were still my Knicks. The appointment is bittersweet. My father died three years ago. I only wish he had been around to share this with me."[6]

William Stern had been an orphan and maintained a tireless work ethic to protect his family from the difficulties of his childhood in

Russia. But William combined his hard work with a self-effacing and open nature. It was a posture Stern would emulate. As Halberstam wrote of William Stern working at Stern's, "It would have been hard for any customer to know that he was the owner. He knew the importance of elemental courtesy, of offering people, in addition to the things they purchased, some sense of dignity and self importance. He treated everyone who came in well, and his son learned to do that as well, and he learned that all too often in comparable stores the owners and staff tended to respond to the customers based on a quick reading of their clothes and what those clothes seemingly revealed about a person's status. The Stern deli did not judge people on their clothing, and it had been a very useful lesson for [David] as he began to move from the simplest part of American society to a place where almost everyone was significantly more privileged, and where he dealt with titans of business and industry every day."[7]

When David was a boy, William moved his family to New Jersey. Stern graduated from Teaneck High School before attending Rutgers as an undergraduate. From Rutgers it was on to Columbia Law School. In 1966, after graduation, Stern got a job that paid him $7,800 a month—as an associate at the law firm of Proskauer, Rose, Goetz, and Mendelsohn. It was one of the top Jewish law firms—in the mid-1960s, such a thing still existed.[8]

At Proskauer, Stern worked closely with George Gallantz. Gallantz was the source of what would become the largest employer-side sports law practice in America, and it occurred almost entirely by accident. In the early 1950s, basketball was rocked by point shaving scandals, and the NBA was not immune. Jack Molinas, a star in the NBA, had been caught in a scandal. The NBA wanted to ban him from the league but knew that litigation would come. Commissioner Maurice Podoloff asked the Knicks owner, Ned Irish, who his lawyers were, to represent the league in a case to ban Molinas. The case ended up with Gallantz. Gallantz won the Molinas case and became the NBA's regular lawyer. When he joined Proskauer in 1963, he took the NBA with him as a client.

As a young associate at Proskauer, Stern volunteered to Gallantz to work on NBA matters when an opening arose. When Stern began working with the NBA, the league had only six employees—there was not even a general counsel. The first in-house attorney, a young man by the name of Russ Granik, would not be hired until the mid-1970s.

For Stern, the NBA work grew. In the late 1960s and 1970s Stern made his bones working with the league mostly on litigation matters. He made his first appearances on the Connie Hawkins case, a case the NBA was defending that Stern believed to be wrong.[9] Hawkins, who had been kept out of the NBA for being associated with point shaving (the case was unfounded), brought a lawsuit that the league was in violation of the antitrust laws. The NBA was vulnerable; Stern, a young lawyer, pushed the league to settle with Hawkins.[10] As part of that settlement Hawkins agreed not to sue the NBA again. He was the only player not to sign onto the *Robertson* lawsuit for that reason.

Much like Fleisher, Stern had principles—liberal principles. From a young age Stern was focused on fairness and civil rights—an important tenet for someone working in a league that was mostly African American. In college, Stern was in a Jewish fraternity. He pushed for change in the brotherhood and was known as being a part of the "liberal" wing of the fraternity at Rutgers. He wanted different types of people in the fraternity—African Americans and non-Jews.[11] As a young man, before he went to work at the NBA, he became the head of Teaneck's Fair Housing Commission, hoping to draft laws to end the housing discrimination in the leafy New Jersey suburb where he lived.[12] Even later in life, after he had become commissioner, Stern was known to give money to Democratic candidates and support liberal causes.[13] When the NBA began to grow internationally in earnest—a move he spearheaded and championed as commissioner—Stern publicly expressed doubts about working with authoritarian regimes in China and Russia. He still worked with them, but he expressed concerns.

When the *Robertson* case was eventually filed, Stern was heavily involved, often acting as the lead litigator on the case. He would argue motions in court, sign the affidavits, handle the mountains of depositions the NBA was forcing on the players to try and wear them out. When O'Brien became commissioner in 1975, one of his first briefings was with his team from Proskauer—Gallantz, Stern, Ganz—about the pending litigation, which then appeared to be an albatross. The legal costs were exploding and the likely outcome at trial was a loss. Just a month into his reign, O'Brien wanted to revisit whether Proskauer should be the exclusive representative of the NBA. Stern, along with Gallantz and several others, briefed O'Brien on the status of the circumstances. It appears that O'Brien never did revisit Proskauer's representation (though O'Brien and Stern would go back and forth quite a bit about the bills Stern would send the NBA for his firm's services).

Not long after O'Brien was in place as commissioner, so was Stern as his consigliere. As Gallantz, who remained on the work with the NBA in those years, said, "When O'Brien wanted to call his lawyer, he called David Stern. David would keep me informed."[14] In the mid-1970s Stern was handling everything for the NBA—well beyond the scope of a traditional outside counsel. On the *Robertson* settlement, in addition to being the litigator, Stern was the creative dealmaker. As the parties prepped to negotiate a settlement in late January 1976, it was Stern whose name was on a memo outlining a number of possible solutions to the economic future of the NBA. When the ABA and NBA merged, though it was O'Brien who received the credit, Stern was integral. Mike Goldberg, who was counsel to the ABA said, "O'Brien was given a lot of latitude by the NBA owners to get the deal done, and O'Brien relied a lot on Stern for legal advice."[15]

Beyond legal tasks, Stern's portfolio with the NBA was considerable. Stern, along with Granik, had helped negotiate the nuts and bolts of the television agreement with CBS in 1976.[16] As outside counsel, Stern was also regularly involved in Board of Governors meetings, intra-league politics, governance, and even helping the NBA investigate and negotiate nascent cable deals with HBO. There was very little that went on that he did not touch. One of O'Brien's first actions as commissioner was to ask all of the departments to write up brief memos about what they did. It was Stern who advised O'Brien on what the general counsel's office of the NBA did. At the time, however, the NBA had no general counsel—only Stern. When Granik was hired by O'Brien, becoming the first staff lawyer at the NBA, O'Brien told him there may not be enough legal work to keep him busy—everything complicated was handled by Stern.[17]

In 1978 O'Brien made Stern what was an inevitable offer to come to work at the NBA full time. By then a partner at Proskauer, Stern had a decision to make. When Stern went to speak to Gallantz—his mentor—about O'Brien's offer, Gallantz said, "Well you schmuck, he's not that nice of a guy to work for." Gallantz, who had spent a lifetime in New York law firms, asked, "How can you put your life in the hands of *one* client?" Stern responded, "I'll give it a try."[18] Stern accepted the offer and became the NBA's twenty-fourth employee.[19] He said later, "I was afraid that if I didn't go in-house, Larry would hire somebody else and I wouldn't be doing the legal work at all."[20]

Stern spent two years as general counsel (with a spell as deputy commissioner), until O'Brien created a new position for him in December 1980—executive vice president of business and legal affairs. In his promotion, it was clear that Stern's new role went beyond simple legal obligations; Stern was in charge of marketing, public relations, and, yes, television.[21] As O'Brien said in his announcement in a telex to the owners (such an announcement was not of interest to the public in those days): "In this new position, he will be responsible for all business-related matters involving the league, and the departments of marketing, communications and broadcasting will function under his direction." When Stern was promoted, so was Granik, to Stern's old gig—general counsel.[22]

Stern believed in a number of things: First, he believed fundamentally that the NBA should be successful. The sport and its players were top rate—its lack of popularity was incongruous with that. Second, he believed that for the NBA to succeed economically, it was crucial for the NBA to have true corporate relationships and television partners. Third, he believed that the hold up to the NBA reaching its potential was the race of the players on the court—rather, others' inaccurate perceptions of those on the court.

Stern found when he spoke with advertisers and networks that even though they would advertise with college basketball, the NBA was somehow different. He would face tremendous resistance. In the pros, players were lazy, they were overpaid, they were on drugs. The reality was that it was about race. One advertising agency told Stern that they had been instructed to focus on college rather than the NBA because the NBA was too black.[23] The players in college— the *best* players in college—played in the NBA. Shouldn't that matter regardless of race? Stern and one of his first hires, Rick Welts, would

David

plead with agencies, showing demographic information: the fans were there! They were young and devoted! It did not matter.

At one point during this time, David Stern sat in the editorial offices of the *Boston Globe* where he was told that his sport would never succeed because a white America will not accept a black sport.[24] Stern did not understand why the NFL who had just as many African Americans as the NBA did not have the same perception. Was it really as stupid as the helmets? Stern said, "There was a fair amount of discussion of the fact that the NBA was predominantly black on the playing court. It became fashionable to discuss whether a black league could ever succeed in a predominantly white country." Stern hated that argument. "We never had a doubt that that was a non-issue but that's something that was widely dealt with in the press."[25]

Stern, in his new role, threw himself into all of it, even then, not focusing on the legal side. Later, when Stern became commissioner, Fleisher was legitimately surprised at Stern's abilities in marketing—he hadn't seen it. He should have, Stern was doing it in the 1970s, trying to rebuild the NBA's image against some difficult headwinds. On the marketing side, Stern aggressively built out the NBA's footprint. Stern maintained an ambitious agenda, seeking to hire more experts for NBA properties, the arm that handled marketing and licensing.[26] He did. In 1982 he greatly expanded the team of executives under him, hiring Ed Desser from the Lakers to become the NBA director of broadcasting. As O'Brien stated, Desser's role was not only to work with the networks but "in our stepped up efforts to ensure the uniformity and quality of our more than 700 local telecasts." The NBA hired Brian McIntyre of the Chicago Bulls as PR director and Alex Sachare from the Associated Press.[27] This was a long way from when O'Brien took over and the NBA had no public relations director at all.

Stern also had a major hand in television and in the NBA's plans moving forward both with cable and CBS. Stern was more than the point of contact with CBS. Stern was shaping the broadcasts nationally, even locally. He negotiated deals with cable operators. He was monitoring the advertising on the cable networks, even the companies who were advertising, to check the growth. In the early 1980s, it was Stern who pushed the NBA to develop "uniform game format" and the "extended timeouts" program with the Board of Governors.

His goal: to make the broadcast of the NBA consistent and reliable and to allow teams to make more money off of advertisements during time outs. He was trying to both professionalize the league and centralize the power. More responsibility was coming into the league office. He was making progress too—NBA properties was growing in the early 1980s, and Stern's efforts were having an impact. Stern was also leading negotiations for cable. The future. While the dreams of cable were tremendous, the reality was still that the overwhelming majority of the money the NBA received from television was from broadcast television—namely CBS.

And in the fall of 1981, before he could turn to the collective bargaining agreement with the players set to expire the following spring, Stern and O'Brien had to negotiate a new deal with CBS, or, they hoped, anyone else. Once again, as it had been in 1976 and 1978, network negotiations were a struggle. Though ratings were up on CBS and interest was improving with the NBA, the NBA was still clearly the third sport.

The NBA had been negotiating with CBS for a new deal as far back as April 1981. As in the previous two negotiations, interest for the NBA on television was tepid at best. Though NBC had expressed interest throughout the summer of 1981 and had several meetings throughout 1981, they did not go any further than NBC wanting to discuss the NBA on a cable property. On September 30, 1981, O'Brien, Stern, Art Watson, and Don Ohlmeyer of NBC (who would later be a great collaborator with Stern when both were leading the meetings) met in O'Brien's office. After some initial interest over the summer, there had been phone calls with NBC in which their interest had declined prior to this meeting. In O'Brien's office Watson expressed, according to O'Brien's notes, "continuing interest in NBA package but great emphasis on cable."[28] It appeared that the NBA would once again be stuck with CBS.

After negotiations with NBC flopped, the NBA went back to CBS. CBS cancelled several meetings with the NBA over the course of October. On October 30, the last day of their exclusive period, O'Brien, Stern, and Granik finally met with CBS Sports. Their partner. CBS made an offer—four years, $88 million. Twenty-two million was the same yearly rate they received in the last year of their previous agree-

David

ment. Disappointing. Stern and O'Brien tried to shop it with NBC, who said that "anything like 100 million is too high."[29]

About a week after CBS made its offer, in early November 1981, there was, once again, a change at the top of CBS Sports. Neal Pilson was named head of CBS Sports and paid an informal visit to O'Brien. Pilson advised O'Brien that the $88 million offer was a final one and that it "wouldn't have been put on the table so early had Pilson then been in charge."[30] It was the same tune CBS had told him four years earlier. The NBA met one more time with Watson from NBC, who again said that the NBA's offer was too high, but that he wanted to negotiate cable. Once again, the NBA was stuck.

This time, at least, the NBA was able to accept an offer that was on the table before they spun a loss as a victory. "We have just signed the largest TV contract in the league's history," O'Brien said in December 1981. Whether or not it was, was not clear. In reality, four-year, $88 million, and the $22 million yearly sum was flat from the last year of the previous contract, for the next four years. With inflation as high as it was in the late 1970s and early 1980s, it was arguable that the actual amount was declining.[31] More importantly, the NBA was falling behind other sports who were doubling the value of their rights in each agreement. Major League Baseball, who signed their deal in 1980, received $184 million, double their previous agreement. College football had agreed to a deal that raised their national television contract from $120 million to $263.5 million. Even college basketball, who had signed a deal with CBS, got a larger increase to its value. And, of course, the NBA paled in comparison with the NFL—who saw their TV rights quadruple. The NFL had gone from $656 million in their previous contract to $2.1 billion. So, yes, O'Brien was correct, the $88 million was the largest, and they had improved their rights by $14 million over the life of the contract.

Furthermore, it was troubling that no matter what the payment from the network, the league's exposure under the new agreement would be considerably lower. The NBA was now mostly off the air during the regular season. Though the payout was unchanged, they gave considerably fewer games to CBS—decreasing from forty-one to only twenty-eight on the new contract—than they had on the previous deal. If they were trying to grow the sport, surely it was no victory to barely be on television.

There was concern that the new deal could cause the country to lose entire teams and superstars on broadcast. What would happen to, say, Ralph Sampson? The top player in the upcoming draft was likely going to be drafted by a terrible team. CBS, now only broadcasting a few games a year, would not want to broadcast a bottom-feeding team. As a result, the next generation of stars would be off television, even though in college Sampson had been a fixture. Stern defended the deal, "I'm not apprehensive about fans losing interest. Pro basketball is going to be televised more than ever before. Because of cable and having watched games in local markets, fans will tune in to playoff games on the networks."[32] As they had done four years earlier, the NBA spun defeat as victory.

O'Brien said that the lack of games on CBS gave the NBA the "vital flexibility we wanted, to more fully explore the expanding fields of cable and pay television, both on a network and an individual market basis."[33] The *Boston Globe* saw through the NBA's spin. Their headline on this story: "Less Is More: CBS Slashes Its NBA Coverage."

• • •

"Now that we have concluded our negotiations for network broadcast and cable television agreements, it is time to begin to focus upon the upcoming collective bargaining with the Players Association," O'Brien wrote in a telex to the NBA owners on February 5, 1982. "As you know, our current collective bargaining agreement will expire at the end of this season, and the Players Association has begun to announce publicly a number of its future demands, the most notable of which is a share of cable television revenues. I predict that our negotiations for a new agreement will be extremely difficult, perhaps the most difficult the league has ever faced."[34]

If the fall of 1981 was about the NBA being squeezed by the networks, then the spring of 1982 was about the NBA preparing to lean on its players. By the time Stern arrived at the hotel, on July 29, 1982, for negotiations with Fleisher, the NBA had done months of studious preparations, and the owners had spent years seething. Between the *Robertson* settlement, the failed television negotiations, the sagging ratings, the instability in ownership, the right of first refusal, rising salaries, the climate in sports, the race of the players, all of them led the NBA owners to expect and demand deep concessions from the players.

The proposal that Stern put on the table in July 1982 was their initial one; and they had long since considered many possibilities, including a framework that would later be in the 1983 agreement and even agreements and concepts reaching decades into the future.

The NBA's preparation for negotiations in the winter and spring of 1982 was methodical and comprehensive. In late February and early March 1982, O'Brien, Stern, and Granik met with the owners from each conference separately.[35] When the owners met, the issue, obviously, was money. At these meetings, the owners wanted what they had pushed for before—a cap per team rather than a traditional salary scale, moving away from the failed proposals from 1980. Most of them recognized, according to Granik, that to get such a cap, they would have to make a significant concession. The believed tradeoff would be "a guarantee to the players as a whole of a fixed amount, either as a percentage of some revenue source or a specific dollar amount."[36] They were expecting to propose the concept Garvey was arguing for in football that the NFL had rejected out of hand.

The owners, in these initial discussions, also discussed the impact of a strike on the league. According to Granik's memo about the meetings, "There was general agreement that it was vital to the survival of the league that there be some retrenchment in terms of player salary and benefits and that all clubs were prepared to suffer a strike in order to obtain that goal." However, the teams still did not trust each other. When discussing a league strike fund, Granik wrote, "A number of owners stated flatly that they would be unwilling to place their credit on the line to assist weaker clubs in borrowing necessary funding."[37]

After the meetings with the owners, O'Brien issued a telex to owners about negotiations. As in each of the previous negotiations, the NBA had a new negotiating team for collective bargaining. For the NBA, it would be O'Brien, Stern, Granik, and Bettman.[38]

On March 15, 1982, David Stern, chief negotiator, issued a memo to file to begin his preparations in earnest. He outlined what he wanted in his file and all of the tasks that had to be accomplished before his meeting with the Labor Relations Committee on March 29. It was an ambitious and comprehensive list of tasks.

First, Stern, Granik, and Bettman wanted to be informed and organized throughout negotiations. They wanted the collective bargaining agreements and proposals from the negotiations in the NFL, who were in the midst of their negotiations, and MLB, who had recently completed their bargaining the year before.

Stern also wanted to know how the NBA was perceived publicly. He wanted press clippings not only from the NBA negotiations but from the NFL negotiations as well. The NFL would be going first—perhaps there were ways to learn from their experience. Stern wanted a list of all articles about the "'problems' in the NBA," and particularly "financial problems of our teams and . . . letters to the editor concerning the status of salaries and other factors in the NBA." Stern also wanted a clippings-file about the broader labor movement, "containing newspaper and magazine articles about collective bargaining negotiations in industry, particularly those involving 'give backs' (UAW and Ford negotiations)."[39] There was a narrative to be crafted, and Stern, Granik, and Bettman wanted to be prepared to do it. The times in America were hard—the NBA was not immune. If workers at UAW could provide givebacks, why not basketball players?

Each member of Stern's negotiating team would have a specific role and tasks, both initially and throughout negotiations. Bettman would be in charge of the first draft of proposals for bargaining, taking ownership of "both those generated by the NBA office and those that [had] been suggested during the recent meetings and during prior Collective Bargaining Negotiations."[40]

Jeff Mishkin, outside counsel, would be responsible for identifying the interrelationship between bargaining and the *Robertson* settlement, "including the drafting of such proposals so that they do not run afoul of the Settlement Agreement."[41] They would have to tread carefully to avoid problems with the court, especially if they wanted to propose anything that could limit free agency.

Stern knew there would be public relations considerations in negotiations and he wanted someone to craft a memo outlining the public relations approaches the league could take, "including suggestions for the designation of appropriate spokesmen and fines for any unautho-rized statements by people other than the persons so designated."[42]

Most of the rest of the team, prepared for worst-case scenarios—a work stoppage. With the contract set to expire in a few months, so would the no-strike clause. As a result, the power would shift to the players, and they would be able to strike—Fleisher had threatened a strike in nearly every collective bargaining cycle since before they had agreements. Stern wanted a memo prepared for teams to out-line a budget in the event of a work stoppage, "including a variety of worst case analyses, such as: a) A stoppage in the preseason; b) A stoppage beginning with the regular season; c) A stoppage at some point during the regular season (December); and d) In connection with all of the above, there should be an assumption that the stop-page lasts all season and an alternative assumption that games are played with employees who are not members of the Collective Bar-gaining unit."[43]

Russ Granik, the NBA's general counsel, was in charge of having dialogue with the Merchants Bank of New England to secure a line of credit, even if the owners did not want one. He was also in charge of understanding the options "available to Labor and Management in connection with the strike/lockout situation" and the "rights of Management to unilaterally implement Collective Bargaining pro-posals in the absence of an Agreement."[44]

Other legal considerations would have to be researched as well: if there was a strike, what would happen to players under contract? Would they become free agents? "Alternatively," Stern wrote, "can a team 'selectively renounce' contracts on the grounds that a work stop-page is a violation of those contracts." Leaving no stone unturned, Stern wanted to know if the players went on strike: What were the ob-ligations of the referees if the NBA used replacement players—would they cross the picket line?[45] Stern wanted to be prepared for anything.

So, with all of those tasks being delegated to others, what exactly was Stern going to do? Stern put himself in charge of investigating what the cable revenues would be for the next five years and meeting with the league's accountant, Arthur Anderson, to compile financial information for bargaining.[46]

On March 29, O'Brien, Stern, Granik, and Bettman met with the full Labor Relations Committee at the Berkshire Place Hotel, room 2003.[47] In February O'Brien had expanded the committee due to his expectation that negotiations with the players would be "extremely difficult and demanding."[48] Initially, the committee was made up of nine members—in addition to Alan Cohen and Angelo Drossos, there was Abe Pollin (Washington Bullets), Harry Mangurian (Boston Celtics), James Fitzgerald (Milwaukee Bucks), J. Michael Gearon (Atlanta Hawks), Harry Glickman (Portland Trailblazers), Doug Adkins (Dallas Mavericks), and Larry Weinberg (Portland Trailblazers); Harold Katz of the Sixers would join later. For the meeting, O'Brien issued a memo detailing all of the potential proposals to be approved by the Board of Governors in June. There were thirty-three proposals on March 29, and the goal was not a mystery: reduce costs—transfer them to players and limit the growth of player salaries.

The first topic for negotiation was entitled "limitation of player salaries." They were not beating around the bush. The memo began: "There appears to be a general consensus that the NBA obtain in collective bargaining a limitation on player salaries. The limitation most often suggested in one that would limit each team's total player payroll, rather than one which created a salary scale for players. This issue will require significant background information and will be dealt with at length as a separate matter."[49] At the meeting on March 29, the committee was unanimous "that a meaningful limitation of player salaries must be adopted," according to Bettman's notes of the meeting.[50]

There were other potential proposals: elimination of guarantees, a 'taxi squad' that included a few lower-paid players at the end of the bench, prohibition on no-trade provisions, elimination of first class travel, and players paying for their benefits. All of them were intended to reduce costs. This was the owners' wish list! They even had a proposal that per diems for players should be reduced if players received food on planes![51]

There were a few the commissioner and the committee removed, namely that the NBA would not propose "confirmation by Players Association that the NBA and its Member Teams are not liable for the Salary Obligations of any other Member Team."[52] There was deep

David

mistrust of revenue sharing in the NBA, especially from the more stable clubs to the weaker ones.

The Labor Committee met again on May 13 in New York City. While the March 29 meeting was devoted to creating proposals for bargaining, the May 13 meeting was about looking at economic data of the NBA. There was a detailed presentation distributed outlining the economic circumstance in the NBA. The data reflected that NBA player salaries had reached a high point in 1981–82, at 63.9 percent of total revenue, up from 56.7 percent the year before the right of first refusal, and up from 52.2 percent in 1977–78. Players' salaries had grown considerably in just the one year since the Stepien/Buss bonanza of 1981. The average salary had increased by $24,000 over the previous year.[53] The documents also showed which teams were in trouble on one metric—the amount of gate receipts relative to salary. In the early 1980s, with the limited television revenues, gate receipts were still important to the NBA. While most teams were under 100 percent, two teams—San Diego and Cleveland—were spending over two times as much on salaries as they were bringing in.

After the meeting on the thirteenth, the NBA was working to finalize its proposals for the Board of Governors meeting in June. During this period, teams were involved in an almost constitutional convention of structures and theories for how the NBA should proceed to reel in salaries. One example, sent in by Atlanta Hawks general manager Stan Kasten and Hawks owner Michael Gearon, outlined a very detailed proposal.

Kasten said there were two options to fix the NBA's problems: a rigid cap or a flexible one—in modern NBA parlance, a hard cap or a soft one. Kasten and Gearon argued against a rigid one, stating, "A rigid cap in an industry which is economically flexible will not work. Current salaries are so far out of line, it would take years and years to get it back in kilter, without giving the players an opportunity, real or imagined, to make greater money through some percentage arrangement. We, therefore, must be committed to some form of adjustable cap."[54]

Kasten's proposal advocated that the teams would put 40 percent "of all its revenue from all sources into a central fund." That central fund would then be divided equally among the teams to be used for salary and benefits. Kasten proposed that teams would directly spend other teams' money—even if 40 percent of a team's (say the Cavaliers) earnings were not enough to field the team, you would take that amount out from the central pool. With revenue sharing a dirty word among NBA owners, Kasten claimed his proposal was different. "This plan has none of the disadvantages of revenue sharing plans, because no team will be able to reap a cash windfall at the expense of another team's financial success," he said. "Since all money received must be plowed back into player salaries . . . there will be no disincentive to continue to actively promote and build one's team because each team will still retain a full 60% of its revenues."[55] The other piece of their proposal was to do away with guaranteed contracts— something many of the proposals attempted to do. They thought it was achievable because if the teams were required to spend money every year at the same rate, it would be more palatable to Fleisher.

Kasten and Gearon saw their proposal as positive. "The cap proposed above, in many respects, makes the players our partners. But a two way street is our only possible chance for success. Anything we come up with which benefits both sides represent a major victory for the owners, because right now, the players literally have all the marbles. And this formula will benefit the owners greatly."[56]

Kasten believed his proposal could be sold to Fleisher and the players. Kasten even tried to frame Fleisher's argument to the players. "Fleisher can say that the revenue cap is not just a three year price life, but a long-term cut of all the action. He has now achieved a major goal by getting part of our cable money—in fact 40%—greater than he ever imagined. At the same time, we are assured that at some point in time, we will not be paying more than 40% of our revenue in salaries." Kasten thought his proposal was crucial, saying, "Our history tells us that if we do not act now, we will ultimately wind up giving away a lot more than that. If we continue to allow 'survival of the richest' as our policy, even the rich will not survive." Many aspects of Kasten's proposal would appear in the NBA negotiations in 1982–83 and beyond.

On June 1, 1982, the day the CBA expired, the NBA had still not finalized its proposals and was looking at three options to propose to the players in their first negotiation. On June 4 the Labor Relations

Committee issued their report to the Board of Governors in advance of the owners meeting on June 15, including their proposals. The report stated: "Because of the serious financial position of many NBA teams, this year's negotiations with the Players Association, beginning in July, will be the most crucial in NBA history. Accordingly, over the past eight weeks the Labor Relations Committee has engaged in extensive efforts to develop a comprehensive and effective negotiations program for your consideration."[57]

The memo, sent to all of the NBA Board of Governors, laid out the NBA's approach to bargaining: "It is the unanimous view of the Committee, and we assume all of you concur, that immediate steps must be taken to remedy what has become a completely untenable situation that threatens the survival of many of our teams and perhaps the NBA itself. Thus we plan to present and fight for an array of proposals aimed at achieving financial stability for the league." The NBA believed, as it stated, that they could get Fleisher to agree to a cap if "at the same time the NBA create[d] a central fund that would be distributed either to those teams that need[ed] additional funds for player salaries or to the players directly, or both."[58]

The NBA also wanted its teams to know they had a special assessment for the coming year. The memo said, "One additional feature of the salary moderation incentive plan we are proposing for inclusion in the new agreement could be of considerable importance to you in your contract negotiations this summer. Under the plan, if a team incurs, before the execution of the agreement, new salary obligations that increase the team's total salary above the salary limit applicable to that team, the team would be assessed the difference between its total salary and the applicable limit. These assessments would be placed into a fund to be divided among the players in the NBA."[59] The proposals were coming together. Though they would not propose this fund initially, the NBA was setting the stage.

On June 14, 1982, Larry O'Brien flew to the annual owners meeting in San Diego, where the NBA would finalize its proposals and set the NBA up to begin negotiating with Fleisher and the players in late July. While the process to finalize the proposals was businesslike, this was still the NBA. And, as O'Brien was attempting to prepare the owners for the most difficult negotiation in NBA history, it was not the only drama that O'Brien was dealing with.

• • •

In fact, there were two major topics at the owners meeting in San Diego. First was the NBA's internal squabble with owner Donald Sterling and the city of Los Angeles over their joint attempt to move the Clippers from San Diego to Los Angeles. Second, was how the NBA intended to handle its upcoming labor negotiations with the players.

Sterling, yet another semi-eccentric NBA owner, had been an embarrassment to the league from the minute he purchased the San Diego Clippers the year before. According to the *Los Angeles Times*, when Sterling bought the Clippers "it was generally assumed that (1) Sterling knew next to nothing about pro basketball and (2) he was in it to make a name for himself."[60]

Sterling's ownership had started with promise. He was approved unanimously by the NBA's Board of Governors in June 1981 and described as a "real estate magnate" when he purchased the team for a little more than $13.7 million.[61] In what would be a hallmark of Sterling's ownership, he had only put up $99,812 of his own money, less than 1 percent of the purchase price.[62]

On the day he purchased the team, Sterling granted a wide-ranging interview with the *Los Angeles Times*. Sterling held forth from his office as he sipped white wine from a Styrofoam cup, which he refilled at least once during the meeting. In basketball terms, Sterling was confident, proclaiming, "I won't fail." He envisioned "pouring champagne over the heads of [his] players when they [won] the NBA championship." Sterling also claimed a moral compass that would guide his ownership. He expressed a message for the children of San Diego, saying, "I believe an owner has a responsibility to kids. So, I stopped smoking the day I bought the Clippers." Sterling, who would later refuse to make basic payments, said, "I care what people think of me. I don't want to be controversial. I want to be trusted, to be an extension of the people, of the fans." Though he would later be involved in a myriad of sex scandals, he said he preferred San Diego to Los Angeles: "San Diego represents more of what I am than LA. The people [in Los Angeles] are too liberal. There's a permissiveness here that's greater than San Francisco or San Diego—and it's contrary to my philosophy."[63] Several days later, when Sterling was asked if he cared about the Clippers, Sterling responded, "Very much . . . Pride is the greatest motivator in the world. Second is the desire for security. Then would come sex, I suppose . . . We're committed to winning."[64] Sterling clearly relished the status that came with owning an NBA franchise.

The good feeling did not last long. Almost immediately stories began to leak out about not only Sterling's peculiar ownership style but also his uglier business practices. When the season started, the Clippers flopped on the court and off. Sterling engaged in several odd marketing techniques: putting *his* face on billboards advertising for the team; kissing his coach, Paul Silas, at center court after the Clippers' first victory; and entering into promotional agreements with a local casino, which earned him particular reprimand from O'Brien and the league office.[65]

Then, in January 1982, Sterling publicly stated he wanted his team to lose. Speaking at a press conference, Sterling said, "We have to bite the bullet. We must end up last in order to draw first and get a franchise maker, like Ralph Sampson of Virginia."[66] Sterling didn't stop there, saying, "I guarantee we'll have the first or second or third pick in the draft . . . I don't think we'll have to work very hard to have the worst record." The NBA immediately distanced itself from Sterling's statements, stating, "Obviously the last thing we would want would be a team going out to intentionally lose games."[67]

The Clippers' players, who lost to the Dallas Mavericks the night of Sterling's statement by one point, were furious. While now the idea of tanking to get a higher draft pick may be seen as a viable way to rebuild a team, Sterling's comment undermined the credibility of a team that was already struggling. Forward Tom Chambers, the team's leading scorer, was blunt in his words: "Maybe it's better for him not to talk anymore. Maybe it's best to be quiet."[68]

The NBA fined Sterling $10,000 for "conduct prejudicial and detrimental to the NBA."[69] Behind the scenes, the *Los Angeles Times* reported that the "NBA had suggested [Sterling] tone down his act, presumably for the betterment of himself, his franchise and the league itself." Sterling withdrew from the public eye, at the request of the NBA.[70]

Then the money problems started. Three weeks after his fine, Sterling advised Granik that he had financial problems and asked to meet with the league's advisory committee.[71] The Clippers laid off six marketing employees and cut back on other staff, including advising scouting director Pete Babcock there was no more money to send him to scout college prospects. Sterling stiffed hotel bills, payments to players, program printers; all kinds of basic payments the Clippers owed were made late or not at all, further undermining the credibility of a weak team in a weak league.[72]

Sterling's penny pinching also impacted Fleisher and the NBPA. The Clippers were failing to make owed payments and insisting players fly coach, despite the fact that the CBA required first class travel. Fleisher threatened to shut down the league if the payments were not made, CBA or not.[73] Fleisher gave Stern a two-week deadline; Stern got it done.[74] Fleisher said of Sterling, "His ownership activities up to now aren't good for the league. If he has financial troubles, they arise out of a misunderstanding of what he was buying, because nothing has happened that would cause this disaster. I have no sympathy for his problems . . . and I would say some owners seem unhappy, they feel he hasn't given the league stability there." Sterling did have his protectors. Ted Stepien said of Sterling, "He's a thoughtful guy . . . Don's one of my favorites. You know he has your interest at heart, where some other [owners] don't."[75]

Sterling or not, the Clippers were struggling in San Diego. They had the second-worst record, the lowest attendance, and were on pace to lose $2 million per season.[76] By the end of the season Sterling didn't even think he could sell the Clippers. "Nobody's as stupid as me," Sterling said. "Nobody's going to invest in this team."[77]

Sterling created his largest mess to date as the owners converged on the Coronado Resort in San Diego for the owners meeting. Sterling had signed a lease to move his team to Los Angeles without league approval. He had done so in part because Los Angeles agreed to pick up the tab on any litigation associated with the move.[78] Sterling always found a way to stick someone else with the bill.

Unfortunately, this chaos was not how franchise movements worked in the NBA, nor was it how the Stern and O'Brien wanted franchise movement to work. Under the NBA constitution, movements re-

David

quired the approval of ¾ of member clubs, which Sterling, obviously, never requested prior to signing a lease.[79] Additionally, making things worse, San Diego, despite its low attendance numbers, was not going to lose its team lying down. Both cities, Los Angeles and San Diego, told the NBA they planned to pursue legal action over the Clippers if the outcome did not work out in their favor, leaving the NBA in the middle of two warring factions with an owner who had abdicated responsibility for the result.

More importantly, despite signing a lease and a public announcement to move the Clippers the following season, Sterling seemed completely unprepared to actually move the Clippers to Los Angeles. Sterling had sold no season tickets in either Los Angeles or San Diego.[80] Despite the bold action, it was not clear there was even interest in a second team in Los Angeles. The Los Angeles Sports Arena, who had been driving the Clippers' move and pushing for the team, said that they had been keeping track of the number of individuals interested, but that the list numbered only about one thousand people. As Bob Ryan stated, "The NBA is appalled, first of all, because anarchy is generally intolerable. Secondly, there is no unanimity of opinion of Los Angeles' ability to support two professional basketball teams. Finally, the league is skeptical of Sterling's credentials to operate a team anywhere, be it San Diego, Los Angeles, or Block Island."

In a meeting with the Board of Governors, O'Brien said, "I was and remain deeply concerned about allowing this franchise to continue operations. The timing of the Clippers proposed move to Los Angeles is both ironic and unfortunate."[81] Stern voiced frustration with the situation but focused his ire on the LA Coliseum Commission, stating, "Instead of telling us they wanted a team, they signed a lease with the Clippers then sent their attorney to say they'd sue if we didn't approve the move." Stern went further, stating, "The Coliseum's primary focus seems to be litigation. They spent millions to pursue the Oakland Raiders and seem willing to spend millions more to try to get the Clippers. Maybe it's time the people of Los Angeles became concerned over the spending of a public agency, which the Coliseum Commissioner is. They're even picking up the legal fees of Sterling."[82] Larry O'Brien doubled down, stating, "I'm not going to be intimidated, our owners are not going to be intimidated and the tax payers of Los Angeles should not be intimidated into spending millions of dollars to support the egos of their own public officials and the attorney the Commission has selected."[83]

The next day, the NBA went into district court for a declaration of its rights regarding the Clippers' move to Los Angeles and postponed its internal vote on Sterling's move. The NBA suit went after Sterling personally, including in its complaint: "The actions (of Sterling) have caused the NBA and its members to suffer substantial injury and have brought into question (Sterling's) ability to operate effectively as a member and in the best interest of the NBA." The suit was also over Sterling's refusal to pay $225,000 owed the NBA office; $300,000 owed to former players; and another $300,000 to third parties. NBA attorney Michael Cardozo said, "We want clarification, since we've been told we'll be sued if we allow or don't allow the move."[84]

The truth was, many in the league were seething over Sterling's maneuver. As the *Boston Globe* reported, "Private discussion with some owners reveal a negative feeling about Sterling, ranging from polite skepticism to loathing."[85] As one owner said, "We're out for blood."

While the owners were fighting each other over Sterling's maneuver, they were publicly aligned over the other major issue discussed at the owners meetings—upcoming collective bargaining negotiations. Despite the fact that the league had taken the extreme step of going into court to sue one of its owners, everyone agreed that CBA negotiations were the bigger story. Sam Schulman of the Sonics said, "Things like this Sterling business are transitory they have a way of working themselves out. A more important thing is this stuff with the players."[86]

First, the Board of Governors had to approve the proposals to the NBPA. O'Brien personally advocated for them. In approving the proposals, "Commissioner O'Brien reiterated to the board the need for unity and strength as the League embarks upon the difficult task of readjusting the inequities of the current financial position of the Players and the NBA." The proposals were approved 19 to 4. The four were Chicago, Indiana, Los Angeles, and New York, who "requested to have recorded their support of the League's collective bargaining proposals, with the exception of that aspect of the Salary Moderation Plan requiring the creation of a fund from a percentage of team gross revenue."[87]

The abstention of those teams was over revenue sharing, not the proposals themselves. Both the Knicks and the Bulls sent letters explaining their abstention. Jack Krumpe wrote to O'Brien after the meeting: "The salary moderation incentive plan . . . includes reference to a central fund, which would apparently be subsidized through a pooling of 'total revenues' generated by each member club. The creation of this fund would therefore, in our opinion, constitute a limited form of revenue-sharing with respect to local television, as well as gate, receipts. As you know, it is the position of the Knickerbockers that such revenue sharing may be implemented by the National Basketball Association only through a unanimous vote of the Board." Krumpe was clear, however: "We wish to document our general support of the program described . . . which is, in our opinion, responsive to the current needs of the National Basketball Association."[88] The Bulls raised the same argument.

Stern recognized that this was an issue—especially convincing big markets to engage in revenue sharing. He said years later, "There were two things we had to persuade—we had to persuade the players, but it was actually persuading the owners . . . We had to preach to the players and the owners that it was good to have a competitive league. And if you didn't you couldn't survive. You wouldn't want the Indiana Pacers, at the time, with a payroll of $1 million or thereabouts coming into your building, with a roster that was not competitive."[89]

It was in that framework that Stern went into the initial negotiations with Fleisher, with his intent to remake the business of basketball. It was no surprise that both sides engaged in pleasantries and unpleasantries.

10

The Moses Signing, September 1982

I'd rather lose a few dollars and win than
make a few dollars and lose.

—HAROLD KATZ

As the summer of 1982 rolled on, so did the NBA offseason. The NBA had undergone a spending spree in 1981, due in part to rule changes resulting from the *Robertson* settlement and in part to the aggressiveness of certain ownership groups—shrewd (Buss) and silly (Stepien). It was not clear what would happen in '82. The economics for the league had improved. CBA negotiations were ongoing, but no deal was close. Stern and O'Brien were very public that teams and the league were losing money, but no one believed owners could show restraint when confronted with the ability to make their teams better. Despite the uncertainty over the collective bargaining agreement, teams prepared for the next season, jockeying to keep up with the young, fast-paced Lakers.

Though everyone was trying to get more athletic, the most valuable commodity on the market that off-season was size. No free agent was as big, as good, or as valuable as Moses Malone, then of the Houston Rockets. Still just twenty-seven and improving every season, Moses was, according to the *Los Angeles Times*, "the most attractive free agent in the history of the NBA."[1] Because he was the reigning league MVP, interest in Malone was expected to be intense when he hit the market.[2] There were rumors that nearly every team could sign Moses.[3] In June of 1981, a full year before he hit free agency, Jerry Buss said of Malone: "He's the player I want and I'm going to get him. He becomes a free agent after next season. Believe me, he'll be a Laker."[4] When other teams accused Buss of tampering with a player under contract, O'Brien sent Buss a stern letter regarding tampering. Rockets GM Ray Patterson said, "What Buss is saying in print is what all the owners and GMs are saying to themselves . . . It really doesn't bother me. What advantage to charging him with tampering? It's a dead issue."[5]

Moses's future loomed large over the rest of the NBA—both on and off the court. He was available, and signing him would make any team an immediate contender, but he was not going to be cheap. He was a test case for the economic problems facing the NBA.

Malone had spent years trying to get an extension in Houston before he became a free agent after the 1981–82 season. Negotiations between Lee Fentress, Malone's agent, and Rockets owner George Maloof began in November 1980, years before his contract was up. "Moses never wanted to be a free agent in the first place," Fentress said. "He asked me to start negotiations back in 1980 so that it would all be cleared up before his contract expired. He was very happy in Houston."[6]

Maloof, who bought the Rockets a year earlier, had made his money in a variety of businesses—beer distributorships, hotels, banking. He had a modern view of the NBA, believing the league was on the cusp of a renaissance, saying, "professional basketball is the sport of the 80s." Though he was new to the NBA, Maloof wanted to win and was willing to spend to do so. "I play to win," he said, when he bought the team, "and you win by the bottom line."[7]

Maloof wanted to sign Malone, and he sat down with Fentress to work out an extension. After ten days of bargaining, Fentress believed the parties were "pretty damn close to a deal." Then, on November 29, 1980, right in the middle of negotiations over a new deal for Moses, Maloof suddenly died of a heart attack. George was replaced by his twenty-four-year-old son, Gavin Maloof. Gavin said that George's last words were, "How many points did Moses score?"[8]

Gavin became the youngest owner in sports and tried hard to establish himself as a serious person. He hired a public relations firm to build his image as a businessman, despite the fact that he was younger than nine of the players on the team he owned. He gave interviews that he claimed were intended to promote the NBA but really seemed intended to make him appear humble and approachable in his new public-facing role. "I don't have a yacht," he said, "or a plane or a beachfront house. I'm dedicated to the family and the business." The only problem was, in separate interviews, Gavin gave the exact same quote to the *Boston Globe* and the *Los Angeles Times*. Not exactly the epitome of authenticity. He did express one idea to benefit the league: a naming contest. "My idea is to run a nationwide contest to pick a name for the NBA finals. Football has the Super Bowl, baseball has the World Series and hockey has the Stanley Cup. . . . Maybe we could call it the Round Bowl. . . . In 35 years, you'd think some of the NBA masterminds would have come up with that."[9] With the focus on establishing the "Round Bowl," Moses's contract was not Gavin's priority, so Moses simply played ball, increasing his value.

Throughout the 1981–82 season, Malone publicly said he was not focused on contract negotiations and wanted to stay with the Rockets. "I just want to finish this season strong and see what happens. I'm not interested in negotiating right now," Malone said in February of 1982. "I'm interested in winning. A couple of reporters asked me and I just told them my number one place is Houston. The Rockets have been fair to me and I want them to have the first shot."[10] Rockets general manager Ray Patterson echoed Moses's statements, saying, "We're going to sign him. I have no idea what it will take. Moses makes us a stable and a complete franchise. It makes good judgment and business sense to sign him."[11]

When the 1981–82 season ended with a first-round playoff exit, the Rockets were clear that they wanted to keep Malone. They had dawdled before, but they pushed to get it done before he hit the open market for real. On June 6, two weeks before Malone would win his second consecutive MVP award, Gavin Maloof said he was going to make Malone the highest-paid professional athlete in history. He said he had already made a number of offers that would make Malone the highest-paid player in the NBA. Fentress confirmed the offer, saying, "I have not had time to consider it or talk to Moses about it . . . if they are trying to avoid having him become a free agent, it does seem a little late in the day." Patterson was desperate to keep Malone: "Houston will not lose him. There are enough people in this city who won't let him leave. Houston has never lost an asset. It was happy to lose hockey, soccer and women's basketball, but it will not lose a thing of great quality. If we start next year without Moses, we might as well forget it. We're dead."[12]

The next day, the Rockets continued their pro-Moses press tour. Maloof said, "We'll do whatever it takes to keep Malone in Houston. We're optimists. I think he likes the city. He's told us he wants to return." Ray Patterson was even blunter about resigning Malone and besting other offers from bigger markets: "I don't care what anybody says in New York, New Jersey or Los Angeles. I'm going to sign Moses Malone and keep him in the Houston franchise. I've heard all the rumors about what [New Jersey Nets owner] Joe Taub is gonna' do and how much Jerry Buss is gonna' offer Moses. They can offer $2 million or they can offer $3 million or they can offer $4 million. We'll still be here in the end of negotiating."[13]

Then, two weeks later, the Rockets abruptly announced that Maloof sold the team to Charlie Thomas, a local car dealer.[14] For the second time in three years, the Maloof family cut out on Malone mid-deal— though only one of them was voluntary. The new owner claimed to share the Maloofs' interest in keeping Malone, as did the team. "The sale will not affect our pledge to sign Moses," Patterson said. "We had the same budget before the sale that we're operating under now." However, Fentress was dubious, stating, "Moses' desire to stay in Houston would seem to exceed their interest in keeping him."[15]

No matter what they said publicly, the new Rockets owner took a hard line with Malone. The summer continued with no signing. Malone stayed in shape by playing basketball at the local rec center and waited. His agent went on vacation. As *Sports Illustrated*'s Alexander Wolff put it, "What was supposed to be a summer of bidding has become a summer of biding, and as a result, Malone will probably not be jumping ship."[16] By August Malone had yet to receive a single offer from another team even though several, like the Nets, were obvious choices.

Beyond Malone, the rest of the players' market was very slow. The players, the union, and Fleisher were concerned by the lack of movement. Teams delayed signing draft picks and free agents and were chalking it up to the collective bargaining negotiations. There were sixty-four free agents at the start of the offseason, and almost none had signed by late summer. Draft picks were not completing their deals, and Moses had not yet found a home. Pistons general manager Jack McCloskey said that the CBA negotiation was one of the factors delaying the signing of their first-round picks and that it would "take a long time" before they were signed. *Sports Illustrated* speculated that the owners "may have already begun their own salary moderation plan by not bidding on free agents."[17]

The conspiratorial concerns of Fleisher and *Sports Illustrated* were not paranoid delusions—albeit there was not clear collusion, either. When the owners approved the NBA's collective bargaining proposals at the owners meetings in June, the proposal included a note that signings made before the new agreement could lead to assessments in the new world order. The uncertainty would spur hesitance of a major outlay in any front office. In addition, in a memo to owners, general managers, and team counsel about collective bargaining in late August, O'Brien warned against signing players. He said, "The NBA is proposing, as a cost-saving measure, the reduction of Active Lists to 10 players. If rosters are ultimately reduced, which is a distinct possibility in light of the cost-savings that would thereby be effected and the players intransigence in refusing even to discuss other cost-savings proposals, teams will be required to cut additional players; accordingly clubs should consider this possibility in determining the number of guaranteed contracts for which they should become obligated."[18] He didn't say not to sign players, he could not do that. But front offices could read between the lines.

• • •

It took a flamboyant owner like Harold Katz of the Philadelphia 76ers to end the stalled bidding war over players like Malone. The Sixers had reached the NBA finals three times in the previous six seasons, including 1981–82, but they had never won a championship. The core of the Sixers, led by Julius Erving, was not getting any younger, and Katz's window for a title was closing.

For most of the off-season the Sixers were not in need of Malone's services. Then, the Sixers started making changes. In August they traded their starting center, Daryl "Chocolate Thunder" Dawkins, to the Nets for their 1983 first-round pick and $700,000 in cash.[19] The trade set the Sixers up for the future; they now had three picks in the upcoming draft, including one from Stepien's moribund Cleveland Cavaliers. Katz, desperate to improve his team, protected that pick with everything he had, saying, "that pick could be Ralph Sampson or Pat Ewing," the two-generational big men dominating college basketball who were expected to enter the NBA draft the next season.[20] These picks, coupled with a strong core of Julius Erving, Maurice Cheeks, and Bobby Jones gave the Sixers a bright present and future.

Katz was an active owner on the court and off. He frequently watched film with coaches and waded heavily into players' personnel decisions. Though Katz had made his money by owning the Nutrisystem diet company, when on the road for business, he scouted college games, looking for prospects for the Sixers to draft, and regaled the local press with descriptions of the time he played against Wilt Chamberlain in high school. As Sixers general manager Pat Williams said, "He's a fan. He was a longtime vocal season-ticket holder before he bought the team." Katz also coveted the press and was the subject of a *New York Times* article dubiously titled "76er Owner Is Conspicuous."[21]

Because of his hands-on approach, the Dawkins trade, and the decision to make it, felt personal. Ordinarily, such a trade would be quizzical—trading a young, elite talent for what amounted to a future pick to add to a large stockpile seemed to be selling low. However, Dawkins, who had struggled in Game Six of the Finals the previous season, seemed an obvious choice for dismissal. Katz took an especially active role in Dawkins's development in 1981–82. He also signed him to a long-term contract and frequently huddled with him after games.[22]

During the Eastern Conference Finals against the Celtics, Dawkins had played poorly and the Sixers lost the first game by forty points. Dawkins attributed his poor play to his injured leg. Katz was skeptical: "The doctors told me his leg had mended. I have done a lot for that kid. I'm trying to motivate him. You don't win without big centers. But we're playing for the championship now and this is no time to talk about Daryl." Dawkins, when asked about Katz, was not critical. As the *New York Times* reported, "When Dawkins was asked about Katz, he smiled and put a hand to his mouth as if to prevent him from saying something he might later regret."[23] It was no surprise when Katz moved him in the off-season. Dawkins said later of Katz , "I often thought his daughter was sweet on me and that freaked him out. He must have hated the thought of any player ever messing with his daughter."[24]

However, when Katz traded Dawkins to the Nets, he asserted that the decision was not based on Dawkins's play. He also was clear it was not personal. Instead, Katz said, it was an economic decision. After trading Dawkins, Katz "espoused what he called a renewed sense of fiscal responsibility in a 'league that [wasn't] making any money' and said that he and other owners had decided to hold the line on salaries."[25] Katz's statements must have been music to Stern and O'Brien's ears, as it clearly proved their point—even successful big market teams like the Sixers had to make cuts in the new economy of the NBA. Surely, this proved that Fleisher and the NBPA should accept the salary moderation proposal in the hopes of saving the league. Katz made it clear publicly that even though he paid "far less than the reported $12 million" for the franchise, he had run his team based on "pure economics."[26]

Katz walked his talk about fiscal responsibility and focus on the future—for about a week. Then the owner who had just proclaimed he never made rash decisions signed Moses Malone to an offer sheet worth a reported $13.2 million, potentially as much as $15 million, a sum greater than what Katz had paid for the entire Sixers franchise just a year earlier.[27] It made Malone the highest paid player in the NBA.

When he signed Malone, Katz's tune changed regarding the nature of the business. "I got deeper into it with my staff and accountants and they all felt very confident that what we'd pay Moses would come back to us," Katz said. "We spent, I can say, at least 60 hours thinking out every possibility of this deal and I was convinced through my lawyers and accountants that the deal makes financial sense for us. If I wasn't, I wouldn't have made the deal."[28]

Malone was available because the new Rockets' owner, Charles Thomas, had taken a hard line with Fentress. Thomas made an offer to Malone at a lower rate than what the Rockets' previously proposed. For some reason, other teams had not entered into the fray.

Fentress said, "The Rockets had taken a tough position because they knew I didn't have any other offers. They didn't have to go as high as before."[29] A far cry from the fawning statements Patterson made before the ownership change.

The Rockets' loss was the Sixers gain, and between the Dawkins trade and the frustration with the Rockets, Fentress went to Katz and a deal came together quickly. The Sixers main concern was whether Moses, the reigning MVP, could coexist with Sixers star Julius Erving and play a faster style than he had in Houston. Before signing a deal, Moses met with Sixers brass, including Katz and Coach Billy Cunningham, in New York City. After an hour meeting, Cunningham was convinced. Malone said later, "What does that mean 'ego'? I left all my ego on the playground."[30]

Economic restraint was no longer a part of the equation. "There is good money and bad money and spending this type of money for Moses Malone is good money," Katz said. "This is a good business deal for Philadelphia. He'll put more people in the seats and that justifies the cost."[31]

Malone signed with the Sixers mostly because of the lack of interest from the Rockets. As the *Washington Post* reported, "Malone . . . sounded a bit irked that two years of negotiations with the Rockets over a new contract had not worked out, causing him to become a free agent."[32] "Moses was puzzled by Houston's attitude," Fentress said. "He told me he couldn't understand why the owners couldn't make up their minds whether to re-sign him."[33] Malone said, "I just wanted to get a contract so I could concentrate on playing ball. The main thing with me was not how much money I could get from a team."[34]

Malone's deal spread like an earthquake through the NBA and coaches, managers, and owners went on the record. Jack McCloskey, GM of the Pistons, called the deal "catastrophic for the league."[35] McCloskey said of Katz: "He can do whatever he wants, and he's done it within the rules, but I don't think it's good for the League."[36] Don Nelson, coach of the Milwaukee Bucks commented, "There are only a few teams that could do something like that. My whole payroll is less than two men on that team. That makes it awfully difficult for us in smaller cities, and I think it hurts the league a great deal."[37] Jerry

Colangelo of Phoenix said, "Offer sheets like this just raise everyone's payroll. Some teams simply can't afford to compete on this level."[38]

Jerry Buss, who had been the subject of complaints from his fellow owners the previous season, said, "We had kept a clipping in which Philadelphia's general manager was quoted as saying 'this is madness' speaking about us. We circled the quote, attached it to a copy of a story about Moses' contract, and sent it back to them."[39]

For his part, Malone did not understand the outrage. "I don't know why people are making such a big deal out of it," he said, though he had privately expressed concern for how the Rockets' fans would respond to his decamping to Philadelphia. "I don't see why it's a crime for me to make big bucks. Lots of people in this league make big bucks. No one is talking about them," Malone said. "The owner thought I deserved it. I don't care what people are saying. Let 'em talk. That's the way life goes." When asked why the Sixers had offered so much, Malone said, "It isn't because I need the money. It's because they thought that was a fair price for me. My lawyers negotiated the price; I just accepted it."[40]

Though Malone had signed with the Sixers, the Rockets still had the right of first refusal. They could match the offer sheet from the Sixers and retain Malone. Initially the Rockets were clear that they intended to match. "We have no choice but to match it," Patterson said. "There is no doubt we have to sign him, then make a judgment. You just can't give up a major asset for nothing." Moses said he had no preference as to which team he ended up with.[41]

Katz, having heard rumors that the Rockets intended to match any offer Malone signed, had seen to that. First, Malone's offer sheet was all cash, no deferred money. On the one hand, it was what Malone wanted. "He must have told me ten times 'no 'ferred no 'ferred,'" Katz said of his negotiations with Malone.[42] More importantly, making Malone's contract all cash made it difficult for a new owner like Thomas to swallow. In addition, Malone's contract with the Sixers was complicated—extremely complicated. It provided for a number of poison-pill provisions that were designed to be difficult for the Rockets to match, built around attendance and other players.[43] Katz, in announcing the signing of the offer sheet, also lobbied the Rockets owner not to match, saying that he would not if he were the owner of

The Moses Signing

the Rockets. "This is a good business deal for Philadelphia, but I'm not sure it's a good deal for Houston," he said. Katz said that even if the Rockets matched, he would be open to trading with them, but that his starters and the draft picks, especially the Cavaliers' choice, were untouchable.[44]

The NBA and the Rockets challenged Katz's offer sheet with the special master as violating the *Robertson* settlement. They argued Katz's deal was in bad faith because it was specifically designed to be impossible for the Rockets to match.[45] They challenged five of Moses's bonus provisions. To make sure that Malone's deal went through, Fleisher stepped in to assist Katz in the litigation. It was an alliance of convenience. "I find it bothersome that we finally saw a free agent get an offer sheet, after a summer of virtually no activity, and the first thing that happens is, it's attacked by the league," Fleisher said. "This is really a continuing, concerted effort to discourage teams from signing free agents. The attitude, in effect, is 'don't waste your time signing somebody, fellas'—that's the nuts and bolts of it. And the more this goes on, the less attractive it becomes to a team to try and sign someone else in the future."[46]

The Malone case was a proxy war between the league and its players. Within a week the special master issued his decision: one term was invalidated, the rest stayed. Fleisher and Katz had won. The Rockets had a decision to make and it was looking favorable to Katz.

Within a week of the decision, Moses was a Sixer: Malone was traded for Caldwell Jones and the Cleveland Cavaliers' number one draft choice in the next year's draft. Katz had said that both Jones and the pick were untouchable days earlier.[47] "When I want something, I go and get it," Katz said after the trade was announced.[48]

Basketball aside, by signing Malone the 76ers were undercutting the NBA's argument about difficulties for the league and proving Fleisher's point. Fleisher had no intention of saving teams from themselves. A week earlier, Katz, outspoken about the economic problems of the NBA, said the league was not making money. It was insane. Drossos said after the Malone deal was finalized, "How can we as a league tell the world, the players, and the fans that we're in financial trouble when one of our partners, who was apparently sane at the time, offers a player $13 million and gives up a draft choice and another quality player worth $20 million? How can you explain doing that unless somebody is holding a gun at your head? I don't blame the players and the Players Association for laughing when we say we're losing money."[49] The truth was, Katz told the *New York Times*, "I'd rather lose a few dollars and win than make a few dollars and lose." Fleisher's point that it was not the players' job to save owners from themselves was cemented when Katz signed Malone. Though expensive, the Sixers were now the favorites to win the championship—finally—the following season. "I think this will make me a better player, playing on a team where I'm not the only star," Malone said, speaking to reporters at a Phillies game a few days after the signing. "It's the Doc's [Julius Erving] show and I'm just going to enjoy the show. I'm not coming here to take over nothing."[50]

After Malone signed, other dominos fell into place. Bernard King signed a free-agent deal with the New York Knicks to leave the Golden State Warriors. The league claimed it was in real financial trouble, regularly citing the teams that were likely to fold and the possibility of problems for the league moving forward, but teams were continuing to sign players and were willing to spend exorbitant amounts of money to make their teams better.

• • •

Four days after Malone's signing with the Sixers, the league and the union got a response on the legality of the NBA's salary moderation proposal and whether it violated the *Robertson* settlement. Special Master Kingman Brewster, who oversaw the *Robertson* settlement in court, made a confusing determination. He held that while the NBA's *proposed* cap was not a violation, if it was implemented it certainly would be.

First, Brewster noted that the owners' salary moderation proposal itself was not illegal—it was simply a proposal. Brewster held that "the NBA argues with some merit . . . that all that is before me is a proposal, which by itself cannot violate anything."[51] The NBPA had argued that if the proposal was allowed, the NBA could and would attempt to force the plan by asserting an impasse over it. Brewster did not buy it, saying, "Although much has been made of the possibility of the NBA unilaterally imposing the Salary Budget Cap, they

The Moses Signing

have not done so, and I have no factual basis for inferring their ultimate intentions."

While the proposal itself was okay, Brewster also said, however, that, "if given effect by the collective bargaining agreement or otherwise" the salary moderation proposal "would violate the purpose, structure and some of the explicit positions of the Robertson Settlement Agreement."[52] Brewster was saying that the *Robertson* settlement could be modified to meet the NBA's proposal, but that would require the agreement of the players in writing and judicial approval of the class. So, the NBA couldn't implement it unilaterally.

Brewster's decision recognized that the parties could reach an agreement on the cap. Brewster said, "Much has been made of the unshakeable opposition of the Players to the Salary Budget Cap and their assertion that they would never agree to it either in collective bargaining or otherwise. I can take their assertions at face value, but I cannot possibly say there might not arise some circumstance in the future in which they might decide differently and they would be free to do so."[53] Brewster was not going to assume that Fleisher's initial position in the first negotiation was his only one.

The NBA declared victory—publicly. After Brewster's decision, the NBA released a statement entitled "NBA Proposal for Salary Moderation Plan Held Legal." In the statement, O'Brien said, "Now that the Special Master has said we can discuss a salary moderation plan, I hope we can proceed with good-faith negotiations with the players association that will lead to a new collective bargaining agreement that is fair to all parties involved."[54] Privately, the NBA was much less bullish. In a telex to the owners by Granik after the decision, he said, "In essence the Special Master has ruled that the NBA may seek to obtain agreement from the players with respect to a salary moderation plan, but the implementation of such a plan without consent of the players would violate the *Robertson* settlement agreement . . . The Labor Relations Committee will be considering the ramifications of this decision."[55] Fleisher said, "It's ludicrous for the NBA to take the position that Special Master Brewster approved their salary cap proposal. It's directly opposite."[56] The NBA could only get the cap if it got the players to agree to it—they couldn't impose it no matter what happened. They were back to the drawing board—strategically, if nothing else.

Although the league and its players were far apart, neither side believed a player strike was imminent. After the Brewster decision, Fleisher reiterated that a strike vote had not been taken and that none was planned. "It's always a possibility, but we're not even there yet," Fleisher said. The NBA agreed, believing that the lack of an agreement would not stop the season. As NBA spokesman Alex Sachare said, "When there is no contract, there's always the possibility (of a strike) but three out of the last four years player have played with no contract."[57]

• • •

On September 9, just days after the special master's decision, the NBA and the NBPA met in New York for the first time in weeks. The meeting was tense. There were no pleasantries this time. Fleisher demanded that the NBA remove the salary moderation proposal. Stern refused—stating that the proposal remained on the table and urged the players to consider it. Fleisher, in a stronger legal position than he had been a few weeks earlier, said that the players were prepared to file an unfair labor practice charge, that the owners could not implement such a proposal, and that "we will never agree to any form of salary cap under any circumstances."[58] Fleisher knew what was coming down the pike—that the owners would argue there was an impasse and implement—and he wanted to stake out his position early.

Stern was clear that no deal would be reached unless the players accepted the economic problems the NBA was facing. Fleisher said the players could negotiate over issues that related to improving the economic situation, but he would like to know the specifics. Stern advised that they were compiling that data but there could be no doubt that the NBA was losing money.

Fleisher said he believed the NBA was "crying wolf" and that the players would not give back what they had achieved, even if it cost them jobs. Fleisher told Stern that if teams folded "so be it—the players are not prepared to give up what they have gained to protect 50 jobs." Stern suggested the players make a proposal that would save the NBA money. Fleisher responded, "Get better owners, with more money, who market better." Stern said that in light of the economic situation the NBA was in, the players' proposals were "embarrassing."[59]

Stern said that the league needed to chart a course. Fleisher shot back, "We did in 1976." Stern said that the current NBA was different, that pro basketball was not healthy and had gotten worse. Stern said, "Maybe there shouldn't be collective bargaining, maybe your Players should get everything they can from individual negotiation."[60] Fleisher, in a unique position to accept such a proposal, said, "This is a possibility."

At the end of the session, Stern said, "We are not at impasse but we're getting there." Fleisher's response was not encouraging: "The players have no intention of changing their style of living to bail out Donald Sterling."[61] The parties planned to meet again the following week—the players planned to bring their executive committee and the owners the Labor Relations Committee.

As Stern said of negotiations in the fall of 1982, "We think we are going into this from two different perspectives and we have a gap. A very large one."[62]

• • •

On September 20, 1982, professional football shut down. Three weeks into the NFL season, Ed Garvey announced that the NFLPA was going on strike in order to get a percentage of the gross profits of the NFL. After the first midseason strike in baseball history in 1981, this strike was the first time that an NFL regular-season game was lost to a labor dispute. The NFLPA did not have a proper strike fund to keep players afloat due to Garvey's spending on his sports federation, and the union hoped that three paychecks would be enough to hold players over.[63]

After a failed strike in 1974, Garvey believed the union was much stronger in 1982. "Our communications are far superior than they were then," he said. "The input from players is better than before, our staff is large and experienced enough to handle essential contacts." Most importantly, Garvey said, "The key point is, we have the right issue. All the players can see how much is involved . . . they can see a percentage of the gross will help virtually every player. If it means strike, it means strike. We're not going to get it unless the owners believe the players will strike. No one gives up money or power for the fun of it."[64]

Garvey was committed to the percentage of gross. The NFL was as unwilling to agree after a strike as they were before. The NFL's negotiator, Jack Donlan, said, "The percentage of the gross concept is alien to American business. It would turn over control of the business to the players. The owners believe pro football is the most successful of all sports entertainment businesses because of the business decisions made by the owners over the years, and the owners don't want to give up the right to make those decisions."[65]

Neither side was able to move. "Garvey didn't try to pull the wool over our eyes," Donlan said. "He was very predictable. The things he said were the things he kept saying. We kept waiting for his real position and it turned out to be the first one."[66]

The owners blamed Garvey for the strike and believed that when he was done the game would come back. "I think when Mr. Ed Garvey wants a settlement," Hugh Culverhouse, owner of the Tampa Bay Buccaneers, said, "You'll have settlement."[67]

11

The Big Item, October 1982

At some point, there was no reason to be arguing
about what the facts were.

—DAVID STERN

Though the NBA had attempted to maintain an aggressive posture
publicly and at the table with Fleisher, the Brewster decision was a
huge blow. The NBA was stuck. The owners could propose the cap,
but if Fleisher rejected it, what could they do? They couldn't implement their proposal even if they got to a legal impasse because the
court would not allow it. They needed Fleisher to agree and he had
been clear that he would not.

As a result, the NBA did something they probably did not anticipate doing—they withdrew their salary moderation proposal.[1] As
O'Brien wrote in a memo to NBA owners, general managers, and
team counsel in late September 1982, "The Labor Relations/Insurance
Committee was advised by counsel that, although the NBA was not
prohibited from proposing a Salary Moderation Plan, and the Players Association could legally agree to such a Plan, the Special Master's
decision . . . made it unlikely that fruitful negotiations could be conducted at this time. Accordingly, the Committee decided to set aside
the proposal of a Salary Moderation Plan and to instruct counsel to
withdraw without prejudice the NBA's unfair labor practice charge
against the Players Association."[2]

Without proposing a cap, what was the NBA going to do? They decided to aggressively pursue other proposals, a series of them, that

were meant to identify considerable areas to cut costs or raise revenue. Some were already in their initial set of proposals and some were new.

O'Brien, in a note to owners outlining the new strategy, said the plan was charted "in light of the fact that the Players' position effectively precluded serious negotiations over the Salary Moderation Plan." As a result, O'Brien said that the NBA had decided to "supplement . . . proposals in two ways, as a further effort to cut player costs; first, by seeking the complete elimination of all collectively bargained benefits (pension, severance, and disability, health and life insurance); and second, by requesting the return to the NBA of certain ancillary commercial rights, such as the right to require the players to wear basketball shoes selected by the teams as part of the team uniform (and the consequent right of the teams to enter into licensing arrangements on that basis with shoe manufacturers)."[3]

Specifically, the league proposed to:

1) reduce roster size from twelve players to ten;

2) require players to pay for their own medical and pension plans;

3) eliminate guaranteed contracts, deferred payments, no-trade clauses, incentive bonuses, and severance payments;

4) prohibit renegotiated pacts;

5) prohibit players from owning interest in a club or subsidiary;

6) allow clubs to extend contracts one year under the same terms if a player is injured or refuses to play;

7) allow the league to increase the number of playoff teams from twelve to sixteen and total playoff games allowed per team from twenty-four to twenty-eight;

8) allow clubs the right to control sneaker endorsements, either through the league or by receiving a percentage from each player; and

9) require players to fly coach instead of first class.[4]

In addition to cutting costs, these new proposals served another purpose. After losing at the special master, the NBA wanted to get away from issues that were covered by the *Robertson* settlement—where what the NBA could do was limited and subject to oversight. The new set of proposals they were making were unrelated to player movement, meant to be unquestionably mandatory subjects of bargaining, outside of the realm of the *Robertson* settlement, and thus, the league could implement these proposals if they were unable to get the players to agree and had reached an impasse. They were also meant to be offensive to the union, so noxious in fact that it would push the union back to its salary moderation plan, or some other version of a salary cap, as being a more workable alternative. Both sides agreed that these were the most drastic proposals ever made by the owners.[5]

The owners chose to articulate their new posture at their next negotiation on September 16, 1982, about a week after the special master's decision. The meeting was held at the New York Hilton and was a full house on both sides. Larry O'Brien and the owners on the Labor Committee attended the September 16 negotiation—the first time they were present—in order to advise the players of the new negotiating posture.[6] For the players, they had their full committee as well—Fleisher, Grantham, Lanier, Bridgeman, Brown, Mix, and Suns forward Maurice Lucas.[7]

O'Brien began the meeting by stating that even though the owners were there, negotiations would be chaired by the staff, namely Stern. Then Abe Pollin, the owner of the Washington Bullets and the head of the Labor Relations Committee, began to speak.

Pollin had been an owner in the NBA for decades—part of the original group that brought the Baltimore Bullets to Washington DC, in the 1960s. By 1982, with decades in the league, he was wistful—concerned that as the league had gotten more expensive, he was having difficulty keeping up. After the dust settled on the offseason in 1981, Pollin said, "Now is not the time to be the owner." As the *Washington Post* reported, after the Lakers' signing of Magic Johnson and Mitch Kupchak, a Pollin favorite, in 1981, Pollin was putting his ownership of the Bullets at issue: "Abe has said that he is reevaluating his entire commercial life . . . He's accomplished an awful lot in sports . . . it's a very deep and traumatic decision to make and he doesn't want to make it without a great deal of thought."[8] Abe Pollin's family would eventually sell the team in 2010, after his death in 2009.

Pollin told Fleisher and the players that the NBA wanted to negotiate a contract with the players in good faith, they wanted all of the teams in the league to survive, but they needed to find ways to save money. Pollin said that the salary moderation proposal would be "set aside," but that all of the other proposals the NBA were making were not only on the table but required. Pollin said he did not believe that setting aside the cap would mean a smooth negotiation, and that the NBA recognized that it would likely lead to a more contentious cycle. After laying out the NBA's new stance he said that "the NBA anticipate[d] a long and tough negotiation and that the League [was] prepared for it."[9]

Fleisher said he was "shocked" by the new proposals and was unsure how to proceed in negotiations. He believed there was a philosophical difference between the NBA and its players. Pollin responded that the league needed to operate as a business and in an economically viable fashion. Fleisher countered Pollin, as he often did, by saying there was nothing in the current system that stopped teams from acting as businesses, and that it was fully within each team's control to decide how much to spend.

O'Brien said that the league's losses were a "joint problem" and that the league had no intention of continuing or increasing them. Lanier jumped in and asked an obvious question: Just two weeks after Moses Malone had signed a gigantic contract, how could Philadelphia afford to pay Malone $2 million a year if the losses were so bad? Stern said that the league revenue was not high enough to cover those expenses. Bob Batterman, then a young Proskauer attorney who would later be known as "lockout Bob" for his penchant for locking out players in the NFL, said there must be player "give backs."[10] Fleisher said that the issue was not player costs but underperforming teams, such as Stepien's Cavaliers and Sterling's Clippers. Both sides were talking past each other.

Grantham asked if the league would return givebacks if the NBA stabilized; Batterman said to make the proposal and they would consider it. At one point, O'Brien asked Fleisher if it was the players' position to not want to negotiate "toward the stability of the league, but simply to increase player benefits."[11] Fleisher, always unafraid to take an unpopular position, said that was a reasonable view. Fleisher ended the meeting. "We are not going to get anywhere today!" he exclaimed. He had heard the owners' position but it was not well received.

The NBA's proposals were nonstarters. Many of them had been in the NBA's initial proposals, the one Lanier said he expected from the "Neanderthals," but in light of the salary moderation proposal neither side had focused on them—now they were. To the players, these proposals were insulting. "If you look at the proposals from our viewpoint, you can see how ridiculous they are. They are trying to take back what we have gained over 23 years," Grantham said.[12] Fleisher agreed, stating, "It is inconceivable that they are serious that any union would accept the elimination of the benefits they are asking for."[13]

Some of these proposals were not only shortsighted but not functional. For example, the NBA proposed decreasing the number of roster spots per team from twelve to ten, which may have appealed to the accountants, but would have been a disaster to implement. Stern said that the proposal was intended to save money, and the NBA believed that going to a ten-man roster could save between $3.6 and $11 million league wide. (In fact, in their bargaining notes, the NBA negotiators had gone through every team in the league looking at minutes played by the eleventh and twelfth man on each roster.) Fleisher said the proposal was a disaster and not realistic. He also said that NBA doctors believed decreased roster size increased the likelihood of player injury.[14]

Stern lined up a few owners behind it, mostly the old hawks. James Fitzgerald of the Bucks said he would cut his roster to ten. Sam Schulman of the Supersonics, who wanted replacement players, said he would cut his roster to eleven, the number of guaranteed contracts they had. And, of course, Angelo Drossos of the Spurs voiced strong support for this proposal, saying, "There is no longer a lineup of eager buyers waiting for the opportunity to invest in professional basketball. Something is going to have to give . . . we have 15 guaranteed players on our roster, but if we decide to go to 10, I'll waive, cut and eat contracts. That's what every team is going to have to do."[15] While some owners talked tough, the support beyond that small group was thin. Harold Katz did not think the proposal was likely to go through, stating, "It is my opinion, and only my opinion, that we'll probably start the season with the 12-man roster."[16]

Beyond ownership, everyone was against it. As the *New York Times* reported, "Most coaches, general managers, team doctors and trainers are against a reduction to 10-man rosters." Jack Ramsay, then the coach of the Portland Trail Blazers, was against it, stating, "I'm certainly not for it and our owner is not for it. Going with 10 players would be hard." Sixers coach Billy Cunningham was more blunt: "I don't know how they expect us to practice with 10 players. Somebody always has a bump or a bruise, and if one guy sits out, we can't scrimmage."[17] Even Red Auerbach did not agree with it, stating, "I've been against it all along. I can see their point, but you can do other things. I don't approve anything that would affect the game. It would make a mockery of the injury list. Every team would start throwing two or three guys on there."[18] The criticism of the roster-limits proposal drew the ire of the league office. In a memo to owners, O'Brien reminded them that the league office would control the narrative saying, "You should be aware that last week a member of the Labor Relations Committee was reprimanded for comments made to a reporter about the NBA's proposals regarding roster size. You are advised that, henceforth, *indiscretions of this nature will result in the imposition of substantial penalties.*"[19]

O'Brien did not want to hear the snark from the peanut gallery, or read it in the papers, but it was clear that some of the proposals were duds. In an update to owners discussing the new course of action, O'Brien said after the session on the sixteenth, "It is clear to me that negotiations with the Players will be difficult. It is essential that our negotiating team, and the proposals they are asserting on our behalf, continue to have the full support of every team."[20]

• • •

The season tip-off on October 29 loomed large, and it remained unclear whether the NBA would start the season without a finalized deal. The NBA had entered the season in 1977 and in 1980 without an agreement, but this time was different—the stakes were higher. Just as the players were happy to maintain the status quo, it was the owners who wanted to pressure the players to have the deal completed before the start of the season. If there was no deal, would the owners lock out the players? Would the owners try to simply implement their proposals? If they did, would it lead to a work stoppage by the

The Big Item

players?[21] After the owners laid out their new position, the rhetoric and the action on both sides heated up.

Though high-profile players like Malone and Bernard King had signed big-money deals, many players remained unsigned late into the offseason. A week before training camp was set to open, fifty-one of the sixty-four veteran free agents were unsigned, including Lakers star Bob McAdoo and Spurs guard Johnny Moore, who had led the league in assists. It wasn't just veterans either—when camps opened, only three of the first round choices from June's draft had signed and only Dominique Wilkins of Georgia, the third overall pick, signed from the top fifteen players drafted.[22]

Fleisher was concerned that the NBA was colluding to suppress demand for players. "In my 20 years of being associated with pro basketball," he said, "this is the first time I saw so few first round picks unsigned so close to the opening of the camps. Tied together with about 50 free agents who are still unsigned, the training camps will surely not be representative with the best pro basketball can provide."[23] Fleisher did not make claims of collusion lightly. In 1980, when several first-round picks were not signed in mid-September and calls of collusion were loud, Fleisher tamped them down. "There's no collusion," he said then, chalking the delay in signing up to overaggressive agents.[24] Now, Fleisher believed it to be coordinated. "It is clear that this is a concerted effort on the part of club owners to thwart free agency and to dramatically reduce salaries of rookie contracts," he said. "It's also definitely tied to the current collective-bargaining negotiations and is meant to intimidate players into panic signings. This has not happened."[25] *Sports Illustrated* speculated that the owners "may have already begun their own salary moderation plan by not bidding on free agents."[26]

Granik publicly countered Fleisher's accusation: "I think such a statement by Mr. Fleisher is outrageous. If players have not signed as quickly as in the past, it is not the product of any concerted action, but perhaps because NBA teams do not have the funds to meet the ever-escalating demands of the players involved."[27] Bullets general manager Bob Ferry said this was simply a market correction, stating, "There are a lot of good reliable players out there, but not too many who are going to turn your team around." Within a week of Fleisher's outcry, however, players began to sign in larger numbers, including James Worthy, the NBA's top draft pick, who signed with the Lakers on September 29.[28] Worthy said, "It's a relief knowing it's all over. One of my main concerns was to start training camp on time."[29] The Pistons signed Johnny Long, their top scorer who remained unsigned, to a multiyear contract on October 4. Later than usual, but the players were starting to sign.

• • •

Unable to convince the players of the cap or of their draconian proposals, as the season approached, the league publicly raised the pressure. Tired of negotiation, in October, Harry Mangurian, of the Celtics said the league would implement its proposals if there was no deal within thirty days. Stern, though he declined to comment on the rumors of implementation, did say the situation was very serious, and that "lawyers for the league [felt] the owners [didn't] have to honor the expired contract."[30] They were trying to use the start of the season to gain negotiating leverage over the players. O'Brien said, "This isn't garbage time. I think the owners feel very strongly that this situation has to be resolved before October 29. The ultimate responsibility for the start of the season rests with the players."[31] Fleisher saw through the maneuver. "They just can't do that," he said. "[Implementation] would be an unfair labor practice unless we were at a complete impasse and weren't bargaining in good faith. But we are and we'll keep bargaining away and negotiating."[32]

Fleisher was right. Even though the NBA was talking tough in the press about implementing its proposals no matter what the players wanted, it was likely not something they were lawfully entitled to do. Stern, Granik, and Bettman knew that to be true. Even though the collective bargaining agreement had expired the previous June, when such agreements expire the basic terms and conditions live on. As a result, the same rules that had been in place before—minimum salaries, roster composition, free agency, flying first class—all of the problems that caused escalating labor costs, continued. Otherwise, every union would have to negotiate from scratch each time the contract expired, placing them at a huge disadvantage.

As a result, any changes the NBA made unilaterally, even the ones the league wanted, would likely be unlawful. Though the parties had been negotiating, they were certainly not at a lawful impasse in early October—the standard is quite high, and to reach it, parties must exhaust the value of continued negotiation, which was certainly not the case here. Pollin had said in mid-September that they expected a long negotiation and were introducing *new* proposals. Fleisher was unconcerned, saying, "We're going to continue to negotiate and we hope to reach an agreement. If we don't, and the owners try to enforce unilaterally these demands, then there are all sorts of ramifications."[33]

If the NBA tried to make its changes—force players to fly coach, decrease roster size, or the rest—it would violate federal labor law and be an unfair labor practice under the National Labor Relations Act. Additionally, any attempt to unilaterally alter terms and conditions of employment for the players would, in addition to being unlawful, trigger massive economic consequences. The NBA, if found to have not been at a lawful impasse, would have to undo the changes and compensate players for the damages. It could even trigger an injunction request from the NLRB. No matter how bellicose their rhetoric, these were not consequences Stern and company were seeking.

However, just because it was unlawful doesn't meant the owners were not seriously considering doing it or happily willing to tell the press they were doing so, for a number of reasons. First, the press and the public's understanding of the nuances of labor law (and its patience for it) is limited. Also, it was possible that the owners' unilateral implementation, though it would almost certainly be overturned later, could be used to sew seeds of problems within the NBPA. If the owners did implement, it would take time for the NBPA or the NLRB to act to remedy it, and though the players were frustrated, they may have gotten tired of flying coach while waiting for the NLRB to deliberate and push Fleisher to a deal.

Privately, the NBA was preparing for the possibility of implementing their proposals and the reality that that decision could provoke a strike. On October 6, O'Brien sent a memo to the owners and asked them to prepare for the upcoming Board of Governors meeting in two weeks, where the "primary subject" of discussion would be the status of bargaining. "This may well be the most important meeting of the Board in a number of years, as the action taken will likely have a great impact upon the future course of the league."[34]

O'Brien said, "As the Players Association remains totally intransigent in its refusal to consider our various proposals for cost reductions, we must be prepared for the possibility of a players' strike. In the event of a strike one of the most important issues confronting us will be whether the League should continue to operate with replacement players." O'Brien asked teams to look into the impact of a strike, the use of replacement players, and the "degree of cooperation you are likely to receive from your arena with regard to potential problems from other unions involved."[35] O'Brien was clear, however: "In no event should any team at this time enter into any agreements with replacement players."[36]

Fleisher, fundamentally was unimpressed with the employers' threats of implementation. "I don't anticipate it will happen," Fleisher said to the *Boston Globe*. "I paid no attention to that when I heard it, and we have no intention of operating with a gun to our heads. If they were to implement those things, they'd have to face labor charges and the wrath of the players."[37]

Rather than frighten players, the NBA's threats angered them and pushed them closer to a strike—or at least threatening one. There were reports that the players felt as if the league was daring them to strike by threatening to decrease roster size, and they believed, according to the *Los Angeles Times*, "If it comes to that they are likely to accept the dare."[38] O'Brien said he had heard that the owners wanted a strike. Stern said, "We don't have any owners who want a strike for the sake of a strike. But it's going to be relatively painless for some of them. If you're running at a loss, then a strike could actually prove to be a profitable experience."[39]

• • •

On October 8, two days after O'Brien asked his owners to look into the feasibility of replacement players, Fleisher said, for the first time, that he was prepared to discuss "the big item." The cap. At negotiations at the Berkshire Place Hotel, Fleisher made the reversal to a small group—Fleisher and Grantham for the players; Stern, Granik, Bettman, and Batterman for the owners. The NBA began the meeting by providing revised proposals. Fleisher was not interested. He said, "Since the league contends that the players are receiving too much in benefits and salaries, relative to revenues, the Players are prepared to discuss proposals aimed at limiting the amount of money payable to the Players, provided the Players are entitled to a share of gross revenues."[40] With the NFL shutdown over a percentage of gross, Fleisher was prepared to discuss it. The players had been thinking about this for a while. Grantham had been going around to the locker rooms discussing the issue, trying to see where the players were.

Stern was surprised by Fleisher's sudden change of heart—the week before Fleisher was pushing to go through the players proposals. "We were under the impression that [you were] not prepared to have such discussions, but we are prepared to do so," Stern said.[41] Batterman said the parties should negotiate on two tracks—on both the cap proposal and the new proposals the NBA had presented that day. Fleisher had no interest in this, saying the revised proposals were "a bunch of bullshit."

Stern and Fleisher kept the focus on the cap. The negotiations in that session moved quickly in terms of concepts. Stern attempted to clarify Fleisher's position that the union would be open to a cap if it was tied to revenues. Fleisher said that was part of it, but there was an additional facet—the deal would have to focus not only on a percentage of revenue but also on revenue sharing, to help the weaker teams as well. Stern and Granik said that in their view there would be two sources of payment to players: salaries and "something" to make up for any difference between negotiated salaries and the formula they agreed on.[42]

Fleisher raised a possibility that the NBA had been considering—and frankly approved something similar at the Board of Governors in June—that each team would put a fixed percentage of its team revenues into a pool that would be divided into twenty-three equal parts and would be the maximum (and minimum) payable to players on each team.[43] Every team would spend the same. Stern nixed it, saying that it would be hard to get certain teams, especially the larger markets, to agree to give up a fixed percentage of revenue to be shared, or to share their revenue rates.

Stern then asked Fleisher a reasonable question: Did it matter to him how the NBA raised the money for the players to be paid? It stood to reason that how the money was raised was management's concern, and beyond the scope of Fleisher's authority. Fleisher was too smart for that—he said yes. If he was getting into a game of limiting player salaries, he was going to be involved in how it was calculated, too. He also reiterated that he wanted the NBA to allocate a certain amount of money to make sure that all teams were competitive; Fleisher said that "any plan must help Utah, San Diego or Kansas City," the weakest franchises, presumably those actually in danger of going under.[44] If the proposal was about simply limiting salary, Fleisher was not interested.

After a series of questions and answers, Stern and Fleisher figured out next steps. Stern and Fleisher agreed to make a written proposal, with both handling certain pieces. Stern outlined the five questions that remained to be answered:

1) Percentage of revenues payable to players in salary and benefits

2) How the NBA raises and allocates the money payable to players

3) How much each team must pay to players

4) Maximum (limit on how much each team can pay to players)

5) What happens to the difference between what is actually paid in salary and benefits and what the players are entitled to.[45]

The NBA was to make proposals for one through four, Fleisher would handle number five. The parties agreed to meet again the following week. After several months, there was progress.

When the parties met again, on October 15, both sides brought their full group. Fleisher had Grantham, Lanier, Mix, Bridgeman, and Quinn. Stern was flanked by O'Brien and a number of owners—Alan Cohen of the Nets, Pollin of the Bullets, and Larry Weinberg of the Portland Trailblazers. O'Brien started the meeting by saying that in light of the progress made at the last session he had appointed the group before him, who were "truly representative," to pursue these discussions in advance of the Board of Governors meeting set for October 20. Angelo Drossos was not present.

Stern summarized the last session, saying that the question was "whether the parties could agree upon a plan which could help con-

The Big Item

trol salaries, as an item of expense, and at the same time enable the Players to share in the NBA's projected growth." Fleisher confirmed that the players were interested in the same discussions and that he was interested in a plan that would allocate equally among *teams* a portion of revenues which must be spent on player salaries and benefits.[46] He wanted to make sure that the smaller market teams could and would be forced to spend.

Now that they had agreed to discuss a broad concept—a limitation on salary in exchange for a percentage of the revenues the league brought in—the parties began to move toward basic themes that would make up what the cap would become. The basic features—much of which still exists today—came together quickly. *What would constitute gross revenues?* Abe Pollin of the Bullets proposed that gross revenue should consist primarily of gate receipts and television revenues. *How much would teams be required to spend?* They agreed that teams would have to spend some minimum on players as well. *If players retained a free market, and teams didn't spend, what would happen if there was a shortfall in what players were entitled?* They also understood that if there was a shortfall, the teams would contribute the deficiency in accordance with a formula of some sort. Pollin said that such a proposal would keep teams competitive; Lanier said that if the minimum was high enough, it could be a good proposal.[47] The two sides were making progress.

Fleisher was more hesitant: if the percentage of gross was too low, would there be cuts? Stern said there would be grandfathering of existing contracts. Fleisher said that he would need projections of the revenues for the league before engaging in such a plan. He asked if the NBA had undertaken any plans; Stern said no firm projections had been done. They had. Quinn asked if there had been any cable projections done; Cohen said that they had done projections through 1990, and the players could see them. After a caucus, Stern told the players that the league's projected revenue was $250 million, and Stern introduced their cable consultant Paul Bortz, who confirmed what Stern had said.

While the parties were making progress, Bridgeman asked if the players would be involved in decision making on an ownership level. It was a reasonable question—under the proposal they were considering, the players would be semi-partners with the owners. Stern responded, "Definitely no . . . the players will not be our partners."[48]

So, how to proceed? They were two weeks from the start of the season and just a few days from the Board of Governors meeting. Fleisher said he needed financial information to evaluate, formulate, and consider any proposal. Pollin said he needed to report to the Board of Governors and asked whether they should recommend to continue these discussions. Fleisher said they should. Stern said, "Time is of the essence."[49]

After the meeting there was, for the first time, hope a deal was in reach. Bulls owner John Kovler believed it could even come before the start of the season.[50] However, despite the modification and the optimism, the league kept one foot in the more draconian proposals it had been pushing. It was possible that Fleisher was playing possum—considering the proposal to avoid implementation before the start of the season. Once the season started, Fleisher's power rose tremendously. On October 18, Fleisher sent Stern a letter requesting detailed financial records.

The Board of Governors meeting on October 20 was the owners' last chance before the season started to implement its proposals. Though Fleisher was willing to negotiate over the cap, there was not yet a deal with the players. At the meeting, Stern was preparing his constituency to consider implementing the owners' proposal. Stern's notes for that meeting reflect: "Counsel is satisfied that we have negotiated fully with respect to the subjects of collective bargaining so that, if the Board were to instruct on October 20, we would announce to the Players Association, in the context of collective bargaining, that, based upon the impasse, we were unilaterally implementing our last contract offer (or at least some components of it.)" However, they were also confident that if they did implement, "it [was] likely that such unilateral implementation would result in a strike by the players."[51]

O'Brien advised the Board of Governors as to the status of negotiations and the progress that had been made. In response the Board of Governors passed a resolution allowing the league to implement its proposals upon reaching impasse. After such a motion was approved, Stern advised the Board of Governors as to why they were being recommended, and he explained the proposed cap in detail. He also, along with Paul Bortz, the league's cable consultant, explained how their proposed salary cap would impact different types of teams. However, they also passed a resolution in the case of a strike—to allow teams to borrow with the franchise as collateral in the event of a strike.[52]

Stern had another matter to be approved by the Board of Governors. He had been working on identifying a uniform game-timing format. He was not simply a labor negotiator—he was trying to build a business. Uniform game times would allow teams to increase revenue and to make the local broadcasts more professional. It also brought more control under the league office. Such approval was unanimous.[53]

As the league emerged from the Board of Governors meeting, it said two things: the league reaffirmed its commitment to bargaining over the proposed cap while also threatening to implement its proposals. The Board of Governors passed a resolution that the NBA was at an impasse with its players, and that they could implement their proposals immediately or "defer implementation of the items specified above, on a week-to-week basis during the pendency of negotiations," for the next thirty days. They also passed a resolution allowing the Commissioner to impose a fine of up to $250,000 "for any unauthorized statement by any Governor or employee of any member relating to the current collective bargaining negotiations with the Players Association."[54]

O'Brien released a statement to the press: "In the past two weeks there has been an important development in the collective bargaining negotiations between the NBA and the Players Association. For the first time, we have engaged in discussions with the players concerning an entirely new approach to the way in which player compensation is structured."[55] He continued, "Although we hope these negotiations will be successful, the Board of Governors reaffirmed its resolve to implement a variety of cost-saving measures in the event of an impasse with the players. . . . We expect that within the next week we will be better able to judge whether these discussions may be productive. If it appears that they are not likely to succeed, we will proceed to implement the cost-saving measures."[56] O'Brien sent the statement as a telex to all NBA owners, general managers, head coaches, and team counsel, with a reminder about the potential for fines, saying, "Please be reminded that no one, with the exception of me or someone designated by me, is permitted to publicly comment on our negotiations with the players. If you are contacted by the press, you should respond with 'no comment' or by reference to the following press release . . . You are requested to inform all members of your staff of this directive. Your total participation is both anticipated and appreciated."[57]

Fleisher, who was authorized to speak publicly, shut it down quickly: "We have discussed some things but they are far away from being decided on. I'm bothered by the commissioner's statements because it seems like on one hand he's trying to be very hopeful and on the other hand he's threatening us."[58]

Regardless of O'Brien's statements, Fleisher proposed a solution with the season approaching. "We're willing to continue to negotiate into the season," Fleisher said. "We have done that in the past two or three collective bargaining agreements and we see no reason why we can't continue in good faith to bargain the issues to a satisfactory conclusion."[59]

The parties met again on October 27, two days before the start of the season. Stern began the meeting by giving the players Arthur Anderson's financial audits for the 1980–81 and 1981–82 seasons. Stern also provided a proposal called the *Guaranteed Compensation Plan*.[60]

The *Guaranteed Compensation Plan* was a breakthrough. It was the first version of the salary cap that was fixed to league revenues, different from the salary moderation plan the NBA had been pushing before. "The following is a description of the principal features of a plan which could have the effect of stabilizing the financial situation in the NBA and allowing all teams to compete for players, while at the same time permitting all players to share in the growth of the league by guaranteeing them a percentage of the NBA's gross revenues," the document began.[61]

The biggest sell of Stern's proposal for the players was that they would be guaranteed to receive a fixed percentage of gross revenue. Previous contracts would be grandfathered and teams would not be forced to shed salary.[62] Stern offered Fleisher and the players 40 percent of gross revenues up to $250,000,000 and 30 percent of all revenues in excess of $250,000,000. This was similar to Kasten's proposal a few months earlier. The maximum team salary would be 1/23 of the fixed

The Big Item

percentages of revenues. No team would be permitted to go above the cap in salary or benefits. Coupled with the maximum was a minimum team salary—equal to 50 percent of the capped amount.[63] If there was a shortfall (i.e., if the salaries did not meet the minimums required), there would be an assessment to pay the players. The NBA categorized the proposal as ending up at a cap worth about $2.8 million per team. Fleisher was dubious about those calculations. He said, based on the previous year's revenues, the salary would only be $2.1 million per team, leaving teams with little or no money to bid for free agents or rookies. All but five teams were over that rate.[64] The breakthrough in the new proposal was not that it would be agreed to by the union, it certainly would not. But for the first time, the cap—conceptually— the NBA was putting forward something worth considering.

Having understood the employers' proposal, both parties also used the session to focus on the biggest issue that would be impacting revenue moving forward—television. Stern asked if the PA had hired a cable consultant, Fleisher hadn't but was looking at a few. Fleisher asked if the NBA's proposed definition of revenue from television included pay, cable, theaters, and over-the-air. Stern said that it did, and that it was intended to include "any mode by which people view the game."[65]

Once they dug in and began to discuss the proposal, Stern moved toward an additional concession—he began to soften on the idea of a "hard" cap. Fleisher attacked the concept by asking questions. Fleisher—both in bargaining and in public—would identify issues (and the flaws in the other side's position) by citing specific examples of players who would be harmed (or benefitted) by the issue being discussed. It was very effective. Fleisher asked a few questions about Stern's proposal. It didn't hurt that he named them after three of the league's biggest (and future) stars. Fleisher asked:

1) how a team at the cap would sign its rookies if they were over the cap (which he called the Ralph Sampson problem);

2) how a team at the cap would replace a retiring superstar (which he called the Kareem Abdul-Jabbar problem); and

3) how a team at the cap retains its superstar who becomes a free agent (which he called the Larry Bird problem).

Fleisher's brilliance was in identifying the goals of the other side. Each one of these problems was of particular interest to *owners* who, while excited about the possibility of decreased costs through a cap, would still want to have a competitive team on the floor. The Celtics would not want to lose Bird, the Lakers would not want to be hamstrung in replacing Abdul-Jabbar, and all of the bad teams would want to be able to sign Sampson. Fleisher framed the problem brilliantly.

Having raised the questions a few sessions later, on November 10, Stern asked Fleisher how he would address those circumstances. Stern asked the question, but said, "Fleisher should assume that the NBA's position is that there are no exceptions to the team salary limitation," a hard cap with no movement. Fleisher had already considered the problems and had solutions. Fleisher said that the Abdul-Jabbar and Bird problems were bigger issues than the Sampson problem. For the Sampson issue, he said "if the minimum were high enough, and if the player could only be subjected to a short-term contract, he could live with a rookie making the minimum."[66] Both sides coalesced around the idea that if a player retired (i.e., the Abdul-Jabbar situation), the team should be allowed to replace them for more than the minimum but less than what the retiring player was earning. With regard to the Bird exception, Fleisher said that continuity for a team is important and that veteran free agents need freedom to negotiate. Though they did not come to an agreement, it was the start of what would become the Bird exception, the most important right under the NBA salary cap system. Fleisher—by virtue of raising perfect examples—had moved the owners off of a deeply frustrating position.

• • •

In the end, the tumultuous off-season ended with basketball on the court. On October 29, 1982, the thirty-seventh NBA season started. Twenty-two of the twenty-three teams were in action on opening night. As the *Washington Post* said, "There are new looks—on the court, where three league MVPs are playing for new teams, on television, since cable will provide most of the national coverage of regular-season games, and in labor negotiations, with the season beginning without a new collective bargaining agreement between the players and management."[67]

The Big Item

Moses Malone, whose signing shocked the league six weeks earlier, started his first game for the 76ers and scored twenty-one points and grabbed seventeen rebounds in a fifteen-point victory over the Knicks at Madison Square Garden.[68] In the preseason Pat Williams, the Sixers' general manager, said, "In last Spring's series against Boston, we were the downtrodden team, David against Goliath. The whole nation was sympathetic to us. Now we're back to being Goliath."[69]

The defending champion Los Angeles Lakers lost at home to the Golden State Warriors. Lakers coach Pat Riley described the concerns about repeating, saying, "There are two major reasons why it's so hard to repeat as champion. First, everyone plays harder against you every night. Games in December become like championship games and it's difficult to sustain that through the playoffs. Second is the mental attitude. The team has to grow closer and form a solidarity." Riley, in assessing his team, said, "We have no weaknesses and our greatest strength is our abundance of talent. We have quality players who can both play and think. We're versatile; we have great quickness, shooting and leaping ability and we have the most dominating center in the game. We are the champions and we aren't giving up anything. All those who want to take our crown know where to find us."[70] O'Brien, at the game to hand out championship rings to the Lakers, assessed the progress in labor negotiations but said that "if there was not further evidence of progress within the next two weeks the owners would arbitrarily implement cost-saving measures without seeking approval from the players."[71] Stepien's Cavaliers, who had lost their last nineteen games of the 1981–82 season, had little hope in the new season. Two players had walked out of training camp. The Cavaliers would lose their first five games and twelve of their first thirteen.[72] Lanier's Bucks were the only team in the NBA not playing opening night. As he started his thirteenth NBA season, potentially his last, the president of the NBPA was hoping that this would be the season in which he finally got that elusive championship. His Bucks—along with the Sixers, Lakers, and Celtics—were the team with the best case to have that hope.

The season began, just as the last one ended, without a collective bargaining agreement in place. Fleisher and Stern agreed to do what they had done in prior negotiations—if a deal could not be reached they would maintain the old agreement in force until a new one was reached, as long as the parties continued to bargain in good faith.[73] The owners had squandered their leverage, but the players were considering a salary cap.

As the season started, the feeling in the media was clear—the NBA had bluffed about its intention of implementing its offer and did not intend to follow through. As Dan Shaughnessy wrote in the *Boston Globe*, "As long as talks continue and the players continue to play without a contract, the owners probably won't bother to implement changes which could provoke a strike or a lawsuit."[74]

• • •

Though they were unable to force the players to agree, the NBA had taken steps to solidify at least two of its troubled franchises—one with a carrot and one with a stick. Slowly but surely the league was getting its house in order.

For the hapless Ted Stepien, the NBA gave a lifeline. On November 18, 1982, Ted Stepien admitted defeat and asked for help in a letter to Commissioner O'Brien. "My proposal," he wrote, "which Harry Mangurian of Boston once suggested I broach, but I was too proud to do so is that the League permit the Cavaliers to receive a first round pick in each of the next three seasons." Stepien could only have so much humility—he blamed the prior Cavs administration for trading picks, and the league for allowing Drossos to steal his coach, calling the first-round picks "a just reparation for the league's silence." Stepien concluded, "I'm looking to the future, Larry, and I need your support behind my proposal."[75]

For the Clippers, and their owner Donald Sterling, the NBA had a stick. Following the lawsuit in June, after his attempt to move the Clippers to Los Angeles, the NBA created a special committee to investigate the situation Sterling created, and in late September that committee, composed of six owners, voted unanimously to oust him. Such an act was unprecedented, and the NBA had never reached the point before of terminating ownership. Fleisher welcomed the news, saying, "I'm surprised at the act of courage taken by the NBA. It's a very, very necessary strong move. It showed that a willful violation of contractual obligations will not be tolerated. They were willing to

The Big Item

stand up to the guy and say you can't do it anymore." The Greater San Diego Sports Association, who had fought to keep the Clippers, was elated. "When we think of the hours and hours we spent working on getting this franchise and then having it end up with some jerk, this is a thrilling announcement," the association's president, Vinnie Vinson said. "I'm just thrilled to death."[76]

Soon after, Sterling intimated he would sell. In October 1982 his attorney said, "Don has a sincere desire to sell, but it may take one heck of a long time."[77] Sterling sold his team in August 2014. Heck of a long time indeed.

• • •

For the NBA and its players, the collective bargaining negotiations went on a brief hiatus in late November to allow Fleisher, his lawyers, consultants and accountants time to review the finances of the NBA and its teams in details.

Fleisher believed any losses were due to mismanagement on the part of owners. Fleisher had said, throughout negotiations, that the economic situation in the NBA was not nearly as dire as Stern and O'Brien made it out to be.

In every negotiation the NBA claimed it was losing money. In every negotiation Fleisher ignored it. "When I started there were eight teams in the league, and every time we had to negotiate a collective bargaining agreement we heard how they were losing money and how teams would fold," Fleisher said in 1982. "Well, from eight teams they've gone to 23 and they're still saying the same thing."

"In some cases, owners are very shortsighted," Grantham said in the fall of 1982. "A business in sports is not unlike a business elsewhere. When you make a decision it entails marketing, projections, studies." Grantham also said, "There are losses. But it doesn't mean they will quit right now. Hockey teams lose money. Baseball teams lose money. You just don't read about it."[78] Fleisher, citing the Malone signing, said, "It's hard to give that much credence when I see guys signing for $13 million (Moses Malone) or $5 million (Bernard King)."[79] The union had conducted its own survey, without economic data, and believed only between 4 and 9 of the NBA teams lost money at all. Bob Lanier, president of the NBPA, said, "The owners have got to keep tabs on themselves. If they would stop paying these humongous salaries, there wouldn't be a problem."[80] When asked if teams might fold, Lanier said, "It might improve the league. We may have to lose some player in the process, but it might make a more quality league."

While the NBA was public with its economic woes, not everyone associated with the league believed it was in such tremendous trouble. Auerbach, in response to worries that the league was in dire straits, said, "They pay their bills, don't they? Who says [the NBA] is not financially sound." The belief, more broadly, according to economists interviewed by the *Hartford Courant*, was, "Though it is possible one or two franchises may collapse, the league appears basically sound."[81]

In negotiations, the NBA's bargaining team continually argued that the league was losing money, but Fleisher would not put much stake in their claims without getting real financials to back it up. As Quinn said, "There had been a tradition over the years that they would whine and moan and say how much they were losing and blah blah blah. Big crocodile tears. And we would say fine show us your audited financials, team financials . . . and we'll consider. And they would never show us the financials. And we always said if you won't show us the financials, then it's obviously bullshit and you know we'll ignore your whining and crying. Which we did."[82]

This negotiation cycle, however, Stern was not as resistant to providing economic information. Several times in September and October, Stern said they would provide the information. When they began to discuss the reality of a cap in October 1982, Fleisher got specific in what he needed. On October 18, he made it official. In a letter to Stern, Fleisher said, "In view of: (i) the NBA's claims of financial distress in negotiations and in public statements and (ii) the NBA's recent proposal of revenue-sharing, we believe it necessary to our collective bargaining position to examine all relevant financial information and projections. Necessarily, meaningful discussion of the revenue-sharing proposal requires that the Players Association be fully informed as to the financial situation of all NBA members. Without detailed financial information, we would not be able to ascertain the consequences of revenue-sharing on the players. NBA negotiators have stated on a number of occasions, and as recently as this past Friday's meeting, that the NBA would be willing to substantiate its claims of financial incapacity by supplying financial information concerning NBA members for our review." Fleisher continued, "We believe that such examination is of particular importance since the NBA has proposed substantial league-wide takebacks. For example, it is necessary that we understand the precise financial consequences of and justification for your proposal for overall reduction of team size." The letter contained a two-page attachment in which Fleisher requested all kinds of information—gate receipts, concessions income, parking licensing, radio and television, and any other expenses. They wanted to know what the expenses teams made—stadium rental, interest, depreciation, travel, etc. Most important were the last two things that Fleisher requested—"all studies, analyses, projections or other writings in the possession of the NBA or its members reflecting future revenues from any and all sources, including, but not limited to, cable television, pay cable television and similar media." Fleisher also asked for "copies of all network and local broadcast and cable television contracts currently in effect between the NBA and/or its member clubs and any broadcast and/or cable television company."[83] He was going for the full boat.

When Fleisher showed up for bargaining on October 27, he was given the Arthur Anderson projections. According to Quinn, they never expected to receive anything. He said, "I remember looking at Larry and saying, 'I don't know Larry, I think that may be their financials. We may be in deep shit here.'"

While a big move, this was insufficient. Fleisher requested detailed information from the team so he could understand the economics better. Fleisher believed he needed each part of every player's contract. Stern and Granik protested—they expressed concern because Fleisher was also an agent. Fleisher responded that they could simply give the information to Grantham, who was not an agent. Fleisher was clear: "There cannot be a deal until I know what all of the numbers are. I must be able to sit with my group and tell them why to accept this proposal and what it all means."[84]

The parties met the next day; this time Stern, Granik, Bettman, and Batterman were joined by Jack Krumpe of the Knicks, Alan Cohen of the Nets, and Angelo Drossos of the Spurs. Stern asked how Fleisher proposed they should proceed. Fleisher reiterated his demand for information. "You must understand," Fleisher said, "we have a responsibility to all members and to represent them fairly. We are quite happy with the system today, but you have told us that disaster looms. As a result, we have jointly come up with a dramatic change to the way the system operates. For me to talk to my own group intelligently, I must be able to satisfy them on two accounts; explaining why the world is coming to an end and why they must change the system, and what can be projected for the future. You have claimed on the one hand that you're going bankrupt and, on the other, that revenue will double over the next few years. Our accountants must look at your books. The Arthur Andersen report has no meaning. Someone must review the books and records of each team. This is not a fishing expedition—we have better things to do with our time."[85]

Drossos responded, "Assume there are $20 million in losses and lots of teams losing money." Fleisher didn't take the bait. "I won't negotiate until I have the numbers," he said. "I am anxious to negotiate and make a deal, but I've got to see what the numbers say. I won't negotiate on assumptions. Let's first determine the losses and make the projections and then we can debate the size and reason for the losses, whether to include concessions, etc. in income and what's fair to the players."[86]

Stern asked about the possibility of the accountants looking at the Arthur Anderson material, but Fleisher said it was insufficient. Drossos grew impatient. He said that time was growing short and "there were only three weeks within which to get the numbers and strike a deal," referring to the Board of Governors deadline to implement its last offer. Fleisher, who was tired of Drossos's antics, said so. "We are not limited to three weeks. I know about the Board of Governors deadline, and that pisses us off, but we'll talk and we'll go and do whatever we have to do. Don't put us under a deadline. We'll get the numbers as quickly as possible and we'll negotiate."[87] Cohen said the time frame should be done by the accountants.

Fleisher met again with the full labor committee on November 19. Fleisher reiterated his approach on reviewing the information and stated that he needed to know "how bad the League's financial condition [was] and what potential there [was] for the players before there could any agreement."[88] Fleisher could not agree without the details. The NBA claimed it needed Fleisher to agree to a cap. Something had to give.

The NBA relented. As a result, the NBPA spent two months reviewing the NBA's books. As Fleisher said in a note to his members, the NBA provided "full and complete financial data from each team." In addition: "The Players Association has arranged for the independent audit of six of the teams to insure that the figures presented to us are correct. Also, we have made a complete review and analysis of all television contracts of each team, including pay TV, cable TV, subscription TV, regular TV, and have made an analysis of the potential of cable television. The data gathered will enable your committee to negotiate intelligently with the club owners for a new collective agreement based upon the use of all available information. This collective bargaining period is critical based upon the position taken by the club owners of abject poverty, financial disaster and destruction of the league."[89]

And so, the books were opened and negotiations went on a hiatus in late 1982. It was an unprecedented act of cooperation. As Stern said later of the decision to provide the economic information, "At some point, there was no reason to be fighting about what the facts were."[90]

• • •

The NFL strike, which began on September 20, 1982, continued into the start of the NBA season. The NFL's loss was the NBA's gain. CBS, without the NFL, needed programming to fill. Where did they turn? The NBA. The NBA took a game between Milwaukee and Seattle and moved it up on November 2. CBS showed two games. As O'Brien said in his newsletter to owners, "During the NFL players strike, two NBA games were carried by CBS. Not only did these games bring in additional revenues, but they also provided an excellent opportunity to promote the beginning of the 1982–83 season." As November continued and the strike went on, CBS asked the NBA to expand the number of games it intended to show if the strike continued. Regardless, for the NBA, those two broadcasts had drawn strong ratings, and each of them had been watched in about 5.6 million households.[91]

By mid-November the deal was done and the NFL was coming back. Garvey had not gotten his percentage of gross. He had gotten the same offer the league had made before the strike began. The players had lost $72 million in wages in the fifty-seven-day strike, and the owners had lost $240 million in television and gate revenue. "The strike was a complete failure," one NFL player rep said. On the owners' side, the strike had taken its toll, too. "Nobody did any handsprings," Art Modell, owner of the Cleveland Browns, said of the owners' vote, "and there was no elation." There was no elation, but there was tremendous bitterness. "It was bizarre there at the end," one NFL player rep said, "Garvey had a terrible cold and it was obvious he'd just had it. The strike collapsed from the top down."[92]

12

Strike Date, January 1983

If the league goes under. It goes under.

—LARRY BIRD

By January 1983 the CBA had been expired for seven months and neither side wanted negotiations to continue much longer. The longer the negotiations dragged out, the greater the risk was to both sides. The owners were worried Fleisher would do what Fleisher had done before—threaten a strike at the end of the regular season, when revenues were at its highest and when he had the most leverage. The owners had good reason to fear this—Fleisher had utilized this tactic many times over the years to great success. The players were worried that if they waited too long the owners would simply run out the clock and impose their terms if negotiations went into the summer when *they* had the most leverage. The players had good reason to fear this as well—the owners threatened to do just that in the fall! Though the owners had not followed through, next time, the players feared, they might not hold off.

But, those were worst case scenarios. The parties resumed negotiations in January 1983 following a two-month break to allow the players to look at the NBA's true financials. The time had been productive. As Fleisher wrote to the players as negotiations resumed, the Players Association was in a strong position as a result of the hiatus, and he credited the NBA for being reasonable. "No other sports players association has had as much information concerning the activities of member teams as the basketball players," he wrote to his members. "To the credit of the NBA, this information was provided without legal hassle and is a great tool in helping us in our negotiations."[1]

Fleisher, after reviewing the information, could see that some teams were in real trouble. Fleisher was clear publicly—the salary cap proposal was "still out entirely."[2] He was less clear privately. Fleisher and Quinn were trying to come up with a way to help with the league's economic problems without agreeing to a salary cap. A cap felt extreme. They tried coming up with ways to tweak the right of first refusal or other mechanisms or have a different compensation system. The difficulty they faced was that Fleisher and Quinn knew (and hoped) that free agency would continue to push salaries upward because the teams in the league, fundamentally, wanted to win. Cutting that off in another way would cut off their strongest engine of continued salary growth.[3] Though they were unsure where it would go, they had been laying the groundwork for a cap with the players and discussing the possibility. Grantham had spent hours in locker rooms in the previous months, speaking with players, preparing them for the possibility of a cap.

The League was holding to its position. "The NBA is set on getting the salary cap," Celtics owner Harry Mangurian said in early January, before negotiations resumed. "There is very serious discussion about that. The whole thrust of the NBA's proposal is to get a salary cap."[4] Fleisher, subtly, tried to build leverage as negotiations resumed. There were rumors the players would strike the All-Star Game. Fleisher refuted them, but not as forcefully as he had in the past. "I've heard the rumors too and they're not correct," he said about a strike in December, but he provided a caveat. "All that's been said is, that at some point, if you're not getting anywhere, you have to think about your alternatives. We've now had time to gather a lot of information, to research situations, and begin to negotiate. The major issue, simply, is that the owners say they are going bankrupt. If that's not true, we'll negotiate one way, and if it is true, we'll negotiate another way. If they can show us they're having real financial difficulties, we'll be reasonable."[5]

Still, when negotiations resumed at the Detroit Airport Hilton on January 18, 1983 there was renewed vigor, and some optimism.[6] Fleisher was joined by Grantham, Lanier, Bridgeman and Steve Mix.

For the NBA, it was O'Brien, who would now be playing a larger role, Stern, Granik, and Bettman.

Larry Fleisher began the first meeting, after a two month break, on a positive note. Fleisher provided the NBA's negotiating team with an update and an assessment. "After pulling teeth," Fleisher said, "the information we got was terrific and we will provide our conclusions to you to let you know more about your business."[7]

Fleisher was able to honestly acknowledge that several NBA teams were losing money. Though he had hired accountants, consultants, and lawyers to assist, Fleisher was uniquely able to review the information. Unlike Marvin Miller, Ed Garvey, or even David Stern, Fleisher was a CPA and a tax lawyer.

Fleisher also said that the data was not conclusive. There was a wide disparity among teams, and the circumstance was not as dire as the league was making it in the press. As a result, based on his assessment, the losses that did exist were not, in fact, due to player salaries.[8]

For example, Fleisher said, Cleveland was a disaster—Stepien's outlays for advertising outpaced the entire team's revenues. While the players were prepared to be reasonable, the players should not be obligated to subsidize Stepien's incompetence. Stern and Granik said that the Cavs were an outlier—it had been impossible to sell the Cavaliers and Granik said there seemed to be a total absence of new purchasers for teams.[9]

Fleisher also had concerns about allocations for teams with complex ownership groups. If Jerry Buss owned the Lakers, the Kings, *and* the LA Forum, how would income be allocated? Several owners were in business together. How would the NBA ensure that the percentage of gross that went to the players was a true gross? Such an issue could be a major loophole, especially given what Fleisher knew about NBA owners. Stern and Granik said that "phantom income" could be included to make them fair.[10]

While Fleisher acknowledged teams were losing money now, the future for basketball was bright. The NBPA had also used the hiatus to retain a cable consultant—and the consultant believed that cable television would yield profits of $45 million in three years and $60 million in five. Fleisher believed that any issue regarding losses was simply temporary.

After making his presentation—the good and the bad—Fleisher said he would discuss the guaranteed compensation plan if he knew it would "solve the problem." Fleisher said that the worst thing would be to "adopt a radical plan that doesn't work."[11] Fleisher was framing the issue on his terms. Yes, he could acknowledge that teams were losing money, but it was not as bad as it seemed. Yes, he wanted to help fix it, but he wanted to make sure it would actually fix the issue—he did not want to limit salaries based on a short-term reality and then watch revenue explode.

Stern said that the cap was just one piece of a broader effort to improve things. It was true. He had been working on marketing, on cable, on television. Stern said, if "the players are against the Plan we could limp along with a basic agreement dealing with per diems and pensions." Fleisher demurred, saying they could negotiate the plan, but it needed work. Fleisher reiterated his desire to "go down this road" and said, "I'm convinced you're losing money and this is the time to address it. I'm not sure if the cable projections are bullshit, but my guy is very optimistic."[12]

Toward the end of the meeting, O'Brien told Fleisher there were three alternatives for moving forward: 1) to "move immediately to serious negotiations on the concept before us," 2) "remove it from the table and return to negotiations on the original series of demands," or 3) if Fleisher "had alternative proposals to make he should state so now." After a pause, Fleisher said he wanted to pursue the cap proposal. O'Brien said that he would be more involved in these negotiations than he had been in the past because previous negotiations "were confined to standard collective bargaining items." In light of the progress, O'Brien advised Fleisher that he would call a meeting of the Labor Relations Committee to "seriously negotiate."[13] Both sides left feeling optimistic.

After the Detroit meeting, Fleisher and his committee met about a week later with the larger Labor Committee of owners, in New York City. In preparing for the meeting, O'Brien told the owners to focus on big-picture issues, and he said, "If we are to make progress I think it is essential that we refrain from nitty gritty and legal niceties as much as possible in an attempt to get to the guts of the issue."[14]

Fleisher began the meeting by describing the outstanding issues with the cap, once again framing the issue on his terms:

1) They would have to agree on a percentage of gross

2) They would have to define revenue—Fleisher wanted all revenue included

3) There would have to be minimum team salary as well as a maximum

4) They would have to deal with the exceptions of Abdul-Jabbar, Bird, and Sampson

5) There needed to be "consideration given to the 'timing and phasing in' of the Plan"

6) They would need to deal with the proper allocation of revenues for complex ownership situations

7) How to handle overages if free agency did not meet the players guaranteed percentage

Fleisher said that from his perspective there were three reasons the NBA was in favor of the cap: 1) competitive balance, which would make teams more sellable; 2) continuity of team rosters (enabling small market teams to keep their players); and 3) enabling teams to make money. Fleisher said he was "least concerned with reason number three." Fleisher said he was focused on the calculation of gross revenues and wanted to include all revenue "to protect the players as to all growth and keep owners from hiding revenues." In front of an audience of owners, Fleisher wanted to make his concerns about them hiding money clear. Fleisher said there was good news and bad news. He said, a cap plan "will be tremendously difficult to work out but we should go forward with it."[15]

After discussion of the minimums and some outstanding issues, Abe Pollin of the Bullets asked Fleisher what percentage of gross he was seeking. Fleisher had not responded to the NBA's proposal from October, where they had proposed 40 percent and 30 percent. Though the two sides had made progress conceptually in discussing the cap, the issue of the haggle was inevitable. Given that Fleisher had proposed team salary caps of $10 million three years earlier, it was reasonable that Pollin would be concerned about where Fleisher expected to end up. "I could say 70% but that would not advance things," Fleisher said. To anchor the negotiations high he believed "there [were] other issues to raise first." Later in the meeting, Fleisher said, "The players want the same percentage of the gross they are currently getting—57.4%."[16]

The owners took a caucus to discuss. When they resumed, Pollin stated, "We are taking under advisement what you have said. While we have differences, we are pleased that it appears we are on the same wavelength and there is enough room to continue discussions. From this point on, negotiations should be continued through the NBA's negotiating team and they should be continued as soon as possible."[17] Commissioner O'Brien then said, "We should move forward without interruption." Fleisher agreed.

Both sides felt like progress had been made in the first sessions after the hiatus. As Pollin later advised of the amount Fleisher proposed, "That was higher than the number we thought was right, but I told Fleisher personally that I was pleased with his response and the fact that we weren't far apart on the percentage and for the most part were agreeable."[18] Larry O'Brien hit a sunny note publicly on prospects for a deal, saying, "There was a good exchange of views from both sides. I would characterize these discussions as serious in nature and add that the climate remains conducive for continued serious negotiations" after their January 24 meeting.[19] In updating his owners, O'Brien had a similar position.[20]

• • •

Things had gone too smoothly. Between the meeting with the owners on January 24 and his next meeting with Stern and the smaller group on February 1, Fleisher encountered an issue—when the cap would go into effect. Fleisher had raised the issue when he met with the owners on the twenty-fourth. Fleisher met with his outside counsel—Quinn's senior partner Ira Millstein—who told him he couldn't agree to the cap. The issue was the *Robertson* settlement. The cap, if agreed to, would conflict with it. Fleisher knew this issue—he had made this argument many times over the years. Fleisher reveled in quoting the first line of the *Robertson* settlement. Millstein simply was not certain that the judge overseeing the settlement would agree to the system. The union, and Fleisher, could be sued. Millstein believed that Fleisher and the NBPA would lose such a suit. Even when the special master ruled in the NBPA's favor in September, he was clear that any agreement would have to be approved by the court.

Beyond the *Robertson* settlement, Fleisher had another concern—implementing the cap immediately was unfair to upcoming free agents. There were many players who would be eligible for free agency. To agree to a cap now would take the rug out from under them. As Charles Grantham put it, "We . . . felt that the 55 players who will become free agents next year would be hampered in attempts to find their real market value if the proposal was implemented. They can maximize their salary. Are you going to tell them they can't?"[21]

As a result, Fleisher had a problem when the parties met next, on February 1. When negotiations began, Fleisher did not raise this issue of implementation. He started with a concession—saying that he would consider the players taking 55 percent of gross, down from the 57.4 he had proposed the previous meeting, and that he "would recommend to the Players that they take 55% of the gross." Fleisher said, "We can't tell our guys to take less than they're getting."[22]

Fleisher's main concern was the weaker teams. He was concerned about how the "have nots" would be required to pay players—how much would they be obligated to spend and, how exactly, did the NBA plan to make the Sterlings of the world spend money. O'Brien said the system itself would do that. He believed the new plan would "show stability for prospective purchasers of franchises," and that the mere existence of the cap, "so that teams [could] at least project in the future," would lead to more stable ownership groups. Granik seized on the issue and said that was the reason the NBA could not agree to high guarantees. O'Brien proposed that they start the minimum salary low and let it grow over time to allow for these new ownership groups to start to populate the league.[23] The parties took a caucus.

When Fleisher returned, he had a new proposal that set things off and moved the parties off the glide path to a deal. He raised an issue they had not really discussed—when the cap would be introduced. "I have an idea that's earth shatteringly creative," he said. "We've been kicking back and forth the idea of phasing in the plan." Fleisher proposed the following—a seven-year deal, the salary cap would kick in 1986–87 (after the *Robertson* settlement ended) and players could become "free free agents" after *Robertson*. Fleisher said this proposal would do exactly what O'Brien said he wanted. Fleisher said his proposal "would give teams stability because they could plan for the next seven years and takes away concerns about the impact on current players, thereby eliminating the legal problems." Fleisher said, "This proposal is the best of all worlds."[24]

The NBA certainly did not share Fleisher's view. Fleisher's proposal undermined the result they sought to accomplish—immediate savings. After Fleisher's proposal, the NBA's negotiating team caucused. They were furious. To bargain over the distribution of income, they understood. That they expected. But to wait four more years for relief? They had spent months pushing this proposal, had worked with the PA, given them the real access to information, and now that they were actually finally moving toward a deal, Fleisher wanted to argue this would not go into effect for *another* four years? Where was this issue earlier?

When the parties resumed, O'Brien spoke. He said sternly, "We gave thought to your proposal and dismiss it out of hand." He said, "This proposal will keep the league in disarray for the next four years, does nothing to encourage stability in the short run and is not responsive to the league's problems." The NBA's bargaining team relished the ability to scold Fleisher who had spent so much of negotiations admonishing them. Stern said that Fleisher's proposal "cut the guts out of the Plan" and expressed concern that Fleisher could have remotely thought that proposal would be "good" for the NBA.[25] O'Brien said that Fleisher's proposal would lead to the loss of teams and that whatever they ended up agreeing to would have to go into effect immediately.[26] All of them—Stern, O'Brien, and Granik—told Fleisher that this proposal did not address the league's concerns and was a significant departure from the prior discussions.

Stern was exasperated: "We were discussing the Bird, Sampson and Jabbar exceptions—is that off the table?"

"Under my proposal maybe you don't need exceptions," Fleisher said, attempting to work toward a solution—effectively floating a hard cap. The irony was that Stern would spend most of the rest of his career seeking such an arrangement.

At that point O'Brien left the meeting. Fleisher told Stern of Millstein's assessment and the conflict with the *Robertson* settlement. They all knew that any modifications they wanted to make would be subject to Judge Carter's approval, and Fleisher said Millstein did not think that this circumstance would get his approval. Fleisher said that if they agreed to the plan "[they'd] get sued and probably lose." Stern told him he disagreed. Stern told Fleisher he should have raised these issues earlier. Fleisher agreed—he should have—but he said, "That's only part. Phasing in makes more sense for the current players."[27]

Stern said, "We categorically reject your proposal; however, we are prepared to discuss some phasing-in of the Plan."[28] The NBA's team told Fleisher he had to withdraw his proposal to have the cap start in four years or they would be unable to go forward until after the NBA's Board of Governors meeting at the All-Star Game. Fleisher refused to withdraw his proposal.

After the meeting on February 1, tension was rising as the All-Star break approached. The players began flexing their muscle in travel, insisting that teams use first-class travel. Teams began putting coaches in first class, in violation of the agreement. In one circumstance, the Dallas Mavericks had to fly two planes to a game because there were not enough seats in first class.[29]

There was also a theory that emerged later that Fleisher changed his position regarding phasing in the plan because of pressure from agents. Celtics owner Harry Mangurian, who was in the midst of negotiations with star forward Kevin McHale at the time, said, "The agents for those players who are free agents, or who would be free agents in the next couple of years started complaining to Fleisher that their clients would be hurt. That's when he backed off and started talking about doing it four years from now. The agents for those players wanted to hit a home run before it went into effect."[30]

On February 11, Fleisher met with the owners' Labor Relations Committee to explain his position regarding delaying the cap. The meeting had been at Fleisher's suggestion. This was a hostile audience for Fleisher—any audience with Angelo Drossos in the room was a hostile audience for Fleisher. Fleisher was telling them something they did not want to hear—that he believed there should not be any change to the economic circumstance for four more years. Fleisher said that the players were willing to accept the plan, but it would go into effect in four years, in order to make the plan "legal."[31]

Fleisher believed that this would give the owners time to prepare for the new world, and allow players a freer market. As he had several times over the years, Angelo Drossos questioned Fleisher's motives. According to Gary Bettman's notes of the meeting, Drossos gave an "impassioned speech" about the topic.[32]

Fleisher maintained his position that to implement the proposal now, in addition to being illegal, would split the union. Alan Cohen of the Nets, a moderate in these negotiations and a voice of reason, was critical of Fleisher's proposal. He said that the four-year delay would limit the ability of teams to be sold—a crucial point to the long-term stability of the league. O'Brien said that the four-year hiatus would be counterproductive and devastating to the league. Fleisher said he was open to discussing anything to bridge the gap. Fleisher reiterated that the players would agree to the cap if it took effect after *Robertson*. He also said—if there were alternatives for the next four years, before it took effect—"I am prepared to discuss them if they won't hurt the players."[33] As Pollin said after the meeting, "We were disappointed and taken aback, but we said we'd consider it and get back to him."[34]

After the meeting with Fleisher, O'Brien met with the Labor Relations Committee. His notes reflect that they were open to what Fleisher was proposing—identify a plan for the next four years, with the cap to be implemented after that. Such a proposal was also discussed at the Board of Governors meeting a few days later.[35] Pollin also confirmed publicly that they were considering it.[36] This concession (or approach) was, it appears, never communicated to Fleisher and would be undone a few days later when the players announced a strike date.[37]

On the eve of the All-Star break, Fleisher gave a public update on the status of negotiations. Fleisher was beginning to lose faith, saying, "I had hoped that we would have had greater progress than this during the All-Star break. That is my greatest disappointment."[38]

• • •

On February 13, 1983, two days after Fleisher's meeting with the Labor Relations Committee, the NBA held its All-Star festivities in Los
Angeles, California. Just as they had in every aspect of the 1982–83
NBA season, the Sixers dominated the proceedings. The Sixers entered
the All-Star break with a blistering 43-7 record, and Moses Malone,
Julius Erving, and Maurice Cheeks were all All-Star starters, consti-
tuting 60 percent of the starting lineup. Their coach, Billy Cunningham, coached the East squad, and Erving led all players in All-Star
votes. When Malone was told that Sixers guard Andrew Toney would
also be on the team, he said, "I don't see why we don't just take our
whole team."[39] They should have. When the game was over, the East
had won and Erving took home the MVP trophy.

Off the court, the stalled labor negotiations were at the forefront. At
his yearly press conference to discuss the state of the league, O'Brien
was forced to discuss the labor strife. According to the *Philadelphia
Inquirer*, O'Brien's press conference "dealt exclusively with the pro-
liferation of feeble, money-losing franchises and the league's ongoing
labor-relations problems with the NBA Players Association." Just days
removed from the meeting with Fleisher on the eleventh, O'Brien was
candid. He was frustrated. The owners, he said, "have to take deci-
sive action now for the best interests of the league. We just can't sit
around and let nature run its course any longer."[40]

O'Brien was clear: the parties "remain far apart on several matters." O'Brien said, "This has taken a very long time and I had hoped
that we'd have gotten more progress at the All-Star break than we've
had. I'm disappointed that we have not."[41] If nothing else, Fleisher
and O'Brien agreed that they were both disappointed.

O'Brien was asked whether the league had an image problem.
O'Brien went ballistic. "I love this league," he yelled, "thumping his
fist down on the podium." He had one more declaration: "And this
league is in a more stable position today than it's ever been in its
history." With that, O'Brien, ever the optimist, "stormed out of the
room." As the *Philadelphia Inquirer* put it, "In total, the conference
was the single greatest recent indicator of how immense the league's
problems are and also of how confused the owners are, as a group,
in dealing with the issues."[42]

Then came more bad news for O'Brien. The players emerged from their All-Star Game meeting with a deadline for a new agreement of April 1; and if they did not reach one, they could strike.[43] "If we don't have an agreement by then the players will take all the necessary action, including a strike, to protect the interests of all the players," Fleisher said.[44] It was an interesting way to call a strike date without requiring the players strike. Just as he had done many times before, Fleisher used the publicity of the All-Star Game and its proximity to the playoffs—when the NBA made its real money—to make a statement. It was exactly what the owners had feared. Though the date would later be pushed back to April 2, 1983—the players were concerned that calling for an April 1 strike date may have been viewed as a joke—the plan to strike was very serious.[45] Grantham said, "The player reps voted unanimously at the All-Star game meetings to set a deadline for April 2. We are ready to continue to negotiate until that date, but we are willing to take whatever steps are necessary to reach an agreement."[46]

In a letter to players outlining the issues, Grantham said, "The NBA made a proposal to share a percentage of gross revenues through a guaranteed compensation plan with the NBPA. Both sides researched the plan and analyzed the league's financial data. Finally, the plan was rejected by the Executive Board of the NBPA on the basis that: 1. The plan effectively placed a limit on how much an individual could earn in the market as a free agent. This, the NBPA cites, is a violation of the Oscar Robertson Settlement Agreement . . . and would be illegal. 2. If implemented, the plan would have a total negative impact on the movement of free agents, as only a few teams would be able to bid for free agents. Additionally, those players whose contracts expire in the next few years would be deprived of an opportunity to earn a fair salary."[47]

The players lined up behind Fleisher. Quinn Buckner, player representative of the Celtics, said, "Quite simply, we want our contract signed by April 2 or we walk"—the first such threat of the bargaining cycle.[48] "Every now and then you just have to do something," Buckner said. "Now they know we're for real. We're going into this with our eyes open. We're aware it's going to hurt, but we really don't have any alternative."[49] Clint Richardson, the player rep for the Philadelphia 76ers said, "We feel we have to have something done by April

1 . . . something we can live with. I'm new at this, and the meetings we had . . . were more involved, more serious than I had thought. There was a lot of discussion about finances, about how certain teams are being run."[50] In a bit of hyperbole, Fleisher said, "We are no closer to an agreement now than we were last summer."[51]

The players argued that the decision to set a strike date was defensive, not threatening, and intended to spur negotiations forward. Greg Ballard, the Player Representative for the Washington Bullets, said, "Nobody wants a strike but if we let this thing keep on going, no one will get anywhere. We felt we had to do something to get things moving."[52] Ballard cited the same key issues—the owners' requests for rollbacks and the players' interest in cable television revenues. Richardson of the 76ers said, "What we're saying now shouldn't be looked at as any kind of threat. We just want to work out an agreement."[53] There was truth to the defensive posture. Many players said they had been preparing for a strike since early that season.[54] The union believed that if they did not strike, or move the negotiations forward, the owners would either lock them out or unilaterally impose changes to the system, as they threatened to do in October.[55] They simply acted first. While there had been prior strike dates in the NBA, this one carried more heft. The MLBPA had gone on strike the previous year. The NFLPA had only settled its strike a few months earlier. It felt like, in some ways, it was the NBA's turn.

Stars throughout the league voiced support for the union, for Fleisher, and for the strike date. "We're not threatening to go on strike because we want anything," Kareem Abdul-Jabbar said, who moonlighted as the Lakers' player rep, another star with a leadership role in the union. "We're not making any demands. We're just trying to maintain what we have. The owners say we make too much money, but I don't think that can be resolved the way they want it resolved." None of the Lakers were believed to be enthusiastic about a potential strike, as they were well situated to win another title, but supported it. "We've got to do what we've got to do," Magic Johnson said. Kareem went further: "I hope it doesn't come to a strike. We don't want to strike. It won't do us that much good to strike but we have to protect ourselves. It seems that the owners feel we're responsible for the owners' misfortune of overpaying us or spending fortunes for dubious talent. Of course, we'd like to see all the teams survive. They provide jobs for us. But we can't be responsible for mismanagement."[56] This was why Fleisher wanted power at the top—and many teams' player representatives were their best and highest paid players.

David Greenwood, player representative for the Bulls, said that even though his team had not taken a strike vote, "I can guarantee you 100 percent that if we did we would get 11 guys going one way [for a strike]. If the players lose this, the big money contracts could be gone. The league had guys like Chamberlain, West and Robertson fighting for this in the past. We're not going to turn around and give that up."[57]

Danny Ainge of the Celtics cited a "universal" opinion that a strike was necessary. "It's the owners' fault. They need protection against themselves." Larry Bird, with a tremendous amount on the line in these negotiations, got right to the heart of the owners' argument. "If the league goes under," he said, "it goes under."[58] While the NBPA prided itself on communication, it was not absolute. Some teams and players were surprised by the union's strike date. The Hawks had several players respond, "What?" when asked about the potential strike.[59]

Fleisher said that a strike was "a real possibility but not one [he could] measure in terms of percentages. . . . We're willing to remain status quo, we've said that all along." He continued, "What will happen? I can't guess. But we've got six-to-eight weeks to effectively negotiate. It can be done."[60]

• • •

Almost from the moment the Players Association announced their strike date, the owners dug in and struck back—hard. They attacked the players, they attacked Fleisher, and they raised questions about the future viability of the league. "Strike has never been part of our lexicon. We have negotiated in good faith all along," said Brian McIntyre, NBA public relations director.[61] O'Brien said initially, "At no point during the negotiations was there any threat or suggestion of a strike by the players association." He said, "The first the NBA learned of such a threat was in yesterday's press reports. The NBA intends, and stands ready, to continue good faith negotiations."[62] "Frankly, we are surprised to hear of a strike threat emanating from our players," Stern said, despite answering questions about a potential strike for months. "It does not serve a useful purpose. We are in the process of scheduling additional negotiating sessions with our players and stand committed to good-faith negotiations designed to reach an agreement."[63]

The NBA was blindsided. Though they had prepared for the possibility of a strike for months, the NBA was legitimately surprised by Fleisher's strike threat. Furthermore, O'Brien seemed personally angry with Fleisher. As he wrote in a note preparing for a call with owners days after the strike date, "From these reports, it was apparent that Fleisher had totally misrepresented to his players what had transpired in bargaining and had flatly lied to the Labor Relations Committee."[64]

Though they were still under a gag order, several owners spoke out. Some were ready for war. Sam Schulman, of the Supersonics, said, "I dare them to strike. The players are overpaid. A strike would enable us to return to normalcy and start all over again. Larry Fleisher has admitted to us that at least ten teams are in financial trouble. I venture to say there are more."[65] Others preached calm. "I don't think a strike will solve any problems but it's their prerogative," Abe Pollin said. "They can do what they want. I was very disappointed when I heard of a strike, but they have the authority to do it if that's what they want. I hope it isn't. I'm an optimist, and if I weren't, I wouldn't still be in this crazy business at all. I plan to, and encourage all of us to, continue to negotiate in good faith. I think you might find some of our people are disappointed and might harden some of their positions. But I plan to continue to negotiate in good faith."[66] Many were in between. Harry Mangurian, owner of the Celtics, said, "To call a strike could cause havoc in the league. The big problem right now is the kind of losses the bulk of NBA teams are taking. They can't even sell tickets now, which never happened in the past."[67]

Some simply wanted clarity—this was chaos. Harry Glickman of the Portland Trailblazers wrote to O'Brien asking for guidance in dealing with the media. "Are we still muzzled under threat of a $250,000 fine? What kinds of comments are appropriate to make to the press?" Glickman asked. He also took issue with Schulman's combative statements, saying, "I don't believe the quote of one of our owners in this morning's paper 'I dare the players to strike' is helpful in trying to settle this issue."[68]

Harold Katz held his own press conference to question the strike date and to plead and threaten everyone into reaching a solution. His Sixers had the most to lose in a strike. Out of the All-Star break, the Sixers coronation plan was on its way—the league simply had to remain in operation. As the *Philadelphia Inquirer* said, "It would be the crowning irony if, in the year when the Sixers were finally about to realize what they believe is their manifest destiny, the players would hit the bricks and erase the playoffs . . . They have always said that the only way to stop [Moses] Malone is to keep the ball away from him. Now, only the Players Association is in a position to do that."[69] The *Los Angeles Times* did have a potential solution, saying, "The Philadelphia 76ers are making a shambles of the NBA. They may destroy the league before the players have a chance to strike."[70]

Katz who had invested so much in his team to help them win a championship that season could feel it slipping away. He didn't hold back. "I'm sour right now, very sour," he said. "Personally I'm at a point right now—and it may change later—that I don't know if I want to be a part of it."[71] He did not believe the players would have any sympathy from the public, saying, "Most of our money from TV this year depends on the playoffs. It hits us at a time when we're at our most vulnerable position. There is no reason to strike two weeks before the end of the season. Being so close to the playoffs, how can a fan sympathize with the players after they've gone through the season making an average of $258,000? Who's going to have sympathy for that?"[72]

Katz, who had become a member of the NBA's Labor Relations Committee, thought Fleisher had gone back on his word saying, "An agreement in principle had been said to us. We should be dealing with how to work out the terms of the agreement. This is a last-minute job."[73] Katz took aim at Fleisher directly: "I think the Players Association is mismanaged. If Fleisher's interest is in keeping all the jobs, this certainly isn't the way to go about it."[74] He continued, "Maybe we'd be down to 19 or 20 teams. I wonder what Fleisher would accomplish if 36 jobs were lost after three teams folded. I think he is gambling with the players he represents."[75]

Though Fleisher had lined up overwhelming support, not every player was with Fleisher and the NBPA—mainly those with the 76ers, especially their long-suffering star, Julius Erving. "I haven't been following the issues too closely," Erving said, about a week after the strike date was announced. "But we've been doing better than any team. We have the best record in the league. There's definitely a feeling that this could be our year. I would think the concerns of the NBA in 1985, '86 or '87 should not exceed the players' concerns in 1983."[76] Erving continued, "I would not sit around and sacrifice my present livelihood and lifestyle for the NBA and the players who will be in the league in '86 and '87."[77] Moses Malone, who had benefitted tremendously from Fleisher's machinations and free agency as recently as September, when Fleisher helped protect the agreement he had reached with Katz, said, "I'm not thinking about it right now. I'm just thinking about playing ball."[78] The 76ers' player representative, Clint Richardson, was stuck in a difficult position, and he tried to maintain a positive relationship with ownership. "He runs a tight business," Richardson said about Katz, "but a lot of owners don't . . . In Philadelphia . . . we're fortunate to have a good working relationship with our owner. But we're beginning to hear stories from other cities that don't sound nearly as good. We don't want to give up things that guys worked hard to get for us, and we're not asking for everything the other sports have asked for . . . We know both sides of the story, and we're a little scared of what the owners want. The ninth [sic], 10th, 11th, and 12th guys on some teams are worried they might be out of jobs. We don't want to go into next year on the owners' terms. Maybe if I was Harold Katz, I'd think his way, because then it'd be my money directly involved. But from what we saw during our meetings, the salaries aren't the problem, poor management is. We don't want to have to pay for somebody else's mistakes."[79]

When the strike date was announced on February 18, there were no dates scheduled for bargaining between the league and its players. The next bargaining session would not happen until March 1, and in the days between the announcement of the strike date and the next session, both sides postured. The NBA went on the offensive publicly, immediately questioning both Fleisher's word and his integrity. The NBA issued a statement saying that Fleisher had "previously indicated his willingness to accept such a concept," and that

Fleisher had "restated . . . his commitment to the plan" as recently as the previous Friday at the meeting with ownership.[80] O'Brien also said that Fleisher was unable to reach a deal in the best interests of professional basketball because he represented a number of the top players as an agent, and such a deal may harm his personal interests. It was a low blow in a relationship that had long been above the belt.

The union took issue with the statement. "No question the league is trying to deface Larry's credibility," Grantham said. "They want to discredit him. They want to implement this damn plan right now and we said no, we want to wait." He also said, "The announcement is a little misleading. It leads you to think we agreed to a plan and then withdrew. It's not true."[81] Grantham also refuted Fleisher's dual role: "It's not news," he said. "It's been in existence for 15 years, since the conception of the union. That's an academic question people will have to answer for themselves."

• • •

As the trade deadline approached there was a flurry of transactions in the NBA, mostly between weaker financial teams and stronger ones. Many of them involved cash going from strong teams to weak ones in exchange for players. There were concerns that Stepien, desperate to sell the Cavs, might hold a fire sale before dumping the team, in the interests of getting a small cash infusion on his way out the door. There was apprehension even though Stepien had already gutted the team of most of its talent. One of the players he was looking to move was Scott Wedman, one of his prized signings from the 1981 off-season. To stop him, the NBA then took the tremendously unusual step of imposing a twenty-four-hour review period for any trade the Cavaliers made.[82] O'Brien sent Stepien a telex saying, "I remain deeply concerned about the on-going status of the Cleveland Franchise and since I understand that you are in the process of negotiating with a potential purchasers of the club, I have concluded that it would be in the best interest of the Cavaliers and the league for the Cavaliers not to have any further trades . . . Please note that this notice is being sent only to you, and other clubs will not be notified of this decision unless they attempt to gain approval of a trade with Cleveland."[83]

Strike Date

There was dimming hope that Stepien would be able to sell at all. He had come close to a deal with a Cleveland real estate developer, John Ferchill. At the last minute, with Ferchill waiting for a signed agreement, Stepien changed the terms. The deal fell through.[84] At one point they were being courted by boxing promoter Don King, who was from Cleveland. King said, "I'm coming to lift them up from the muck and mire and to put them back in the place where they belong. I would be a promoter of friendship, unanimity and zeal and constricting negativism to its narrowest form."[85]

The next bargaining date between the NBA and the NBPA, and the first since the strike date and the public tensions, was scheduled to be in New York on March 1. It was expected to be a very tense session. Katz, who expected to be at negotiations, said, "From our end there's only aggravation on the table. One thing we're going to do, though, is ask Larry Fleisher if a strike is a legitimate possibility. He's used the word, but never directly to us. We want to see exactly where he stands."[86]

• • •

While the labor front in the NBA was heating up, Marvin Miller quietly exited the stage. On January 3, 1983, Marvin Miller, after eighteen years of making MLB players rich and owners miserable, left the post of executive director of the Major League Baseball Players Association. He was replaced by Ken Moffett, the former federal mediator who had acted as a facilitator in negotiating several baseball collective bargaining agreements. Major League Baseball and its players had just signed a new collective bargaining agreement, and the union had some time to break in a new executive director before things got heavy. Moffett had been chosen over Don Fehr—who, for all of his intelligence and skill, was seen as needing to improve his media relationship and his ability to communicate with the rank and file.[87]

By February it was unclear whether Miller would be able to let go of the organization he built and the industry he conquered. He was still regularly in the office. The plan was that when spring training started, "the transition [would] enter phase two: exit Miller as full-time boss, enter Miller as full-time advisor and historian."[88]

"Ken started on January 3, but all through January, I've been there every day," Miller said. "Now, I'm digging out the files of 17 years, and I'm on call. I'm available as a consultant. But I'm leaving the organization in good shape. And I'm in good shape. It's an ideal time to leave."[89]

"It's possible we're entering a period of truce," Miller said. "This time, I think even the hardliners have had enough."[90]

13

War, February 1983

The owners are using scare tactics and it is those very
tactics which could in the long run force a strike.

—LARRY FLEISHER

On the basis of where we are, we're all going to wind
up sitting on a torpedo and it may explode.

—DAVID STERN

While baseball may have believed it was entering a period of truce,
professional basketball was not. The Players had issued a strike date
at the All-Star Game, they said, to increase pressure on ownership.
After an All-Star weekend full of players speaking about the status
of negotiations and their disappointment with the NBA and its proposals, the NBA was prepared to fight back. Though there had been
some sporadic statements from owners and the league, and some
off-the-cuff comments from Stern and O'Brien, within a few days
the NBA had created a coordinated response. As the *Atlanta Constitution* said, "The best defense, according to the National Basketball
Association, is a good offense."[1]

The next negotiation date was set for March 1, about two weeks
after the NBPA's announcement. Fleisher had attempted to schedule
an earlier date, but O'Brien refused to respond to him, as he told his
Labor Relations Committee, "until we had an opportunity to set the
record straight with the press, the public and the players."[2]

The "setting the record straight" O'Brien referred to was an aggressive PR and action campaign designed to highlight the NBA's position and intimidate players. Though the players had the first shot, the NBA sought to raise pressure publicly and privately, nationally and locally, on all of the parties on the other side—players, the union, and Fleisher. In the end, some of it worked while some of it failed, miserably. Regardless, with about six weeks left before the players threatened strike to avoid a salary cap, from the NBA's perspective, the gloves were certainly off.

Within a day of the players' strike date, team employees and national and local media received a bevy of information from the league's headquarters in New York. The information was intended to show how reasonable the NBA had been, how awful Larry Fleisher was, how imperiled the NBA was financially, and how devastating a strike would be. The NBA issued a press release that filled six legal-size pages, outlining in excruciating detail the NBA's position on the negotiations to date, explaining the salary cap proposal, and providing the public with detailed specifics of Fleisher's misdeeds. Having held back publicly, the NBA wanted to convey that they had been fair and reasonable, and that it was Fleisher who had broken the deal.

Just as the league had gone public about the salary cap, so did Fleisher. Before the strike date, Fleisher was measured in his public comments about the cap. However, after the NBA's public comments, Fleisher responded in kind. He ridiculed the salary cap plan. Fleisher said the system was unworkable and was being improperly reported in the press. He said the deal as currently constituted would cause havoc in the market and greatly decrease free agency and competitive balance. Most important, he did not want to agree to anything before the *Robertson* settlement expired in 1987.

Fleisher was frustrated by the owners' conduct. "What they're trying to do is castrate the union," he said. "This is a negotiation that is taking place under enormous threats by the other side. They've shown that teams are in financial trouble, but they haven't shown that the reason is because the players make too much money."[3] Fleisher explained the union's actions saying, "The reason for a strike deadline is that we've gone 10 months without a contract and we don't want to go into next season."

Fleisher did not dispute that the NBPA was open to the concept of a cap, in theory, but that they didn't want it to take effect until after the *Robertson* settlement expired, and to do so otherwise would be unfair. "We signed a court order when we made that settlement," said Fleisher, "and we aren't going to change it because some immature and egomaniacal owners can't control themselves."[4] Fleisher continued, "It took us six long years to get that settlement and we aren't going to give it up now. More than 200 players will become free agents in the next three years and we aren't going to take that away from them. If we waited four years to implement the plan, all of the players would have a chance to plan ahead, and the gross revenues in the league would be high enough so as no players would get hurt by it. We can live with the plan—we just can't live with it now."

Fleisher also attacked the distribution of revenue. The 40 percent of revenues would work out to about $1.6 million payroll per team, well below what several teams were already at. He said, "We've told them it makes zero sense. The income generated and projected would not be sufficient for players to become free agents. It would be a disaster for our players and it wouldn't be long before a lawsuit would challenge it."[5]

Most importantly, Fleisher said he believed the NBA's economic problems were temporary and that revenues in the NBA were going to rise over the next few seasons. He said, "We believe that gross revenues in the league four years from now will be substantially higher, and would allow the players to earn what they are earning now, even more. But even if all of this was agreed on—and it hasn't been—there's still a far, far way to go in our negotiations. There are 100 other items that would have to be agreed on. Could the plan work? In my opinion, in '86–'87, it could."[6] Fleisher believed that in light of their inability to reach agreement, they should simply move on from the cap. "Since we can't get together on the [timing of the cap] we're going to sit down now and talk about our original proposals—things such as a cost of living increase."[7]

Once the details of the plan were public, every city began to analyze how it would impact their teams. The issues seemed to mirror exactly the Abdul-Jabbar, Sampson, and Bird problems that Fleisher had raised months earlier. The *Los Angeles Times* worried whether the Lakers could keep Kareem. As they reported, "A free agent following this season, he figures to command about $1.5 million a year when he signs a new contract. But if teams can pay only $1.6 million in salaries for their entire roster, none will be able to afford Abdul-Jabbar at his price. His price would have to come down considerably. Even then, the Lakers wouldn't be able to compete for him. They already are several million dollars over the $1.6 million limit and will be for a number of years because of their extended contracts. They wouldn't be forced to trade or waive players to get down to the limit, but they would not be able to sign any new players more than the $40,000 minimum salary. It's doubtful Abdul-Jabbar would have signed for that."[8] The *Boston Herald* ran an article entitled "Bird Could Escape Salary Cap," highlighting that his agent, Bob Woolf, hoped that Bird could get paid considerably under the plan.[9] The *Washington Post* investigated what would happen with Ralph Sampson, the projected top pick in the draft. The Houston Rockets, who were most likely to get him, were over the $1.6 million salary limit and, under the NBA's proposal, Sampson would not be able to make more than $40,000, much less than the five-year, $3.5 million contract that James Worthy had signed the previous season.[10] In response, Fleisher said, "And there would be nothing Ralph could do about that. And we don't think that's right."[11]

Beyond the public pressure, the NBA privately threatened players with what could happen in a strike. Along with the release, the NBA distributed a memorandum to all NBA general managers from the League Office outlining the consequences of the strike.[12] The memo began by advising general managers of what was going on, "in light of all the apparent misinformation being distributed to the players and press by the Players Association about the status of collective bargaining."[13]

Though the memo was intended to "educate" general managers, in fact it seemed to outline issues that would never be relevant to a team general manager. This was meant for the press and, especially, the players. "Before a strike becomes a reality," the memo read, "it is important that the players understand what the potential consequences may be, so that their willingness to strike will not be based on some misguided notion that their salary payments are somehow assured, and that only management would suffer."[14]

The memo said that the impact of a strike could be greater than the players were stating.[15] "Despite Fleisher's public pronouncements on the subject," the memo said that if there were a strike, players would lose any deferred monies in their contracts that year, in addition to lost salary.[16] The memo also advised that if teams went out of business as a result of the strike, "neither the NBA, nor any of its teams [were] responsible for the salary obligations of another NBA team."[17] The memo also said that teams would be forced to terminate insurance provided to the players, that players would be disqualified from incentive clauses in their contracts, and that teams would have claims against players for a return of salary attributable to the remainder of the season and playoffs.[18] The memo went after Fleisher personally, saying, "If these press reports and interviews are accurate, Fleisher is deliberately misleading his membership in order to generate a strike."[19] While the memo painted a bleak reality, it was not clear that it was accurate. While some owners, like the pugilistic Sam Schulman of the Supersonics and the cost conscious Sam Nassi of the Indiana Pacers, believed they would be better served by having a strike, several teams, including the Celtics, believed they may have to pay player salaries even if the league closed due to a strike.[20]

After privately giving NBA teams the ammunition to threaten its players and publicly giving their side of the story, the NBA gave its proxies the ability to speak to the public and players directly. The teams received the memo and the press release accompanied by a telex from O'Brien, advising that the gag rule they had passed in October was off. Teams were now not only allowed but *encouraged* to publicly state their displeasure with negotiations, and especially with Fleisher. "In view of the fact that the Players Association has abandoned all attempts to maintain the confidentiality of collective bargaining negotiations and has resorted to public strike threats by some players," O'Brien said, "there no longer appears to be any purpose served by restricting your comments on this subject. Accordingly, until further notice, you are authorized and encouraged to keep your local media informed on the facts relating to negotiations to date."[21]

Not that they had really held back, but with the fines dropped, owners started talking, especially the regular cast of characters—Katz and Drossos. "I agree with every point," Katz—the diet magnate—said of the legal assertions in the memo. "If the players strike, they've violated their contractual rights. If all they want is the status quo, as they've said, then what's the difference in waiting six or eight weeks? We'd have the whole summer to reach an agreement. I know they think they can hurt us more now, because of losses of revenue from the playoffs, but I believe we can hurt them more than they can hurt us."[22] Drossos, who had a habit of signing players to agreements with incentives for team wins, thought he would be able to withhold large segments of players' salaries if they went on strike. "All that money would stay with me," Drossos told the *Boston Herald*. "I've made clear to the players what they'll lose out on."[23]

Next, the NBA convened a meeting of its special committee to investigate the financial viability of teams, scheduled for February 28, one day before negotiations were set to resume with Fleisher after a three-week hiatus. As part of its PR barrage, the NBA and its owners had spent much of the previous week publicly discussing the likelihood that teams would go under without an agreement, and especially if there was a strike. The four-man committee, appointed in mid-February by O'Brien, before the strike date was announced, was charged with "identifying those franchises in difficulty, the severity of their problems and the problems they [were] causing for the league."[24] In describing the outcome of the committee's meeting, the league announced, "Several specific proposals were discussed that could reduce the size of the league by five or more teams."[25] The analysis of dropping five teams, according to the NBA, was "explored significantly."[26] They were empowered to relocate franchises, merge two franchises, or dissolve them.[27] The NBA admitted that one of the factors the committee considered in its deliberations was the NBA threat of a strike.[28]

Fleisher was obviously and reasonably skeptical of all the management conduct. "It's interesting and fascinating that these kind [*sic*] of words would come out of a meeting the night before resumption of collective bargaining," Fleisher said in response to the committee's findings on February 28, mocking the timing.[29]

For all of the machinations, the NBA fear machine did not have the public impact they had hoped for.[30] Dan Shaughnessy, in the *Boston Globe*, said on February 27, about ten days after the onslaught and a few days before negotiations, that the NBA's conduct had not worked, and that "management [had] kept the presses running day and night, issuing one release after another, each longer and more boring than the last."[31]

. . .

"To open, the Players should clarify what we have been reading and hearing with respect to the Players' April 2 strike deadline," Larry O'Brien said, speaking directly to Fleisher. "We have heard it from the press but we have never heard it from you."[32] The parties resumed negotiating on March 1, 1983, in New York. It was the parties' eighteenth bargaining session and the first under the strike deadline. All that had been going on the prior month—the memo to the GMs, the strike date from the players, the announcements regarding the contraction of clubs, saber rattling from players and owners—made for the disaster it became. Even before O'Brien spoke, the mood in the room was tense. When Fleisher, Grantham, and Lanier arrived at the Berkshire Palace Hotel in Midtown, where they had met several times over the last few months, they were greeted by the press. The NBA's public relations director was there, as well as photographers, cameramen, and reporters. Fleisher advised he would not meet with them there, nor would he allow any pictures to be taken.[33] Not a good sign.

O'Brien was angry from the start. He had not wanted to meet at all, and in a conference call with the Labor Relations Committee on February 25, O'Brien viewed this meeting as purely theater. According to his notes for that call, he believed, "We should meet with Fleisher simply to obtain clarification of his position. If, in fact, the players have imposed an April 2 deadline, I think we should walk out immediately. That is my personal view—but of course, the decision on how to proceed is up to your committee."[34]

Fleisher was forthright in responding to O'Brien's statement. Fleisher said that when he met with the owners before the All-Star break, he "listened to harangue and abuse from . . . owners, especially Angelo Drossos." He said that after that meeting he believed that the NBA and its players were at an impasse. The owners insisted on implementing the cap immediately, and the players needed to wait until after the *Robertson* settlement was completed. Fleisher said, "It was apparent to me from statements at that meeting that we were not going to work anything out with respect to the Players proposal." Fleisher said he met with the players on Saturday at All-Star weekend, and that he had laid out the potential next steps. Fleisher told them the owners' position: they needed to have a cap in effect immediately. Fleisher said, "The players response was unless we have an agreement by April 2, that will be it—the players will strike before the end of the season."[35]

Both Stern and O'Brien said they felt blindsided by the strike date. Stern said he thought they had maintained an open dialogue and were working through outstanding issues—why escalate matters with a strike threat? Fleisher reiterated that they would strike absent an agreement.

Stern said, "We don't have the ability to negotiate."

"Why?" Fleisher shot back. "You threatened us in October with taking away our benefits and some jobs."[36]

Stern said relations had improved since then, and there had been no threats. Fleisher was clear—they would not change *Robertson*. He proposed either reaching a short-term traditional labor agreement or waiting until after *Robertson* ended. Stern said waiting four years wouldn't fix the NBA's problems. Fleisher responded that they could use that time to plan for the future. The exchange brought Stern to a reasonable question in light of Fleisher's conduct. "Are you saying that the status quo is all the players are prepared to do for now?" Stern asked.

"Correct, we are not willing to change *Robertson*."

O'Brien stepped in. "I had construed the good faith aspect of the past few months as good faith on both sides. We gave you the numbers you requested in good faith. You then said you would negotiate the concept. Our chain was pulled," he said.[37]

"If that's your belief that's wonderful," Fleisher responded.

"You think you have us in a spot. Since you have a pressure point you are going to squeeze, so go ahead," Granik said.

"You did it," Fleisher responded, referring to the owners' attempts to implement the previous fall. "Now you complain that we do it."[38]

"If you won't address the League's problems now, there is nothing to talk about," O'Brien said. "You've said to us you know that ten teams are in trouble but your answer is to strike."

"You said we must change the system," Fleisher said. "We won't."

Lanier jumped in, the only person who actually had to play the game at issue. "What does this mean, no more talks?" he asked.

Stern responded, "Yes."

"When you want to address our problems, give us a call," Granik said.

When Fleisher asked what that meant, Stern said, "On the basis of where we are, we're all going to wind up sitting on a torpedo and it may explode."

"There is nothing further to discuss," O'Brien said.[39] Just as he had walked out when Fleisher had asked to delay implementation, and with the press at the All-Star break, O'Brien stormed out of the negotiation—just as he had orchestrated. For a dealmaker, it was becoming a trend. "No purpose was served under the circumstances to continue the meeting," O'Brien said after. "It is depressing to me that this set of circumstances arises given the history of sports in this country and strikes in the last year."[40] O'Brien said publicly what he had said privately, that talks were effectively cut off, stating, "The players are free at any time to respond to the problems of this league. They have been invited to contact us if they have thoughts or recommendations in this area."[41] The entire session lasted less than thirty minutes.[42] There were no additional meetings scheduled.[43]

Later that day O'Brien circulated a memo to the Board of Governors summarizing the session. O'Brien said, "Fleisher responded unequivocally that the players would not agree to any proposal addressing the league's financial problems which would take affect prior to 1987, at the expiration of the *Robertson* settlement agreement." O'Brien said, "In view of the players' unwillingness to discuss any such proposals and its imposition of a strike deadline, there was no basis for further discussion . . . No further meetings have been scheduled, but the players were advised that we would meet at such time as they were prepared to consider any meaningful proposal."[44]

After the meeting, Fleisher was angry. "I have a tendency to get upset," Fleisher admitted to the *New York Times*, who reported that he could be heard yelling at the league's negotiating team.[45] Fleisher believed that the meeting was a show for a press. "That was a charade, a setup," he said. "The press has never known where our meetings have been held, but when we walked in yesterday there were reporters and television cameras. The first thing Bob Lanier said was 'this is the first time I've been to a meeting where everybody kept their jackets on. Three of them jumped up and took off their jackets then."[46] Fleisher, in a memo to players after the meeting said, "As we predicted, the NBA set it up as a total game."[47]

As to substance, Fleisher was also clear. "They said that unless we agree to something that will relieve them of their financial problems, there is nothing to talk about," he told the *Washington Post*. "We told them that if it involves giving up free agency, we couldn't do that. That ended the meeting."[48] As Lanier said, "I think the length of this meeting has to tell you something. The players are going to do what they have to do, and the All-Stars and the big money players are going to be right out in front."[49]

Collective bargaining is like marriage without the possibility of divorce, and angry feelings or not, the parties were required to come back to the table. On March 3, two days after that explosive session, Fleisher sent a letter to O'Brien demanding bargaining dates and admonishing him for claiming there would be no more talks. "I am surprised and somewhat dismayed by the position you and the NBA took during the negotiating session of March 1, 1983," he wrote. "As I understand that position, communicated to me and to the press, you and the league will not agree to hold any further collective bargaining meetings with the Players Association unless and until (i) the Players Association withdraws its strike deadline of April 2, 1983 and (ii) the Players Association commits to come to the bargaining table with a specific new proposal to address the financial condition of certain NBA teams. Obviously, any NBA refusal (for whatever reason) to sit down and talk is counterproductive . . . Nor, under the National Labor Relations Act, can any preconditions be imposed on the collective bargaining process. I sincerely hope that the NBA's statements to the contrary were made in the heat of the moment."[50] O'Brien responded the next day, saying that Fleisher had "misconstrued" the NBA's position, but they were seeking dates for bargaining as soon as possible.[51] They planned to meet the following week.

• • •

While the parties were posturing, time was running short, and the strike date came into focus. As April 2 drew closer, the press and the fans were not sympathetic to either side. Players were receiving threats, especially in Philadelphia. Clint Richardson, player representative of the Sixers, said, "I've been getting hate letters. Haven't gotten any letters supporting us. They're letters from factory workers mostly. And I go out to home games and a whole section of fans behind our bench has started yelling at me."[52] Fleisher did not expect to win a public relations war. "We're the third sport," he told the *Boston Globe*. "Baseball and football have had their strikes. We have highly paid players and 75 percent of them are black. Those are all negatives, but hopefully people will understand that we're not trying to change anything."[53]

Beyond owners and players, Fleisher was also fighting public opinion of the deal itself. Fleisher was being second-guessed for even considering a salary cap. Bob Woolf, who represented many players, including Larry Bird, said of the proposed cap, "I don't know. I'm afraid." Agents, columnists, union leaders—all of them were arguing that Fleisher should not even consider it. Ira Berkow, longtime sports writer in the *New York Times*, said, "A salary cap seems a strange thing for a union to accept—establishing, in effect, a maximum wage. But Fleisher believes that revenue sharing from future cable and pay television would make it at least as profitable for the players as the current arrangement." Berkow was skeptical, "A salary cap is anathema to the free-enterprise system and smacks of antitrust violation. The owners are capable of getting out of their own muddy mess—if, in fact, it is a mess—by themselves."[54]

Fleisher was feeling the heat from the players as well—especially those desperate for a championship. On Saturday, March 5, Fleisher went to the Meadowlands Hilton to meet with the Sixers to discuss negotiations. In the midst of the playoff hunt, uninterested in losing the opportunity to win their elusive title, the players were not excited about striking. While the Lakers and Celtics, and other contenders, were publicly behind the union, the Sixers were less so. Player representative Clint Richardson said, "Our position is the same as it has been . . . We haven't taken a formal vote, but we've talked about supporting a strike, and even though we don't want one, we'd do what we had to do. We have a union, and we're involved in trying to reach a settlement. It wouldn't work at all if we weren't unified."[55] Not a ringing endorsement.

After hearing about the meeting, Katz couldn't help himself: "I don't know if, before this, they really knew the consequences of what they were planning. If they go on strike, it's not as if they're just going to lose two weeks' salary. I don't think Larry Fleisher has laid out the true picture."[56]

The NBA also used the time between their March 1 and March 8 negotiations to try to raise the pressure on players. First, they initiated a special master proceeding to approve their position that if a players strike occurred there would be no free agency. It was not a strong argument. Once again, as it had been doing since the strike date, the NBA coupled its filing with a press release. As the league announced, "The NBA has commenced an enforcement proceeding against the players association to obtain a declaration confirming that any player who fails to complete his playing contract because of a strike, will not become a veteran free agent. As a result, players who otherwise would be eligible to negotiate with new teams this summer will be prohibited from doing so."[57]

In addition, in early March, a number of owners decided to take their case to their players directly. The Philadelphia 76ers, Denver Nuggets, San Antonio Spurs, Phoenix Suns, and Seattle Supersonics were all teams whose owners pulled them aside to discuss the impact of a strike. For the New Jersey Nets, the GM met with players individually.[58] There was a league-wide effort to meet with players to discuss the cost of a strike.[59] In Phoenix, Jerry Colangelo told the Suns he met with the hope that the meeting "enlightens you on what the owners are doing and what they want to do."[60] In Philadelphia, Harold Katz decided to meet with his team for a "very relaxed session" to discuss the ongoing negotiations.[61] The seventy-minute meeting, which included the Sixers players, Katz, GM Pat Williams, and Assistant GM John Nash was apparently very relaxed. So relaxed, in fact, that the word relaxed comes up in everything club officials said.

Though Katz had called the meeting, both sides pressed their positions. The players attempted to convince Katz to delay implementation of the salary cap. Katz tried to convince the players to accept

the owners' offer and not to strike. After the meeting, Billy Cunningham, coach of the team, and a player during the threatened strike of
1967, said, "I think we should just let Larry Fleisher and Harold Katz
sit down together and it'd be over in an hour. . . . And anyway, I don't
think there'll be a strike. We had the same kind of situation before the
1966–67 season where we were threatening to strike, but we settled."
As the *Inquirer* put it, "Yesterday's meeting at least signaled that the
Sixers owner remained on speaking terms with the team's players,
unlike the owners of several teams around the league."[62]

In San Antonio, however, things were less tranquil. Angelo Drossos
of the Spurs held a twenty-five-minute meeting with his players, after
a victory, to distribute the memo from the league office. Drossos then
used the meeting to engage in a combination of threats and bribes.

Drossos said, "A possible strike would affect everyone. A strike the
last month of the season would substantially affect teams more because the playoffs and the last part of the season bring in more revenue than the first part of the year." Drossos then opined, "If a player
has a contract to play for the full year, we expect him to honor that
contract. If the players don't play, they can expect to lose from 30–50
percent of their salaries."[63] Drossos also said that if the players voted
as a team not to strike, that he would pay them their full salary even
if other teams went on strike and they played no games at all.[64] He
said that if anyone refused to give the money back to him, he had
some advice: "I hope he has a lawyer."[65]

The players were dubious of Drossos's claims. Spurs forward and
player representative Mike Dunleavy said, "Legally, I don't think that's
possible. It may have to go to a court of law. You get paid for the games
you play. I believe it's an intimidation move by the owners and the
general managers."[66] Drossos said in response to Dunleavy's comments, "If someone takes it that way I'm sorry."[67]

Fleisher objected to Drossos's behavior. He called the meeting "an
empty threat, an illegal threat and an illegal meeting." He said, "We
may take necessary actions but I also don't want to get involved filing [unfair labor practice suits] all over the country. He clearly violated the labor laws, but I'm not going to get all charged up about
it."[68] The next day, Fleisher sent Drossos a letter saying, "The fore-
going statements made by you in your official capacity constitute a

clear, indeed flagrant, violation of the rights accorded to your players under the National Labor Relations Act."[69] Even though other
teams held similar meetings, it does not appear that Fleisher sent
any other owners letters.

Regardless of what Fleisher said, Drossos' conduct had its intended
effect of intimidating players. Gene Banks, a second year player, wanted
to get away from the entire negotiation. "I'm not going to mess with
it. I'm not going to touch it. The whole thing is crazy," he said. George
Gervin and Artis Gilmore, the highest paid Spurs players, would not
comment on the Drossos meeting. Gervin said, regarding the strike
date, "I'm not going to worry about it until it's time."[70] These conversa-
tions were enough of an issue that when the Board of Governors met
a few days later, league attorneys provided guidance on what could
or could not be said to players regarding a strike under labor law.[71]

If Philadelphia was a discussion, and if San Antonio was a threat,
then Seattle was a war zone. After a 126–103 win over the Rockets,
Sonics owner Sam Schulman met with his team behind closed doors.
Schulman told the players, "If they go on strike, we'll have another
team on the floor the week after April 2. I told the players their names
would be forgotten in no more than two years if we can put a moti-
vated, fighting team out there, and I think we can." He said, "I came
here as a friend to tell them to forget about all the details and consider what they're doing from a moral and ethical standard."[72] It is
doubtful the players saw Schulman's meeting as friendly.

Jack Sikma, the Sonics' All-Star and NBPA player representative,
who lost a tooth during the Sonics win, said of Schulman, "He didn't
come across as if he was throwing it down our throats. It was low key
but it still doesn't change what he said." When Fred Brown, a Sonics
guard and NBPA vice president, was asked about Schulman's comments he said, "We talked about this possibility way last summer. It's
not a big surprise. These things happen a lot in labor negotiations—
unions threaten a strike and management brings in scabs." When
asked whether he was concerned the scabs would be able to replace
NBA players, Brown said, "I wonder how CBS would feel about that?"
Schulman tried to play it down but was unsuccessful: "I didn't come
here to threaten and I didn't come representing anyone but myself
as an owner. But I felt it necessary to travel all day, which I don't rel-

ish, to tell the players what they're facing and to consider not creating a holocaust for themselves."[73]

Fleisher called it as he saw it, saying, "The owners are using scare tactics and it is those very tactics which could in the long run force a strike." Fleisher believed the league was "wrong, just like . . . in all of its legal maneuverings. [The NBA owners were] determined to use every conceivable threat to confuse the issue."[74] Fleisher even went so far as to circulate a memo to NBA general managers in response to the one distributed to players, in which he said: the league's correspondence was a "clearly unlawful threat concerning salary and deferred payments owed to NBA players which may have serious consequences for your team." The memo said, in response to Drossos's threats, "You should be aware that in any event any salary or deferred payment *already earned* are withheld from players, the Players Association will take immediate and expedited legal action which may result in the declaration that a player is a free agent with no remaining obligations to the team."[75] If the NBA could send a memo to "educate" GMS but threaten his members, Fleisher figured he could do the same.

• • •

For all of the attacks and threats, Fleisher had predicted all of this and prepared his players for it, like a good union leader. After the fiery session on March 1, Fleisher sent a memo to players to keep their spirits up, reminding them that they had planned for this.

He wrote, "I indicated to you during the summer and at our various team meetings in the fall, if we ever reached a period of 'strike dates' we would have to be faced with various attacks by the NBA owners. My predictions have proved correct. The first thing I said would be that they would threaten you, and the teams have done so. They have done it, first, with a memorandum from the NBA office to each of the General Managers, with directions that their memorandum be delivered to you. Some teams have done it by putting a three-page memorandum in your lockers; some have had the General Manager talk to you; some have had the owners talk to you. The purpose of it was clearly to threaten you. They have stated improperly from a legal point of view, that they would withhold your pay, either current or deferred. . . . Some of the owners have attempted to bribe their players."[76]

He predicted, "My judgement is that continuing threats will be made over the next few weeks. Obviously, they have also threatened you by indicating that teams would fold. Nothing was more transparent than their holding a meeting the night before our collective bargaining session to announce they were studying plans for folding five teams. This threat is intended to scare players with the loss of jobs. You shouldn't be surprised at any of this. We have discussed it before, and the threats will probably get greater as time goes on."[77]

Fleisher also prepared the players for what was coming: "I have indicated to you that they are going to try and divide us. The initial attempts on their part were to discredit me. They have run their whole campaign that way. Also implicit in the report they gave you was a credibility attack on our negotiating group, more specifically directed at me. The next step will be to try to divide us by team, by years of experience, by salary, by trying to differentiate between the higher-paid and the lower-paid players, and by other means. Again, this is something I told you would happen at our meetings and it has occurred."[78]

In closing his memo, Fleisher identified the importance of their solidarity. He concluded by saying, "The most important aspect of all of this is that you continue to display the unity that has occurred as of this date. While we will probably never convince the public or the media in total of our position, we have done a remarkable job of blunting the League's attacks. In the New York area particularly, more and more of the press has come around to our way of thinking. While nobody supports a strike, the media understand why we are taking the position we are taking, and I believe you should start seeing some of the comments in your local papers, but one thing that has come across in our discussions with various reporters around the country is their amazement at the unanimity of the position of the players. A writer from the *Washington Post* traveled to seven cities and came back and said that the support was even greater than it was in baseball and totally the opposite of what happened in football. If we can continue that, and obviously there is no reason why we can't, the fear injected into the owners will be the surest way of resolving this dispute. Any crack in the ranks will only serve to strengthen the owners' resolve and make a settlement that much more difficult."[79]

14

Unbounded Pessimism and Cautious Optimism, March 1983

If you're looking for a villain in the tense labor negotiations between
National Basketball Association players and owners, you can start by
pointing a finger at San Antonio owner Angelo Drossos.

—Randy Harvey, *Los Angeles Times*, March 1983

With the tension rising on both sides, the NBA and its players resumed negotiations on March 8, 1983, in New York. For all of the public and private posturing, there was still an incredibly complex and
novel agreement to negotiate. There were large issues on both sides,
and simply threatening one another was not moving things forward.

Fleisher had low expectations entering the meeting with management, telling *USA Today*, "If it's a meaningless meeting, it's a meaningless meeting. But at least we'll go ahead and meet."[1] Fleisher, Grantham,
and Fred Brown were there for the players. For the league were O'Brien,
Stern, Granik, Bettman, and Batterman. The talks were intended
to clarify the parties' positions before the owners' meetings scheduled for that weekend in Los Angeles, but at the start there was little hope of progress.[2] O'Brien started by asking Fleisher to "kick off"
the meeting, since he had demanded it. Fleisher had admonished
O'Brien for cutting off negotiations after their blowup on March 1.
Fleisher responded that he had no ideas and that "the negotiations
were going nowhere."[3]

Fleisher reiterated his position that the cap not go into effect for
four years—but this time he had a solution. Fleisher proposed starting the cap in four years, but making it at "today's levels." Stern was
unclear what that meant: If they did that, what would occur in terms

of exceptions—Bird, Sampson, and Jabbar? Fleisher seemed to be willing to waive those exceptions, saying, "it could be worked out."[4] This was the second time Fleisher seemed to be proposing a hard cap. Bettman expressed concern with this arrangement: Could teams front-load all of their salary now, believing they would be able to get under the cap later? Fleisher said they could allocate money to reflect that. The NBA rejected Fleisher's proposal. The owners gave away a hard salary cap to insist on immediate relief.

Stern asked Fleisher if he had a plan to save the troubled franchises—the Clippers and Cavaliers. Fleisher said, "Nothing we do will protect those teams—those teams will be in trouble with or without a collective bargaining agreement." O'Brien told Fleisher, "There is a view held by many in the League that the NBA should be a twelve team league and that the Krumpe Committee would be studying the manner."[5] There was discussion of marketing difficulties, which Fleisher said were the league's problem and not the players'.

With the strike date approaching and progress slowed, Fleisher proposed signing a basic deal and not worrying about the salary cap, or as he called it, the "master plan." "The NBA should sign a regular collective bargaining agreement and forget the master plan," he said. "I'll take a two-year agreement, while you work on your problems. Deal with your other problems first."[6] It was a reasonable position. What they were negotiating was novel, especially in sports. Though Fleisher admitted teams were losing money, he did not really believe the league would be in peril if they came back to the topic in two years. They had made some progress, kicked around good ideas—maybe it was time to move on, the way they had in 1980. O'Brien declined, saying, "The status quo from the players was not good enough." Fleisher reiterated his position. In two years it could be different—it probably would be. Cable television provided hope—maybe they should just sign a cost of living deal and see where they were in two years? Stern said that the projections skewed toward the large markets, and that "nothing in the league's history would indicate that the owners [would] do anything but pay it to the players."

Late in the day on the eighth, Fleisher made a new proposal—a comprehensive one; one that could move the parties to a deal. After a day trying to get them off of it, he returned to the master plan.

Fleisher proposed that the players would get 55 percent of gross, teams would have to spend 1/23 of the cap—no team could spend more or less, the NBA would guarantee 276 jobs and guarantee that team payrolls are at least $3.5 million. Fleisher also proposed that the plan take effect immediately after the 1982–83 season. Stern said the 55 percent was "too much to help the league." Fleisher said that the 55 percent was firm and "the players [would] not take less." Fleisher said the NBA should consider the proposal and that he was open to modifications. With that, they prepared to end for the day.

As the meeting ended, Stern said to Fleisher, "You have a hell of a lot of nerve making complex proposals and expecting us to respond to them and make a deal by April 2, since the players took six months with the guaranteed compensation plan."[7] Stern was right—but unless someone made a complex proposal, how else would a deal like this ever get done?

After the meeting, the parties were positive but cagey. Fleisher said that day's negotiation "was basically a clarification meeting. We are no closer than we were before, but I think both sides understand the issues better. When they get back from the Board of Governors meeting, we'll meet again." Fred Brown of the Supersonics, who was at the meeting, said, "The only thing you can say positive was that we were together for five hours. We discussed all of the issues and made sure that each side understood the position of the other."[8] Fleisher said, "As Fred said after the meeting, anytime you talk you're encouraged."[9]

From the owners' side, the view was the same—cautious, optimistic, and vague. O'Brien told the *Washington Post*, "We reviewed the elements of and the proposals. It was a true business session."[10] The meeting on the eighth, he said, "reminded me of the type of meetings we had up until a couple of weeks ago," referring to the strike threat—still clearly smarting from the union's action. "We're going to review these two sessions with our Board of Governors, who are scheduled to meet Friday in Los Angeles, and we'll probably schedule more bargaining talks next week."[11]

• • •

Though there was progress, the strike date still loomed large. When the Board of Governors met at the Century Plaza Hotel in Los Angeles for a special meeting on the morning of March 11, there was only one issue on the agenda, regardless of the meeting a few days earlier. This was the first time that the owners had met since the strike date, and when the meeting was called to order, O'Brien advised that the issues for discussion were collective bargaining, the players strike date of April 2, and what the NBA would do in case of a strike.[12]

O'Brien began by asking Stern to update the owners on the status of negotiations. Stern provided a six-point history of negotiations to that point. His summary made it appear as if there was no reason whatsoever for Fleisher and the players to call a strike date. After Stern's presentation, O'Brien asked Abe Pollin, owner of the Bullets and chairman of the Labor Committee, to address the assembled ownership as to the status of the Labor Committee's thinking. The night before, the eleven-member Labor Committee had met and debated what to do in case of a strike by the players. They had considered two alternatives: 1) they could complete the 1982–83 season with replacement players; or 2) the NBA could forego the playoffs and cease operations for the 1982–83 season if a strike was called and begin the next season with replacement players.[13] If there was a strike, it likely would upend the season, especially given the timing. Though there had not been a strike in the NBA, the other leagues had done so recently. When the MLBPA went on strike in 1981, it lasted fifty days. When the NFLPA went on strike the previous fall, it lasted fifty-seven. Both strikes were in season and impacted scheduling. Pollin said that with the strike scheduled to begin on April 2, the committee recommended that they cease operations for the rest of the season and, if the strike continued, begin 1983–84 with replacement players.

Several owners objected vigorously to ceasing operations. The contingent, led by Schulman, Drossos, and, amazingly, Jerry Buss of the Lakers, presented the idea of identifying potential replacement players from the Continental Basketball Association immediately. They believed the league should continue to operate the rest of the season.[14] When put up to a vote, Pollin's recommendation barely passed, 13–10, revealing deep divisions among the owners as to how to proceed.[15] The Board of Governors resolved that if "the players of the NBA engage[d] in a strike, then the NBA regular season and playoffs [would] be cancelled and plans [would] be implemented to play the 1983–84 season with replacement players."[16]

While they were divided as to how to handle a strike, they were not divided about what they wanted to see in a collective bargaining agreement. They voted unanimously to reject any contract that "would not help solve the league's financial problems," and directed its Labor Relations Committee to remain firm in negotiations with the NBPA and to bargain in good faith.[17]

The owners tried to convey strength out of the Board of Governors meeting, even though they were divided about what came next. "Twenty three to nothing," Harry Mangurian said of the owners' resolution about what would be in the agreement, selectively ignoring the divisions over replacements. "There were no objections by any of the owners," he continued, in a blatantly false statement. "Everyone was willing to accept the strike. The attitude is: if it is going to come, let it come now. We may as well go under now as later. Why not find the answer right now?"[18]

The threat of replacement players was met with a literal shrug from the players. The night of the Board of Governors meeting, for all of the frustrations on the West Coast as owners fought with how to best attack their players, there was still basketball to be played, and the Nets and Celtics were set to play the Meadowlands in New Jersey. As the *Boston Globe* reported, "Forty-five minutes before last night's Celtics-Nets game, Quinn Buckner and Foots Walker (player reps of the Celtics and Nets) came together at midcourt to hear what the owners had resolved. After listening to the owners' resolution, Buckner and Walker looked at each other, shrugged, and went their separate ways with a duet of 'No comment.'"[19]

After the Board of Governors meeting, Fleisher remained confident in the strength of the strike, now just three weeks away. "My history with these fellows is that they never do anything unless they're under pressure. I'm sure if you polled them now, they'd say 'good, let 'em strike' but let's wait and see what happens in the next three weeks."[20]

Fleisher was dubious that the league would fold without such a plan. "I went back and looked at clips of things that were said in the past, and except for the dates and the names, this could be 1964. They said the league would go bankrupt then if the players' pension proposal went through. Yes, there are teams losing money in the NBA today but it's not just because of player salaries. There has been total mismanagement in some cases, undercapitalization in some cases and greed on the part of the owners—such as the entry fee they made ABA teams pay to join the league. Indiana and Denver have never recovered."[21]

Rhetoric aside, both sides had a lot to lose from a strike. According to the NBA's internal documents, they pegged the total losses of revenue at $11.7 million for the regular season simply calculating for gate, local revenues, and network revenues if all ninety-six remaining regular season games were lost. The postseason would be much worse—each of the twenty-three playoff games set for broadcast on CBS would cost the league nearly $800,000 a piece. Between CBS, ESPN, and USA, the league stood to lose about $20 million on television revenue alone if the playoffs were lost to a strike. Including gate, that number rose to $29 million. The total potential impact of a strike was about $41 million dollars if the league simply ceased operations.[22] For a league that was teetering economically, that was a massive and potentially fatal loss for the business. While the economics were daunting, Fleisher was pragmatic, and there was a belief he would not put the NBA in such jeopardy. As the *Boston Globe* reported, "People who know him doubt that Fleisher would force a strike if he believed it would blow the league apart and put his people on the street for good."[23] One team official said, Fleisher "is a great poker player. He takes it right to the brink, and in the past the owners have always backed off."[24]

• • •

On March 15, amid the heightening strike rhetoric, a story emerged that Ted Stepien was planning to move the Cavaliers to Toronto at the end of the 1982–83 season. Stepien said he would do it even if other owners objected. He had tried to sell the Cavaliers throughout the season and was growing desperate. "My first obligation is to myself and my family and my business. I have invested $15 million in the Cavaliers. I can't take the losses anymore." He would need eighteen of the twenty-three clubs to vote to move the team to Toronto. It was not likely he would be able to do so.[25]

• • •

Coming off the Board of Governors meeting, the parties met again on March 16 in New York. Fleisher had called O'Brien a few days earlier, making an "urgent" request. Fleisher asked O'Brien to have a "representative" group of owners at negotiations. O'Brien wrote in notes for himself that he saw this as a positive sign for "meaningful progress" because Fleisher wanted to move closer to a deal. Fleisher also said that staff would be there—which O'Brien also took as a good sign because that meant Fleisher would do less grandstanding.

There were owners at the meeting, from both the big markets and the small—Jack Krumpe of Knicks, Alan Cohen of the Nets, Harry Mangurian of the Celtics, and Larry Weinberg of the Trail Blazers.[26] For the players, Bob Lanier, who had a game that night in Milwaukee, was in for negotiations as well.

As for the negotiation itself, O'Brien's positive public position belied a general rejection of the players' position. Fleisher had proposed two tracks for a cap: 1) a "7 year plan," with the cap set to take effect after the *Robertson* settlement ended, and 2) a "second year implementation plan" that would allow the cap to go into effect after the 1984–85 season but required teams to pay the full amount of the cap and guarantee 276 player jobs. The NBA rejected them both, saying, both proposals are "unacceptable in that they totally fail to address the League's current financial plan."[27]

The NBA did make a counter. First, they raised the guaranteed percentage of defined revenue from 40 to 50 percent. They also set the minimum required team salary at 2/3 of the cap from ½. These numbers were still too low—especially on the minimums. Fleisher thought it was imperative that every team would need to spend, and simply restraining high paying teams was not a positive solution. This was the NBA moving into the realm of what could actually become a deal. The NBA's bargaining notes also stated that they wanted to "reiterate to the Players Association that the NBA is prepared to discuss any and all proposals which are aimed at addressing the League's current financial problems," and that "so long as the parties remain in good faith negotiations, NBA teams will continue to provide all existing collectively bargained benefits."[28] This was the NBA's way of trying to move Fleisher off the strike date. They were indicating that they did not intend to implement their proposals as they had in October. Now, they were making real progress.

Fleisher sounded a positive note. "I'm becoming a little more optimistic," Fleisher said of negotiations. "I feel a little better than I did at one time. We've stopped all of this nonsense about meeting once and then not getting together again for two weeks. More owners are taking part in the discussions lately, too, and that's a good sign."[29] Fleisher continued, "I'm very encouraged. We've been talking a long time and we're still talking. It's nothing I can put my finger on and I don't know how close we are to a settlement, but I am encouraged."[30] Fleisher said that he expected the two sides to continue to speak, "unless either side gets angry."[31]

After the meeting, Lanier was rushed to the airport to fly to Milwaukee for the game that night, in which he would score 10 points in a loss.[32] "It's not a fineable offense," Coach Don Nelson said of Lanier's being in New York for negotiations. "I was going to start him so it hurt a little bit, but we had him for the second quarter."[33]

The parties agreed that they would meet again six days later, and in light of the progress, they reinstituted their media blackout.[34] "The policy agreed upon by the parties is to make no comment on what takes place at the meetings," said Alex Sachare, public relations spokesman for the league.[35] Fleisher said, "The only way any real news will come out of Monday's meeting will be if there's a settlement, which I doubt will happen, or if talks break off."[36]

While the strike date was fast approaching, optimism for a deal was growing. On March 21 and 22, Fleisher and Grantham met with the subcommittee of owners—Mangurian, Cohen, Krumpe, and Weinberg, of the Portland Trailblazers, in secret. (The NBA was surprised that they had actually been able to keep it a secret.)[37] They made tremendous progress. The twelve hours of meetings over two days led both sides to believe a deal was close. Fleisher was optimistic. He had even called all of the player representatives and said he believed a deal was close at hand.[38] The league and its players agreed upon the concept of the cap—they had agreed that there would be minimums and guarantees. The heavy lifting, at least they hoped, was over.

The team maximum they were discussing was about $4 million per team and a minimum of about $3.2 million.[39] Fleisher's view was that if they were going to rein in the Philadelphia 76ers, who had just the previous season spent as much money as possible, Fleisher and the NBPA wanted the Indiana Pacers to pay more than the $1.1 million on their current payroll, and even Pollin's Bullets would have to pay more than their $2 million. "If the minimum and maximum salary were high enough," Fleisher said, "at least 18 teams would be forced to spend a considerable amount more for salaries than they are presently doing, and there would no longer be any need for the *Robertson* settlement."[40]

To require a push to the minimum would have a second component—revenue sharing. As the *Globe and Mail* reported, "A source close to the negotiations said such a plan would probably entail some form of revenue sharing among the clubs for the first time in NBA history. That would enable a financially troubled club to meet the minimum payroll. It also might bring the league closer to parity on the court because it would allow troubled clubs to spend more freely for player talent."[41] There were a few issues left: 1) when the cap would be implemented; 2) what the parties would do in terms of crediting deferred compensation against the cap; and, most importantly, 3) what percentage of revenues the players would get. After nine months of bargaining, given the complexity of the circumstance and where they started, that was not a long list of outstanding issues.

Regarding timing, the parties had made progress from the hurt feelings around the All-Star Game. There were reports that the NBA, who wanted implementation of the cap immediately, and the NBPA, who wanted it in four years, would meet in the middle and implement it in two years. That would allow a freer market until after some of the bigger names—Kareem Abdul-Jabbar, Kevin McHale, Larry Bird, and Kelly Tripucka—completed free agency and got their chance to make money.[42]

Deferred compensation was another issue. The league as a whole owed between $80 and $90 million in deferred compensation to players. It was a popular trick for both weaker and stronger owners. The players liked it because it allowed them to have more stability over a longer period of time. Weaker owners hoped to get someone else to pay when the bill came due. Shrewd owners like Jerry Buss also used deferred compensation to push things off into the future. For cap purposes, the difficulty was twofold: How do you calculate deferred compensation for purposes of a salary cap, and, more importantly, what would happen if this did not work and teams folded? "Our position," Fleisher said, "is that the league is really a partnership among owners," but if shaky teams folded, the league would be responsible for the payments.[43] Some owners, like Harry Mangurian of the Celtics, disagreed, "Why should I have to pay for Magic Johnson's salary if Jerry Buss decides he wants to give him a $25 million deal?"[44] This remained outstanding.

The last issue—the biggest issue—was the percentage of revenues that would have to be spent. The owners were tremendously interested in identifying the maximums the teams would be able to spend but significantly less interested in identifying how much revenue the teams would have to share, and what the minimum salary would be. Fleisher was focused on ensuring that all teams would have to spend. The parties set a meeting for March 25, which they hoped would be to finish their collective bargaining agreement.

After the progress with the smaller group, the owners scheduled a meeting in New York with the entire Labor Committee on March 24 to discuss the framework they hoped would stabilize the NBA and revolutionize sports.

• • •

"If you're looking for a villain in the tense labor negotiations between National Basketball Association players and owners," the *Los Angeles Times* reported, "you can start by pointing a finger at San Antonio owner Angelo Drossos."[45]

For the negotiation on March 25, after weeks of progress, all eleven members of the NBA Labor Relations Committee came to New York. Drossos flew in to New York a day early and began to campaign. Drossos simply did not believe the players would really strike, and he was certain there was a better deal on the table than the one Stern had negotiated. The *Los Angeles Times* reported that Drossos "began campaigning among the owners to hold out for a better settlement. He had been convinced all along that the players were bluffing when they set an April 2 strike deadline" and believed the owners should take a harder line rather than capitulating to a phony strike date.[46]

Drossos was persuasive, and the owners came into the meeting on the twenty-fifth with a different proposal than what Fleisher and Stern had spent the last few weeks negotiating that had spurred such optimism. The new proposal had two major changes. First, Drossos convinced the owners to not only bring down the team caps they were discussing but the minimums as well.[47] Gone were the $3.5–4 million caps and the $3 million minimums. Fleisher said management reduced its minimum salary to as low as $1.5 million per team and the maximum to $2.8 million. The problem was a proposal of $1.5 million minimum was beneath the current minimum for most teams, making it a worthless proposal. There was a second issue as well. The new NBA proposal removed large amounts of money from what constituted the gross revenue, further reducing the players' share. The NBA removed parking, concessions, exhibitions, and the playoffs from the revenue, estimated at being worth $15 to $18 million dollars.[48] Not only did they not have a deal, but in Fleisher's mind, the owners went back on what they had proposed. Fleisher said afterward that they "backed off everything that had been agreed to and their offer would effectively remove the players' right of free agency."[49]

The meeting itself was a disaster. "Angelo and his guys came in and busted the meeting up," Fleisher said. Drossos and Fleisher got into it, with Drossos, the former boxer, saying there would be a confrontation the next time he met with Fleisher. When asked if that was accurate, Drossos said only, "I was there." Fleisher stormed out in less than thirty minutes. As one source closed to the negotiations said, "If we could keep Angelo away from the meetings, we might reach a settlement."[50]

Drossos's maneuver had blown up months of work. One of the owners called the Drossos meeting a "serious setback."[51] Fleisher was furious. "We're back to square one," he said to the press.[52] Fleisher said, "The NBA proposal today was a change in gross income from what was originally discussed and what the teams had to spend. They said $1.5 to $1.6 million a year. That's ludicrous. It would eliminate all free agency. The intent of the owners was apparent today. They want to take away free agency and we won't go for that."[53] Fleisher said he simply did not see how the NBA could avert a strike.[54]

Stern was embarrassed. He normally had his constituents in line and could move them to a deal, but this had blown up what should have been an agreement. Quinn thought it was a tactic by the owners— they wanted to see how desperate the players were to reach a deal, and whether the owners would push them.[55] Grantham had a different theory, "After negotiating with the group for three days we felt there was movement. But when they went to their full committee, they either couldn't sell it or some of the (most militant) owners rejected it."[56]

Publicly, the NBA said that the union rejected the owners' offer of 50 percent of the gross revenues, demanded 53 percent, then broke off discussions and left the meeting.[57] Fleisher characterized the NBA's explanation as "absolute nonsense. It was a catch all way to make the public think we walked out over very minor differences."[58] Grantham seconded Fleisher's comments, "The real issue is not whether it's for 50 percent or 53 percent. Players will not strike over three percent. The issue is the definition of gross income. That will significantly change the amount."[59] "It was as if we never had the meetings I had characterized as productive," Fleisher said.[60] The NBPA simply couldn't agree to the proposal. Drossos's proposal would hamstring the market. "We have felt the gross would have to be big enough to allow players to enjoy a competitive free market," Grantham said.[61]

The owners tried to spin it as an overreaction by the players, but it rang hollow. Harry Mangurian said, "I thought I understood (the players' position), but after all the owners flew into New York for this meeting and Fleisher walked out, I liken it to the guy who kills the goose that's about to lay the golden egg."[62] Mangurian said, "Watching the whole exhibition was a little too much to take."[63] Colangelo, who had a strong relationship with Larry Fleisher, fought back, "I think Larry Fleisher is trying to manipulate the media. The severity of the problem is there. Nobody is trying to break the union. All we're asking is that the union understand that we have problems. A strike would put everything in disarray and put more jobs in jeopardy."[64]

After negotiations on the twenty-fifth, things looked grim. Fleisher said, "It is clear to us that based on today, we've been wasting our time the last few weeks. My feeling is that there is no alternative. There will be a strike April 2. I will be shocked if it didn't occur."[65] It was not the outcome Fleisher wanted. "We don't want a strike," he said. "It wouldn't be good for anybody but we have to protect our rights. When somebody sets a fire at your door and you throw water on it, you shouldn't be the bad guy just for getting things wet."[66]

While Fleisher believed there would be a strike, the NBA felt confident about a settlement, even with Drossos's explosion. According to a management source, after the meeting, "From where we stand, we've come 90 percent of the way. We've covered a lot of ground. The players have changed their position. They are finally talking about a salary cap and a minimum. That's a major step. I wouldn't say we're close-close but we've got between now and Thursday to make this deal." Another anonymous source told the *Boston Globe*, "These are grown men with the same interests. With what we're taking about, nobody loses and the game gets better. Nobody wants a strike. Thursday's meeting of owners will be very important because either the board votes to re-affirm and allow a strike, or they'll vote on something that will get negotiated."[67] A source close to negotiations told the *Washington Post* that avoiding a strike "would be in the best interests of everyone," and that a settlement "is possible, and even likely, if everyone is reasonable."[68]

After a weekend of press, the parties resumed negotiations on Sunday amid a media blackout. Larry O'Brien was there for the owners, along with David Stern, and Jack Krumpe and Alan Cohen, of the Knicks and Nets respectively. For the NBPA was Fleisher, Grantham, Lanier, and Bridgeman.[69] Drossos was gone, and the hope was that they would get down to business. The representative group went back to the table.

While negotiations continued, in the league's mind, everyone turned to the potential of a strike, which was set to start in a few days. With negotiations troubled, the concern became whether the players would actually strike. The *Hartford Courant* reported, "Player solidarity appears strong. Some owners question whether Fleisher is a Pied Piper and the players' children who don't comprehend the League's financial problems."[70]

Greg Ballard of the Bullets said of a strike, "We will vote to if it comes to that. None of us wants to strike, but there are things we must protect."[71] "Too many great players in the NBA have worked too hard in the past for the benefits we have," Bulls player representative David Greenwood said. "We have to stand up for what we've already earned." Larry Drew of Kansas City agreed, "I don't want to do it [strike]," he said. "I would rather play it out but you've got to do what you've got to do. We've got to protect certain things."[72] Elvin Hayes, a fifteen-year veteran, blamed the owners: "I didn't realize it would come to this. Eventually we've always settled disputes in the past. We're not asking for any more. The owners have created this mess. They must unite and stop fighting because some teams can't compete. Some teams will survive, some will not." Joe Merriweather, the player rep for Kansas City, said, "I don't think they will split us up. I think we will all be together. I don't think we should give back what we've worked for. Free agency is the main thing that will hurt a lot of guys."[73]

Celtics coach Bill Fitch was more clear: "I don't care what side you're on," he said. "If anyone just thinks of the consequences they'd realize in a second that a strike would be the height of stupidity. Nobody could possibly gain a blessed thing, even in the long run."[74]

Oscar Robertson, in attendance at a Lakers-Rockets game just days before the strike was set to commence, was asked about the situation his lawsuit helped start. "I think it would behoove both parties to sit down and settle the situation before a strike," Robertson said. "But the players shouldn't give back what we won in court. They have rights in this situation. It's time that the owners recognized that. From my dealing with owners in the past, though, I'm not optimistic. I'm sure a lot of them don't think yet that the players will strike. Until they take the players seriously, there will be a problem."[75]

Fleisher did not expect public sympathy: "People take the view that the players are overpaid. You've got a racist element there too. *Hey they're overpaid black players*. Plus, nobody likes a striker under any circumstances. We're the third sport. People are tired of it. So we're never going to convince the fans."[76] There were only a few days before the proposed strike date, and they were already looking at a Golden State-Kansas City game on April 1 as the last before a strike would take place.[77] The players were trying to figure out how they would get home from their games in case of a strike.

• • •

The small group met again on March 28, and both sides agreed the talks had gotten back on track—regardless of Drossos. The group—Stern, Granik, Bettman, along with Krumpe and Alan Cohen for the owners; Fleisher, Grantham, Lanier, and Bridgeman for the players—was getting things done. "We're having serious talks," Alan Cohen said. "The fact that we are still talking indicates there is at least a possibility that a strike can be averted. But to say that there is anything more definitive than hope at this time is premature." Fleisher, calmly told the *New York Times*, "I share Mr. Cohen's views after what has occurred to date."[78]

Though the sides were progressing, the union did not slow down as the April 1 date approached. The players were taking strike votes team by team. The Knicks voted 12–0 after a practice, before a game against the Clippers. "The vote took five minutes," said Marvin Webster, the captain, player representative, and longtime Fleisher client who had won a compensation hearing in the 1970s. "We don't have any other choice. There was very little discussion. The guys felt they knew the issue and if they had to strike they would."[79] The Lakers, who were also playing for a championship, voted 12–0 to side with the players association, even if it was against their interests. "It was more of a vote of confidence for Fleisher," Jamal Wilkes said, another player who had benefitted personally from Fleisher's machinations over the years. "But we don't want to strike here. We're in an unusual situation. We're making good money. We're looking forward to the playoffs. Us and Philly don't want to strike. But we're going to do what is best for all the players."[80]

But there was progress at the table, and hope. After the first meeting on the twenty-eighth, the parties met again on March 29 and 30, furiously working toward a deal. A source told the *New York Times*, "We continue to talk about profit sharing and finding a formula that would allow free agency to continue and yet find a way to curb the escalating salaries. If we can agree on minimum and maximum salary caps that each team must spend, I think we can avert a strike."[81] There were a few issues still outstanding in negotiations. Fleisher wanted several things included in revenue for the cap, including gate sharing, and it appeared to be the answer to the logjam. "If there is a settlement, gate sharing will have to be included," a source told the *New York Times.*[82]

The *Boston Globe* reported that there was optimism. The *Boston Herald* reported on March 30 that the parties had a deal. "I'd like to know where they got their information," Alan Cohen responded. "Negotiations are continuing and they are serious, but we can't go beyond that." Fleisher concurred, "There's no reason why there can't be a settlement but that's not the same as predicting there will be a settlement."[83]

The owners began arriving in New York for a Board of Governors meeting on March 31, with hope there would be a pending resolution on the agreement. Or . . . there would be a strike. Angelo Drossos, who was approached while checking in at the Waldorf Astoria for the meeting, said, "There won't be a strike. I have always felt that way. We'll get this solved." Katz of the Sixers said, "I think progress has been made, but I don't discuss the areas." Greg Ballard, player representative for the Bullets, said he had spoken with Fleisher, saying, "Larry Fleisher and the officers of the players association, have been very happy so far today. We feel we will reach an agreement before the weekend. I would say it's 80 percent against the strike, 20 percent for the strike."[84]

As the *Associated Press'* William Barnard said on the eve of the Board of Governors meeting, "Unbounded pessimism is being replaced by cautious optimism at the National Basketball Association contract talks."[85]

15

Peace, April 1983

Lanier had two speeches prepared: the one he made
and the one that said the war was on.

—LARRY FLEISHER

And then . . . it was over.

"Thank you all for your patience. I appreciate you being here. I think you will find out what I have to announce to have been worth your wait," O'Brien said in his prepared notes for the press conference on April 1, 1983, from the fourth floor of the Waldorf Astoria.[1] Instead of announcing the NBA's response to a strike, which was called for that day, O'Brien was there to announce a new collective bargaining agreement with the players that provided for a salary cap, the first in all of sports. "This agreement contains many unique aspects which will be enormously helpful to management in planning a stable future for the league while also assuring the continuity and protection of players rights. It represents what I fully believe to be a dramatic new approach to the conduct of a professional sports league. Did the owners get everything they wanted when the negotiations began nine long months ago? The answer is no. Did the players get everything they wanted? The answer, once again is no. Was an agreement reached which represents a revolutionary advance for professional basketball. The answer, I believe, is a firm and resounding yes."[2]

Fleisher was also generous in his description. "The key to our agreement," he said, "is that we share in the revenues of the league, but we keep free agency as well. Even with the shared revenues, the players still have individual negotiating rights."[3] He was also clear, however, that it was a compromise. "In any settlement," Fleisher said, "there are various interests affected, but usually each side thinks only of what they have gained. This settlement, I believe, is unique in the history of sports."[4] "We're in this sport together and this agreement proves it," said Larry O'Brien.

Both sides acknowledged there was pressure to reach an agreement. "Lanier had two speeches," Fleisher said, "the one he made and the one that said the war was on."[5] Junior Bridgeman believed the specter of the strike vote had pushed the groups to a deal. "Things just started falling into place after that. Both sides started seeing the other one's point better."[6] Fleisher was also clear that the strike, or the threat of it, had an impact: "The thing that triggered this deal was the belief among the owners that we seriously would strike. We wanted a share of the receipts, they wanted the cap, we compromised in some areas, and so did they. I feel like we've been working on it forever."[7]

Part of the reason for the strength of the deal was also Fleisher's reaction to Drossos's maneuver the previous week. "The owners came in with a lot of new proposals that day," Steve Mix said. "They did it to test our strength, and we showed them our convictions. When they realized how strongly we felt, we came back to the bargaining table and began getting things done." Katz tried to downplay it, saying, "Their walkout was a game but I understood the game. I've been negotiating in business for 20 years and it wasn't something I hadn't seen before. As soon as it happened, I accepted it as the first sign that we were going to make a deal. We tested them, they tested us, then we got it done."[8] Regardless, everyone was happy to have a deal. "Most teams didn't see a light at the end of the tunnel," said Larry Weinberg of the Blazers. "With this Agreement, I believe that now they will be able to see a light at the end of the tunnel."[9]

Fleisher was clear he was happy with the deal. "I feel sensational," he said. "First, in the public's eye, we've created a better sport, forcing a form of revenue sharing among the teams that makes the bottom teams spend more money for better players. We're no longer in a situation where, say, a Philadelphia spends five times what an Indiana spends. The result has to be a more competitive league, contingent on the decisions of each individual management group. Next, the players now have the best of all worlds, because we've not only maintained, but enhanced, the competition for their services. And getting 53 percent of the revenue, if we're all correct about the future of cable, that could be a bonanza."[10] Lanier concurred, saying, "By requiring each team to be competitive in bidding for players and in spending money, it greatly enhances the possibility of equality of talent and play."[11]

Many owners were ecstatic. "I think this is the most important thing that has happened to the NBA since the merger and it may be even more important than that," Abe Pollin said. "It takes a lot of craziness out of the sport. Teams can now plan their futures better and have some projections on where they're going, and it's going to make the game more competitive for the fans."[12]

The last few days of negotiations had been intense. O'Brien attempted to keep the owners informed, but it was difficult—he was unsure of when they would meet with the players and how long it would go. The final flurry of negotiations had the largest impact on the Milwaukee Bucks, who were fighting for playoff position. Lanier, Bridgeman, and Mix were all officers of the NBPA and Milwaukee Bucks. They attended more negotiations than any other players in the league. "In the last two weeks I've done a lot of traveling," Bridgeman said when the deal was reached. "Since last Tuesday, I've stayed in seven or eight different hotels to go back and forth between games and negotiations. That really wears you down both physically and mentally."[13] Though they hadn't missed any games for the Bucks, Fred Brown of the Supersonics did miss a game—which the Sonics lost by 2 points—to attend to negotiations in New York toward the end of bargaining. The team's president advised the coach, former NBPA member and Fleisher client Lenny Wilkens, "to tell Fred that his participation in any meeting will have to be on nongame days or by conference telephone."[14] The leadership of players in negotiations was crucial—in all forms. "Larry is definitely more skilled in arguing back and forth with the other side, so the players didn't do too much of that. I believe our number one contribution was knowing how the rank and file players feel," Bridgeman said.[15]

The owners had debated the proposed agreement at a Board of Governors meeting the day before O'Brien's press conference at the Waldorf Astoria. O'Brien proudly advised the owners that they had reached a tentative agreement. Stern advised the teams "line by line" of the agreement. There was a lengthy discussion of the agreement, and owners were given an opportunity to ask questions. Because this involved revenue sharing among the clubs, it required an amendment to the by-laws of the NBA itself. Stern, just as he had a few months earlier, had his consultant present an economic model to show the impact of the agreement based on various revenue and salary projections moving forward.

O'Brien, pushing for the agreement's passage among the owners, chose to start from the beginning. O'Brien, according to the Board of Governors minutes, "reviewed for the Board the mandate given to the Labor Relations Committee at the Annual Meeting las June." O'Brien said that "the tentative agreement comports with that mandate and was the result of the NBA's firm stand over many months." He noted extensive owner involvement and said, "Despite some imperfections, the proposed agreement is a quantum leap forward for the league."[16]

The owners voted in favor of the agreement twenty-two to one, with the only dissent coming from Sam Schulman, owner of the Seattle Supersonics. Even Drossos voted for it. Schulman was furious at the deal and claimed he intended to file lawsuits to derail it, saying that Fleisher had "raped the league."[17] "The union made no concessions of any substance," Schulman said. "When we go into negotiations we deal from weakness and fear and make concessions. This is a repeat of what has happened each time in collective bargaining. We are shutting our eyes to reality." Schulman credited Fleisher, calling the agreement an "indisputable" victory for the players. "The strike was an intimidating factor. There's no question Larry Fleisher had this whole scenario mapped out . . . He delayed and delayed this thing until now. He took two months to study our books, then said that up to 10 teams were in trouble but he didn't care. Then he cut off negotiations after the All-Star break and said there would be a strike April 2. The whole scenario was obvious to an 11-year-old."[18]

Fleisher had a ratification vote scheduled but believed "ratification is only a formality."[19] Of all the players, no one was more excited than Clint Richardson, the player rep for the 76ers. "We either had to get it done or we were going on strike, and neither side wanted that. Coming up with an agreement takes the weight off us, especially me. This was easily the hardest situation an NBA player rep in Philly had ever faced. Maybe people in other businesses can now use us as an example. We didn't strike, we didn't need a mediator, we got it solved on our own."[20]

The players were pleased. "There's no question about us being satisfied," Steve Mix said. "In my case, I've already played 13 years and the sport has given me a good life. I'm not going to reap the benefits of this agreement, but the future of the sport is meaningful to me. I was elected to this position, and up to now it's been pretty easy. When it got harder, we all felt an obligation to do the best possible job. The average guy on the street can't relate to us because of our salary level, but we're a union and we needed a contract. We had a right to do what we did."[21] David Greenwood, player rep for the Bulls, said, "We kept our free agency and that was the main thing. I know the Bulls are under the $3.6 million level for player salaries, they'll have to go out and get some other higher priced players or give us all raises. We also got a piece of the cable money, which is something we fought for."[22]

O'Brien was happy to take a victory lap. "I never had the slightest question as to whether I should be involved," he said about negotiations. "That's not the sort of thing that's in the job description, it was just something that seemed obvious to me. When we started on this road nine months ago, examined the intricacies and the revolutionary aspects of what we had in mind, we knew it represented a completely different way of conducting a sports league. I can't remember how many times I said, 'Why did we ever get into this? It's impossible.' Yet, as I was saying that I knew if we could do it, it would advance the NBA immeasurably."[23]

With the deal signed, the threatened strike was quickly forgotten and Fleisher received plaudits from management. As the *Los Angeles Times* reported, "Fleisher was highly respected by management before the strike threat and remains so." Jerry Buss said, "In three or four years, the league would have been down to 8 or 10 teams . . . Weighing that correctly, Fleisher decided to make a contract. He visualized correctly that he was saving basketball."[24] Unlike the NFL and MLB, the NBA reached an agreement without a work stoppage.

Even CBS was pleased that the NBA had reached a deal. In a letter to O'Brien and Stern, Neal Pilson, head of CBS Sports, said, "Just a quick note to express my congratulations on the professional manner in which you conducted the negotiations with the NBA Players Association and the results which you achieved." Pilson found the NBA's success impressive, especially "when you compare the outcome of your negotiations with the recent disasters experienced by the NFL and Major League Baseball."[25]

When the CBA deal was reached, Clint Richardson had hope that he and the NBA would not be in this situation again. "Maybe the owners will run their teams better now," he said. "They have to, because there will be more competition than ever. You can't make anybody make the right decisions on players for a particular team, but these are smart men. They didn't make the millions that allowed them to buy a team by being dummies."[26]

• • •

The final agreement was enormously complex. The cap itself, unrelated to the rest of the CBA, became a thirty-one-page document that could not be distributed for another six weeks as it continued to be negotiated. In the end, on most of the issues that were truly in conflict, Fleisher was able to get much of what he wanted.

The owners would be required to give the players 53 percent of revenue. Crucially, Fleisher got contract language requiring that "the NBA and each NBA team shall in good faith act and use their best efforts" to maximize their revenues.[27] He was able to achieve a broad definition of revenue that, although it excluded the All-Star Game, concessions, and parking, included money earned from "all sources, whether known or unknown, derived from, relating or arising out of the performance of players in NBA basketball games."[28] For parking and concessions, the players agreed to $1 million dollars in benefits, despite the fact that the league says these receipts exceeded $5 million the previous season.[29] That compromise sealed the deal; it allowed the owners to give the players 53 percent, and the owners to save some money from the players.

Most importantly, revenue included "proceeds from the sale, license or other conveyance of the right to broadcast or exhibit NBA pre-season, regular season and playoff games on radio and television, including, without limitation, network, local, cable and pay television, and all other means of distribution."[30] Finally, the players had a piece of cable revenues of the NBA.

The cap would go into effect after the 1983–84 season. For 1983–84, the teams with the top five payrolls—Los Angeles, New Jersey, New York, Philadelphia, and Seattle—would be frozen at the place where they were, kind of. They could still sign draft picks and trade players for players whose combined salary was no greater than 100 percent of what they traded away.[31] For the other teams, there would be no cap or minimum, but if they went above the cap, they would lose some of the cap exceptions.

Then, beginning in 1984–85, the salary cap would go into effect. In the end, it was close to the compromise Fleisher had been offering months earlier, it just took the owners a little while to get there. How they would determine the cap would be to find the total gross receipts based on a number of factors. Then players would get 53 percent of the gross revenue formula divided by the twenty-three teams. They would then get the greater of the number from the formula, or $3.6 million in 1984–85, $3.8 million in 1985–86, and $4 million in 1986–87.

Compared to the modern cap, with its exceptions and circumstances, the original cap seems quaint. But, it did include some of the hallmarks and policies that would be refined over time. First, it was a soft cap—teams could go above it under certain circumstances. Second, it included "Bird rights" to fix the Larry Bird problem. This allowed a team, even if it was at or above the cap, to match any offer sheet extended to one of its payers or to enter into an agreement at any cost. Next, the cap also dealt with the Abdul-Jabbar problem—if players were waived or retired, they could be replaced at 50 percent of their worth.[32] If a free agent left? The team could replace that salary up to 100 percent of their value. There were also protections in the event of injury or otherwise being unable to play.

There was also a provision for rookies—to deal with the Sampson problem. Teams could sign rookies to any salary they wanted. If a team was at or above the cap, they could sign a rookie to $65,000/$70,000/$75,000 each year of the contract, well below the amount that first-rounders were making at the time. Here was where Fleisher protected the rookies: if a rookie signed to a team he could sign a one-year contract then become a free agent—the Sampson problem.

The NBA said it would guarantee 253 jobs (eleven players per team), even if teams folded. Fleisher was not concerned about teams folding, but he had the protections. If a team folded, "the then remaining NBA teams shall carry an aggregate of least 253 players on their Active Lists for such playing season."[33]

How would they deal with allocations among ownership groups? The parties agreed that what occurred as of the date thereof was reasonable. The deferred money issue? It had a simple solution: if the player's contract said which season the deferred payments were for, they would be attributable to that season for cap purposes. If not, ascribed per rata in each season.[34] What about benefits? The NBA would continue to pay, and they would not count against the cap. All of these were victories for Fleisher.

And here was the last part: if the team could not meet the minimum, "the difference will be made up from a pool of shared revenues."[35] The NBA agreed, as part of the memorandum of agreement, that if there was a judgment that any team had failed to make its payments, the NBA shall either make the payment on behalf of the team or "promptly commence proceedings to terminate said Team's franchise pursuant to the NBA constitution."[36] There would not be any more Sterling missing payments or wildcat strikes. As Lanier said, "Teams will be able to compete with each other on an equal basis. The large teams like Los Angeles and New York would be bidding basically at the same level as all the other teams in the league."[37]

There were complex monitoring proposals on both sides to ensure they complied with the cap. The NBA agreed, as part of the deal, that during each year the NBA teams would allow the PA "access to all the books and records including audited financials, accountants work papers, any contracts and documents relevant to making the determinations, computations, valuations or allocations."[38] The NBA agreed to advise the PA on June 1 of the salary of each team for the previous season, and the accurate numbers would be provided by July 31. If they could not calculate it in time, what would they do? They would simply take the previous year's number and project a 10 percent increase. What if it was too low and players were over or underpaid?

The money would either be added to or taken out of the benefits the players received.[39]

There would certainly be loopholes (and Fleisher invited them)—but what about circumvention of the agreement itself? "Neither the parties hereto, nor any Team or player shall enter into any agreement, player contract, offer sheet or other transaction which includes any terms that are designed to serve the purpose of defeating or circumventing the intention of the parties."[40]

Fleisher was not certain what was going to happen with the *Robertson* settlement. He was concerned about being sued and whether the court would approve the deal. As part of the agreement, the NBA agreed to pay all reasonable fees of the players association that could be incurred as a result of the salary cap.[41] It didn't matter—Judge Carter would approve the modifications the sides agreed to.

Now the focus could return to the court, and no one wanted that more than the Philadelphia 76ers. Pat Williams, the Sixers' general manager, said, "Our season has been so great that anything that would have detracted from it would have been devastating. It would have been too much for our fans to absorb. I don't think they could have come back from that. It's been too great a struggle to win their hearts. And they won't care about the details either." Williams said, "They want the games. They're sick of all the labor talk, as I am."

• • •

There were no final victories in the NBA. Even as both the NBA and Fleisher were praising the likelihood of victory, there were those questioning them. For Stern, the issue was revenue sharing. "Most NBA owners cringe at the thought of revenue sharing," the *Boston Globe* declared. Celtics owner Harry Mangurian said, "I'm just thinking about it. It's based on the supposition that there's going to be increases in the gross revenues. Both sides project increases, but you've got to show me. I don't like to be negative, but[. . .]."[42] Jerry Buss saw the other side. Buss, who had opposed gate sharing, said, "Now that every team will be required to spend a minimum in salaries, they will be able to go out and get better players. With better players, there is more parity. Better teams bring in more paying customers. So you see, I didn't do it for socialistic reasons."[43] When asked about revenue sharing, Stern demurred: "It's a league-wide commitment to getting teams up to whatever the minimum is. It'll be internal revenue sharing on a broader basis, but I don't want to get into that now."[44]

Fleisher got criticism from his side of the aisle as well. "We knew we'd get some shit," Quinn said of the expected blowback for agreeing to the cap. As Dan Shaughnessy wrote in the *Boston Globe*, "There were varied reactions and much confusion when the structure of the contract was outlined. O'Brien, Fleisher, and several owners were quick to point out that this is an agreement "in principle" only, but even in principle it appears more complex than blueprints for the neutron bomb." Bob Woolf, Larry Bird's agent who had loved Fleisher's machinations when he was able to negotiate Otis Birdsong's deal with Stepien, was unsure of the impact on his prized client: "I couldn't really give you an intelligent answer as to how this affects Larry because I haven't studied the agreement. I only hope there isn't anything devised that won't give Larry his worth."[45]

Bird wasn't the only one. Kevin McHale, one of the top upcoming free agents, was limited from being signed by the top-payroll teams. As one Celtic official told the *Boston Globe*, "If I were to pick five clubs that I'd not want to be bidding for McHale, four of them are in that group."[46] Even David Greenwood, the Bulls' player rep, was not sure how the deal would impact his free agency, as he was set to hit the open market after the following season. "This whole situation is something we'll all have to sit down and evaluate. That's really going to put me in a fix. This agreement is best for the whole league, but I'll have to do what's best for me."[47]

In the end, both sides achieved what they wanted. Fleisher had his hands on the long-term viability of the league, cable revenues, television, and a minimum floor that teams could not go beneath. He also had something that bound all of the owners together: if a Ted Stepien or a Donald Sterling didn't want to run their team or spend money reasonably, his members would be protected and paid.

David Stern also had what he wanted. He had a league—and he had something that unified ownership. "Each team will have to spend the minimum, no exceptions," Stern said at the time. "What this does is make teams in the smaller markets now able to compete for players."[48] He also knew that this would solidify the market for individuals who wanted to buy teams. Don King would not be an NBA owner. "We expect teams to be sold before they'll fold. That is because prospective buyers can project what they will have to spend and won't have to worry about having its best players taken by rich teams."[49] Stern said, "I think what this agreement does is it gives our teams a chance to look at the immediate and long-range future, look over their budgets and attract new capital."[50]

Lanier, ever the survivor, saw the big picture: "The key to this agreement is that we were able to maintain player movement. I'm getting along in years, and I may not reap the benefits of this agreement, but we have worked on behalf of the younger brothers and those who are still to come. Guys like Oscar Robertson and Paul Silas sacrificed for me. We won because the guys stuck together."[51]

Epilogue

On April 8, 1983, about a week after O'Brien appeared to announce the agreement with the Players Association, a sale was announced for the Cleveland Cavaliers. Ted Stepien had found a buyer in Gordon Gund. Finally.

In order to unload the Cavaliers, Stepien had to sell not only the Cavaliers but his advertising company as well, the one he had founded with $500 he borrowed from his father. "I didn't expect them to want Nationwide as part of the package," Stepien said. "It had to be tied into the deal. I couldn't keep losing money." A part of the deal was that Stepien was not allowed to remain with either company, even the agency he founded. "They wanted me out immediately," he said.[1]

Gund was who the new NBA wanted—well funded, sophisticated, and not Ted Stepien. On April 29, 1983, O'Brien sent a telex calling a special meeting of the Board of Governors to approve the transfer of two of the weakest franchises—Cleveland and Indiana—to new, stronger, more reliable ownership.[2] The cap was beginning to do its work. As O'Brien would say at the owners meeting in June, "It's not coincidence that shortly after this collective bargaining agreement was announced, successful businessmen with strong backgrounds and substantial local ties came forth to purchase two of our so-called trouble franchises, those in Cleveland and Indiana."[3]

When the sale was approved on May 13, 1983, Stepien was quietly out of the NBA. The kindest words about Stepien were written in the *Hartford Courant* by Bob Sudyk: "It took this first generation American just three years in the NBA to blow a Horatio Alger success story of 36 years, a classified advertising empire that included 27 offices in the United States and Canada." Bob Sudyk wrote, "Stepien is a modern American tragedy."[4]

Sudyk asked Stepien if he thought it was worth it. "Oh, I'd do it again," [Stepien] said in the subdued voice of a youngster just cut from his Little League team. "But I'd do a lot of things differently." He had a plan for the future. "I'm looking to get a Continental Basketball League franchise for Toronto."[5]

Soon after, the NBA would pass a rule to ensure that a reign like Stepien's would never happen again, limiting the ability of teams to trade draft picks in consecutive years. It would be known as "the Stepien rule."

· · ·

"Fo', fo', fo'." Though it is not clear when or where he said it, fo', fo', fo', will forever be known as the answer Moses Malone gave when asked how the 76ers would do in the playoffs—fo', fo', fo', in each round. A clean sweep. Though it sounds brash, Malone did not mean it that way. "We had played so many games during the regular season, and I just felt, why play 21 more in the playoffs? Just win 12 more and go home and rest up for the next year. I spoke to a group of writers, and I was serious. It was no joke, because I felt we could go fo', fo', fo', and have a big ending," Moses said.[6]

Both Doc and Moses felt good entering the playoffs. "With Moses and the chemistry of this team, the type of players we have. I have a different role. I'm a supporting player," Erving said. "We have a purpose, which is to win the championship, and we have a quiet subdued confidence. We expect to win. This has been a fun year for me too. In fact, so fun that I look forward to playing several more years now."[7]

Moses had spent a career barely speaking to the media. "Moses don't talk in Denver," he said once. "Moses don't talk on Tuesdays," he said another time. But as his team pushed toward a title, the elusive one for Julius, Moses became more talkative: "Moses is just a player, that's all Moses is. This is Doc's team, not Moses' team. Moses is just here to help him win."[8] And he did. "I can win a championship with this team," he said. "I've got all the money I want. Moses can buy anything he wants, but he can't buy the championship. Got to win that. That's why I'm here."[9]

The NBA, for the first time, was pushing to market the playoffs. They created a special logo and a catchphrase, "Showdown '83," that was sent to media outlets around the country. As O'Brien said to the owners, "The NBA's Public Relations Department has intensified its ongoing effort to build the playoffs as a truly major event." Working with their outside PR firm, the NBA sent information to both NBA and non-NBA cities, trying to build the reach of the league. They were careful, however, to wait to send their information—until after the NCAA tournament, MLB opening day, and the Masters.[10] They were optimistic, sure, but not delusional. They were still the NBA and this was still 1983.

However, nearly every playoff game was set to be broadcast— many on CBS, but others on USA and ESPN. Members of the NBA PR Department were expected to play a major role both in the Conference Finals and the Finals, in order to help "in servicing the increased number of media members who cover these playoff rounds." The NBA was getting stronger. They were making a hard push to increase exposure. As O'Brien told his owners at the dawn of the playoffs, "A special effort will be made, by both the PR and Broadcasting departments, to be of service to CBS, USA and ESPN in their playoff coverage. With virtually every game of our playoffs receiving some form of national television coverage, this is our best opportunity to expand the number of NBA fans in the general public and to intensify the loyalties of those who are already NBA fans."[11]

The Sixers swept their first round opponent, the New York Knicks, with almost no problem whatsoever. In the second round, they were met by Bob Lanier and the Bucks. The Bucks had swept their first round opponent as well, the Boston Celtics. After years of futility, this was the farthest Lanier had ever gotten in the playoffs, the Eastern Conference Finals. "I never saw a happier face than Lanier's in the dressing room after we swept the Celtics," Garry St. Jean, the Bucks' assistant coach, said. "He was like a sentimental kid. He just walked around yelling 'wow.'"[12] "It's just like being on a cloud," Lanier said, after the sweep of the Celtics. "It's the greatest feeling of my three years here. The last time I was involved in winning and moving on was back in college at St. Bonaventure. My knees feel the way my knees feel. That's the way it is. We're moving on to the next series and I hope

I can make as much of a contribution as I made to this one."[13] Paul Silas, Lanier's predecessor as NBPA president, said, "I spoke to Bob the other day and he was ecstatic. He is really getting himself mentally ready to play. He doesn't know whether he will be able to play another season and he wants that championship."[14]

After the sweep, the Bucks' thoughts turned to the mighty Sixers and the important matchup between their big men—Lanier and Moses. "We were confident we could beat them," forward Marques Jonson said. "We felt if we could beat Philly in Game 1, we had an excellent chance to upset them. We believed that if we won that game, it would knock them back on their heels," Junior Bridgeman said.

The Sixers were a team of destiny. The Bucks were no match. After an overtime loss in Game One, the Bucks held close to the Sixers in Game Two. However, after a disputed play in which the refs did not call a foul (Lanier would hold onto it for years), the Bucks lost again, and were down 2–0 to Philadelphia. Every game was close. Back in Milwaukee, the Bucks could feel their season on the brink. Back-to-back games were scheduled for Games Three and Four. The question was how much Lanier would play—he did not regularly play back-to-back games because of his knees. Sixers coach Billy Cunningham said before Game Three, "The big question is how many minutes Lanier will be able to play." Cunningham, knowing Lanier, answered his own question, "I think, given the competitive nature of Bob Lanier, that he'll somehow play as many minutes as he can and still contribute to his team." As the *Philadelphia Inquirer* said, "It is almost certain that, for the Bucks to win today, either the Sixers will have to collapse or Lanier's knees will have to hold up."[15]

Lanier played thirty minutes in Game Three, but the Bucks lost anyway. The next day, on the brink of elimination, Milwaukee won Game Four, as Lanier nearly willed the team to victory himself. It was only his second back-to-back game of the entire season. "After 13 seasons in the National Basketball Association, five knee operations and countless frustrations, Bob Lanier today showed a sellout crowd of 11,052 fans and the Philadelphia 76ers just how badly he wants his first championship ring," the *New York Times* wrote. During the fourth quarter, Lanier entered the game with a little over seven minutes to play and the Bucks down 3. The Bucks ran their plays for Lanier—

they called them four-series or six-series plays—to get him the ball inside. Lanier was guarded by Moses Malone. When the ball came into the paint, Lanier expected the double team. It didn't come. Lanier took advantage. He scored eleven points in the last eight minutes of the game. "They weren't doubling down," Lanier said after the game. "Not much, anyway. If you don't do something to affect a guy's shot, he'll beat you in this league."[16]

Despite the win, Lanier was not happy after the game. "Don't make nothing more of this than what it was," Lanier warned. "I didn't feel great—I never feel great—but I wanted to be a part of it, especially since we were one win away from going out."[17] Lanier's heroics helped win the game, and the Bucks stayed alive, even though there was no expectation that they would win the series. Lanier was proud, a survivor. There would be no fo', fo', fo' for the Sixers.

His moment was not enough to bring the Bucks back. The Sixers won Game Five, ending the series with the Bucks and setting up a finals rematch with Magic and the Lakers, who had bested Drossos's Spurs in the Western Conference Finals. "They're the next world championship team, in my opinion," Bucks coach Don Nelson said of the Sixers. "They play a different style in the West, but I can't see any team touching them."[18]

The Sixers took the first two from the Lakers in Philadelphia. Then they won Game Three in Los Angeles. "We want LA in four. We want people to remember this team," Cunningham said after the first three Sixers victories.[19] The Sixers were not going to let up. Asked what he would do in Los Angeles between Games Three and Four Moses said, "Stay in the room and get ready for the next game . . . There will be plenty of time to go to the beach after we win."[20] After Game Three, Cunningham returned to his hotel room to a knock at the door. It was Harold Katz. "We're going to Vegas," he said. "Let's go." Cunningham declined.[21] They were too close to a title.

Just as the Sixers' character had been excoriated after their failure in the Finals the previous year, in 1983 it was the Lakers' turn to have their mettle questioned. Bob Ryan referred to the Lakers as "a glitter team—a California team if you will . . . It's pretty clear that a healthy Laker team would not have affected the outcome, only the number of games it would have taken."[22] The team that looked unbeatable twelve months earlier, now looked soft. There were no final victories in the NBA.

The Sixers won Game Four and the NBA championship on May 31, 1983. The Sixers came back from a sixteen-point deficit, led by, who else, Julius Erving and Moses Malone, to win 115–108. Fo', five, fo'.

It was pandemonium. Finally—the Sixers won a championship. Malone was named the unanimous MVP.[23] Outside of the locker room, Erving was contemplative and emotional. "After coming in second three times (since coming to the Sixers in 1976), you start to ask why it happens. I would like to give thanks to the Creator, not only for the time we were victorious, but for the times we lost. Those times built our character as men. Without what happened then, we wouldn't be the same now." Erving thanked his wife, who, as he said, "has had trial after trial after seeing me come home in second place for six years."[24]

Larry O'Brien handed the championship trophy to owner Harold Katz. "The Sixers own this forever," O'Brien said.[25] Erving embraced O'Brien and Katz. Erving said, "Rather than look at Julius Erving and say he finally won one, I think you should look at our team and our owner and our commitment."[26] The championship was cathartic for Erving—he had exorcised the hex. Erving went back to the previous year's failure. "I cried here last year, for the first time since my brother died in 1969 but Mr. Katz took one look at the tears in my eye and he said 'you won't have to cry again.'"[27] Billy Cunningham said, "I thought this was a picture-book ending. Doc has worked so hard and has come so close, now it's ours. I can't think of anything else but to enjoy this."[28]

Steve Mix, then a member of the Lakers, went to the Sixers locker room after their victory to celebrate. He had spent nine seasons in Philadelphia and had been through the frustrations with them. The cover of the *Philadelphia Daily News* would show Mix, who had played the game on the other team, pouring champagne on his former teammates. He was happy for them. "I do remember going in immediately and congratulating everybody. I was happy for those guys," he said.[29]

The morning after the Sixers won the championship was June 1, 1983. On June 1, 1983, the NBA was in some ways a very different place and in some ways exactly the same as the year before. June 1, 1982, was the day the CBA expired—with the Sixers and Lakers playing in the Finals. On June 1, 1983, however, the perspective had flipped. The Philadelphia 76ers, with their owner Harold Katz; their best player, Julius Erving; and their free agent acquisition, Moses Malone were basking in the victory of their first NBA championship.

Within a week, Moses would be named the MVP of the NBA, again. He finished the season as the highest paid player in the history of the NBA—earning $2.965 million in salary, $27,258 in playoff share, and, to top it off, a Pontiac Trans-Am for being the MVP of the finals. When he was presented with the car, Malone was asked whether he had expected a championship when he was traded to the Sixers. "When I signed the offer sheet," Malone said with a huge smile.[30]

The post-hoc analysis of the Malone signing was very different than at the time. As the *New York Times* said, "At the time, a lot of people second guessed Harold Katz for making a deal like that but now when you look back at the dramatic rise in 76er attendance, the increased ticket prices and the championship, Katz made a shrewd business decision. He got his money back."[31]

Katz, it was said, "Has been accused of being the George Steinbrenner of basketball, in that he has tried to buy a championship team."[32] As the *Boston Globe* wrote, "If you subscribe to the fair-play school of sport, there's something repugnant about this but a depressing reality of professional athletics in the 80s is that championships can be bought. There can be no doubt that 76ers owner Harold Katz locked up the NBA title last September when he signed free agent Malone to a six year, $13.2 million contract."[33] As Bob Ryan wrote, "And so Philadelphia owner Harold Katz will be right, and much of the basketball world was wrong. Count me among those who scoffed when Katz brought Malone to the 76ers."[34]

Katz had been right about Malone's impact on the court and in the stands. The Sixers were the top road attraction with Moses, drawing five thousand more fans per game than the average. At home, the Sixers, who had made the Finals the previous season, saw their attendance rise by three thousand people. Katz said, "This is a business and signing Malone was a business decision. It cost a lot of money to get him, but he's been worth it, both on the court and at the gate—not just in Philadelphia but throughout the league." Katz, who had said a few months earlier that he would rather lose a few, was the subject of a new article. This time, it was "Money's Nice, Malone's Better."[35]

A few months after threatening to sell because he was so sour about the labor situation in the NBA, Katz was feeling pretty good about the business. Katz said that he wanted to get President Reagan to sign the telegram he had sent the team after their championship, and that he wanted to get him to come and see the Sixers the following season. "As I think about it, I don't recall seeing a President at an NBA game in the past. But perhaps we're reaching the stage where basketball will be on equal footing with football and baseball in that regard."[36] Perhaps they were.

• • •

On June 11, Ed Garvey announced his resignation as executive director of the NFLPA, leaving behind a complicated legacy. He resigned to become the deputy state attorney general in Wisconsin. "It was a matter of coming home," Garvey said. "I'm proud of what we accomplished. But I simply wanted to get into public service." His counterpart at the NFL, Jack Donlan, was not kind. "He followed a litigious path, and that's the earmark of an immature organization. He'd rather be in court than at the bargaining table. During the life of the contract, most union leaders support the industry. He was always attacking the industry." Donlan couldn't even acknowledge the progress that Garvey had made, saying sarcastically, "We're not that enthusiastic to see him leave. Everybody in the NFL enjoyed the contracts we've gotten with him."[37]

When the NBA agreement was reached and the players got a percentage of revenues, Garvey took credit. As the *New York Times* reported, "If Larry Fleisher, chief negotiator for the National Basketball Players Association, was the happiest man around after last week's handshake on a revolutionary new basketball agreement, his opposite number in the National Football League Players Association, Ed Garvey, ran him a close second."[38]

"I tore my rotator cuff patting myself on the back," Garvey said after the deal.[39] He told the *Sporting News*, "I guess I'm conservative again," he said. "Sensible businessmen realize this is the most reasonable way of compensating players for the future. People fear change, particularly in the NFL, where they hate to say they gave in. The basketball owners decided they couldn't live with the way they don't share revenues. The idea was not exactly born out of Karl Marx's brain."[40] Garvey was not sure if the NFL would agree to the framework the NBA did in 1987, when the next NFL agreement would be up.

Garvey, even after the NBA deal was signed, was pushing that there should be a basic union scale. Both Fleisher and Stern disagreed with Garvey's premise. Fleisher said, "The agreement only made sense for us if there was competition for players services. It's no catastrophe for the NBA, just a way to ensure more competitive balance. If the teams get better, there'll be more interest at the gate and on TV and revenues will go up."[41] Stern was even more blunt, "We sell a Larry Bird or a Julius Erving to the public as unique. These are very special performers. You can't put them into an assembly line mold and treat them as identical with everyone else."[42]

There were rumors that Garvey was setting the stage for a political career. Garvey did not deny his ambition, saying, "At some point, down the road, who knows what could happen? But I'm here now to be the Deputy Attorney General."[43]

He was soon replaced as NFLPA executive director by Gene Upshaw, a recently retired offensive lineman from the Oakland Raiders and a staunch union advocate. He had long been a Garvey supporter. He saw it as a new beginning. "It's reconstruction, sort of like after the Civil War," he said after Garvey's resignation. "I think we need a change in philosophy in our approach . . . I want our image changed." After he left, Garvey was known to be referred to in NFLPA circles as "that bastard."[44]

• • •

"A warm welcome to you," Larry O'Brien started the NBA's annual meetings in June 1983. "From the newest members of the NBA family to the most grizzled veterans of the basketball wars, welcome to our 1983 annual meetings."[45] In mid-June everything was looking different and all the same. The NBA held its awards luncheon to celebrate. The NBA draft, for the first time, was going to be broadcast on USA.

O'Brien announced that the entire Finals had been broadcast live, that they had increased their revenue and were in strong shape. He said that their CBS ratings were up by 6 percent and had been each of the previous four years. "Think about that," O'Brien said, "the next time someone tells you pro basketball is a dying sport on network television."[46]

O'Brien was also able to announce success on the commercial side. The NBA achieved renewals of corporate sponsorships with Miller Highlife (at 3x the amount) and Spalding (5x the amount.). He also announced that through cable and other forms of television, they had earned $17 million the previous season from broadcasting, in addition to the CBS deal. O'Brien told his fellow owners, "We can be proud that the NBA has been in the forefront of the quest for ways to tap the growing cable market, a position that should reap benefits for us all in the future."[47]

He also referenced the collective bargaining negotiations with the players as one of the most satisfying things he had done. "By instituting a salary cap, we have taken a major step to insure that the rich will not be able to rob the poor. This should make for more competitive teams and a more exciting product on the court, which can only help the league to grow and prosper."[48]

The owners also began the process of holding one another accountable. In June the NBA's Board of Governors authorized massive fines for trying to circumvent the salary cap, of up to $500,000. The fines would be at the discretion of the commissioner, if any team would submit a player contract that violated the CBA. There was an additional provision: if a team negotiated any "under the table" clauses—such as hidden payments—the commissioner could impose a fine of up to $1 million. O'Brien was also allowed to award cash, draft choices, or another team's players in the event of such an infraction. They were establishing steep penalties to ensure the cap's success.

The annual meetings were also when teams looked to the next season. The Chicago Bulls were looking to sign the greatest free agent of them all, Kareem Abdul-Jabbar. The thirty-six-year-old was seeking a three-year, $6 million offer, less than Malone's, but still the top of the market. The Bulls, desperate for relevance, were looking to sign him. "It's our last chance to sign the big free agents before the salary cap goes into effect," Bulls GM Rod Thorn said. "So why shouldn't I take a guy like Kareem? He's the second best center in the league, and he's a guy the fans will talk about." Abdul-Jabbar's agent was clear that he was interested in the Bulls, but the conventional wisdom was that Jerry Buss would match any offer on Kareem.[49] The cap would go into effect the following year. "It's the last year of real freedom so people are taking advantage of it," Joe Axelson, now of the Kings, said. "I don't think this was foreseen."[50]

• • •

"The subject of this news conference, as you all know, is drugs," Larry O'Brien said. On September 28, 1983, Larry O'Brien announced a deal for drug testing in the NBA. "At this time the National Basketball Association, the National Basketball Players Association, are pleased to announce an agreement on what we can honestly call the most comprehensive program for dealing with the problem of drug use that any sport has developed."[51]

"Our message today is a simple one: Drugs and the NBA do not mix," O'Brien said. "If you want to get involved in drugs, you will not be involved with the NBA."[52] After the CBA negotiations were done, the NBA and its Players Association negotiated a deal to rid the NBA of drugs.

During negotiations the players had resisted a drug program. Lanier was public that the players would not agree to drug testing. "I ain't no damned guinea pig," he said early in negotiations. "Drug testing would be an invasion of a guy's personal and private life."[53] Larry Fleisher agreed that the union was "totally against testing."[54] Fleisher quoted Tom Landry saying, "We have not yet reached a police state in this country."

However, everyone recognized that drugs were a major issue in the NBA—both in reality and in perception of the league. The league and the union, even before negotiations, had recognized the potential issue. In 1981 the NBA and the NBPA agreed to establish a twenty-four-hour counseling service, the first of its kind in professional sports. O'Brien said, "Players may avail themselves of the program with the knowledge that their participation will be kept completely confidential. Neither the league office, nor their respective teams will know about it. The counseling program is an extension of and broadening of an ongoing education program."[55]

Testing, however, was different. Stern believed that a drug agreement was crucial to the economic growth of the NBA. "What we were dealing with at the time was a different America," Stern said of the issue in 2018. "The assumption was of course these guys are using drugs. They're black, they're making too much money . . . and if they were wearing afros they must be bad."[56] It was not only Stern. Lanier changed as well, becoming a hawk on the issue. Drugs became a crucial issue to Lanier, who was simply sick of the perception of the NBA as being drug addled. Later, Stern recalled a conversation with Lanier in which they negotiated this issue. Lanier said, "Well we catch a guy doing drugs we should throw him out for life." Stern responded, "Bob, life is a long time."

The agreement they reached was harsh. Players could be tested without notice. The first time a player voluntarily came forward to seek treatment, they would be paid their salary. A second time, he would be suspended but treated. If there was a third violation, the player would be disqualified from the league.[57] The disqualification would be independent of any guarantees and could reapply for reinstatement after two years.[58] The list of prohibited drugs only contained two substances—cocaine and heroin.[59]

After the deal was reached, Lanier penned an op-ed in the *New York Times*, in which he said, "Support for the program is overwhelming among the membership." The players interest in such a harsh program was threefold: 1) They wanted the public to know the players did not do drugs; 2) Healthier players would increase revenue; and 3) "[They] all felt [they] had a responsibility, as role models, to change the trend" with drugs.[60]

"I'm as liberal as the next guy," Fleisher said, "but these guys were mad at being portrayed as junkies. Most of our players didn't even want a two-year review, because it would seem like just a two-year suspension. It's not. It's a lifetime review. But Bob Lanier wanted the two year review, so we did it."[61] Grantham said that the harshness was necessary—for racial reasons. "It is important that we in the NBA take a leadership role in the solution of these problems," Grantham said. "Every time you see a story about drugs in the media, it happens that the person involved is black. That's unfortunate because it confirms attitudes that white America has about us. We would like to destroy that." Lanier said, "We're role models to these kids. That's particularly true in the ghetto, where sometimes the other role models are pimps and hustlers."[62]

There was a concern that the program was so strict it would harm troubled players who had not yet been able to turn themselves in. Michael Ray Richardson, a player who had undergone treatment for drug addiction, thought the agreement missed the point: "The NBA doesn't understand it's not drugs. It's a disease. It's like cancer or something. Guys need help."[63] As the *New York Times* reported, "The lifetime ban needs to be examined with some skepticism. If a player who asks for help can go back to work after being treated, presumably within a month or two, should a player who is caught be banned for two years at a minimum? In theory, the penalty should scare young players who stand to lose their golden chance if they mess with drugs. But this is assuming a rational mode of thinking, and people who take drugs are doing so to blot out pain, confusion, fear and anger in the first place." Fleisher defended the plan, saying, "If we didn't have a growing problem, we could think more about the individuals. For some individuals, it could be sad, but we do protect the overwhelming interest or the few?"[64]

• • •

On November 10, 1983, Larry O'Brien stepped down as commissioner of the NBA. "There comes a time when you have to move on," O'Brien said. "I think the eight and one-half years I spent as Commissioner was the longest I have ever spent concentrating on a particular situation or subject. If you told me eight and a half years ago when I came in that I'd be standing here today, I wouldn't have believed it for a minute."[65] To the *Washington Post* O'Brien was blunt, saying, "Basketball just isn't the most important thing in the world to me anymore. I think my job here is done."[66]

It had not been a simple retirement. O'Brien had sought a new contract for an additional five years. He was offered two years as commissioner and three as consultant. He declined, expecting a better offer. The NBA's offer didn't change. O'Brien submitted a letter of resignation. "I intend to keep the same good relations with the owners and to be of service to them. As far as reconsidering my action, the deed is done," he said.[67]

O'Brien was asked what the high points were of his tenure as commissioner. All of them were related to deals he cut with Fleisher—the *Robertson* settlement, the drug program, and the creation of the salary cap. There were some concerns about the state he left the league in, but as one anonymous source told *Sports Illustrated*, "The commissioner has no real power over which yo-yos will own an NBA team. It's up to the other yo-yos."[68]

In terms of who would succeed O'Brien, the *New York Times* said Stern was considered the odds-on favorite. Larry Weinberg of the Trailblazers said, "I certainly would advocate for David Stern. If the board chooses him, he will make an excellent Commissioner."[69]

The decision to name a new commissioner was not even on the agenda for the Board of Governors when they met in November 1983—just an opaque entry listed as "Commissioner's Business." Toward the end of the meeting, O'Brien excused the rest of the staff—Stern, Granik, and Bettman often sat in on these meetings. O'Brien addressed the owners. According to the minutes of the meeting, taken by Richard Bloch of the Suns, "[O'Brien] stated that he felt that it would not be in the best interest of the League to delay in choosing his successor and recommended that the Board act today to elect a new Commissioner to assume office effective February 1, 1984. Commissioner O'Brien then advised that it was his strong personal recommendation that the board elect David J. Stern."[70]

When O'Brien announced his resignation the owners did not even bother to convene a search committee to replace him, they simply voted unanimously for Stern. As O'Brien said, "I firmly believe the state of the league is such that we needed a man from within to run it into the future. Clearly the best man available was David Stern. I couldn't be more pleased."[71]

It was a new world in the NBA. As the *Philadelphia Inquirer* put it, "The search for a successor to outgoing baseball commissioner Bowie Kuhn has assumed soap-opera length and complexity. Meanwhile, the NBA owners, widely perceived as the most shortsighted, buccaneering band of renegades this side of Donald Trump and the United States Football League, settles its War of Succession without a shot."[72]

As the *Washington Post* reported, "The person practically everyone concerned felt should and would get the job, did."[73] When Stern was elected, it was very quick. "He has earned our respect," Suns owner Richard Bloch said. "Not a dissenting voice was heard."[74]

Stern was surprised at the speed with which the owners selected him. "I was aware there was sentiment behind me and I'm ready to do the best I can and continue in the manner of Larry O'Brien."[75] Stern said, "I'm happy that [the governors] decided to stay within the house, so to speak. They could have gone for a big name in this situation, but they chose to stay with someone who is familiar with the problems. I appreciate that."[76]

For all of the public knowledge of Stern now, at the time he was appointed commissioner Stern was practically unknown publicly. The *Boston Globe* reported, "David Stern is a name not many people outside the NBA inner circle would recognize."[77] He was described as some who "was always a man who did his best work behind the scenes." As the *Boston Globe* said, in an editorial intended to push for public support for Stern, "You probably haven't heard of Stern because he's never won a slam-dunk contest, starred in a television sitcom or served as Secretary of the Treasury. He's merely a low-profile guy who has been the NBA's de facto commissioner for the last couple of years." Later in that same article, Dan Shaughnessy defined Stern's qualifications: "No one knows more about NBA marketing, television and law than David Stern."[78] It was true.

A large part of Stern's ascension in the NBA was the recent television deal, but more importantly, his deals with cable. "Cable is an area that sports is hugely involved in and having David at the top, the owners felt they would be in a better position to deal with cable," the NBA's spokesman said after Stern was appointed.[79] They were right—he had been doing it for years. At the time of his appointment, Stern said that fifteen of the twenty-three NBA teams had specific deals with cable systems and "that all 23 teams [would] have one form or another in the future."[80]

Stern was asked what he wanted to accomplish as commissioner. "I want a period of stability, where we can turn the focus, you know, from the image of the renegade NBA with Ted Stepien to one that is on the game," said Stern.[81] He was succinct in identifying what the future held: "I see our teams at the lower end getting stronger. I see the salary cap, combined with additional cable revenues making our teams more profitable. I look forward to sharing that profit with the players, who have 53 percent of the gross. Ultimately, we will put emphasis on international competition. There is interest in pro basketball all over the world."

Later, when Stern had become a tremendous success, Fleisher was asked about Stern's appointment. Fleisher said, "I think he's done a good job. I was not enthusiastic about him when he took over. I thought he lacked marketing skills and was strictly a litigator. But he recognized he didn't have those skills and that became his strength. He hired good people. He's smart, very smart." When asked about Stern's future in 1989, Fleisher said, "If he's smart enough not to let his ego get carried away, he'll continue to do well."[82]

• • •

A month after his appointment, Stern was asked about the recently completed collective bargaining agreement and whether the changes they had made were working. Before the cap was even in effect, Stern said, "We're going to have some arguments with the players and arguments among the teams because there's always a loophole, always an exception you didn't think about. But the framework itself, I believe, is absolutely the best for the survival and the thriving of a professional sports league."[83]

They already had some squabbles. The summer before Stern was appointed commissioner, the NBA and the Players Association had their first spat over the intent of the salary cap. It was written that teams were scouring the document to find loopholes, namely the Knicks. Though the cap would not go into effect until 1984–85, the top five teams, including the Seattle Supersonics, were frozen at their rate of salary—for the Sonics, it was $4.6 million. After the 1982–83 season, the Sonics made a number of trades and brought their salary down below that amount. They then signed a free agent, Reggie King, whose salary put them at $4.42 million, still beneath their salary cap.

At that point, with the rest of their roster full, the Sonics re-signed David Thompson, whose contract had expired, to a $400,000 contract. Thompson's contract put the Sonics way over the cap. Under the Bird exception the Sonics could re-sign their own players to any amount they wanted, they had just timed it in such a way to maximize it. If the Sonics had signed Thompson first, they would not have been able to get their other players.

The NBA called foul and the commissioner refused to approve Thompson's contract. The players union fought to complete the signing, saying that it complied with the CBA. When the case went to arbitration, the NBPA won and Thompson's contract was approved. They had blown a big hole in the salary cap. Other teams began delaying their veteran-free-agent signings until they had the rest of their roster full.

Thompson's agent who orchestrated the maneuver and found a way around the salary cap?—Larry Fleisher, the first capologist.

• • •

In October 1983 Bob Lanier started his fourteenth season in the NBA, and his fifth with the Milwaukee Bucks. It would be his last as a player in the NBA. At the end of the 1983–84 season, when the Bucks were eliminated by the Boston Celtics in the Eastern Conference Finals, Lanier was asked if he was considering retirement. He said, "I would tend to go in that direction."[84] He held off making a decision until September.

When Lanier began the news conference to announce his retirement from the NBA, he tried to start it three different times. Each time, Lanier walked up to the microphone before taking a step back, too overcome with emotion to speak. After the second attempt, Lanier said softly to himself, "I thought I had it together. I can't even talk right now." Lanier said he was retiring to spend more time with his family. "It's been kind of a difficult decision to make," he said. "I've been a basketball player for a great many years and had to deal with a lot of pain and aggravation." Lanier admitted that he had considered one more season—one more, as he said it, "quest for that all-elusive ring"—but decided against it. In the end, Lanier said, "Because of giving so much to basketball, it's caused a lot of difficulty in my life. I realized it was interfering with my family. I think I have things a little better in focus."[85] Lanier never won an NBA championship.

• • •

In 1991 Larry Fleisher was inducted into the Basketball Hall of Fame. Fleisher was inducted the same night as Larry O'Brien. Fleisher, who had passed away a few years earlier, was inducted by his wife and his first client, then senator Bill Bradley.

Bradley walked up to the microphone to talk of his old friend on the night of his celebration. He told a story from when they were preparing for one of their collective bargaining sessions. "Larry Fleisher once asked me," Bradley said, "'Did you ever see the movie the organizer?'" Bradley had never seen it. He asked what it was. Fleisher said, "It's a movie about a labor leader who comes to town, organizes a plant, gets major benefits and higher salaries for the workers." Bradley paused. "Then, the union members vote him out of office and he leaves town unrecognized and unappreciated." Bradley paused again. He said Fleisher said, "'That's why in this business, only your work sustains you. The knowledge of what you've done for other people.'" Pause. "'Because you never know when it will end.'" Bradley paused once more as he described what Fleisher did next: "Then he looked up at me." Pause. "And smiled."[86]

Acknowledgments

Writing a book is hard. I had read that many times and believed it to be true. However, I had not actually lived it until I tried to write a book. You want everything to be perfect, you fall in love with every single detail, but in the end, you have to adjust. Sometimes forty pages about NBA ownership swaps in the '70s ends up on the cutting room floor (even though it is fascinating!). I certainly would not have been able to write what you are reading without the wonderful support of family, friends, and colleagues, whom I would like to thank.

This book is dedicated to my wife (and I'll thank her at the end), but it certainly would not have happened without many people. Most importantly, my dad, Richard. My father is a philosophy professor with no particular love or interest in sports. For example, once, as we left the theater after seeing a Broadway show, I whispered to my Dad excitedly that David Stern was standing in front of us at the exit. This being long before I began (and he read) this book, my dad turned and said very loudly, thinking David Stern was probably a friend of mine from summer camp, "WHO IS DAVID STERN?" Stern turned and waved at us. I was mortified.

My father's field is the philosophy of language; and while he is the world's expert on Gottlob Frege, he approached Larry Fleisher, David Stern, and the NBA with the same passion and interest he would a nineteenth-century German philosopher. He always helped me and always listened. He was encouraging when what I wrote was good and honest when what I wrote was not. Of course, his love and support are not confined to this book but are a part of everything I have ever done professionally and personally. Thanks, Dad.

Thank you to my mom, Marsha, who has always been my biggest fan, had my back, and believed in me. No matter what I have ever tried to do—even if it was not the brightest endeavor—my mom has always been supportive. Thanks to my entire family—Mom, Dad, Robin, Shimmy, Steve, Cheryl, Lauren, Ryan, Lainie, and Ellie. Thank you to my friends who read initial drafts, tried to help, or acted as sounding boards through this process, even if they didn't know it—Howie Wexler, Sean Lally, Matt Rocco, Ben Green, Bezzy Stern, Cary McLelland, Scott Wachs, Andrew Zizmor, Asaf Davidov, Dan Bushansky, Mike Prasad, Rich Larkin, Jennifer Peat, and Aliza Reicher. Thanks to Andy Weisel, who spent untold hours with me watching terrible basketball from the upper deck of Nets games over the last decade. Thanks to Eliz, Peter, Graham, and Crosby for letting me use their house when I tried (unsuccessfully) to lock myself away and complete the book.

This book changed when I uncovered Larry O'Brien's papers at Springfield College. Thank you to the wonderful staff there, including Jeff Monseau, who let me set up shop whenever I wanted, on very short notice, to review thousands of pages. Thank you to Rob Taylor at the University of Nebraska Press for agreeing to buy a book by someone who has no business writing a book. Thank you to the people who lived through these times and were generous with their time—Jim Quinn, Charlie Grantham, Marc Fleisher. Thank you to all the people who helped me with my interest in these topics over the years and have been generous with advice and opportunities— Jeff Fannell, Dave Prouty, Bob Lenaghan, and Ron Klempner. Of course, I was impacted as well by Mike Weiner, whom I met when I was very young and who will always be a model of how I want to carry myself as a lawyer and a person. It was not lost on me that it was Larry Fleisher who recommended Mike to the MLBPA when he was a young man. If I didn't respect, like, and admire the people who did this work in real life, I probably would not have spent the time to try to learn so much about it.

Thank you to my wife, Jen, who was certainly the most immediately impacted by the total domination this book had on my mind for most of our relationship but married me anyway. She is kind and supportive, but also pragmatic. She helped me finish something I was not sure I could. You're the best, and I am very lucky to have you.

Notes

1. No Final Victories

1. Adrian Wojnarowski Tweet, July, 1, 2016, https://twitter.com/wojespn/status /748729966922113024.

2. Mark Medina, "NBA Free Agency: Timofey Mozgov Sold on Luke Walton's Promise of a Significant Role," *Los Angeles Daily News*, July 4, 2016.

3. "NBA Player Salaries—2015–2016," ESPN.com, http://www.espn.com/nba/salaries, accessed August 6, 2018.

4. Tim Bontemps, "Timofey Mozgov's Insane Lakers Contract Inspires Incredulous Reaction," *Washington Post*, July 1, 2016.

5. Medina, "NBA Free Agency."

6. "Auerbach, Schaus Agree: West All-Stars Were 'Hot,'" *Chicago Daily Defender*, January 12, 1967.

7. Robertson, *Big O*, 216.

8. Robertson, *Big O*, 194.

9. "NBA Owners Bar Players' Attorney," *Boston Globe*, June 11, 1965.

10. "NBA Plans for Expansion, Seeks 10th Team for 66," *Chicago Daily Defender*, January 10, 1965.

11. "NBA Vote to Take In Two Cities," *Baltimore Sun*, June 8, 1966.

12. "NBA Vote."

13. "NBA Vote."

14. Thomas Heinsohn, "Time's Right for Players Demands, Says Former President Heinsohn," *Boston Globe*, March 1, 1967.

15. "NBA Players Lose Opening Move," *Washington Post*, June 11, 1965.

16. Alan Goldstein, "Pro Cagers Seek Advances through Six Point Program," *Baltimore Sun*, January 11, 1967.

17. Ray Fitzgerald, "NBA Players against Adding to Schedule," *Boston Globe*, January 11, 1967.

18. Goldstein, "Pro Cagers."

19. Fitzgerald, "NBA Players."

20. Alan Goldstein, "Cagers Seek End to Reserve Plan: Robertson Leads Revolt for Negotiating Freedom," *Baltimore Sun*, June 9, 1966.

21. "KC Doubts NBA Owners Will Junk Reserve Clause," *Boston Globe*, June 12, 1966.

22. Goldstein, "Cagers Seek."

23. Goldstein, "Pro Cagers."

24. Goldstein, "Pro Cagers."

25. Goldstein, "Pro Cagers."

26. Fitzgerald, "NBA Players."

27. "Wilt May Jump NBA to Play in New ABA," *Hartford Courant*, January 19, 1967.

28. "10 Team A.B.A Official Entry in Pro Sports," *Chicago Tribune*, February 3, 1967; "No Raids planned on NBA Players," *New York Times*, February 5, 1967.

29. "10 Team A.B.A."

30. "New Basketball Loop Launched; Mikan Is Named Commissioner," *Baltimore Sun*, February 3, 1967.

31. "No Raids Planned."

32. Alan Goldstein, "Another Day," *Baltimore Sun*, February 4, 1976.

33. Halberstam, *Breaks of the Game*, 293.

34. Bob Ryan, "For Money . . . and Respect," *Boston Globe*, May 16, 1975.

35. Goldstein, "Another Day."

36. Bob Ryan, "NBA Owners Settle for Less of Two Evils," *Boston Globe*, February 8, 1976.

37. "Players, NBA Settle Suit Out of Court," *Los Angeles Times*, February 4, 1976.

38. Bob Logan, "Owners, Players Make Peace in NBA: NBA Owners 'Free' Players," *Chicago Tribune*, February 4, 1976.

39. Fred Rothenberg, "NBA Didn't Surrender to Players—O'Brien," *Boston Globe*, February 22, 1976.

40. Goldstein, "Another Day."

41. Logan, "Owners, Players."

42. "Players, NBA Sign New Pact," *Baltimore Sun*, April 13, 1976.

43. Sam Goldaper, "Revenue Sharing Instituted," *New York Times*, April 1, 1983.

44. "Equality Goal in New NBA Pact," *Sporting News*, April 11, 1983.

45. Kevin Draper, "Michele Roberts on N.B.A. Competitive Balance: Don't Blame the Players," *New York Times*, July 9, 2018.

46. Mike Littwin, "The Kupchak Gamble: Lakers Are Set to Bite a $5.6 Million Bullet," *Los Angeles Times*, July 28, 1981.

2. Pleasantries and Unpleasantries

1. Bruce Newman, "The Gospel According to Hubie," *Sports Illustrated*, October 31, 1983.

2. "Lakers Drop Westhead as Coach," *New York Times*, November 20, 1981.

3. Randy Harvey, "Magic's Bombshell: He Wants to Be Traded," *Los Angeles Times*, November 19, 1981.

4. Harvey, "Magic's Bombshell."

5. Harvey, "Magic's Bombshell."

6. Steve Hershey, "Paul Westhead's Vanishing Wasn't Done by 'Magic,'" *Washington Post*, December 15, 1981.

7. Bruce Newman, "LA's Streak Goes by the Boards," *Sports Illustrated*, June 7, 1982.

8. Anthony Cotton, "I Can Do So Many Things," *Sports Illustrated*, November 1, 1982.

9. Newman, "LA's Streak."

10. "76er Owner Is Conspicuous," *New York Times*, June 2, 1982.

11. Roy S. Johnson, "NBA Thinks about Changes," *New York Times*, January 31, 1982.

12. Johnson, "NBA Thinks."

13. David DuPree, "Major Trades Make NBA Season Even More Volatile Than Usual: NBA Ready to Begin Unpredictable Season," *Washington Post*, October 26, 1982.

14. Randy Harvey, "Lane Now Clear for the Start of NBA Season," *Los Angeles Times*, October 30, 1981.

15. Sam Goldaper, "Financial Difficulties in Sight for N.B.A," *New York Times*, June 14, 1981.

16. David Israel, "Stagnant NBA Wonders if It Should Change to College-Style Game," *Chicago Tribune*, March 26, 1981.

17. Chris Cobbs, "40–75% Usage: NBA and Cocaine: Nothing to Snort At," *Los Angeles Times*, August 19, 1980.

18. Mary Hynes, "NBA's No Longer a Basket Case: Stern Measures Guided League through Troubles," *Globe and Mail*, December 26, 1988.

19. Israel, "Stagnant NBA Wonders."

20. LOB. Lawrence F. O'Brien National Basketball Association Papers, Springfield College, Springfield Massachusetts.

21. Israel, "Stagnant NBA Wonders."

22. Goldaper, "Financial Difficulties."

23. Dan Shaughnessy, "The National Basketball Affliction: Owners Have League in an Overlapping Grip," *Boston Globe*, March 28, 1982.

24. Ray Kennedy, "Who Are These Guys?" *Sports Illustrated*, January 31, 1977.

25. Will McDonough, "NBA Ship of Fools Near Rocks," *Boston Globe*, March 17, 1983.

26. Joe Axelson, memo to Larry O'Brien, November 10, 1981, LOB.

27. Johnson, "NBA Thinks."

28. Johnson, "NBA Thinks."

29. Interview with Jim Quinn.

30. Bob Ryan, "A Strike? A San Diego Move? What's NBA to Do?" *Boston Globe*, June 27, 1982.

31. Bruce Newman, "Can the NBA Save Itself?" *Sports Illustrated*, November 1, 1982.

32. Russ Granik, memo, March 1, 1982, LOB.

33. *Hearings before the Subcommittee on Monopolies and Commercial Law*, H.R. 823, 3287, 6747, 97th Cong., July 15, 1981, 155.

34. Gary Bettman's Bargaining Notes, September 23, 1982, LOB.

35. Gerald Eskenazi, "Familiar Foes in NBA Talks," *New York Times*, October 24, 1982.

36. Jeffrey Mishkin, notes, July 29, 1982, LOB, 1.

37. Larry Whiteside, "Inside Choice: Stern Takes Over NBA Center Stage," *Boston Globe*, November 17, 1983.

38. Mishkin, notes, 1–2.

39. Mishkin, notes, 2.

40. Mishkin, notes, 2.

41. Eskenazi, "Familiar Foes."

42. Mishkin, notes, 2.

43. Mishkin, notes, 2–3.

44. Mishkin, notes, 3.

45. NBA proposals, August 4, 1982, LOB, 1–2.

46. NBA proposals, 2.

47. "NBA Proposes Contract Terms," *New York Times*, August 6, 1982.

48. Mishkin, notes, 4.

49. Lawrie Mifflin and Sam Goldaper, "Scouting; NBA Talks Start Quietly," *New York Times*, July 29, 1982.

3. Survivors

1. Interview of Charles Grantham.

2. David Stern Hall of Fame Induction Speech, https://www.youtube.com/watch?v=CjuJqR-UmS0.

3. David DuPree, "Lanier: Winding Down in Pain and in Growth," *Washington Post*, May 14, 1983.

4. Dupree, "Lanier: Winding."

5. Ira Berkow, "For Bob Lanier, a Tough Season," *New York Times*, April 6, 1981.

6. DuPree, "Lanier: Winding."

7. Peter Simon, "Coach Who Cut Lanier at Bennett Tells His Side of It," *Buffalo News*, March 11, 1990.

8. Simon, "Coach Who Cut."

9. Kenneth Denlinger, "Bonnies Win 97–74, but Lose Bob Lanier," *Washington Post*, March 15, 1970.

10. Denlinger, "Bonnies Win."

11. William F. Reed, "Bonny Year for Buffalo Bob," *Sports Illustrated*, January 19, 1970.

12. Sam Goldaper, "Threat of Merger Spurs Top College Stars to Grab Pro Dollars," *New York Times*, March 23, 1975.

13. Mark Asher, "Pipers Land Mike Malloy of Davidson," *Washington Post*, March 12, 1970.

14. Redd, "Bonny Year."

15. Asher, "Pipers Land."

16. "Recent Signings Render Pro Draft Anticlimactical," *Hartford Courant*, March 23, 1970.

17. "Lanier Spurns ABA for Detroit," *Chicago Daily Defender*, March 26, 1970.

18. Bob Ryan, "NBA Will Draft Amid Intrigue," *Boston Globe*, March 23, 1970.

19. "N.B.A Pistons Draft Lanier No. 1; Pistol Pete to Atlanta," *Chicago Tribune*, March 24, 1970.

20. "Lanier Spurns."

21. Goldaper, "Threat of Merger."

22. "Pistons Win Lanier in Price War," *Washington Times*, March 25, 1970.

23. "Pistons Pin Lanier for 5 Years," *Washington Post*, March 26, 1970.

24. "Lanier Spurns."

25. "Instant Millionaire," *Hartford Courant*, March 26, 1970.

26. "Lanier's Father Likes Rich Pact," *Chicago Daily Defender*, March 30, 1970.

27. Mark Asher, "ABA Plans Resumption of Raids in Two Weeks: Unless Merger Is Effected," *Washington Post*, March 28, 1970.

28. "Maravich, Lanier Coup Not Stopping Talks," *Hartford Courant*, March 29, 1970.

29. Steve Aschburner, "NBA Legend Bob Lanier Reflects on Career, Current Game, and Impact off the Floor," *NBA.com*, September 10, 2018.

30. Tom Flaherty, "Lanier: Big on the Outside and the Inside," *Milwaukee Journal*, May 10, 1992.

31. Leonard Koppett, "N.B.A. All-Stars Ready to Resist Fines," *New York Times*, May 27, 1972.

32. "NBA Counsel Terms Talks Breakdown a Ploy," *Hartford Courant*, July 11, 1975.

33. "Players Approve Pact," *Washington Post*, February 5, 1980.

34. George Shirk, "Bucks' Hopes Ride on Lanier's Knees," *Philadelphia Inquirer*, May 14, 1983.

35. Sam Goldaper, "Malone-Lanier Is Key Matchup in Series," *New York Times*, May 8, 1983.

36. Berkow, "For Bob Lanier."

37. Barry McDermott, "Big Boost from Big Bob," *Sports Illustrated*, April 7, 1980.

38. Berkow, "For Bob Lanier."

39. Berkow, "For Bob Lanier."

40. "Bob Lanier—Starring in a Tough Season," *New York Times*, April 6, 1981.

41. "Federal Judge Robert L. Carter Rejected a National Basketball Players Request," *United Press International*, July 30, 1982.

42. Memo to NBA owners, general managers, and team counsel, July 30, 1982, LOB.

43. "Players Rebuffed on Pay Proposal," *New York Times*, July 31, 1982.

44. Memo to NBA owners, general managers, and team counsel, 4.

45. Bob Ryan, "A Strike? A San Diego Move? What's NBA to Do?" *Boston Globe*, June 27, 1982.

46. NBA proposals, August 4, 1982, LOB, 1.

47. NBA proposals, August 4, 1982, LOB, 2–4.

48. NBA proposals, August 4, 1982, LOB, 4–6.

49. O'Brien, *No Final Victories*, 246.

50. Fred Rothenberg, "NBA Didn't Surrender to Players—O'Brien," *Boston Globe*, February 22, 1976.

51. Bob Logan, "NBA's O'Brien a Miracle Worker," *Chicago Tribune*, February 8, 1976.

52. Interview with Charles Grantham.

53. Halberstam, *Playing for Keeps*, 117.

54. Larry O'Brien, telex, February 5, 1982, LOB.

55. Board of Governors minutes, June 1982, LOB.

56. Larry O'Brien, letter to Bob Lanier, August 5, 1982, LOB, 1.

57. Bob Lanier, letter to Larry O'Brien, August 6, 1982, LOB.

58. Lanier, letter to O'Brien.

59. Lanier, letter to O'Brien, 1–2.

60. Lanier, letter to O'Brien, 2.

61. Larry O'Brien, memo August 31, 1982, LOB, 2.

62. Lawrie Mifflin and Sam Goldaper, "Scouting; NBA Talks Start Quietly," *New York Times*, July 29, 1982.

4. That Brave Group of Guys

1. Heinsohn and Lewin, *Heinsohn*, 120.

2. Heinsohn and Lewin, *Heinsohn*, 120.

3. Wilkens and Pluto, *Unguarded*, 104.

4. Reynolds, *Cousy*, 150.

5. Reynolds, *Cousy*, 148–49.

6. Reynolds, *Cousy*, 150.

7. "Podoloff's Plea Heads Off Union," *New York Times*, January 16, 1957.

8. Harold Kaese, "Pro Players Air Labor Grievances: Showdown Possible Today as Cousy, Podoloff Meet," *Boston Globe*, January 15, 1957.

9. Will McDonough, "Pro Hoop Pension Rift Widens: Players Threaten Holdouts If Plan Not OKd by Next Season," *Boston Globe*, January 16, 1964.

10. Heinsohn and Lewin, *Heinsohn*, 121.

11. McDonough, "Pro Hoop Pension."

12. "Los Angeles to Seek NBA Team Today," *Boston Globe*, January 21, 1960.

13. "Pension Plan Started by NBA Players," *Washington Post*, January 10, 1961.

14. Charles Maher, "NBA Players Militant . . . Still Get Along with Owners," *Los Angeles Times*, February 14, 1973.

15. Heinsohn and Lewin, *Heinsohn*, 121.

16. Robertson, *Big O*, 181.

17. Heinsohn and Lewin, *Heinsohn*, 121.

18. Heinsohn and Lewin, *Heinsohn*, 120.

19. Richard Hoffer, "The Black Pioneers: They Changed League for Good; Now NBA Has Forgotten Lloyd, Cooper, and Clifton," *Los Angeles Times*, January 27, 1986.

20. "The Anti-Donald Sterling: Remembering the Boston Celtics Own Walter Brown," WBUR, May 23, 2014.

21. Heinsohn and Lewin, *Heinsohn*, 121.

22. Heinsohn and Lewin, *Heinsohn*, 122.

23. McDonough, "Pro Hoop Pension."

24. "NBA Prexy Hits Stars" *United Press International,* January 21, 1964.

25. Leonard Koppett, "NBA Players Threaten Strike in Dispute over Pension Plan," *New York Times,* January 15, 1964.

26. Heinsohn and Lewin, *Heinsohn,* 122.

27. Robertson, *Big O,* 182.

28. Jack Barry, "Brown Again Flays Heinsohn," *Boston Globe,* January 18, 1964.

29. McDonough, "Pro Hoop Pension."

30. Embry and Schmitt Boyer, *Inside Game,* 127.

31. McDonough, "Pro Hoop Pension."

32. Heinsohn and Lewin, *Heinsohn,* 122; Wilkens, *Unguarded,* 105.

33. "NBA Star Game Almost Ruined by Threatened Strike of Players," *Globe and Mail,* January 15, 1964.

34. Wilkens, *Unguarded,* 105.

35. Heinsohn and Lewin, *Heinsohn,* 122.

36. "NBA Prexy Hits."

37. Embry, *Inside Game,* 128.

38. Heinsohn and Lewin, *Heinsohn,* 122.

39. Heinsohn and Lewin, *Heinsohn,* 122–23.

40. Heinsohn and Lewin, *Heinsohn,* 123.

41. Embry, *Inside Game,* 128.

42. Heinsohn and Lewin, *Heinsohn,* 123.

43. Heinsohn and Lewin, *Heinsohn,* 123.

44. Heinsohn and Lewin, *Heinsohn,* 123.

45. Dan Hafner, "Lakers Can Receive Pension on Request," *Los Angeles Times,* January 17, 1964.

46. Araton and Bondy, *Selling of the Green,* 67.

47. Robertson, *Big O,* 183.

48. "NBA Star Game."

49. Embry, *Inside Game,* 128.

50. Heinsohn and Lewin, *Heinsohn,* 123.

51. Heinsohn and Lewin, *Heinsohn,* 124.

52. Heinsohn and Lewin, *Heinsohn,* 124.

53. "NBA Assured of Pension Considerations," *Washington Post,* January 15, 1964.

54. McDonough, "Pro Hoop Pension."

55. Dan Hafner, "East Wins All-Star Classic Delayed by Player Revolt," *Los Angeles Times,* January 15, 1964.

56. "NBA Players Threaten Strike in Dispute over Pension Plan," *New York Times,* January 15, 1964.

57. "Russell Says League Has Negro Quota," *Hartford Courant,* January 15, 1964.

58. "NBA Assured of Pension Considerations."

59. "Boston Quint's Owner Still Mad at Heinsohn," *Baltimore Sun,* January 18, 1964.

60. "East Wins by 111–107 in Boston," *Hartford Courant,* January 15, 1964.

61. Embry, *Inside Man,* 128.

62. Leonard Koppett, "East All-Stars Protect Early Lead and Defeat Surging West Five, 111 to 107," January 15, 1964.

63. "Robertson Paces East Pro Cagers to 111–107 Triumph," *Baltimore Sun*, January 15, 1964.

64. Koppett, "East All-Stars."

65. Bud Collins, "Listen! Player Tells His Story," *Boston Globe*, January 16, 1964.

66. Koppett, "East All-Stars."

67. Will McDonough, "Pro Hoop Pension Rift Widens," *Boston Globe*, January 16, 1964.

68. McDonough, "Pro Hoop Pension."

69. Dan Hafner, "Lakers Can Receive Pension on Request," *Los Angeles Times*, January 17, 1964.

70. Bud Collins, "Players Pension Stand Breaking Brown's Heart," *Boston Globe*, January 18, 1964.

71. Oscar Robertson, interview with Charles Korr.

72. Cliff Keane, "Pension Vote Angers Brown," *Boston Globe*, January 17, 1964.

73. "Heinsohn No. 1 Heel, Says Boss: Heinsohn Feud" *Los Angeles Times*, January 18, 1964.

74. Keane, "Pension Vote Angers."

75. Keane, "Pension Vote Angers."

76. "Heinsohn No. 1 Heel."

77. "Heinsohn 'Heel' Says Celtic Owner," *Boston Globe*, January 18, 1964.

78. Keane, "Pension Vote Angers."

79. "Heinsohn No. 1 Heel."

80. Keane, "Pension Vote Angers."

81. "Heinsohn 'Heel' Says Celtic Owner"; "Boston Quint's Owner Still Mad."

82. Collins, "Players Pension Stand."

83. "Boston Quint's Owner Still Mad."

84. Collins, "Players Pension Stand."

85. "Heinsohn 'Heel' Says Celtic Owner."

86. "Boston Quint's Owner Still Mad."

87. Barry, "Brown Again Flays Heinsohn."

88. "NBA Confirms Player Pensions, Start Next Year," *Washington Post*, February 26, 1964.

89. "NBA Okays Pension Plan," *Boston Globe*, May 27, 1964.

90. "NBA Approves Pension Plan, Sets Television Program for 1964–65," *Hartford Courant*, May 27, 1964.

91. "NBA Approves Pension."

92. "NBA Players OK Pension Plan," *Hartford Courant*, June 24, 1964.

93. Quinn, *Don't Be Afraid*, 14.

94. Smith, *Hard Labor*, 119.

5. Larry

1. "Larry Fleisher; Led NBA Players Union," *Newsday*, May 5, 1989.

2. Cosell, *What's Wrong with Sports*, 203.

3. Larry Fleisher, memo to players, 1987.

4. Gary Chester, "The Disappearing Act," *Sports, Inc.*, March 28, 1988.

5. Sam Goldaper, "Pro Basketball: Stern Hopes for Talks Despite New Union Move," *New York Times*, February 7, 1988.

6. "NBA Union Is Voted Out," *Washington Post*, February 6, 1988.

7. Chester, "Disappearing Act."

8. Goldaper, "Pro Basketball."

9. "Union May Die in NBA: Player Reps Vote to Decertify," *Philadelphia Inquirer*, February 6, 1988.

10. "NBA Union."

11. Bob Ryan, "NBA Ahead of the Game: Agreement Is Model of Sensible, Lucrative Compromise," *Boston Globe*, May 1, 1988.

12. Marc Fleisher, interview.

13. Sam Goldaper, "Fleisher Finds a New Career: NBA," *New York Times*, October 5, 1988.

14. Jim Quinn, interview.

15. Marc Fleisher, interview.

16. Marc Fleisher, interview.

17. "Fleisher's Roll Slowed by Soviets—Even Super Agent Having Problems," *Seattle Times*, December 25, 1988.

18. Cosell, *What's Wrong*, 204.

19. Cosell, *What's Wrong*, 204; Kenneth Denlinger, "Fleisher Leaves a Wealth of Progress for Players," *Washington Post*, May 14, 1989.

20. "Former NBA Players Remember Impact Fleisher Had on Game," *Baltimore Sun*, May 9, 1989.

21. Ira Berkow, "When 15 7-Footers Trailed Him," *New York Times*, May 11, 1989.

22. "Former NBA Players Remember Impact."

23. Cosell, *What's Wrong*, 204.

24. Wikipedia Entry (https://en.wikipedia.org/wiki/Larry_Fleisher); Alexander Wolf, "NBA Players Counsel Fleisher Wears a Second Hat as an Agent," *Sports Illustrated*, February 11, 1985.

25. Wolf, "NBA Players Counsel"; Marc Fleisher, interview.

26. Wolf, "NBA Players Counsel."

27. "A Power off the Court," *Chicago Tribune*, January 30, 1977.

28. Marc Fleisher, interview.

29. Marc Fleisher, interview.

30. Jim Quinn, interview.

31. Quinn, interview.

32. Cosell, *What's Wrong*, 208.

33. Bob Ryan, "Fleisher NBA Players Man," *Boston Globe*, May 5, 1989.

34. Bradley, *Life on the Run*, 147–48.

35. John Powers, "New Deal, Old Dealer: Larry Fleisher, the Players' Point Guard, Runs the Break," *Boston Globe*, March 29, 1983.

36. Frederick Klein, "Fun and Folly in the National Basketball Asylum," *Wall Street Journal*, October 28, 1982.

37. Wolf, "NBA Players Counsel."

38. Neil Amdur, "Pro Agents Play the Recruiting Game," *New York Times*, May 25, 1981.

39. Marc Fleisher, interview.

40. Bob Ryan and Bob Kinsley, "Chaney Spurns Celtics, 'Spirited' off to St. Louis," *Boston Globe*, September 28, 1974.

41. Bob Ryan, "Celtics Put Chaney on Suspension," *Boston Globe*, September 24, 1974.

42. "Chaney Uses His Option: He'll Join the ABA," *Los Angeles Times*, September 28, 1974.

43. Bob Ryan, "Chaney Owes Thank-Yous to Red and Bill and Tom," *Boston Globe*, September 29, 1974.

44. Ray Fitzgerald, "Don't Blame the Duck," *Boston Globe*, October 3, 1974.

45. John Powers, "Auerbach, Fleisher Bury Their Hatchets," *Boston Globe*, September 25, 1977.

46. Power, "New Deal, Old Dealer."

47. Jim Quinn interview.

48. Marc Fleisher, interview.

49. "NBA Players Attempt to Stop Merger Plan," *Globe and Mail*, April 17, 1970.

50. "NBA Players Attempt."

51. Robertson, *Big O*, 213.

52. Oscar Robertson, interview with Charles Korr.

53. Robertson, interview with Korr.

54. Robertson, interview with Korr.

55. Peter Gruenberger, affidavit in support of application for attorneys fees, costs, and disbursements, ROB, 3–4.

56. Gruenberger, affidavit in support of application, 4.

57. Robertson interview with Korr.

58. Wolf, "NBA Counsel Larry."

59. Gruenberger, affidavit in support of application, 3–5.

60. Charles Maher, "Sports Option Clauses: The Issue Is Freedom," *Los Angeles Times*, June 29, 1972.

61. Red Smith, "Athletes Stand Up for Their Rights," *Washington Post*, April 22, 1970.

62. *Hearings before the Subcommittee on Antitrust and Monopoly of the Committee on the Judiciary*, S.2373, 92nd Cong., January 25, 1972, 228.

63. Pluto, *Loose Balls*, 424.

64. Pluto, *Loose Balls*, 424.

65. Charles Maher, "Clubs' Counsel, Ed Silver, Says Owners Are Hesitant of Collective Bargaining," *Los Angeles Times*, February 14, 1973.

66. Charles Maher, "NBA Players Militant . . . Still Get Along with Owners," *Los Angeles Times*, February 14, 1973.

67. Jim Quinn, interview.

68. Smith, *Hard Labor*, 119.

69. Charles Maher, "Pro Basketball: Suit Threatens Life of the NBA," *Los Angeles Times*, October 30, 1975.

70. Robertson v. National Basketball Association, 389 F. Supp. 867 (1975).

71. Maher, "Pro Basketball."

72. Maher, "Pro Basketball."

73. "NBA Owners Get a Deadline," *New York Times*, January 9, 1976.

74. "Robertson Case Tops NBA Meeting Agenda," *Baltimore Sun*, January 9, 1976.

75. Bob Logan, "NBA's O'Brien a Miracle Worker," *Chicago Tribune*, February 8, 1976.

76. "NBA Players, Owners Surprisingly Agreeable," *Atlanta Constitution*, February 3, 1976.

77. Alan Goldstein, "Another Day," *Baltimore Sun*, February 4, 1976.

78. "NBA Management Votes Freedom," *Atlanta Constitution*, February 4, 1976.

79. Bob Logan, "Owners, Players Make Peace in NBA," *Chicago Tribune*, February 4, 1976.

80. Logan, "Owners, Players Make Peace."

81. "NBA Management Votes."

82. "Pro Cagers, Diamond Stars Won 'Dignity' in 1976," *Baltimore Sun*, December 26, 1976.

83. Logan, "NBA's O'Brien."

84. Gruenberger, affidavit in support of application, 5.

85. Gruenberger, affidavit in support of application, 2.

86. Logan, "Owners, Players Make Peace."

6. The Sport of the '70s

1. Halberstam, *Breaks of the Game*, 207.

2. Roone Arledge, "It's Sport . . . It's Money . . . It's TV." *Sports Illustrated*, April 25, 1966.

3. Arledge, "It's Sport."

4. Arledge, *A Memoir*. 140–42.

5. Arledge, "It's Sport."

6. Arledge, *A Memoir*, 140–42.

7. Jack Craig, "Study Predicts Basketball Will Be Sport of 70s," *Boston Globe*, February 28, 1971.

8. Ronald Buel, "Pro Basketball Gets Tips from Football, Rises to New Heights," *Wall Street Journal*, January 12, 1966.

9. Seymour Smith, "Prime TV Time Possible for NBA: ABC Ponders Change to Monday Night in the Future," *Baltimore Sun*, September 28, 1969.

10. Craig, "Study Predicts Basketball."

11. "NBA, ABC Signs 3 Year Contract," *Hartford Courant*, February 18, 1970.

12. Bob Logan, "ABC Expected to Sign a New NBA Contract," *Chicago Tribune*, February 14, 1973.

13. Charles Maher, "ABC Sues CBS Over TV Rights: NBA Would Rather Switch, but Fight Due," *Los Angeles Times*, June 2, 1973.

14. Halberstam, *Breaks of the Game*, 211.

15. Arledge *A Memoir*, 140–42.

16. Jack Craig, "NBA Sheds ABC Affiliation Fast When CBS Quotes a Higher Figure," *Boston Globe*, March 11, 1973.

17. Maher, "ABC Sues CBS."

18. Gary Deeb, "Roone's Revenge: Jilted ABC Makes the Most of Sundays," *Chicago Tribune*, April 27, 1979.

19. Maher, "ABC Sues CBS."

20. Jack Craig, "The National Basketball Affliction: TV's Slow Fade," *Boston Globe*, March 30, 1982.

21. Bob Kinsley, "The Sports Log," *Boston Globe*, November 3, 1973.

22. "NBA Players Upset with CBS Decision," *Hartford Courant* November 3, 1973.

23. "CBS Hands Pro Basketball Players the Best Deal in Sports," *Chicago Tribune*, December 6, 1973.

24. Jack Craig, "CBS Tries NBA Again," *Boston Globe*, October 29, 1978.

25. Gary Deeb, "ABC Sports Plans Savage Competition," *Chicago Tribune*, November 16, 1973.

26. Craig, "CBS Tries NBA."

27. Craig, "National Basketball Affliction."

28. Craig, "CBS Tries NBA."

29. "NBA, CBS Sign Four-Year Pact," *Chicago Tribune*, May 25, 1976.

30. Alan Rothenberg, memo, May 7, 1976, LOB.

31. Russ Granik, memo, October 25, 1976, LOB.

32. Russ Granik, memo, November 1 1976, LOB.

33. Russ Granik, memo October 26, 1976, LOB.

34. Paul Attner, "The NBA's Puzzle: Interest Is Lagging and the Problem Is That Nobody Knows What the Problem is," *Los Angeles Times*, February 22, 1979.

35. Craig, "National Basketball Affliction."

36. Larry O'Brien, telex to owners, May 3, 1978, LOB.

37. Larry O'Brien, notes of call with Board of Governors, May 3, 1978, LOB.

38. Craig, "National Basketball Affliction."

39. Larry O'Brien, notes for teleconference, May 3, 1978, LOB.

40. George Faust, memo to Larry O'Brien, April 20, 1978, LOB.

41. O'Brien, notes for teleconference, May 3, 1978, LOB.

42. O'Brien, notes for teleconference, May 3, 1978, LOB.

43. Russ Granik, memo, April 21, 1978, LOB.

44. Faust, memo to O'Brien.

45. Faust, memo to O'Brien.

46. Faust, memo to O'Brien.

47. Larry Stewart, "Cable TV: A Bonanza Awaits the Sports Junkie," *Los Angeles Times*, May 25, 1979.

48. Stewart, "Cable TV."

49. Bob Ryan podcast with David Stern.

50. Stewart, "Cable TV."

51. Les Brown, "Garden Cable Network Is Going Beyond Sports," *New York Times*, April 7, 1978.

52. Brown, "Garden Cable."

53. Bill Jauss, "The Future of Sports Television Connected to a Cable," *Chicago Tribune*, June 13, 1979.

54. Russ Granik, memo, August 2, 1977, LOB.

55. Jauss, "The Future."

56. UA Cablevision, letter to David Stern, LOB.

57. Memo to television committee from David Stern, June 13, 1979, LOB; Letter from ESPN to Larry O'Brien, May 29, 1979, LOB.

58. Memorandum to Board of Governors, July 6, 1979, LOB.

59. David Stern, letter to Joseph Vaerio, ESPN, September 12, 1980, LOB.

60. Board of Governors minutes, May, 1980, LOB.

7. The Cap

1. Seymour Smith, "NBA's Free Agents Find Market Slow; Court Action Threatened," *Baltimore Sun*, August 3, 1977.

2. "Owner Promises Salary Cuts," *Atlanta Constitution*, June 22, 1979.

3. Bob Logan, "Payroll Lid Could Cause NBA Strike," *Chicago Tribune*, September 21, 1979.

4. Bob Logan, "NBA Salary Lid Could Bring Strike Before Playoffs," *Chicago Tribune*, September 28, 1979.

5. Quinn, *Don't Be Afraid*.

6. "Owner Promises Salary Cuts."

7. Memo to Commissioner O'Brien, September 11, 1979, LOB.

8. Alan Rothenberg, memo to Board of Governors, September 20, 1979, LOB.

9. Howard Ganz, memo to Larry O'Brien, September 11, 1979, LOB.

10. Howard Ganz, memo to NBA negotiators, November 1, 1979, LOB.

11. Ganz, memo to NBA negotiators.

12. Interview with Jim Quinn.

13. "NBA Politics Upset O'Brien," *Atlanta Constitution*, November 9, 1979.

14. Alan Rothenberg, letter to Larry O'Brien, September 17, 1979, LOB.

15. Logan, "NBA Salary."

16. Ganz, memo to NBA negotiators.

17. Howard Ganz, memo to Commissioner O'Brien, September 11, 1979, LOB.

18. Ganz, memo to O'Brien.

19. Ganz, memo to O'Brien.

20. Rothenberg, memo to Board of Governors.

21. Ganz, memo to O'Brien.

22. Simon Gourdine, memo to Commissioner O'Brien, September 27, 1979, LOB.

23. Johnny Ludden, "McCombs Loses a 'Loyal Friend,'" *San Antonio Express-News*, January 11, 1997.

24. Pluto, *Loose Balls*, 289.

25. Barry Robinson, "The Great Escape," *San Antonio Express-News*, June 16, 1999.

26. Ludden, "McCombs Loses."

27. Pluto, *Loose Balls*, 295.

28. Van Hasselt, *High Wire Act*, 170.

29. Pluto, *Loose Balls*, 429.

30. Glenn Rogers, "Friends, Foes Recall Drossos' Fierce Loyalty to Spurs," *San Antonio Express-News*, January 11, 1997.

31. Dan Cook, "What NBA Needs: Drossos in Charge," *San Antonio Express-News*, July 2, 1995.

32. Pluto, *Loose Balls*, 295.

33. Pluto, *Loose Balls*, 302.

34. Pluto, *Loose Balls*, 429–30.

35. Robinson, "Great Escape."

36. Pluto, *Loose Balls*, 430.

37. Pluto, *Loose Balls*, 433.

38. Glenn Rogers, "Spurs and Drossos Hard Work Made Drossos Influential around League," *San Antonio Express-News*, April 15, 1993.

39. Interview with Charles Grantham.

40. Ganz, memo to O'Brien.

41. Memo to Commissioner O'Brien, September 11, 1979, LOB.

42. Memo to Commissioner O'Brien.

43. Memo to Commissioner O'Brien.

44. Howard Ganz, memo, September 11, 1979, LOB.

45. Memo to Commissioner O'Brien, September 20, 1979, LOB.

46. Howard Ganz, memo, September 20, 1979, LOB.

47. Gourdine, memo to O'Brien.

48. Memo to Commissioner O'Brien, September 20, 1979, LOB.

49. Logan, "NBA Salary Lid."

50. Logan, "Payroll Lid."

51. Board of Governors minutes, September 28, 1979, LOB.

52. Ganz, memo to NBA negotiators.

53. Memo from Ed Silver and Howard Ganz, January 16, 1980, LOB.

54. Bob Logan, "NBA Players Ready to Strike over Pay Limits," *Chicago Tribune*, February 2, 1980.

55. Bob Logan, "NBA Player Reps Rubber-Stamp Contract," *Chicago Tribune*, February 5, 1980.

56. Board of Governors minutes, February 3, 1980, LOB.

57. Howard Ganz, memo outlining CBA, November 5, 1980, LOB.

58. Bob Logan, "NBA Approves Pact with Players, Expansion to Dallas," *Chicago Tribune*, February 3, 1980.

59. "NBA Expands; Players Close to Pact," *Boston Globe*, February 3, 1980.

60. Logan, "NBA Approves Pact."

61. David DuPree, "NBA, Union Agree; Expansion to Dallas Is Voted," *Washington Post*, February 3, 1980.

62. Interview with Grantham.

63. Meg Algren, "Full Court Press Pays off for Nationwide," *Crain's Cleveland Business*.

64. Stephen Steiner, "The New Kid in the NBA," *Sport*.

65. George Vecsey, "White Heroes and Professional Basketball," *New York Times*, June 9, 1980.

66. Vecsey, "White Heroes."

67. Steiner, "New Kid."

68. Vecsey, "White Heroes."

69. Vecsey, "White Heroes."

70. Vecsey, "White Heroes."

71. Steiner, "New Kid."

72. Vecsey, "White Heroes."

73. Vecsey, "White Heroes."

74. Linda Kay, "New Cavs Boss Makes Presence Felt," *Chicago Tribune*, June 16, 1980.

75. Vecsey, "White Heroes."

76. Bob Ryan, "NBA Wraps Up Good Time Meeting," *Boston Globe*, June 5, 1980.

77. "Another Owner for Cavaliers," *New York Times*, April 14, 1980.

78. "Zingale Rejects Offer to Buy NBA Cavs," *Hartford Courant*, April 20, 1980.

79. Kay, "New Cavs Boss."

80. Ryan, "NBA Wraps Up."

8. The Right of First Refusal

1. Marc Stein, "Q&A with the Commish," Espn.com, January 22, 2004, https://www.espn.com/nba/columns/story?columnist=stein_marc&id=1715470.

2. Helyar, *Lords of the Realm*, 26.

3. Helyar, *Lords of the Realm*, 29.

4. Helyar, *Lords of the Realm*, 115.

5. Kuhn, *Hardball*, 77–78.

6. Helyar, *Lords of the Realm*, 33.

7. Helyar, *Lords of the Realm*, 33.

8. Mark Heisler, "Here's an Idea Worth Talking About," *Los Angeles Times*, June 17, 1981.

9. Cosell, What's Wrong with Sports, 208.

10. Charles Maher, "NBA Players Militant . . . Still Get Along with Owners," *Los Angeles Times*, February 14, 1973.

11. Ian Thomsen, "Questions Remain, but Lakers Always Know They Can Count on Kobe." *Sports Illustrated*, March 7, 2013.

12. Helyar, *Lords of the Realm*, 276.

13. Charles Maher, "A Challenge to Rozelle: Professional Football Players Want to Cut Commissioner's Power in Judging Grievances," *Los Angeles Times*, February 13, 1973.

14. Alan Goldstein, "Another Day," *Baltimore Sun*, February 4, 1976.

15. Michael Madden, "Garvey the Great," *Boston Globe*, April 23, 1983.

16. Marvin Miller, letter to Ed Garvey, August 11, 1976.

17. Robert H. Boyle, "The 55% Solution," *Sports Illustrated*, February 1, 1982.

18. George Solomon, "'Dignity,' 'Liberty' Drive Ed Garvey: NFL Strike: A Walkout for Dignity," *Washington Post*, July 21, 1974.

19. Madden, "Garvey the Great."

20. Leonard Shapiro, "Garvey: Share the Wealth," *Washington Post*, January 23, 1981. Alan Goldstein, "NFLers Make Note of Baseball Brethren," *Baltimore Sun*, June 17, 1981.

21. "Halas Blasts Garvey; Many Changes Seen," *Hartford Courant*, July 31, 1974.

22. "NFL Players Seek Support from Other Trade Unions," *Baltimore Sun*, July 7, 1974.

23. Don Pierson, "First Bears' Vet Crosses Line," *Chicago Tribune*, July 31, 1974.

24. "Staubach 'Sacks' Garvey," *Los Angeles Times*, August 7, 1974.

25. Bob Oates, "Mack Turns on Garvey for Slap at Staubach: Garvey Rapped," *Los Angeles Times*, August 8, 1974.

26. Oates, "Mack Turns."

27. Robert Markus, "It's 'Cold War' Haggling between Owners, Players," *Chicago Tribune*, August 20, 1974.

28. "Garvey Optimistic Despite Strike Loss," *Globe and Mail*, November 15, 1974.

29. "NFL Players Group Is $200,000 in Debt," *Chicago Tribune*, July 9, 1975.

30. "NFL Union in Debt for $200,000," *Washington Post*, July 9, 1975.

31. "NFL Union."

32. "NFL Players Group."

33. Robert Markus, "Garvey Offers Union's Side in NFL Squabbles," *Chicago Tribune*, January 18, 1976.

34. Interviews in collective bargaining in sports project; Ed Garvey, interview, 1977.

35. Paul Attner, "What's Next? Football in the NFL, More Teams, New Divisions—and, Possibly, a Strike," *Washington Post*, July 5, 1981.

36. Alan Goldstein, "NFLers Make Note of Baseball Brethren," *Baltimore Sun*, June 17, 1981.

37. "Rozelle Lashes Back at Garvey on Charge of Racism in NFL," *Los Angeles Times*, November 19, 1979.

38. Jane Gross, "Unions See Benefit in Strike," *New York Times*, July 23, 1981.

39. "Free Agency Is 'Dead' in the NFL, Garvey Says," *Washington Post*, June 27, 1981.

40. Paul Attner, "What's Next? Football in the NFL, More Teams, New Divisions—and, Possibly, a Strike," *Washington Post*, July 5, 1981.

41. Leonard Shapiro, "Garvey: Share the Wealth," *Washington Post*, January 23, 1981.

42. Mike Kiley, "NFL Players Group Fires 1st Salvo," *Chicago Tribune*, July 1, 1981.

43. Bart Barnes, "Garvey: Players May Seek 65% of NFL Gross Revenues," *Washington Post*, November 25, 1981.

44. "Garvey Says NFL Players Monitoring Baseball Strike," *Boston Globe*, June 28, 1981.

45. "Real Free Agentry in NFL Far Off," *Hartford Courant*, June 7, 1981.

46. Boyle, "The 55% Solution."

47. Boyle, "The 55% Solution."

48. "Lambert Would Ignore Pickets," *Hartford Courant*, August 6, 1981.

49. Leonard Shapiro, "Garvey Denies Union Wants Strike," *Washington Post*, January 24, 1982.

50. Attner, "What's Next?"

51. Gary Pomerantz, "NBA's New Free-Agent System: A Bullish Market for Players," *Washington Post*, June 28, 1981.

52. Mike Littwin, "Moneyball: The Owners Moan and Then Sell the Teams for a Profit," *Los Angeles Times*, March 17, 1981.

53. Anthony Cotton, "Those Agents Are Hardly Free," *Sports Illustrated*, June 8, 1981.

54. Cotton "Those Agents."

55. Ted Green, "Dr. J Moves into the Forum," *Los Angeles Times*, May 30, 1979.

56. Ted Green, "Magic's New Numbers Are $25 Million for 25 Years," *Los Angeles Times*, June 26, 1981.

57. Green, "Magic's New Numbers."

58. Green, "Magic's New Numbers."

59. Malcolm Moran, "With Johnson Out, the Lakers Are Having Their Problems," *New York Times*, January 12, 1981.

60. Mike Littwin, "The Lakers Other Guard: Norm Nixon Remains a Spectacular Talent Who Has This Nagging Idea That He Isn't Being Used Correctly," *Los Angeles Times*, March 31, 1981.

61. Basketball reference standings, https://www.basketball-reference.com/leagues/NBA_1981_standings.html.

62. Mike Littwin, "Magic Gone? Johnson Feels Some Lakers Are Resentful," *Los Angeles Times*, April 4, 1981.

63. Littwin, "Magic Gone?"

64. Littwin, "Magic Gone?"

65. Scott Ostler, "Stop the Music: The Party's Over," *Los Angeles Times*, April 6, 1981.

66. George Vecsey, "Rockets Win 89–86 and Eliminate Lakers from the Playoffs" *New York Times*, April 6, 1981.

67. Ostler, "Stop the Music."

68. "Editorial: Buss vs. the Press," *Los Angeles Times*, April 11, 1981.

69. Mike Littwin, "Buss Begins the Laker Autopsy, Saying There'll Be Some Changes Made," *Los Angeles Times*, April 9,1981.

70. "Catching Buss," *Los Angeles Times*, May 14, 1981.

71. Littwin, "Buss Begins."

72. "Buss Was Only Saying What Other General Managers Are Thinking," *Los Angeles Times*, April 14, 1981.

73. Alan Greenberg, "Ted Stepien: Some Say He Means Well, but in Only 20 Months, He Has Turned Cavaliers into Laughingstock," *Los Angeles Times*, February 24, 1982.

74. Bob Ryan, "A Franchise in Trouble: NBA Takes a Dim View of Stepien's and Musselman's Cavalier Attitudes," *Boston Globe*, November 30, 1980.

75. Ryan, "Franchise in Trouble."

76. "Cavs Owner Asks NBA to Probe Albeck," *Hartford Courant*, June 13, 1980.

77. "Albeck Signs to Coach Spurs; Cavaliers Seek Compensation," *Los Angeles Times*, June 12, 1981.

78. "Musselman to Coach Cavs," *Chicago Tribune*, June 14, 1980.

79. Thomas Rogers, "NBA to Take Role in Cavaliers Trades," *New York Times*, November 7, 1980.

80. Gary Bettman, memo, "Status of Cleveland Cavaliers Draft Picks," February 1, 1983, LOB.

81. Bob Ryan, "Rescuing the Cavaliers from Their Own Fate," *Boston Globe*, November 9, 1980.

82. "Owners of Cavs Irate Over NBA Orders," *New York Times*, November 7, 1980; Ryan, "Rescuing the Cavaliers."

83. "Owner of Cavs."

84. Rogers, "NBA to Take Role."

85. "Owner of Cavs."

86. "Cavs Can Trade with Approval," *New York Times*, November 26, 1980.

87. Ryan, "Franchise in Trouble."

88. Ryan, "Franchise in Trouble."

89. "Cavalier Treatment," *Chicago Tribune*, November 21, 1980.

90. "Ex-Arizona State Coach Reportedly Arranged for Payment to Athlete," *Los Angeles Times*, November 20, 1980.

91. "It's Your Move, Chief," *Chicago Tribune*, December 18, 1980.

92. "Cav Owners File Suit Against Radio Station," *Hartford Courant*, February 4, 1981; Craig, Jack, "Cleveland Has Mouth that Roars," *Boston Globe* February 14, 1981.

93. Chuck Melvin, "He Huffs and Puffs, Blows Their Doors in on Sports Talk Show," *Hartford Courant*, March 1, 1981.

94. "Cleveland Cavaliers Owner Ted Stepien Is Again Threatening," *United Press International*, February 22, 1981.

95. Gerald Eskenazi, "Athletes' Salaries: How High Will the Bidding Go?," *New York Times*, August 16, 1981.

96. Cotton, "Those Agents."

97. "The Kansas City Kings Will Lose Otis Birdsong to . . . ," *United Press International*, May 25, 1981.

98. Bill Livingston, "Ted Stepien's Huge Free Agent Offers Rattle NBA owners," *Philadelphia Inquirer*, June 2, 1981.

99. Byron Rosen, "Stepien Strikes Again, Offers Edwards $3 million," *Washington Post*, May 27, 1981.

100. Pomerantz, "NBA's New Free Agent System."

101. "Sports Briefing: Baseball Union Awaits Ruling from NLRB," *Chicago Tribune*, May 26, 1981.

102. Fred Mitchell, "NBA Salaries Ridiculous but They Just Keep Going Up," *Chicago Tribune*, July 19, 1981.

103. Sam Goldaper, "Financial Difficulties in Sight for NBA," *New York Times,* June 14, 1981.

104. Mike Littwin, "NBA Owners: They're Taking a Second Look at First Refusal," *Los Angeles Times,* July 10, 1981.

105. Mitchell, "NBA Salaries Ridiculous."

106. Pomerantz, "NBA's New Free Agent System."

107. Littwin, "NBA Owners."

108. Goldaper, "Financial Difficulties."

109. Pomerantz, "NBA's New Free Agent System."

110. Goldaper, "Financial Difficulties."

111. Littwin, "NBA Owners."

112. Sam Goldaper, "Pro Basketball Notebook Salaries and Trades Top Menu," *New York Times,* May 31, 1981.

113. Green, "Magic's New Numbers."

114. Johnson and Novak, *My Life,* 151.

115. "Magic Says Trade a Must," *New Pittsburgh Courier,* May 9, 1981.

116. Green, "Magic's New Numbers."

117. Green, "Magic's New Numbers."

118. Bob Clancy, "Lakers Owner Gave 'Magic' Offer He Couldn't Refuse," *Hartford Courant,* July 3, 1981.

119. Green, "Magic's New Numbers."

120. Green, "Magic's New Numbers."

121. Pomerantz, "NBA's New Free Agent System."

122. Green, "Magic's New Numbers."

123. Neil Amdur, "Abdul-Jabbar Said to Want to Play Here," *New York Times,* July 31, 1981.

124. "Buss Says No Deal for Jabbar," *Baltimore Sun,* August 3, 1981.

125. Amdur, "Abdul-Jabbar."

126. Amdur, "Abdul-Jabbar."

127. Scott Ostler, "Forget Those Rumors: Lakers Are Happy as Tall Clams," *Los Angeles Times,* August 5, 1981.

128. Littwin, "NBA Owners."

129. Katz, *Split Season.*

130. Katz, *Split Season,* 106.

131. Jane Leavy, "Baseball Negotiators Do Nothing," *Washington Post,* June 23, 1981.

132. Leavy, "Baseball Negotiations Do Nothing."

133. Gross, Jane, "Unions See Benefit in Strike," *New York Times,* July 23, 1981.

134. Gross, "Unions See Benefit."

135. Katz, *Split Season,* 178.

136. *Hearings before the Subcommittee on Monopolies and Commercial Law,* H.R. 823, 3287, 6747, 97th Cong., July 15, 1981,157.

137. *Hearings before the Subcommittee on Monopolies.*

138. *Hearings before the Subcommittee on Monopolies.*

9. David

1. Alexander Wolf, "NBA Players Counsel Fleisher Wears a Second Hat as an Agent," *Sports Illustrated*, February 11, 1985.

2. Peter May, "Stern Is behind the Metamorphosis," *Hartford Courant*, February 12, 1989.

3. Curt Schleier, "NBA Commissioner David Stern," *Investors Business Daily*, March 11, 1999.

4. Halberstam, *Playing for Keeps*, 121.

5. Brian Mahoney, "NBA Finals: Star Summit Shelved," *Journal-Gazette*, June 4, 2010.

6. Larry Whiteside, "Inside Choice: Stern Takes Over NBA Center Stage," *Boston Globe*, November 17, 1983.

7. Halberstam, *Playing for Keeps*, 121–22.

8. Halberstam, *Playing for Keeps*, 123.

9. Halberstam, *Playing for Keeps*, 123.

10. Bethlehem Shoals and Jacob Weinstein, *FreeDarko Presents: Undisputed Guide*, 104.

11. Keteyian, Araton, and Dardis. *Money Players*, 33.

12. May, "Stern Is Behind."

13. Seth Cline, "All-Star Politics of the NBA," February 24, 2012, https://www.opensecrets.org/news/2012/02/nba/.

14. Keteyian, Araton, and Dardis, *Money Players*, 39.

15. Pluto, *Loose Balls*, 430.

16. Memo from Russ Granik, October 28, 1976, LOB.

17. Bill King, "One of the Good Guys," *Sports Business Journal*, March 26, 2015.

18. Keteyian, Araton, and Dardis, *Money Players*, 39.

19. Bob Ryan, podcast with David Stern, August 4, 2017.

20. Marc Stein, "Q&A with the Commish," Espn.com, January 22, 2004, https://www.espn.com/nba/columns/story?columnist=stein_marc&id=1715470.

21. May, "Stern Is Behind."

22. Larry O'Brien, telex, November 18, 1980, LOB.

23. Halberstam, *Playing for Keeps*, 118.

24. Charles Grantham, interview with David Stern, April 26, 2018.

25. Mary Hynes, "NBA's No Longer a Basket Case: Stern Measures Guided League through Troubles," *Globe and Mail*, December 26, 1988.

26. Board of Governors meeting, June, 1981, LOB.

27. Larry O'Brien, statements, 1982 owners meeting, LOB.

28. Larry O'Brien, notes from "Chronology of Network Negotiations," 1981, LOB.

29. O'Brien, "Chronology of Network Negotiations."

30. O'Brien, "Chronology of Network Negotiations."

31. Jack Craig, "The National Basketball Affliction: TV's Slow Fade," *Boston Globe*, March 30, 1982.

32. Craig, "National Basketball Affliction."

33. Larry Stewart, "Less Is More: CBS Slashes Its NBA coverage," *Los Angeles Times*, December 23, 1981.

34. Larry O'Brien, telex, February 5, 1982, LOB.

35. O'Brien, telex.

36. Memo regarding meeting of Western Conference owners, February 23, 1982, LOB.

37. Memo regarding meeting of Western Conference owners.

38. Larry O'Brien, telex, March 15, 1982, LOB.

39. 1982collective bargaining memo from David Stern, Russ Granik, and Gary Bettman, March 15, 1982, LOB, 2.

40. 1982 collective bargaining memo from David Stern, March 15, 1982, LOB.

41. 1982 collective bargaining memo from David Stern.

42. 1982 collective bargaining memo from David Stern.

43. 1982 collective bargaining memo from David Stern.

44. Stern, memo, March 5, 1982, LOB.

45. 1982 collective bargaining memo from David Stern.

46. 1982 collective bargaining memo from Stern, Granik, and Bettman, 2.

47. Larry O'Brien, telex, March 22, 1982, LOB.

48. Larry O'Brien, telex, February 17, 1982, LOB.

49. 1982 player negotiations: possible NBA proposals, NBA memo, March 29, 1982, LOB.

50. Gary Bettman, memo, May 5, 1982, LOB.

51. 1982 player negotiations, NBA memo.

52. 1982 Player Negotiations, NBA memo; Bettman, memo.

53. NBA economic memo, May 13, 1982, LOB.

54. Stan Kasten, letter, May 27, 1982, LOB, 2.

55. Stan Kasten, letter, 2.

56. Stan Kasten, letter, 2.

57. June 4, 1982, memo, LOB.

58. June 4, 1982, memo.

59. June 4, 1982, memo.

60. Chris Cobbs, "Suddenly, the Silence Is Sterling," *Los Angeles Times*, March 31, 1982.

61. Bob Ryan, "NBA Drops Bonus Throw," *Boston Globe*, June 3, 1981.

62. Draft memo for the files "NBA—San Diego Clippers—Special Engagement," September 17, 1982, LOB.

63. Chris Cobbs, "Clippers New Owner Says He Won't Fail," *Los Angeles Times*, June 6, 1981.

64. Chris Cobbs, "Clippers Think Big for NBA Draft," *Los Angeles Times*, June 9, 1981.

65. "NBA Cites Casino Ties," *New York Times*, November 11, 1981.

66. Dave Distel, "NBA Makes a Move to Oust Sterling," *Los Angeles Times*, September 22, 1982; Chris Cobbs, "Owner Says He Wants Clippers in Last Place," *Los Angeles Times*, January 8, 1982.

67. Cobbs, "Owner Says."

68. Cobbs, "Suddenly, the Silence."

69. "NBA Fines Clippers Owner," *New York Times*, January 9, 1982.

70. Cobbs, "Suddenly, the Silence."

71. "Clippers Owner Tells of Financial Problems," *New York Times*, January 28, 1982.

72. Distel, "NBA Makes."

73. Interview with Jim Quinn, October 23, 2018.

74. Interview with Jim Quinn.

75. Cobbs, "Suddenly, the Silence."

76. Cobbs, "Suddenly, the Silence."

77. "Clipper Owner Admits Having Financial Woes," *Hartford Courant*, January 28, 1982.

78. Chris Cobbs, "Sterling Passes NBA Debt Test; Probe continues" *Los Angeles Times*, June 25, 1982.

79. Bob Ryan, "A Strike? A San Diego Move? What's NBA to Do?" *Boston Globe*, June 27, 1982.

80. Cobbs, "Sterling Passes."

81. Larry O'Brien, "Statement by Commissioner O'Brien to the Advisory/Finance Committee on June 21, 1982," LOB.

82. Cobbs, "Sterling Passes."

83. Ryan, "A Strike?"

84. Chris Cobbs, "NBA Sues Coliseum for $10 Million, Probes Sterling," *Los Angeles Times*, June 23, 1982.

85. Bob Ryan, "Mystery Buyer For Clippers?," *Boston Globe*, June 22, 1982.

86. Ryan, "A Strike?"

87. Board of Governors minutes, June 1982, LOB.

88. Jack Krumpe, letter to Larry O'Brien, July 7, 1982, LOB.

89. Ryan, "A Strike?"

10. The Moses Signing

1. "Moses Might Go but for Now He's One Hot Rocket," *Los Angeles Times*, February 20, 1982.

2. "Nuggets, Rockets Are Sold," *New York Times*, June 16, 1982.

3. "Moses Might Go."

4. "Buss Was Only Saying What Other General Managers Are Thinking," *Los Angeles Times*, April 14, 1981.

5. "Buss Was Only Saying."

6. Steve Hershey, "Malone's Windfall: Many See It as NBA's Downfall," *Washington Post*, September 29, 1982.

7. "At Least 1 Owner Is Gung Ho about the Future," *Chicago Tribune*, March 2, 1980.

8. Hershey, "Malone's Windfall."

9. "Just a Kid on Big Man's Playground: Maloof, an Heir, a Salesman, and the Youngest Owner in Sports," *Los Angeles Times*, May 14, 1981.

10. "Moses Might Go."

11. "Malone Heads List of 66 Free Agents," *New York Times*, April 18, 1982.

12. "Rockets Offer May Be $1.9 Million to Malone," *Chicago Tribune*, June 6, 1982.

13. "Rockets Owner Says He'll Pay What It Takes to Keep Malone," *Los Angeles Times*, June 7, 1982.

14. "Nuggets, Rockets Are Sold," *New York Times*, June 16, 1982.

15. Alexander Wolff, "Searching for a Promised Land," *Sports Illustrated*, August 30, 1982.

16. Wolff, "Searching for a Promised Land."

17. Wolff, "Searching for a Promised Land."

18. Collective bargaining memo from Lawrence O'Brien, August 31, 1982, LOB, 3.

19. "76ers Sign Malone to $13 Million Offer," *New York Times*, September 3, 1982.

20. "76ers Deal Dawkins to Nets," *Chicago Tribune*, August 28, 1982.

21. Sam Goldaper, "76er Owner Is Conspicuous," *New York Times*, June 2, 1982.

22. Goldaper, "76er Owner Is Conspicuous."

23. Goldaper, "76er Owner Is Conspicuous."

24. Dawkins and Rosen, *Chocolate Thunder*, 117.

25. "76ers Sign Malone to $13 Million Offer."

26. Goldaper, "76er Owner Is Conspicuous."

27. Hershey, "Malone's Windfall."

28. "76ers Sign Malone to $13 Million Offer."

29. Hershey, "Malone's Windfall."

30. Williams and Jones, *Tales*, 5.

31. Hershey, "Malone's Windfall."

32. "Malone: I Don't Care What People Are Saying," *Washington Post*, September 6, 1982.

33. Hershey, "Malone's Windfall."

34. "Malone: I Don't Care."

35. Dan Shaughnessy, "No Agreement yet, but No Sweat," *Boston Globe*, October 3, 1982.

36. "Malone's Windfall."

37. Shaughnessy, "No Agreement yet."

38. Hershey, "Malone's Windfall."

39. Bruce Newman, "Can the NBA Save Itself?" *Sports Illustrated*, November 1, 1982.

40. "Malone: I Don't Care."

41. "Rockets to Match Offer by 76ers for Malone"; "Malone: I Don't Care."

42. Williams and Jones, *Tales*, 5.

43. "Malone Contract Could top $15 million," *New York Times*, September 10, 1982.

44. "Rockets to Match Offer."

45. "Malone Contract."

46. Phil Jasner, "Players Group Backs 76ers, Malone," *Philadelphia Daily News*, September 11, 1982.

47. David Dupree, "Major Trades Make NBA Season More Volatile Than Usual," *Washington Post*, October 26, 1982.

48. "76ers Land Malone," *Chicago Tribune*, September 16, 1982.

49. Newman, "Can the NBA Save Itself?"

50. "76ers Land Malone."

51. Report of special master, September 7, 1982, LOB, 3.

52. "NBA Commissioner Lawrence O'Brien Said Tuesday He Hopes a . . . ," *United Press International*, September 7, 1982.

53. Report of special master, 4.

54. NBA press statement, September 7, 1982, LOB.

55. Russ Granik, telex, September 7, 1982, LOB.

56. "NBA Commissioner Lawrence."

57. "NBA Commissioner Lawrence."

58. Gary Bettman, memo, September 23, 1982, LOB.

59. Bettman, memo.

60. Bettman, memo.

61. Bettman, memo.

62. C. L. Smith Muñiz, "NBA Sides Far from Agreement," *Hartford Courant*, October 12, 1982.

63. Harris, *The League*, 544.

64. Harris, *The League*, 543.

65. Harris, *The League*, 544.

66. Harris, *The League*, 545.

67. Harris, *The League*, 542.

11. The Big Item

1. Dan Shaughnessy, "No Agreement yet, but No Sweat," *Boston Globe*, October 3, 1982.

2. Larry O'Brien, memo, September 24, 1982, LOB, 1.

3. O'Brien, memo, 2.

4. C. L. Smith Muñiz, "NBA Sides Far from Agreement," *Hartford Courant*, October 12, 1982.

5. Muñiz, "NBA Sides."

6. O'Brien, memo, 2.

7. Gary Bettman, notes, September 23, 1982, LOB.

8. David DuPree, "Pollin: Rough Time in New World," *Washington Post*, July 7, 1981.

9. Gary Bettman, memo, September 23, 1982, LOB.

10. Bettman, memo.

11. Bettman, memo.

12. Muñiz, "NBA Sides."

13. "NBA Owners Will Be Briefed on Talks," *New York Times*, October 20, 1982.

14. Bettman, memo.

15. Steve Hershey, "NBA Owners Meet Today on Union Negotiations," *Washington Post*, October 20, 1982.

16. George Shirk, "Sixers Ponder Hazards of a 10-Player Roster," *Philadelphia Inquirer*, October 21, 1982.

17. Hershey, "NBA Owners Meet."

18. Dan Shaughnessy, "Owners Won't Rock the Boat During Stalled Negotiations," *Boston Globe*, November 14, 1982.

19. Larry O'Brien, memo, August 31, 1982, LOB.

20. O'Brien, memo, September 24, 1982, LOB.

21. "Owners Seek New Salary Plan," *Chicago Tribune*, October 21, 1982.

22. Sam Goldaper, "Scouting: No Rush to Sign," *New York Times*, September 22, 1982.

23. Goldaper, "Scouting: No Rush."

24. Bob Ryan, "Unsigned Picks: Collusion or Delusion," *Boston Globe*, September 14, 1980.

25. Goldaper, "Scouting: No Rush."

26. Alexander Wolff, "Searching for a Promised Land," *Sports Illustrated*, August 30, 1982.

27. Goldaper, "Scouting: No Rush."

28. "Lakers Sign Worthy," *New York Times*, October 1, 1982.

29. "Worthy Expected to Sign This Week," *Los Angeles Times*, September 28, 1982.

30. C. L. Smith Muñiz, "Roster Reduction Rumors Usher in Owners Meeting," *Hartford Courant*, October 16, 1981.

31. Bruce Newman, "Can the NBA Save Itself?" *Sports Illustrated*, November 1, 1982.

32. "O'Brien: New NBA Plan Ready for Negotiations," *Washington Post*, October 21, 1982.

33. Shirk, "Sixers Ponder Hazards."

34. Larry O'Brien, memo, October 6, 1982, LOB.

35. O'Brien, memo.

36. O'Brien, memo.

37. Shaughnessy, "Owners Won't Rock."

38. Randy Harvey, "Another Sport Strike Looms," *Los Angeles Times*, November 2, 1982.

39. Newman, "Can the NBA."

40. Gary Bettman, memo, October 10, 1982, LOB.

41. Bettman, memo.

42. Bettman, memo.

43. Bettman, memo.

44. Bettman, memo.

45. Bettman, memo.

46. Gary Bettman, memo, October 17, 2019, LOB.

47. Bettman, memo.

48. Bettman, memo.

49. Bettman, memo.

50. "O'Brien: New NBA."

51. Outline for Advisory/Finance Committee presentation, LOB.

52. Board of Governors meeting, October 20, 1982, LOB.

53. Board of Governors meeting.

54. NBA Board of Governors minutes, October 28, 1982, LOB.

55. "O'Brien: New NBA."

56. "Owners Seek New Salary Plan," *Chicago Tribune*, October 21, 1982.

57. Larry O'Brien, telex, October 21, 1982, LOB.

58. "O'Brien: New NBA."

59. Hershey, "NBA Owners Meet."

60. Gary Bettman, player negotiations memo, October 29, 1982, LOB.

61. Guaranteed Compensation Plan, LOB, 1.

62. Chronology of collective bargaining between NBA/NBPA, LOB.

63. Sam Goldaper, "NBA and Players Schedule New Talks," *New York Times*, February 23, 1983.

64. "NBA and Players Schedule New Talks," *New York Times*, February 25, 1983.

65. Gary Bettman, player negotiations memo, October 29, 1982.

66. Bettman, player negotiations memo.

67. David Dupree, "Major Trade Makes NBA Season Even More Volatile Than Usual," *Washington Post*, October 26, 1982.

68. Basketball Reference, https://www.basketball-reference.com/boxscores /198210290NYK.html.

69. Anthony Cotton, "I Can Do So Many Things," *Sports Illustrated*, November 1, 1982.

70. Dupree, "Major Trade."

71. Harvey, "Another Sports."

72. Sam Goldaper, "It's Time to See if Changes Help," *New York Times*, October 24, 1982.

73. Dupree, "Major Trade."

74. Shaughnessy, "Owners Won't Rock."

75. Ted Stepien, letter to Larry O'Brien, November 18, 1982, LOB.

76. Dave Distel, "NBA Makes a Move to Oust Sterling," *Los Angeles Times*, September 22, 1982.

77. Chris Cobbs, "Clippers Do Unexpected—yet Again," *Los Angeles Times*, October 19, 1982.

78. C. L. Smith Muñiz, "Big Bucks Threaten the NBA," *Hartford Courant*, October 29, 1982.

79. Shaughnessy, "No Agreement yet."

80. Newman, "Can the NBA."

81. Muñiz, "Big Bucks Threaten."

82. Interview with Jim Quinn.

83. Larry Fleisher, letter to David Stern, NBPA letter, October 18, 1982, LOB.

84. Gary Bettman, player negotiations memo, October 29, 1982, LOB.

85. Bettman, player negotiations memo.

86. Bettman, player negotiations memo.

87. Bettman, player negotiations memo.

88. Gary Bettman player negotiations memo, November 19, 1982, LOB.

89. *Time-Out*, (NBA players association magazine), February, 1983, LOB.

90. David Stern, interview at Seton Hall.

91. Larry O'Brien's Commissioner's newsletter, January 24, 1983, LOB.

92. Harris, *The League*, 547–48.

12. Strike Date

1. *Time-Out*, (NBA players association magazine), February 1983, LOB.

2. "McHale Is Worth a Mint, but He's Talked Too Much," *Boston Globe*, January 2, 1983.

3. Interview with Jim Quinn.

4. "McHale Is Worth."

5. "Sixers Wary of Cavalier Attitude," *Philadelphia Daily News*, December 15, 1982.

6. "NBA Discusses Bargaining Idea," *New York Times*, January 19, 1983.

7. Gary Bettman, bargaining notes, January 21, 1983, LOB.

8. Bettman, bargaining notes.

9. Bettman, bargaining notes.

10. Bettman, bargaining notes.

11. Bettman, bargaining notes.

12. Bettman, bargaining notes.

13. Larry O'Brien, notes, presumably for February 11, 1983 meeting, LOB.

14. O'Brien, notes.

15. Gary Bettman, bargaining notes, January 26, 1983, LOB.

16. Bettman, bargaining notes.

17. Bettman, bargaining notes.

18. David DuPree, "Pollin Warns of Teams Folding, Strike Threat Backlash in NBA," *Washington Post*, February 20, 1983.

19. "Talks Resume," *New York Times*, January 25, 1983.

20. Larry O'Brien, telex, January 28, 1983, LOB.

21. C. L. Smith Muñiz, "NBA Says Union Reneged," *Hartford Courant*, February 18, 1983.

22. Gary Bettman, bargaining notes, February 1, 1983, LOB.

23. Bettman, bargaining notes.

24. Bettman, bargaining notes.

25. Bettman, bargaining notes.

26. Bettman, bargaining notes.

27. Bettman, bargaining notes.

28. Bettman, bargaining notes.

29. Dan Shaughnessy, "Tune In . . . While You Can," *Boston Globe*, January 30, 1983.

30. Will McDonough, "NBA Ship of Fools Near Rocks," *Boston Globe*, March 17, 1983.

31. Gary Bettman, bargaining notes, February 15, 1983, LOB.

32. Bettman, bargaining notes.

33. Bettman, bargaining notes.

34. Dupree, "Pollin Warns."

35. Board of Governors meeting, February 12, 1983, LOB.

36. DuPree, "Pollin Warns."

37. Larry O'Brien, conference call outline, February 25, 1983, LOB.

38. "Notes: Basketball," *Chicago Tribune*, February 14, 1983.

39. Dan Shaughnessy, "NBA Hoping Restraints Will Force Stepien to Sell," *Boston Globe*, February 6, 1983.

40. George Shirk, "Owners' Meetings at All-Star Game Do Little to Solve NBA's Problems," *Philadelphia Inquirer*, February 14, 1983.

41. Shirk, "Owners' Meetings."

42. Shirk, "Owners' Meetings."

43. O'Brien, conference call outline.

44. Sam Goldaper, "Players in NBA Issue Deadline," *New York Times*, February 17, 1983.

45. "Scorecard," *Sports Illustrated*, March 14, 1983.

46. "Vowing His Union Is Willing to Take Whatever Steps," *United Press International*, February 17, 1983.

47. Charles Grantham, letter, February 15, 1983, LOB.

48. "NBA Players Set April 2 as Deadline," *Hartford Courant*, February 17, 1983.

49. Dan Shaughnessy, "NBA Management Takes the Offensive" *Boston Globe*, February 17, 1983.

50. Phil Jasner, "NBA Talks Strike," *Philadelphia Daily News*, February 16, 1983.

51. "Union Sets Deadline, Hints at April Strike," *Miami Herald*, February 18, 1983.

52. David Dupree, "Strike Date of April 2 Set by NBA Players," *Washington Post*, February 17, 1983.

53. Jasner, "NBA Talks."

54. C. L. Smith Muñiz, "Strike Threat Is Far from Frivolous," *Hartford Courant*, February 20, 1983.

55. "Scorecard," *Sports Illustrated*.

56. Randy Harvey, "Lakers Beat Mavericks; 32 by Jabbar," *Los Angeles Times*, February 18, 1983.

57. "Notes: Bulls," *Chicago Tribune*, March 7, 1983.

58. Muñiz, "Strike Threat."

59. "NBA Blames Fleisher for Strike Possibility," *Atlanta Constitution*, February 18, 1983.

60. Phil Jasner, "Start of Salary Plan Key to Talks," *Philadelphia Daily News*, February 17, 1983.

61. "NBA Players Set April 2 as Deadline," *Hartford Courant*, February 17,1983.

62. Dan Shaughnessy, "NBA Fires Second Salvo in Two Days," *Boston Globe*, February 18, 1983; Dupree, "Strike Date."

63. Goldaper, "Players in NBA."

64. O'Brien, conference call outline, 2.

65. "Owner Dares Union to Strike," *New York Times*, February 18, 1983.

66. Dupree, "Pollin Warns."

67. Dan Shaughnessy, "NBA Management Takes the Offensive," *Boston Globe*, February 17, 1983.

68. Telex from Harry Glickman to Larry O'Brien, February 18, 1983, LOB.

69. Bill Lyon, "Only a Players Strike Is Likely to Stop the Sixers," *Philadelphia Inquirer*, February 19, 1983.

70. Dan Hafner, "76ers Ease toward Record, 133–101," *Los Angeles Times*, February 24, 1983.

71. "Philadelphia 76ers Owner Harold Katz May Be Having a . . ." *United Press International*, February 19, 1983; George Shirk, "Katz Might Consider Getting out of the NBA if Players Go on Strike," *Philadelphia Inquirer*, February 19, 1983.

72. "Philadelphia 76ers Owner."

73. "Philadelphia 76ers Owner."

74. Phil Jasner, "Would NBA Be a Fool to Strike Now?" *Philadelphia Daily News*, February 19, 1983.

75. "Philadelphia 76ers Owner."

76. Bill Livingston, "Richardson: NBA Strike Would Draw Fans' Wrath," *Philadelphia Inquirer*, February 28, 1983.

77. Livingston, "Richardson: NBA Strike."

78. George Shirk, "Katz, Players Air Their Opinions on Dispute but Don't Change Them," *Philadelphia Inquirer*, March 10, 1983.

79. Phil Jasner, "NBA Talks Strike," *Philadelphia Daily News*, February 16, 1983.

80. Shaughnessy, "NBA Management Takes the Offensive."

81. C. L. Smith Muñiz, "NBA Says Union Reneged," *Hartford Courant*, February 18, 1983.

82. Shaughnessy, "NBA Hoping Restraints."

83. O'Brien, telex, February 8, 1983, LOB.

84. "NBA Is Studying a Reduction in Clubs," *New York Times*, March 1, 1983.

85. Dan Shaughnessy, "Money Can't Ease Kupchak's Pain," *Boston Globe*, February 24, 1983.

86. Phil Jasner, "Doc's a Sight for Sore Eyes," *Philadelphia Daily News*, February 28, 1983.

87. Burk, *Marvin Miller*, 221.

88. "Exit Miller, Racquet in Hand" *New York Times*, February 12, 1983.

89. "Exit Miller."

90. "Exit Miller."

13. War

1. "NBA Blames Fleisher for Strike Possibility," *Atlanta Constitution*, February 18, 1983.

2. Larry O'Brien, conference call outline, February 25, 1983, LOB.

3. Dan Shaughnessy, "NBA Management Takes the Offensive" *Boston Globe*, February 17, 1983.

4. David DuPree, "Fleisher Ridicules NBA Ceiling," *Washington Post*, February 22, 1983.

5. Dan Shaughnessy, "Players Mean It—Fleisher," *Boston Globe*, March 13, 1983.

6. Phil Jasner, "Start of Salary Plan Key to Talks," *Philadelphia Daily News*, February 17, 1983.

7. "General Counsel for the NBA Player Association," *United Press International*, February 21, 1983.

8. Randy Harvey, "The Disagreement in the NBA: Owners Want to Limit Their Payrolls to $1,600,000," *Los Angeles Times*, February 22, 1983.

9. Mike Carey, "Bird Could Escape Salary Sap," *Boston Herald* March 9, 1983.

10. Harvey, "Disagreement in the NBA."

11. DuPree, "Fleisher Ridicules."

12. Sam Goldaper, "NBA and Players Schedule New Talks," *New York Times*, February 25, 1983.

13. Memo from NBA negotiating team, February 23, 1983, LOB.

14. Memo from NBA negotiating team.

15. Memo from NBA negotiating team.

16. Goldaper, "NBA and Players"; Memo from NBA negotiating team.

17. Goldaper, "NBA and Players."

18. Phil Jasner, "NBA Owners Voice Striking Words," *Philadelphia Daily News*, March 7, 1983.

19. Memo from NBA negotiating team.

20. C. L. Smith Muñiz, "Strike Threat Is Far from Frivolous," *Hartford Courant*, February 20, 1983.

21. Larry O'Brien, telex to NBA general managers and public relations directors, February 18, 1983, LOB.

22. Jasner, "NBA Owners Voice."

23. Carey, "Bird Could Escape."

24. Goldaper, "NBA and Players."

25. Sam Goldaper, "NBA Is Studying a Reduction in Clubs," *New York Times*, March 1, 1983.

26. "San Diego Safe from NBA Cuts," *Los Angeles Times*, March 1, 1983.

27. Goldaper, "NBA and Players."

28. Goldaper, "NBA Is Studying."

29. Goldaper, "NBA Is Studying."

30. Art Rosenbaum, "No Winners in NBA Players Strike," *San Francisco Chronicle*, March 11, 1983.

31. Dan Shaughnessy, "Money Can't Ease Kupchak's Pain," *Boston Globe*, February 24, 1983.

32. Gary Bettman, negotiations memo, March 2, 1983, LOB.

33. Text of memo from Larry Fleisher to all NBA players, March 3, 1983, LOB.

34. Notes of conference call, February 25, 1983, LOB.

35. Gary Bettman, negotiations memo, March 2, 1983, LOB.

36. Bettman, negotiations memo.

37. Bettman, negotiations memo.

38. Bettman, negotiations memo.

39. Bettman, negotiations memo.

40. David DuPree, "NBA Negotiations Last for 24 Fruitless Minutes," *Washington Post*, March 2 1983.

41. Sam Goldaper, "Brief NBA Labor Talks Held," *New York Times*, March 2, 1983.

42. Dan Shaughnessy, "Players Mean It."

43. David Dupree, "NBA: Strike Would Cancel Free Agency," *Washington Post*, March 6,1983.

44. O'Brien, memo to the Board of Governors, March 1, 1983, LOB.

45. Goldaper, "Brief NBA Labor."

46. "Fleisher: Pay Doesn't Hurt NBA," *Atlanta Journal Constitution*, March 3, 1983.

47. Larry Fleisher, memo to players, March 3, 1983, LOB.

48. Dupree, "NBA Negotiations Last."

49. Goldaper, "Brief NBA Labor."

50. Larry Fleisher, letter to Larry O'Brien, March 3, 1983, LOB.

51. Larry O'Brien, letter, March 4, 1983, LOB.

52. Bill Livingston, "Richardson NBA Strike Would Draw Fans' Wrath," *Philadelphia Inquirer*, February 28, 1983.

53. Shaughnessy, "Players Mean It."

54. Ira Berkow, "Sports of the Times: The NBA Money Game," *New York Times*, March 4, 1983.

55. Jasner, "NBA Owners Voice."

56. Jasner, "NBA Owners Voice."

57. Dupree, "NBA Strike Would."

58. Memo from Scotty Stirling, March 4, 1983, LOB.

59. Jim Hutton, "Spurs Win, Warned about Strike Costs," *San Antonio Express*, March 2, 1983.

60. Steve Weston, "Colangelo Stresses 'Good Faith' in Talks," *Phoenix Gazette*, March 1, 1983.

61. George Shirk, "Katz, Players Air Their Opinions on Dispute but Don't Change Them," *Philadelphia Inquirer*, March 10, 1983.

62. Shirk, "Katz, Players."

63. Jim Hutton, "Strike Would Cost Spurs $2 Million, Drossos Warns," *San Antonio Express-News*, March 1, 1983.

64. Larry Fleisher, letter to Angelo Drossos, March 3, 1983, LOB.

65. Jerry Briggs, "Drossos Threatens Spurs," *San Antonio Light*, March 6, 1983.

66. "NBA Commissioner Larry O'Brien Said Thursday the League . . . ," *United Press International*, March 2, 1983.

67. Briggs, "Drossos Threatens Spurs."

68. Hutton, "Spurs Win, Warned."

69. Fleisher, letter to Drossos.

70. Briggs, "Drossos Threatens Spurs."

71. Board of Governors notes, March 11, 1983, LOB.

72. Thiel, Art, "Sonics Cruise, but More Sam Threats," *Seattle Post-Intelligencer*, March 6, 1983.

73. Thiel, "Sonics Cruise."

74. DuPree, "NBA: Strike Would."

75. Larry Fleisher, memo to general managers, March 4, 1983, LOB.

76. Larry Fleisher, memo to players, March 3, 1983, LOB.

77. Fleisher, memo to players.

78. Fleisher, memo to players.

79. Fleisher, memo to players.

14. Unbounded Pessimism and Cautious Optimism

1. Ron Thomas, "NBA Union and Owners Meet Today," *USA Today*, March 8, 1983.

2. "NBA Talks Last Five Hours," *Washington Post*, March 9, 1983.

3. Gary Bettman, memo, March 12, 1983.

4. Bettman, memo.

5. Bettman, memo.

6. Bettman, memo.

7. Bettman, memo.

8. "NBA Talks Last Five Hours," *Washington Post*, March 9, 1983.

9. "In Sharp Contrast."

10. "NBA Talks Last Five Hours."

11. "In Sharp Contrast."

12. Board of Governors minutes, March 11, 1983, LOB.

13. Board of Governors minutes.

14. "Scouting; Idea Rejected," *New York Times*, March 15, 1983.

15. Board of Governors minutes.

16. Undated Larry O'Brien memo, LOB.

17. "NBA, Players Meet; Talks Continue Today," *Washington Post*, March 22, 1983.

18. Will McDonough, "NBA Ship of Fools Near Rocks," *Boston Globe*, March 17, 1983.

19. Dan Shaughnessy, "Celtics Notebook: No Luck without Bird in Hand," *Boston Globe*, March 12, 1983.

20. Shaughnessy, Dan, "Players Mean It—Fleisher," *Boston Globe*, March 13, 1983.

21. Shaughnessy, "Players Mean It."

22. "Gross basketball income attributable to playoffs and regular season after April 1," memo in Larry O'Brien's notes, LOB.

23. John Powers, "New Deal, Old Dealer: Larry Fleisher, the Players' Point Guard, Runs the Break," *Boston Globe*, March 29, 1983.

24. Powers, "New Deal, Old Dealer."

25. "Stepien Cites Toronto in NBA Cavalier Move," *Globe and Mail*, March 14, 1983.

26. "NBA Talks Last More Than 4 Hours," *New York Times*, March 17, 1983.

27. Points to be made by the NBA: bargaining session, March 16, 1983, LOB.

28. Points to be made by the NBA.

29. David DuPree, "Fleisher: Positive Signs at the Talks," *Washington Post*, March 24, 1983.

30. DuPree, "Fleisher: Positive Signs."

31. "Fleisher Says NBA Reneged On Point," *Baltimore Sun*, March 26, 1983.

32. "NBA Talks Last More Than 4 Hours."

33. "Milwaukee Bucks Center Showed Up in Time," *United Press International*, March 17, 1983.

34. "NBA Talks Last More Than 4 Hours."

35. "Parties Mum after NBA Talks," *Hartford Courant*, March 23, 1983.

36. "Talks Planned Today," *Washington Post*, March 21, 1983.

37. Memo to Larry O'Brien regarding media, March 28, 1983, LOB.

38. DuPree, "NBA's Free Agency, Lone Strike Issue," *Washington Post*, March 27, 1983.

39. DuPree, "NBA's Free Agency."

40. "Union Alters Stance," *New York Times*, March 26, 1983.

41. "Players May Agree to Caps if Payroll Minimum Included," *Globe and Mail*, March 26, 1983.

42. David DuPree, "NBA; Players Meet; Talks Continue Today," *Washington Post*, March 22, 1983.

43. Ira Berkow, "Scouting: N.B.A. Money," *New York Times*, March 24, 1983.

44. McDonough, "NBA Ship of Fools."

45. Randy Harvey, "Drossos Isn't Spurring a Settlement," *Los Angeles Times*, March 29, 1983.

46. Harvey, "Drossos Isn't."

47. Interview with Jim Quinn.

48. Muñiz, "Painting a Picture."

49. "NBA Talks Stall as Strike 'Talk' Rumbles On," *Hartford Courant*, March 25, 1983.

50. Harvey, "Drossos Isn't."

51. David Dupree, "Fleisher: NBA Players Likely to Go on Strike," *Washington Post*, March 25, 1983.

52. "Fleisher Says NBA Reneged on Point," *Baltimore Sun*, March 26, 1983.

53. "NBA Talks Stall as Strike 'Talk' Rumbles On," *Hartford Courant*, March 25, 1983.

54. Phil Jasner, "Fleisher's Daring Move Led to NBA Settlement," *Miami Herald*, April 2, 1983.

55. Interview with Jim Quinn.

56. C. L Smith Muñiz, "Painting a Picture of Doom," *Hartford Courant*, March 28, 1983.

57. Dupree, "Fleisher: NBA Players."

58. "NBA Talks Back to Square 1," *Associated Press*, March 25, 1983.

59. Muñiz, "Painting a Picture."

60. "Fleisher Says NBA."

61. "NBA Talks Break Off," *New York Times*, March 25, 1983.

62. "Talks Aimed at Averting a Scheduled Saturday Night Walkout," *United Press International*, March 28, 1983.

63. Muñiz, "Painting a Picture."

64. "NBA Talks Stall."

65. "NBA Talks Stall."

66. Dupree, "NBA's Free Agency."

67. Dan Shaughnessy, "NBA Strike Saturday? It Ain't Necessarily So," *Boston Globe*, March 28, 1983.

68. David DuPree, "NBA Talks Scheduled to Continue," *Washington Post*, March 29, 1983.

69. DuPree, "NBA Talks Scheduled."

70. Muñiz, "Painting a Picture."

71. Dupree, "NBA Talks Scheduled."

72. Fred Mitchell, "Players Talk Tough on Possible Strike," *Chicago Tribune*, March 20, 1983.

73. "Talks Aimed at Averting."

74. DuPree, "NBA Talks Scheduled."

75. Randy Harvey, "Rockets Make It Easy for the Lakers," *Los Angeles Times*, March 28, 1983.

76. Powers, "New Deal, Old Dealer."

77. "Larry Fleisher Says It's Very Simply," *United Press International*, March 29, 1983.

78. "NBA Talks Called Hopeful," *New York Times*, March 30, 1983.

79. Sam Goldaper, "Progress Reported by NBA in Talks," *New York Times*, March 31, 1983.

80. Harvey, "Rockets Make It."

81. "NBA Talks Called."

82. Goldaper, "Progress Reported."

83. Mike Carey, "Here's the Deal," *Boston Herald*, March 30, 1983.

84. Goldaper, "Progress Reported."

85. *Associated Press*, March 30, 1983, LOB.

15. Peace

1. Larry O'Brien statement, LOB.; Dan Shaughnessy, "NBA Agreement Leaves Questions," *Boston Globe*, April 1, 1983.

2. O'Brien statement.

3. DuPree, "Strike Is Averted as NBA, Players Agree in Principle," *Washington Post*, April 1, 1983.

4. Larry Fleisher, statement, LOB.

5. *Associated Press*, March 31, 1983, LOB.

6. Dupree, "Strike Is Averted."

7. Phil Jasner, "Fleisher's Daring Move Led to NBA Settlement," *Miami Herald*, April 2, 1983.

8. Jasner, "Fleisher's Daring Move."

9. *Associated Press*, March 31, 1983, LOB.

10. Jasner, "Fleisher's Daring Move."

11. "Equality Goal in New NBA Pact," *Sporting News*, April 11, 1983.

12. DuPree, "Strike Is Averted."

13. *Associated Press*, April 4, 1983, LOB.

14. "NBA Talks Called."

15. *Associated Press*, April 4, 1983, LOB.

16. Board of Governors minutes, March 31, 1983, LOB.

17. Dupree, "Strike Is Averted"; Randy Harvey, "One Man, One Vote, One Strange Point of View," *Los Angeles Times*, April 5, 1983.

18. *Associated Press*, April 1, 1983, LOB.

19. Dupree, "Strike Is Averted."

20. Jasner, "Fleisher's Daring Move."

21. Jasner, "Fleisher's Daring Move."

22. "Equality Goal in New NBA Pact" *Sporting News*, April 11, 1983.

23. Jasner, "Fleisher's Daring Move."

24. Harvey, "One Man."

25. Letter to David Stern and Larry O'Brien, April 11, 1983, LOB.

26. Jasner, "Fleisher's Daring Move."

27. NBA/NBPA memorandum of agreement, LOB, 7.

28. NBA/NBPA memorandum of agreement, LOB, 2–3.

29. DuPree, "Strike Is Averted"; Goldaper, "NBA Strike Averted."

30. NBA/NBPA memorandum of agreement, LOB, 4.

31. NBA/NBPA memorandum of agreement, 8, LOB.

32. NBA/NBPA memorandum of agreement, 10.

33. NBA/NBPA memorandum of agreement, 25.

34. NBA/NBPA memorandum of agreement, 4.

35. DuPree, "Strike Is Averted."

36. NBA/NBPA memorandum of agreement, 14.

37. *Associated Press*, March 31, 1983, LOB.

38. NBA/NBPA memorandum of agreement, 29.

39. NBA/NBPA memorandum of agreement, 16.

40. NBA/NBPA memorandum of agreement, 18.

41. NBA/NBPA memorandum of agreement, 30.

42. Shaughnessy, "NBA Agreement."

43. Goldaper, "NBA Strike Averted."

44. Shaughnessy, "NBA Agreement."

45. Shaughnessy, "NBA Agreement."

46. Shaughnessy, "NBA Agreement."

47. Bob Logan, "NBA Owners Get 253 New Partners," *Chicago Tribune*, April 1, 1983.

48. Dupree, "Strike Is Averted."

49. *Associated Press*, March 31, 1983, LOB.

50. Goldaper, "NBA Strikes Averted."

51. Goldaper, "NBA Strikes Averted."

Epilogue

1. Bob Sudyk, "Fame's Costly Flame," *Hartford Courant*, May 13, 1983.

2. Larry O'Brien, telex, April 29, 1983, LOB.

3. Larry O'Brien, opening remarks, NBA owners meeting, June, 1983, LOB.

4. Sudyk, "Fame's Costly Flame."

5. Sudyk, "Fame's Costly Flame."

6. Williams and Jones, *Tales*, 116.

7. DuPree, "Katz: Money's Nice, Malone's Better," *Washington Post*, May 25, 1983.

8. Dan Shaughnessy, "It's Been Wholly Moses," *Boston Globe*, May 31, 1983.

9. DuPree, "Katz: Money's Nice."

10. Larry O'Brien, commissioner's newsletter, April 21, 1983, LOB.

11. O'Brien, commissioner's newsletter.

12. Sam Goldaper, "Malone-Lanier Is Key Matchup in Series," *New York Times*, May 8, 1983.

13. Larry Whiteside, "Bucks Well Tutored to Meet Challenge on Boards," *Boston Globe*, May 3, 1983.

14. Goldaper, "Malone-Lanier."

15. George Shirk, "Bucks' Hopes Ride on Lanier's Knees," *Philadelphia Inquirer*, May 14, 1983.

16. Roy S. Johnson, "Bucks Top 76ers, Trail Series 3–1," *New York Times*, May 6, 1983.

17. Mark Whicker, "Criss, Lanier, Give Bucks Reason to Smile," *Philadelphia Daily News*, May 16, 1983.

18. Williams and Jones, *Tales*, 123.

19. Williams and Jones, *Tales*, 129.

20. Shaughnessy, "It's Been Wholly."

21. Williams and Jones, *Tales*, 129.

22. Bob Ryan, "They're Delightful," *Boston Globe*, May 31, 1983.

23. George Shirk, "76ers Are Kings of the NBA at Last; Lakers Fall in Game 4 Sweep," *Philadelphia Inquirer*, June 1, 1983.

24. Bill Livingston, "Happy Feet—Dr. J Kicks Up His Heels," *Philadelphia Inquirer*, June 1, 1983.

25. Williams and Jones, *Tales*, 134.

26. Shirk, "76ers Are Kings."

27. Livingston, "Happy Feet."

28. Shirk, "76ers Are Kings."

29. Williams and Jones, *Tales*, 134.

30. Sam Goldaper, "Malone's Season Worth $2.96m," *New York Times*, June 8, 1983.

31. Goldaper, "Malone's Season."

32. Dupree, "Katz: Money's Nice."

33. Shaughnessy, "It's Been Wholly."

34. Ryan, "They're Delightful."

35. Dupree, "Katz: Money's Nice."

36. "Reagan Salutes Sixers," *United Press International*, June 8, 1983.

37. Vito Stellino, "Ed Garvey Resigns as Union Head," *Baltimore Sun*, June 11, 1983.

38. A. H. Raskin, "NBA's New Contract: A Statesmanlike Settlement," *New York Times*, April 3, 1983.

39. Raskin, "NBA's New Contract."

40. "Equality Goal."

41. "Equality Goal."

42. Raskin, "NBA's New Contract."

43. Stellino, "Ed Garvey."

44. Harris, *The League*, 551.

45. Larry O'Brien, opening remarks, NBA owners meeting, June 1983, LOB.

46. O'Brien, opening remarks.

47. O'Brien, opening remarks.

48. O'Brien, opening remarks.

49. Roy S. Johnson, "Moves Looming in NBA," *New York Times*, June 16 ,1983.

50. "NBA Votes."

51. Larry O'Brien, notes, September 28, 1983, LOB.

52. O'Brien, notes.

53. "Milwaukee Bucks Center Bob Lanier Saying He Is Not a . . . ,'" *United Press International*, August 2, 1982.

54. "NBA Will Urge Drug Tests," *Washington Post*, July 2, 1982.

55. Sam Goldaper, "NBA Adds Counseling Service," *New York Times*, March 17, 1981.

56. David Stern, Seton Hall interview.

57. Larry O'Brien, memo to owners, October 12, 1983.

58. O'Brien, memo to owners.

59. Larry O'Brien, memo, exhibit 3, LOB.

60. Bob Lanier, "Sports of the Times: Facing the Drug Problem," *New York Times*, October 26, 1983.

61. Lanier, "Sports of the Times."

62. Larry Whiteside, "NBA, Players ASSN Unite to Drive Out Drug Abusers," *Boston Globe*, September 29, 1983.

63. "NBA Announces Crackdown on Illegal Drug Use," *Los Angeles Times*, September 29, 1983.

64. Lanier, "Sports of the Times."

65. Sam Goldaper, "O'Brien Steps Down as Commissioner of NBA," *New York Times*, November 10, 1983.

66. David DuPree, "O'Brien Resigns NBA Post," *Washington Post*, November 10, 1983.

67. Bob Logan, "O'Brien Rejects NBA Offer to Stay," *Chicago Tribune*, November 10, 1983.

68. "Scorecard," *Sports Illustrated*, November 21, 1983.

69. Goldaper, "O'Brien Steps Down."

70. Board of Governors minutes, November 15, 1983, LOB.

71. David DuPree, "Stern Gets Top NBA Job," *Washington Post*, November 16, 1983.

72. Bill Livingston, "Court King—in Naming Stern, NBA Has Smooth Succession in Top Job," *Philadelphia Inquirer*, January 29, 1984.

73. Dupree, "Stern Gets."

74. Livingston, "Court King."

75. Dupree, "Stern Gets."

76. Larry Whiteside, "Stern to Succeed O'Brien as NBA Commissioner," *Boston Globe*, November 16, 1983.

77. Larry Whiteside, "Inside Choice: Stern Takes over NBA Center Stage," *Boston Globe*, November 17, 1983.

78. Dan Shaughnessy, "A Stern Choice for Commissioner," *Boston Globe*, November 13, 1983.

79. Steve Parks, "David Stern Named NBA Chief," *Baltimore Sun*, November 16, 1983.

80. Whiteside, "Inside Choice."

81. Livingston, "Court King."

82. Peter May, "Stern Is behind the Metamorphosis" *Hartford Courant*, February 12, 1989.

83. David DuPree and David Remnick, "NBA Commissioner to Be Stern," *Washington Post*, December 22, 1983.

84. Dan Shaughnessy, "Lanier Hinting at Retirement," *Boston Globe*, May 24, 1984.

85. "Tearfully, Lanier Ends Title Quest," *United Press International*, September 25, 1984.

86. Larry Fleisher, induction into Hall of Fame, https://www.youtube.com/watch?v=InVXTH-_42U&t=162s.

Bibliography

Archives/Manuscript Materials

LOB. Lawrence F. O'Brien National Basketball Association Papers. Springfield College, Springfield MA.

Marvin and Theresa Miller Papers. Tamiment Library/Robert F. Wagner Labor Archives. New York University Library, New York NY.

ROB. *Robertson v. National Basketball Association.* Accession number 21-83-0037, boxes 3–20, New York NY.

Published Works

Arledge, Roone. *A Memoir.* New York: HarperCollins, 2004.

Araton, Harvey, and Filip Bondy. *The Selling of the Green: The Financial Rise and Moral Decline of the Boston Celtics.* New York: HarperCollins, 1992.

Bradley, Bill. *Life on the Run.* Large print edition. New York: Times Books, 1976.

Burk, Robert F. *Marvin Miller: Baseball Revolutionary.* Champaign: University of Illinois Press, 2015.

Cosell, Howard. *What's Wrong with Sports: America's Most Uninhibited Sports Critic Takes Aim at the Scandalous State of Sports Today.* New York: Simon & Schuster, 1991.

Dawkins, Daryl, and Charley Rosen. *Chocolate Thunder.* Toronto: Sport Media Publishing, 2003.

Embry, Wayne, and Mary Schmitt Boyer. *The Inside Game: Race, Power, and Politics in the NBA.* Akron OH: University of Akron Press, 2004.

Halberstam, David. *The Breaks of the Game.* New York: Hyperion, 1981.

———. *Playing for Keeps: Michael Jordan and the World He Made.* New York: Random House, 1999.

Harris, David. *The League: The Rise and Decline of the NFL.* New York: Bantam Books, 1986.

Heinsohn, Tommy, and Leonard Lewin. *Heinsohn, Don't You Ever Smile? The Life and Times of Tommy Heinsohn and the Boston Celtics.* New York: Doubleday, 1976.

Helyar, John. *Lords of the Realm: The Real History of Baseball.* New York: Ballantine Books, 1994.

Johnson, Earvin "Magic," and William Novak. *My Life*. New York: Fawcett Books, 1992.

Katz, Jeff. *Split Season: 1981*. New York: Thomas Dunne Books, 2015.

Keteyian, Armen, Harvey Araton, and Martin F. Dardis. *Money Players: Days and Nights inside the New NBA*. New York: Pocket Books, 1997.

Kuhn, Bowie. *Hardball: The Education of a Baseball Commissioner*. New York: Times Books, 1987.

O'Brien, Lawrence F. *No Final Victories*. Garden City NY: Doubleday, 1974.

Pluto, Terry. *Loose Balls: The Short, Wild Life of the American Basketball Association*. New York: Simon & Schuster, 1990.

Quinn, James W. *Don't Be Afraid to Win*. New York: Radius Book Group, 2019.

Reynolds, Bill. *Cousy: His Life, Career, and the Birth of Big-Time Basketball*. New York: Pocket Star Books, 2005.

Robertson, Oscar. *The Big O: My Life, My Times, My Game*. Lincoln: University of Nebraska Press, 2003.

Shoals, Bethlehem, and Jacob Weinstein. *Freedarko Presents: The Undisputed Guide to Pro Basketball History*. New York: Bloomsbury, 2010.

Smith, Samuel. *Hard Labor: The Battle That Birthed the Billion-Dollar NBA*. Chicago: Triumph Books, 2017.

Van Hasselt, Caroline. *High Wire Act: Ted Rogers and the Empire that Debt Built*, John Wiley & Sons, 2008.

Wilkens, Lenny, and Terry Pluto. *Unguarded: My Forty Years Surviving in the NBA*. New York: Simon & Schuster, 2001.

Williams, Pat, and Gordon Jones. *Tales from the Philadelphia 76ers Locker Room*. New York: Sports Publishing Books, 2013.

Index

ABC (American Broadcasting Company), 54, 69, 93–97, 98, 99, 100, 103

Abdul-Jabbar, Kareem (Lew Alcindor), 38, 233–34; Chicago Bulls and, 294–95; contract of, 141, 148, 153, 243–44; dissatisfaction of, 153; Jerry Buss and, 141, 144, 153; Los Angeles Lakers and, 18. *See also* "Kareem Abdul-Jabbar problem"

Adkins, M. Douglas, xiii, 170

African Americans in the NBA, 23–24, 58–59, 83–84, 87, 99, 124, 163

Ainge, Danny, 234

Albeck, Stan, 144–45

Alcindor, Lew. *See* Abdul-Jabbar, Kareem

All-Star Game, NBA: 1957, 56; 1964, 53–55, 58, 59–66, 69; 1967, 3–4; 1976, 11, 90–91; 1980, 122; 1983, 231; 1988, 72–73

American Basketball Association (ABA): NBA merger with, 11, 27, 83, 85–89, 116–18; NBA teams from, 117; origin of, 9–10; player recruitment tactics of, 11, 38–39, 41. *See also specific teams*

American Broadcasting Company (ABC), 54, 69, 93–97, 98, 99, 100, 103

antitrust lawsuit, 11–13, 31, 71–72, 83–86. See also *Robertson* case

Arledge, Roone, 93–100

Asik, Omer, ix

Auerbach, Red, 11, 67, 99, 106, 216; Don Chaney and, 81–82; ejection of, 3–4, 9; Larry Fleisher and, 11, 75, 81–82; roster viewpoint of, 200; on Walter Brown, 59

Axelson, Joe, xiii, 26, 145–46, 295

Ballard, Greg, 233, 269–70, 272

Banks, Gene, 254

Barbash, Joseph, xiii, 30, 33–34

Barry, Rick, 4, 38, 101

Batterman, Bob, xiii, 198, 204–5, 217, 257

Baylor, Elgin, 53, 60, 64, 101

Bellamy, Walt, 60

Berkow, Ira, 251

Bettman, Gary, 298; collective bargaining work, 71, 167, 168, 169–70, 202, 204–5, 217, 223, 230, 257, 271; hired by NHL, 49

Bird, Larry, 35, 221, 234, 244, 251, 265, 279, 282, 293. *See also* "Larry Bird problem"

Birdsong, Otis, 144, 148–49

Blass, Norman, 40, 41

Bloch, Richard, 298, 299

Board of Governors: approval of 1982 collective bargaining proposals, 50, 170, 171, 173, 178–79; cap proposal to, 230, 249; cost reduction proposals to, 170, 178; deadline of, 218; Donald Sterling and, 174, 177; election of David Stern as Commissioner, 298–99; fines from, 294; March 1983 meetings of, 260–61, 272, 275–76; merger meetings by, 116–17; NBA Properties decision by, 107; 1979–80 negotiations and, 118, 120, 121–22; October 1982 meeting of, 203–4, 206, 208–9; pension plan approval by, 7, 54, 57, 60, 62–67, 69; player attendance with, 56, 61; resolutions of, 209, 260–61; revenue sharing negotiations of,

Board of Governors (*cont.*)
121–22, 205, 208–9; strike discussion by,
120–21, 259–61; Ted Stepien and, 123–26,
150, 285; television rights and, 95–96
Bonnies, St. Bonaventure, 37–38, 287
Boston Celtics, 5, 25, 76, 81–82, 87, 185, 301;
union and, 84; Walter Brown and, 59
Bradley, Bill, 55, 75, 79, 83, 86, 87, 88, 302
Brewster, Kingman, 190–91
Bridgeman, Junior, xiv, 79, 197, 206, 222,
269, 271, 274, 275, 288
Brody, Martin, 76
Brown, Fred, xiv, 254, 257, 259, 275
Brown, Hubie, 18
Brown, Larry, 115
Brown, Walter, 53–54, 58–59, 67–68, 197
Buckner, Quinn, 42, 232, 261
Bucks, Milwaukee, 38, 42–43, 213, 275, 287,
288–89, 301
Bulls, Chicago, ix, 5, 149, 179, 234, 277, 294–95
Bunning, Jim, 127
Buss, Jerry, 18–19, 26, 183, 223, 277, 281;
deferred compensation and, 266; Ka-
reem Abdul-Jabbar and, 141, 152–53, 295;
Magic Johnson and, 143–44, 151–52; re-
placement players proposal by, 260; rev-
enue sharing and, 277, 281; right of first
refusal and, 140–44, 150; spending and,
19, 26, 141–42, 150, 151–53, 171, 188; tampering by, 180–81

cable. *See* television
Cardozo, Michael, 178
Carter, Donald, 27
Carter, Robert (Judge), 45, 46, 89–90, 229, 281
Cavaliers. *See* Cleveland Cavaliers
CBA (collective bargaining agreement): announcement of 1983 agreement, 273–74;
conditions of, 2, 3, 111, 250, 278–81; David
Stern and, 22–23, 31; expiration of, 17, 108,
172–73, 202; Larry Fleisher and, 32, 72, 80,
215; MLB and, 239; NFL and, 137, 138; proposal for, 46–47, 191
CBS: broadcasters of, 101; college basketball
and, 165; NBA agreement with, 21–22, 49,
93, 97–104, 105–6, 219, 277–78; NBA strike
effects on, 262; negotiations with NBA,

163–66; ratings gain within, 293–94; rat-
ings loss of, 100–101
Celtics. *See* Boston Celtics
Chamberlain, Wilt, 4, 9, 10, 60, 63, 94, 185
Chambers, Tom, 175
Chaney, Don, 11, 81–82
Chaparrals, Dallas, 114, 116
Chappell, Lenny, 60, 63
Cheeks, Maurice, 185, 231
Chicago Bulls, ix, 5, 149, 179, 234, 277,
294–95
Chones, Jim, 141
Clarke, Doug, 147
Cleveland Cavaliers: challenges of, 213;
draft and, 214; financial challenges within,
223, 258; in-game presentation changes
within, 146; Otis Birdsong signing, 148;
salaries of, 171; sale of, 123–26, 223, 239,
262, 285; Timofey Mozgov and, 2; trades
of, 145–46, 238. *See also* Stepien, Ted
Clippers, San Diego, 171, 174–79, 214–15, 258
Coca-Cola, 116
cocaine, 23, 296
Cohen, Alan, 271, 272; as Labor Relations
Committee member, xiii, 170, 206, 217, 263,
264, 269; viewpoint of, 109, 113, 119, 230
Cohen, Jeff, 148
Colangelo, Jerry, 16, 117–18, 150, 152, 187–
88, 252, 268
collective bargaining agreement (CBA): announcement of, 273–74; conditions of, 111,
250, 278–81; David Stern and, 22–23, 31;
expiration of, 17, 108, 172–73, 202; Larry
Fleisher and, 32, 72, 80, 215; MLB and, 239;
NFL and, 137, 138; proposal for, 46–47, 191
college basketball, 22, 165
college football, 96–97, 165
commercial rights, 196
Conley, Mike, 3
Continental Basketball Association, 260–61
contracts, guaranteed, 34, 170, 280
Cooke, Jack Kent, 96–97
Cooper, Charles, 58
Cooper, Michael, 141
Cosell, Howard, 78, 132
Cousy, Bob, 54–55, 56, 57, 63

Index

Cunningham, Billy, 187, 200, 231, 253, 288, 289, 290
Curry, Ayesha, 2
Curry, Bill, 133
Curry, Stephen, 2

Dallas Chaparrals, 114, 116
Dawkins, Daryl, 149, 184–86
deferred compensation, 27, 34, 40, 119, 188, 196, 245, 255, 265–66, 280
Delaney, Don, 145, 147
Denver Nuggets, 117, 149, 252
Desser, Ed, 163
Detroit Pistons, 40, 42, 202
Dischinger, Terry, 60
Divac, Vlade, 75
Dolph, Jack, 39
Donlan, Jack, 194, 292
Donovan, Eddie, 152
Drew, Larry, 270
Drossos, Angelo, 108, 189–90, 214; background of, 114–18; captive audience meetings and, 253–54, 257; 1982 collective bargaining negotiations and, 170, 199, 217–18, 229, 230, 240–41, 245–46, 260, 266–68, 269, 272, 276; 1979 collective bargaining negotiations and, 109, 112–13, 118–21, 122; roster viewpoint of, 199
drugs, 23, 34, 295–97
Dunleavy, Mike, 253

Edwards, James, 149
Embry, Wayne, 24, 60, 63–65
English, Alex, 144, 149
Erving, Julius, 20, 21, 184, 185, 190, 231, 286, 290–91, 293; strike and, 237
ESPN, ix, 2, 22, 24–25, 105, 106–7, 112, 262, 287
exhibition games, 8, 54, 55, 137
expansion teams, 5, 25, 27, 117

Faust, George, 103
Fehr, Don, 75, 130, 239
Fentress, Lee, 181, 182, 183, 187–88
Ferchill, John, 239
Ferguson, Steve, 149
Ferry, Bob, 150, 201–2
Finals, 17–21, 22, 185, 287, 289, 290–91
fines, 54, 169, 209–10, 245, 294

Fitch, Bill, 108, 270
Fitzgerald, James, xiii, 108, 109, 110, 118, 120, 170, 199
Fleisher, Larry: as agent, 16, 74–75, 79–81; background of, 32, 76–77; Congressional testimony of, 86–87, 155–56; criticism of, 5, 6, 110, 235–38, 242, 245, 268, 276, 282; David Stern and, 29, 32, 34, 75, 259, 300; death of, 70, 75; decertification plan of, 72–73; Hall of Fame induction of, 302; influence of, x, 10–11, 32–33, 82; as lawyer, 73–74, 79; leadership of, xiv, 4, 63, 78, 131–33, 255–56, 271–72; negotiating style of, 33, 40, 44–45, 77, 85, 111, 198, 203, 204–6, 217, 225, 227–31, 258–59, 263; ownership viewpoint of, 5, 25, 28, 31–32, 57, 192–93, 242, 245, 247–48, 255; quote of, ix, 17, 34, 122, 241, 267–68, 273–74; revenue analyzation by, 205–12, 215–19; strike role of, 69, 82, 118, 128, 154–55, 169, 176, 192, 221, 232–34, 245, 251–53, 260–62, 269–70, 276–77; victories of, 12–13, 69, 70–71, 90–91, 98–99, 108, 140, 189, 274–75, 278–81; vision of, 15
franchise movements, 176–77
Frank, Barry, 96
Franklin, Pete, 146, 147
free agency: achievement of, 128–29; Ed Garvey's viewpoint of, 134–35; Larry Fleisher's viewpoint of, 87–88, 183–84; Major League Baseball and, 29–30; Moses Malone and, 180–81; National Football League and, 30; right of first refusal, 140–41, 150; salaries and, 15, 222, 227

Gallantz, George, 89–90, 159, 161–62
game times, uniform format of, 209
Ganz, Howard, 109–10, 112, 113, 118, 119–20, 121–22, 160
Garvey, Ed, 30, 127, 154; criticism of, 133, 138; leadership style of, 133–34; NBA adoption of Garvey's "percent of gross" proposal, 127, 167, 292–93; NFLPA finances and, 136–38; 1981 "percent of gross" proposal of, 128, 129, 134, 138–39, 155, 193–94, 219–20; 1982 NFL strike and, 193–94, 219–20; 1974 NFL strike and, 134–36, 193; resignation of, 292–93; Roger Staubach and, 135

Gearon, J. Michael, xiii, 170, 171–72
Gervin, George, 254
Glickman, Harry, xiii, 170, 235–36
Gola, Tom, 60
Goldstein, Alan, 133
Gourdine, Simon, 109, 113, 119–20, 123, 145
Granik, Russ: leadership of, xiii, 30; negotiations role of, 46, 71, 100, 161, 164, 168, 169, 205, 217, 223, 227–28, 257, 271; promotion of, 162; quote of, 1, 101, 132–33, 167, 191, 201, 248–49; television and, 100–101, 105–6, 112, 164–65
Grantham, Charles: background, 81; as committee member, xiv, 30, 197, 205, 206, 222, 257, 264, 269, 271; drug testing viewpoint of, 296–97; quote of, 49, 70, 118, 123, 199, 215, 227, 232, 238, 268
Grebey, Ray, 133, 154, 155
Greenwood, David, 234, 270, 277, 282
Greer, Hal, 60
Griffith, Calvin, 154
gross revenues: conditions of, 243, 279; determination of, 207; projections of, 207; proposal for, 139, 155, 193–94, 225–26, 259, 263, 268; rejection of, 232. See also NBA owners central fund; revenue sharing
Guaranteed Compensation Plan, 210–12, 232
guaranteed contracts, 34, 170, 280
Guerin, Richie, 57
Gund, Gordon, 285

Halas, George, 134
Halberstam, David, x, 10, 50, 96, 159
Havlicek, John, 7
Hawkins, Connie, 160
Hayes, Elvin, 270
Heinsohn, Tommy: criticism of, 67–68; Larry Fleisher and, 76, 81–82, 83–84; NBPA leadership of, 55, 57, 60–66, 69, 76, 79; 1964 All-Star Game and, 54, 58, 59–68; viewpoint of, 6; Walter Brown and, 59, 67–68
Houston Rockets, ix, 25, 142–43, 180–83, 187–89, 244
Howell, Bailey, 60
Hughes, Kim, 145
Hunter, Billy, 158

impasse, 45, 120, 190, 193, 195, 197, 202, 203, 208–9, 247
Indiana Pacers, 117, 179, 265
International Management Group (IMG), 70, 74–75
international players, 74–75
intimidation, 241–42
Irish, Ned, 96, 159

Jankowski, Gene, 102
Johnson, Earvin "Magic": 1981 contract of, 151–52; Los Angeles Lakers and, 21, 141–44; quote of, 18, 19, 20, 142–43, 151, 153, 233
Johnson, Marques, 42, 288
Johnson, Steve, 80
Johnston, Bruce, 131
Jones, Bobby, 185
Jones, Caldwell, 189
Jones, KC, 7
Jones, Sam, 60, 67

Kansas City Kings, 148–49
"Kareem Abdul-Jabbar problem," 211, 243–44, 279
Karl, George, 115
Kasten, Stan, 171–72
Katz, Harold: leadership of, xiii, 185, 252–53; Moses Malone and, 188–89, 291–92; quote of, 21, 180, 187, 190, 199, 245–46, 252, 272, 274, 289; roster viewpoint of, 199; strike effects to, 236–37; trading by, 184–86, 291
Kennedy, J. Walter: criticism of, 97; leadership of, 57–58, 60–67; quote of, 5, 87; television involvement of, 69, 95–96, 97, 98; work of, 49
Kennedy family, 48
Kenyon and Eckhardt, 95
King, Bernard, 190, 215
King, Don, 239, 283
King, Reggie, 300
Kings, Kansas City, 148–49
Knicks, New York, 79, 111, 117, 158, 179, 271, 279, 287, 300
Koppet, Leonard, 53, 66
Kovler, Jonathan, 14, 208
Krumpe, Jack, xiii, 179, 217, 263, 264, 269, 271
Kuhn, Bowie, 49, 130–31, 298
Kupchak, Mitch, 1, 2, 15–16, 144, 150

labor law, violations of, 44–46, 203, 250, 254

Labor Relations Committee (NBA): divergent views within, 118–19; members of, xiii–xiv, 170; negotiations of, 122, 171, 197, 224, 229–30, 247, 266–67; report from, 173

LA Coliseum Commission, 177

Lakers. *See* Los Angeles Lakers

Lambert, Jack, 139

Landis, Kennesaw, 48–49

Lanier, Bob: background of, 35–37, 47; David Stern and, 35; drug testing viewpoint of, 295–97; injuries of, 37–38, 41, 42; Larry Fleisher and, 42; as NBPA president, xiv, 30, 35, 42; negotiation role of, 51–52, 111, 197, 199, 206, 222, 247–50, 263–64, 269, 271; personal struggles of, 43–44; professional career of, 38–44, 287, 288–89; quote of, 35, 36, 215–16, 250, 275, 280, 283, 287–88, 289; retirement of, 301; union involvement of, 41–44

"Larry Bird problem," 211, 212, 243–44, 279

lawsuits, antitrust, 11–13, 31, 71–72, 83–86. See also *Robertson* case

Layden, Frank, 23, 152

Lindhorst, Ambrose, 5

line of credit, 27, 167, 169

"Lords of the Realm," 130

Los Angeles Lakers: championship concerns of, 213; drama within, 142–43, 152–53; Finals and, 17–21, 289–91; Kareem Abdul-Jabbar and, 243–44; Mitch Kupchak and, 15–16; Pat Riley and, 20, 213; Paul Westhead and, 18–20; rebuilding of, 1; salaries within, 140–44, 151; salary cap conditions for, 279; strike vote within, 233, 271; success of, 20; system implementation of, 18–19; television coverage of, 96; Timofey Mozgov's contract with, 1–2. *See also* Buss, Jerry; Johnson, Earvin "Magic"

Los Angeles Sports Arena, 177

Loughery, Kevin, 83

Lucas, Jerry, 60

Lucas, Maurice, xiv, 197

luxury tax, 113

Mack, Tom, 135

MacPhail, Bill, 98

Madison Square Garden (MSG) network, 24, 105, 111

Major League Baseball (MLB): free agency within, 29–30; leadership within, 48, 49; "Lords of the Realm" within, 130; MLBPA agreement with, 155, 239, 277; 1981 strike, 29, 45, 130, 154–55, 260; television deal of, 93, 165; television revenue for, 22

Major League Baseball Players Association (MLBPA), 127, 128–29, 155, 239, 260

Malone, Moses: All-Star Game and, 231; contract of, 148, 188–90, 215; as free agent, ix, 149, 180–83; negotiations for, 181; performance of, 213, 289, 290; personality of, 286; Philadelphia 76ers and, 186–87, 213, 290, 291–92; quote of, 188, 190, 213, 237, 286, 289, 291

Maloof, Gavin, 181–82, 183

Maloof, George, 181

mandatory subjects, negotiating for, 44–45

Mangurian, Harry: as committee member, xiii, 170, 263, 264; deferred compensation and, 266; quote of, 25, 222, 229, 235, 261, 268, 281

marketing, playoffs and, 287

Marks, Sean, xi

Markus, Robert, 136

McCarver, Tim, 129–30

McCloskey, Jack, 184, 187

McCombs, Red, 114

McDonough, Will, 66–67

McHale, Kevin, 229, 265, 282

McIntyre, Brian, 163, 234

McKinney, Jack, 18

merger, NBA/ABA, 11, 27, 83, 85–89, 99, 101, 116–18

Mikan, George, 9–10, 63

Miller, Marvin: decertification viewpoint, 72–73; Fleisher and, ix–x, 72–73, 80, 127, 128, 129, 133, 136, 222; "Lords of the Realm" and, 130; MLBPA and, x, 127, 128–33, 136, 154–55; 1981 strike and, 29, 45, 130, 154–55, 260; Ray Grebey and, 154–55; resignation of, 239–40; work of, 80

Miller Highlife, 294

Millstein, Ira, 226–27, 229

Milwaukee Bucks, 38, 42–43, 213, 275, 287, 288–89, 301

Mishkin, Jeff, xiii, 30, 168

Mix, Steve, xiv, 14, 30, 197, 206, 222, 274–75, 277, 290

MLB (Major League Baseball): free agency within, 29–30; leadership within, 48, 49; "Lords of the Realm" within, 130; MLBPA agreement with, 155, 239, 277; strike within, 29, 45, 130, 154–55, 260; television deal of, 93, 165; television revenue for, 22

MLBPA (Major League Baseball Players Association), 127, 128–29, 155, 239, 260

Modell, Art, 220

Moe, Doug, 18

Moffett, Ken, 239–40

Mogavero, Nick, 36–37

Molinas, Jack, 159

Morey, Daryl, ix

Moss, Dick, 130, 131

Mozgov, Timofey, 1–2, 3

MSG (Madison Square Garden) network, 24, 105, 111

Murphy, Dennis, 10

Musselman, Bill, 144, 145, 147

National Basketball Players Association (NBPA): All-Star Game and, 4, 54; Bargaining Committee of, xiv; Bob Lanier and, xiv, 30, 35, 42, 215–16; decertification of, 72–74; founding of, 54–55; lawsuits of, 78–79, 83, 111–12; leadership of, 5, 30, 55, 127, 269, 275; Oscar Robertson and, 4–5, 6–9, 10–13, 84–86; Outside Counsel of, xiv; plan presented by, 4–5, 6–9; presidents of, 78–79; review of NBA financials by, 215–19, 221–24; salary cap proposal and, 113, 186, 190–91, 232, 265–66, 268; television research of, 223; threats of, 128. See also Robertson case

National Broadcasting Corporation (NBC), 56, 97, 100, 164, 165

National Football League (NFL): free agency and, 30; gross revenue proposal for, 139; merger within, 39; negotiations within, 168; race within, 163; racism within, 137–38; salaries within, 134;

strike within, 30, 135–36, 137, 193–94, 219–20, 260; television deal of, 93, 137, 138, 165; television revenue for, 22. *See also* National Football League Players Association (NFLPA)

National Football League Players Association (NFLPA), 30, 127, 128, 136–37, 193–94

National Labor Relations Board, 44–46, 52, 72, 195, 202, 203, 250, 254

Nationwide Advertising Agency, 123–24, 150

NBA/ABA merger, 11, 27, 83, 85–89, 99, 101, 116–18

NBA owners central fund, 171–72, 179, 205–12

NBC (National Broadcasting Corporation), 56, 97, 100, 164, 165

Nelson, Don, 43, 187, 264, 289

New Jersey Nets, 252, 279

New York Knicks, 79, 111, 117, 158, 179, 271, 279, 287, 300

New York Nets, 39, 40, 117, 185

Nixon, Norm, 141, 142–43, 151

Noah, Joakim, 3

Non-Statutory Labor Exemption, 70–71

Nuggets, Denver, 117, 149, 252

O'Brien, Larry: agreement message by, 273–74; Angelo Drossos and, 116–17; background of, 47–48; David Stern and, 161–62, 164; as deal maker, 49–52; installment of, 90–91; Larry Fleisher and, 235, 238, 241–42, 247–48, 263; letter from, 47, 50–51, 52, 166, 181, 219, 238, 245; negotiation role of, 167, 169–70, 173–74, 178–79, 197–200, 203–9, 224–32, 248–49, 257–60, 275–76; playoff efforts of, 287; quote of, 12, 13, 91, 177–78, 184, 191, 213, 234, 247, 277, 285, 287; resignation of, 297–98; revenue sharing negotiations of, 205–12; roster viewpoint of, 184, 200; salary moderation plan and, 195–96; television agreement and, 100, 102–3, 106, 111, 164–66

Ohl, Don, 60

Outside Counsel (NBA), xiii

Outside Counsel (NBPA), xiv

ownership: agreement vote by, 184, 276; allocations for, 280; baseball and, 132, 154; challenges of, 25–26, 128, 260; complexities of,

31–32, 223; criticism of, 4–5, 6, 131, 192–93, 215–16, 270; economic troubles and, 23, 26–28, 137, 222; free agency and, 149–50; Larry Fleisher's viewpoint of, 5, 25, 28, 31–32, 57, 192–93, 242, 245, 247–48, 255; "Lords of the Realm," 130; meeting of, 56–57, 174, 176, 178, 260, 263–64, 272; negotiation role of, 167, 197–98; pension plan and, 61–66; player relationship and, 8, 12, 29, 42, 49, 55, 58, 66–67, 78, 253; resentment of, 108; revenue sharing and, 281–82; strike and, 9, 62, 122, 136, 194, 200–201, 204, 220, 221, 232, 234–38, 260, 274; television and, 69, 96–106, 119; threats from, 241, 252–56, 268; turnover within, 25; unification of, 282–83, 294; wish list of, 170, 172. See also *Robertson* case; *specific owners*

Pacers, Indiana, 117, 179, 265
Parsons, Bob, 135
Parsons, Chandler, 3
Patterson, Ray, 181, 182–83, 188
pension plan, 7, 54, 57, 62–67, 68–69
Pepsi, 116
Petit, Bob, 55, 60, 61, 65
phantom income, 223
Philadelphia 76ers: championship and, 287, 288–91; Moses Malone and, 186–87, 213, 290, 291–92; 1983 All-Star Game and, 231; salary cap conditions for, 279; strike effects to, 236–37, 252; threats to, 251; trading by, 184–85
Phoenix Suns, 252. See also Colangelo, Jerry
Pilson, Neal, 165, 278
Pistons, Detroit, 40, 42, 202
Players Associations, 127–28. See also *specific associations*
playoffs, marketing for, 287
Podoloff, Maurice, 56–57, 159
poison-pill provisions, 188–89
Pollin, Abe: leadership of, xiv, 16, 265; negotiation role of, 170, 197–98, 203, 206–8; quote of, 226, 230, 235, 275; recommendation by, 260
Presti, Sam, xi
public relations, negotiations and, 168–69
Public Relations Department, 287

Quinn, Jim: Larry Fleisher and, 88; lawsuit filing by, 71–73, 111–12; leadership of, xiv,

30; negotiating role of, 33, 51, 77, 78, 206, 222; quote of, 82, 216, 217, 282

race: challenges of, 162; Charles Cooper and, 58–59; David Stern's viewpoint of, 23–24, 162–63; demographics of, 23–24; Larry Fleisher's viewpoint of, 86–87; Ted Stepien's viewpoint of, 124–25
racism, 137–38, 270
"Ralph Sampson problem," 211, 212, 244, 279, 280
Ramsay, Jack, 200
Reed, Willis, 4, 7–8, 41, 83
reserve clause, 6–7
restricted free agency, 140
retirement, 212
revenue sharing: abstention of, 179; conditions of, 278–79, 281–82; proposal for, 171–72, 205–12, 259, 263, 265
Richardson, Clint, 21, 232–33, 237, 251, 276–77, 278
Richardson, Michael Ray, 297
right of first refusal, 96, 97, 103, 131–32, 140–41, 148–50, 188, 222
Riley, Pat, 20, 213
Roberts, Michele, 14–15
Roberts, Robin, 127
Robertson, Oscar: All-Star Game performance of, 4, 60; contract strike by, 67; Larry Fleisher and, 5, 7, 84; lawsuit of, 83; leadership of, 55, 61, 101, 283; MVP award to, 66; NBPA and, 4–5, 6–9, 10–13, 84–86; quote of, 75, 77–78, 83–84, 270
Robertson case: Bob Lanier and, 47; conditions of, 28, 77–78, 85–89, 140, 180; David Stern and, 31, 88–89, 160–61, 168; effects of, 21, 23, 32, 33; expiration of, 70–71, 242–43, 247–49; free agency and, 128; Larry Fleisher and, 82, 132, 133, 227–28, 242; Larry O'Brien and, 47, 49; leadership within, 44; NBA's plan within, 88–89, 191, 196–97; 1981 phase of, 108–9; salary cap confliction with, 226–27, 229; settlement of, 89–92, 100; violation of, 46, 113, 189, 190, 232. See also Robertson, Oscar
Rockets, Houston, ix, 25, 142–43, 180–83, 187–89, 244

Rodgers, Guy, 60

Rosenbloom, Carrol, 135–36

Rosencrans, Robert, 105

rosters, negotiation proposals of, 199

Rothenberg, Alan: negotiation role of, 109, 113; presentation of, 122; proposal of, 110; quote of, 111–12; salary cap negotiation and, 119; work of, 96–97

"Round Bowl," 182

Russell, Bill, 4, 35, 55, 60, 94, 96

Russell, Campy, 125, 145

Ryan, Bob: interview with, ix; quote of, 12, 27, 40, 46, 70, 78, 81, 126, 177, 289, 291

Sachare, Alex, 163, 192, 264

salaries: competition within, 244, 274–75, 277; deferred compensation, 255, 265–66; delay proposal of, 257–58; free agency and, 73–74, 140, 184, 201, 222; Guaranteed Compensation Plan and, 210–12; increases of, 23, 39, 108, 171; introduction proposal of, 13–14, 227–30, 247–48; limitation proposal of, 170; Los Angeles Lakers and, 140–44, 151; as mandatory subject, 45; maximum proposal for, 265, 267; minimum proposal for, 28–29, 202, 211, 227, 263, 265, 267, 280; NFL, 39, 129, 134; racism and, 270; retirement and, 212; revenue and, 172, 205, 206, 207, 210; review proposal of, 110; *Robertson* case settlement and, 91, 108; statistics of, 31, 50, 91, 171; strike and, 245, 246, 253, 255; wage scale for, 39, 110. *See also specific players*

salary cap/salary moderation plan: central fund and, 178–79; conditions of, 46–47, 173, 206, 210–11, 225, 263; details of, 278–82; exceptions, 211, 212, 243–44, 279, 280; Guaranteed Compensation Plan, 210–12, 232; hard cap and, 171, 211, 212, 228–29, 258; introduction of, 33–34; legality of, 190–92; as mandatory subject, 44; NBA withdrawal of proposal, 195–96; rookies and, 279–80

Sampson, Ralph, 166, 244, 279–80

"Sampson problem," 211, 212, 244, 279, 280

San Antonio Spurs, 115–17, 252, 253. *See also* Drossos, Angelo

San Diego Clippers, 171, 174–79, 214–15, 258

Schayes, Dolph, 57

Scheer, Carl, 16, 140, 149

Schulman, Sam, 149, 178, 199, 235, 245, 254–55, 260, 276

Seattle Supersonics, 24, 252, 254, 279, 300. *See also* Schulman, Sam

76ers. *See* Philadelphia 76ers

Shaughnessy, Dan, 214, 246–47, 282, 299

Short, Bob, 64, 67

Sikma, Jack, 254

Silas, Paul, 12, 13, 42, 111, 122, 283, 288

Silver, Adam, 49, 87

Silver, Ed, 87, 121–22, 132

Smith, Frank, 102–3

Snyder, Paul, 90

Spalding, 294

sponsorships, conditions of, 294

Spurs, San Antonio, 115–17, 252, 253. *See also* Drossos, Angelo

Staub, Rusty, 155

Staubach, Roger, 135

St. Bonaventure Bonnies, 37–38, 287

Stepien, Ted: background of, 123–24; criticism of, 26, 146–47, 223, 285–86, 299; deal by, 285; Donald Sterling and, 176; Jerry Buss and, 150, 153; lawsuit from, 147; leadership of, 26, 124–26, 144–50, 262; proposal of ("Stepien Rule"), 214, 286; racial comments by, 124–26; reprimand of, 145–46; right of first refusal and, 140–41, 148–50, 171; sale of Cavaliers, 238–39, 285–86; trading practices of, 145–46, 185. *See also* Cleveland Cavaliers

Sterling, Donald, 26, 174–79, 193, 214–15

Stern, David: as attorney, 88, 159–60; background of, 30–31, 157–59; Board of Governors and, 161, 163; Bob Lanier and, 35; characteristics of, 30–31; drug testing viewpoint of, 296; election as NBA commissioner, 298–99; leadership of, xiii, 14, 27–28, 49, 132, 161–62, 197, 199, 257, 269, 271, 298–300; marketing abilities of, 163; negotiation style of, 30–31, 73, 77, 161, 168–69, 192–93, 268; New York Knicks and, 158; quote of, 17, 24, 31, 34, 69, 75, 127, 195, 241; race viewpoint of, 23–24, 162–63; relationship with Larry Fleisher, 29, 32, 34, 75, 132–33, 259, 300; revenue sharing negotiations of, 205–

12, 215–19, 281–83; strike viewpoint of, 204,
234–35, 248–49; television negotiations by,
21–22, 24–25, 100–101, 105, 106–7, 112, 163–
66, 299; values of, 160; vision of, 162, 179
Stern, William, 158–59
Stern Delicatessen, 157–58, 159
St. Jean, Garry, 287
stretch provision, 113
strike: Board of Governors and, 120–21, 259–
61; concerns of, 82; date for, 232–34, 242,
247–48, 251, 261–62; David Stern's viewpoint of, 204, 234–35, 248–49; effects of,
128, 167, 169, 219–20, 236–37, 244–45, 252,
260, 262; fear of, 221; Larry Fleisher's role
within, 69, 82, 118, 128, 154–55, 169, 176,
192, 221, 232–34, 245, 251–53, 260–62, 269–
70, 276–77; Major League Baseball and,
29, 45, 130, 154–55, 260; NFL and, 30, 135–
36, 137, 193–94, 219–20, 260; ownership
and, 9, 62, 122, 136, 194, 200–201, 204, 220,
221, 232, 234–38, 252–56, 260, 274; replacement players following, 260–61; resolution
for, 209; Roger Staubach and, 135; salaries
and, 245, 246, 253, 255; threat of, 8–9, 62–
67, 120–21, 122, 204, 244; votes for, 233, 271
Sudyk, Bob, 285–86
Suns, Phoenix, 252. See also Colangelo, Jerry
Supersonics, Seattle, 24, 252, 254, 279, 300.
See also Schulman, Sam
Superstars (TV show), 100

Taylor, Telford, 44
television: ABC, 54, 69, 93–97, 98, 99, 100,
103; boom of, 104–9; college basketball
and, 165; college football and, 165; David Stern's role with, 21–22, 24–25, 100–
101, 105, 106–7, 112, 163–66, 299; ESPN,
2–3, 22, 24–25, 105, 106–7, 262; Kent Cooke
and, 96; Larry Fleisher's negotiating role
within, 29, 98–99, 111, 112, 121; Los Angeles Lakers and, 96; Major League Baseball
and, 22, 93, 165; MSG network and, 24, 105,
111; NBA agreement within, 2–3, 105–6, 155;
NBC, 56, 97, 100, 164, 165; NBPA lawsuit regarding, 111–12; negotiations for, 21–22, 111,
119–20, 121, 122–23; NFL and, 22, 93, 137,
138, 165; 1964 All-Star Game and, 53–54;

ownership and, 69, 96–106, 119; pension
plans and, 7; playoffs and, 287; proposal
of, 29; ratings gain within, 293–94; ratings
loss within, 23, 100–101; revenue from,
14, 22, 111; strike effects on, 262; Super-
stars, 100; Turner Broadcasting, 2–3; UA-
Columbia Cablevision and, 105, 106; USA
network, 21–22, 24–25, 262. See also CBS
Thomas, Charlie, 183, 186–87
Thompson, David, 300–301
Thompson, John, 135
Thurmond, Nate, 4
Toney, Andrew, 231
trade deadline, 238
travel, challenges within, 229
Turner, Evan, 3
Turner, Ted, 104–5
Turner Broadcasting, 2–3

UA-Columbia Cablevision, 105, 106
Upshaw, Gene, 293
USA network, 21–22, 24–25, 262
USSR, players from, 75

Vecsey, George, 124

wage scale proposal, collective, 110, 112, 134
Walker, Chet, 60
Walker, Foots, 145, 261
Webster, Marvin, 271
Wedman, Scott, 149, 238
Weil, Gotshal, and Manges, xiv, 30, 88
Weinberg, Larry, xiv, 125, 126, 170, 206, 263,
264, 274, 298
Werblin, Sonny, 24
West, Jerry, 20, 60, 64
Westhead, Paul, 18–20
Wilkens, Lenny, 55, 60, 61–62, 275
Wilkerson, Bobby, 149
Wilkes, Jamal, 141, 144, 271
Wilkins, Dominique, 201
Williams, Pat, 185, 213, 252, 281
Wolff, Alexander, 183
Woolf, Bob, 148, 244, 251, 282
World Series, 22, 94, 97, 182
Worthy, James, 202, 244
Wussler, Robert, 100, 101–2

Zollner, Fred, 55, 56–57, 58, 60, 69

Index